THE WOMEN'S MOVEMENT

THE WOMEN'S MOVEMENT

POLITICAL, SOCIOECONOMIC, AND PSYCHOLOGICAL ISSUES

SECOND EDITION

BARBARA SINCLAIR DECKARD
University of California, Riverside

Harper & Row, Publishers
New York, Hagerstown, San Francisco, London

To Marga and Thornton Sinclair with love and gratitude

Sponsoring Editor: John Greenman
Project Editor: David Nickol
Designer: Gayle Jaeger
Production Supervisor: Kewal K. Sharma
Compositor: Kingsport Press
Printer and binder: The Murray Printing Company
Cover Art: John Sovjani

THE WOMEN'S MOVEMENT: Political, Socioeconomic, and Psychological Issues, Second Edition

Library of Congress Cataloging in Publication Data

Deckard, Barbara Sinclair.
The women's movement, political, socioeconomic, and psychological issues.

Bibliography: p.
Includes index.
1. Women—History. 2. Women—United States—History. 3. Feminism. I. Title.
HQ1154.D35 1979 301.41'2'09 78-16969
ISBN 0-06-041612-2

CONTENTS

PREFACE

In the past few years, the increased activity in the new feminist movement has resulted in a mass of literature about women. The social, economic, and political status of women in past and present societies and their long struggle for liberation has been explored, yet no attempt has been made to synthesize the old knowledge with the new. This book attempts such a synthesis.

Chapter 1 documents prevalent sexual stereotypes and explains how they function as an ideology. It is the explanations of the political functions of this ideology that set the analytical framework for the book. Part One (Chapters 2–7) describes and analyzes the present status of women in the United States. Data on psychological theories about women, sex role socialization, the family, working women, and laws affecting women are analyzed and the theories that have been used to justify this evidence are critiqued. Conservative, liberal, and radical economic theories are examined to see how they explain the patterns of discrimination evident in the data. Part Two (Chapters 8–14) begins with a survey of the status of women from primitive societies through the nineteenth century. The present status of women in a variety of capitalist and socialist societies is then discussed. Chapter 10 focuses on the nineteenth-century women's movement in the United States. The growth of the women's movement is examined in light of the social, economic, and political position of women in the nineteenth century. Chapter 11 analyzes why the movement died after 1920 and describes the changes in women's status between 1920 and 1960. Part Two concludes with an examination of the contemporary women's movement. Its origin, history, and development are traced, and the issues on which feminists have worked and their accomplishments are described. The final chapter presents and analyzes the three major ideological positions in the movement.

This is not a neutral book. I was a feminist when I began working on it and doing the research has made me more so. The book, while not neutral, is, I think, fair.

Alice Amsden and Nancy Hancock read the manuscript and gave me many helpful suggestions. Sara Sheehan and Marcia Keller contributed a great deal to my understanding of feminist issues and theories. Others who reviewed the first edition and provided suggestions for this second edition include Mary Ellin Colten, Survey Research Center, The University of Michigan; Jacqueline J. Snyder, Wichita State University; Mel Steinfield, Department of History, San Diego Mesa College; and Joan Acker, Department of Sociology, University of Oregon. Carmen Mathenga, Janet Gropp and Shirlee Pigeon typed various versions of the manuscript. Howard Sherman helped me understand the intricacies of economic theory, helped with the empirical research, and provided much needed moral support.

I am very much indebted to all of these people. My greatest debt, however, is to the women in the movement—those whom I have met and from whom I have learned, those whose work I have read, and the many thousands whose determination and hard work produced and sustain the feminist movement.

Part one

AMERICAN WOMEN TODAY

INTRODUCTION: SEXUAL STEREOTYPES AS POLITICAL IDEOLOGY

1

What is woman? Writers, past and present, have asked and answered this question over and over again. On the nature of woman everyone seems to consider himself an expert ("himself" because most of the answers come from men).

According to these "experts," woman is emotional rather than logical. In fact, she is not very bright.

> We may thus conclude that it is a general law that there should be naturally ruling elements and elements naturally ruled . . . the rule of the freeman over the slave is one kind of rule; that of the male over the female another. . . . the slave is entirely without the faculty of deliberation; the female indeed possesses it, but in a form which remains inconclusive. . . . [Aristotle]

> Women, then, are only children of larger growth: they have an entertaining tattle, and sometimes wit; but for solid, reasoning good sense, I never knew in my life one that had it, or who reasoned or acted consequentially for four and twenty hours together. [Lord Chesterfield]

> [Woman is] in every respect backward, lacking in reason and true morality . . . a kind of middle step between the child and the man, who is the true human being. [Schopenhauer]

> The chief distinction in the intellectual powers of the two sexes is shown by man attaining to a higher eminence, in whatever he takes up, than woman can attain—whether requiring deep thought, reason, or imagination or merely the use of the senses and hands. [Darwin]

> Feelings, moods and attitudes . . . rule a woman, not facts, reason nor logic. By herself, woman is all mixed up, but superb as an auxiliary. . . . [G. C. Payetter]

Everything relating to exploration and cognition, all the forms and kinds of human culture and aspiration that require a strictly objective approach, are with few exceptions, the domain of the masculine intellect, of man's spiritual power, against which women can rarely compete. [Helen Deutsch]

Man is active and independent; woman, passive and dependent. He does, she is.

Women, in general, want to be loved for what they are and men for what they accomplish. The first for their looks and charm, the latter for their actions. [Theodor Reik]

Women are usually more patient in working at unexciting, repetitive tasks. . . . Women on the average have more passivity in the inborn core of their personality. . . . I believe women are designed in their deeper instincts to get more pleasure out of life—not only sexually but socially, occupationally, maternally—when they are not aggressive. To put it another way I think that when women are encouraged to be competitive too many of them become disagreeable. [Benjamin Spock]

Women must give and give and give again because it is their one and only way to obtain happiness for themselves. [well-known American gynecologist]

It is a hard and hateful thing to see proud men, not to speak of enduring them. But it is annoying and impossible to suffer proud women, because in general Nature has given men proud and high spirits, while it has made women humble in character and submissive, more apt for delicate things than for ruling. [Boccaccio]

Women are naturally mothers; their greatest desire and only true fulfillment lies in maternity. In fact, this is one of the few things women are any good at.

. . . As much as women want to be good scientists and engineers, they want, first and foremost, to be womanly companions of men and to be mothers. [Bruno Bettelheim]

Biologically and temperamentally, I believe, women were made to be concerned first and foremost with child care, husband care and home care. [Benjamin Spock]

. . . Woman is nurturance; . . . anatomy decrees the life of a woman. When women grow up without dread of their biological functions and without the subversion of feminist doctrine and therefore enter upon motherhood with a sense of fulfillment and altruistic sentiment, we shall attain the goal of a good life and a secure world in which to live. [Joseph Rheingold]

If woman is naturally stupid, dependent, and passive, then, of course, she is naturally subordinate to the male.

Wives, submit yourself unto your husbands . . . for the husband is the head of the wife, even as Christ is the head of the church. [Ephesians 5:22–23]

The whole education of women ought to be relative to men. To please them, to be useful to them, to make themselves loved and honored by them, to educate them when young, to care for them when grown, to counsel them, to console them, and to make life sweet and agreeable to them—these are the duties of women at all times and what should be taught them from their infancy. [Jean-Jacques Rousseau]

Nature intended women to be our slaves; . . . they are our property, we are not theirs. They belong to us, just as a tree that bears fruit belongs to a gardener. What a mad idea to demand equality for women! . . . Women are nothing but machines for producing children. [Napoleon Bonaparte]

Man for the field and woman for the hearth:
Man for the sword and for the needle she:
Man with the head and woman with the heart:
Man to command and woman to obey;
All else confusion. [Alfred, Lord Tennyson]

When woman steps out of her natural role, disaster results:

A woman who is guided by the head and not the heart is a social pestilence: she has all the defects of the passionate and affectionate woman, with none of her compensations; she is without pity, without love, without virtue, without sex. [Honoré de Balzac]

Frigidity, as we see it today, is an outgrowth of woman's running away from her biological destiny, which is to be wife, mother, and homemaker. [Dr. Arthur Mandy]

Women's intellectuality is to a large extent paid for by the loss of valuable feminine qualities; it feeds on the sap of the affective life and results in improverishment of this life. . . . All observations point to the fact that the intellectual woman is masculinized; in her, warm intuitive knowledge has yielded to cold unproductive thinking. [Helen Deutsch]

Mom got herself out of the nursery and the kitchen. She then got out of the house. . . . She also got herself the vote, and, although politics never interested her (unless she was exceptionally naive, a hairy foghorn, or a size 40 scorpion) the damage she forthwith did to society was so enormous and so rapid that the best men lost track of things . . . political scurviness, hoodlumism, gangsterism, labor strife, monopolistic thuggery, moral degeneration, civil corruption, smuggling, bribery, theft, murder, homosexuality, drunkenness, financial depression, chaos, and war. [Philip Wylie]

Aside from their often virulent nastiness, the most striking aspect of these quotations is the underlying assumption on which they are based—that all women are alike. The image of women presented is a stereotype—a simple-minded, unexamined notion based on prejudice. Similar statements about blacks (that they all have natural rhythm, for example) are immediately recognized as racist stereotyping. In most circles, racist slurs are no longer socially acceptable. In contrast, sexism is the last socially acceptable prejudice. People still tell and laugh at wife, mother-in-law, and sex jokes that depict women as stupid and empty-headed, unconcerned with anything but their looks, and good for only one thing.

The ideology of sexism is so deeply embedded in our society that, to a considerable extent, most people are unaware they are prejudiced. The notion that women are inferior to or at least extremely different from men is taken as a self-evident truth:

Sexism, then, is an "ideology" in the sense that its beliefs and postulates are well integrated, it functions to direct and guide social and political activity, and it rests on assumptions that are not reliably tested, but that to some degree are accepted on faith.[1]

For example, most tennis pros assumed that Bobby Riggs would beat Billie Jean King even though she was twenty years younger and one of the world's best women players. When she beat him, they dismissed it as an anomaly. When looking at someone, a prejudiced person will interpret whatever behavior occurs in a way that fits with the stereotype. A sociologist points out:

---

[1] Kirsten Amundsen, *The Silenced Majority* (Englewood Cliffs, N.J.: Prentice-Hall, 1971), p. 108.

> Whatever the facts about sex differences, anti-feminism—like any other prejudice—distorts perception and experience. . . . Thus, an anti-Semite watching a Jew may see devious or sneaky behavior. But in a Christian he would regard such behavior only as quiet, reserved, or perhaps even shy.[2]

Since prejudice distorts perception, it is highly resistant to change even in the face of contrary evidence.

As an example of how prejudiced stereotyping affects behavior, imagine an employer interviewing a series of people for an executive job. Suppose he believes in the usual stereotypes of women. Suppose the first woman is sophisticated and careful about speaking. He thinks: She is too passive and "feminine" for the job. Suppose the second woman objects to something he says. He thinks: She is an aggressive bitch. Suppose the third person is a man; he gets the job. Prejudiced stereotypes are not harmless; they lead directly to discrimination.

Even in minor ways and unconsciously, most people believe the myths. For example, if a man and woman order tea and coffee in a restaurant, the man will almost always get the coffee and the woman the tea (sometimes even if you ask for it the other way around). Why? Apparently tea is perceived as a light and delicate and therefore feminine drink. In reality, of course, most American women drink coffee. In the same way, if a man and a woman order a soft drink and a cocktail, the waiter or waitress will almost always give the soft drink to the woman without asking. Another myth.

More dangerous is the myth that most women do not work at paid jobs, and that those who do work only for pin money. Yet in Chapter 5 we shall see that a majority of women of working age now work at two jobs: a paid job in the economy and their traditional job in the home.

Like most stereotypes, the sexist stereotype is internally inconsistent. Depending upon the purpose, two quite different sets of characteristics are attributed to women. Women cannot be statesmen, captains of industry, or even auto mechanics because they are irrational, flighty, overemotional, sentimental, and unmechanical. On the other hand, women cannot be great poets and painters because they are practical, unadventure-

---

[2] Philip Goldberg, "Are Women Prejudiced Against Women," in Athena Theodore, ed., *The Professional Woman* (New York: Schenkman, 1971), p. 168.

some, unspontaneous, and unimaginative.[3] Unfortunately, inconsistency never destroyed a healthy stereotype, and sexism is still all too robust.

Religion has had a particularly important role in advancing and perpetuating sexist notions. The great religions of the world have mostly been pervaded by sexism. Examples:

> . . . And the rib, which the Lord God had taken from man, made he a woman, and brought her unto the man. . . . And the Lord God said unto the woman, What is this that thou hast done? And the woman said, The serpent beguiled me, and I did eat. . . . Unto the woman he said, I will greatly multiply thy sorrow and thy conception; in sorrow thou shalt bring forth children; and thy desire shall be to thy husband, and he shall rule over thee. [Genesis 2–3]

The Christian Saint Paul wrote:

> Let the woman learn in silence with all subjection. But I suffer not a woman to teach, nor to usurp authority over the man, but to be in silence. For Adam was first formed, then Eve. And Adam was not deceived, but the woman, being deceived, was in the transgression. Notwithstanding she shall be saved in childbearing, if they continue in faith and charity and holiness with sobriety. [1 Tim. 2:11–15]

The Christian Bible also declares:

> . . . how can he be clean that is born of a woman? [Job 25:4]

And the Pope says:

> Woman as a person enjoys a dignity equal with men, but she was given different tasks by God and by Nature which perfect and complete the work entrusted to men. [Pope John XXIII]

Christianity is equaled, if not surpassed, by other religions. The male Orthodox Jew recites every morning:

> Blessed art Thou, oh Lord our God, King of the Universe, that I was not born a woman.

The Koran, the Muslim sacred text, says:

> Men are superior to women on account of the qualities in which God has given them pre-eminence.

---

[3] Discussion based on Cynthia Ozick, "Women and Creativity," in Vivian Gornick and Barbara Moran, eds., *Woman in Sexist Society* (New York: Signet, 1971), p. 437.

The Hindu Code of Manu declared:

> In childhood a woman must be subject to her father; in youth to her husband; when her husband is dead, to her sons. A woman must never be free of subjugation.

Finally, there are the profound sayings of Confucius:

> The five worst infirmities that afflict the female are indocility, discontent, slander, jealousy, and silliness. . . . Such is the stupidity of woman's character, that it is incumbent upon her, in every particular, to distrust herself and to obey her husband.

The new high priests of Western society—the psychiatrists—are not much subtler in their sexism, as we shall see in the next chapter. A later examination of the mass media will show that they too perpetuate sexism.

SEXISM IN LANGUAGE

Sexist thinking is deeply embedded in the English language.[4] Anthropologists have discovered that a society's basic and often unconscious mores are often revealed in its language. We can see many reflections of sexist thinking in our own language.

A linguist writes: "The word *man* originally meant human being, but males appropriated it."[5] This equating of men with the human race causes some confusion in very important texts as well as trivial ones. Does "foreman" or "handyman" or "freshman" mean that these positions cannot be filled by women? In fact, the earlier stereotypes implied just that—only men could be supervisory workers, only men are handy, only men should go to college. Or take the sentence "All men are created equal." Many males have argued that this does not apply to women and thus would deny women their democratic rights. In this book we use the language in a sex-neutral way as a reflection of the fact that English is flexible enough to accommodate new ways of thinking without losing fluency or naturalness of expression.

Many words with wicked or evil emotional connotations were

---

[4] See Ethel Strainchamps, "Our Sexist Language," in Gornick and Moran, op. cit., pp. 347–361.

[5] Ibid., p. 350.

sex-neutral in an earlier period. Eventually, however, the wickedness came to be associated with women only. For example, "shrewish" first was applied to either male or female, then became associated with a stereotype of women. By contrast, some words gained a better emotional connotation when associated with men only. For example, "shrewd" (from the same root as "shrewish") originally had an evil connotation; but when it became associated with powerful males, its emotional connotation became much more favorable.

The reason for such developments is that language reflects the dominant ideology of the most powerful group in society; and sexism is the ideology of the male, who is dominant in Western society. More precisely, one linguist writes that "emotive words acquire their connotations by reflecting the sentiments of the dominant group in a society—in our case white Anglo-Saxon males (WASMs). . . ."[6]

"BUT IT'S NATURAL"

The last refuge of people lacking a sound argument is to say: "But it's natural." For example, it is "natural" for a woman to have the whole burden of household and child-rearing chores—even if she has an outside job in addition. It is "natural" for women to be passive and submissive; it is "natural" for men to command. It is "natural" for women to be paid less than men. Before 1920, it was said to be "natural" for American men to vote but "unnatural" for women to do so.

What do people mean when they say "It's natural"? Sometimes, *natural* is construed to mean "that which will happen if untouched by human intervention."[7] Thus, it is natural for a woman to get pregnant from sex, and unnatural for her to use any means of birth control. But then, isn't it natural for a man to grow a beard, and unnatural for him to shave? What about the use of smallpox and polio vaccines? Are these to be considered unnatural? According to this definition, perpetual pregnancy, beards, and dying of smallpox are all natural.

---

[6] Ibid., p. 352.

[7] The argument here follows the excellent discussion in Christine Pierce, "Natural Law, Language and Women," in Gornick and Moran, op. cit., pp. 242–258.

But their being natural in this sense does not mean they are either unchangeable or desirable.

Another argument claims that male dominance is natural because it is based on "innate instincts" or "human nature." But, if women are prevented from doing some things by their nature, why must other barriers be erected? For example, if women's nature prevents them from being doctors, why must many medical schools prohibit the admission of all but a small quota from among all the qualified women applicants? If women's nature prevents them from being lawyers, why did many U.S. state laws have to prohibit qualified women law school graduates from practicing in the nineteenth century? The reality, as will be shown in the next chapter, is that there are no such "natural" barriers in the psychology of women.

As John Stuart Mill observed, "Everything which is usual appears natural. The subjection of women to men being a universal custom, any departure from it quite naturally appears unnatural."[8] Usually a person who says something is natural means that it is not just common but desirable. Such statements contain either a giant illogical leap or are simple assertions of preference. Male supremacy—and poverty, disease, and slavery—have been prevalent in many societies. That certainly does not make them desirable. Arguments based on the naturalness of male supremacy and female subordination should be attributed very little value.

SEXIST IDEOLOGY AND POWER

The sexist ideology is well integrated and elaborate. Its major premise is that woman is inferior to man. It is sufficiently flexible (inconsistent) so that any behavior a woman exhibits can be interpreted to conform with the major premise. The ideology is so pervasive that, until recently, few people were aware of its existence. Its tenets were simply accepted as self-evident truths.

Such an ideology neither develops nor survives without purpose. Its function is to justify and maintain a particular status quo—in this case the dominance of the male over the female. A ruling group always requires an ideology to justify its position

[8] John Stuart Mill, *The Subjection of Women* (1869).

of power. All slave societies, for example, developed a set of beliefs stating that slaves are innately inferior or even nonhuman. In essence, such beliefs put the onus for their condition on the slaves. Their status is decreed by their nature or by the gods; it is certainly not the fault of the slave owner.

The ideology is important as a self-justification for the ruling group. It is equally important in its effects on the subordinate group. Members of the subordinate group are inculcated with the ideology from early childhood. To a considerable extent they believe its claims—that they are, in fact, inferior and thus destined to play a subordinate role.

Sexual stereotyping thus is a *political* ideology. Its function is to maintain the power of the dominant group.

This book deals with the ideology of sexism, with the socioeconomic conditions the ideology seeks to justify, and with women's struggles to free themselves and their society from sexism.

THE NATURE OF WOMAN: PSYCHOLOGICAL THEORIES

2

On the subject of what women are really like, everyone is an expert. As we saw in the last chapter, philosophers and novelists, baby doctors and social critics all know exactly what the nature of woman is. Woman is not very bright; she is emotional and subjective, passive and dependent. Woman is very good at child care and at the sort of repetitive tasks involved in housework. She finds her greatest joy and only true fulfillment in the roles of wife and mother. Woman, clearly, is very, very different from man.

These popular stereotypes should not be accepted without evidence. Perhaps the experts in human psychology have scientifically determined what women are really like. What do the psychologists have to tell us about the nature of women?

PSYCHOLOGICAL SEX DIFFERENCES

Seventy-nine clinically trained psychologists, psychiatrists, and social workers were asked to describe the mature, healthy male and the mature, healthy female.[1] According to these experts, the male is very aggressive, very independent, not at all emotional, very objective, very dominant, not at all easily influenced, and very logical; his feelings are not easily hurt; he can make decisions easily; and he is very self-confident. The normal female is not at all aggressive, not at all independent,

[1] Inge K. Broverman et al., "Sex-Role Stereotypes and Clinical Judgments of Mental Health," in Judith M. Bardwick, ed., *Readings on the Psychology of Women* (New York: Harper & Row, 1972), pp. 320–324.

very emotional, very illogical, very submissive, very sneaky; her feelings are easily hurt; she has difficulty making decisions; and she is not at all self-confident, but very dependent.

The authors of the study remark about the latter description that "this constellation seems a most unusual way of describing any mature, healthy individual."[2] How have these supposed experts come to such conclusions? Remember, they are not describing the average woman but the healthy, mature woman. In effect, they are saying that this is what women should be like. The experts' ideal is remarkably like the popular stereotype. The stereotype, in turn, reflects what men want women to be.

In a male-dominated world, the woman who at least puts on a good show of conforming to the male ideal seems to get along better than her rebellious sisters. Male control of resources means the "good" woman will be rewarded, while the woman who does not "act like a woman," that is, as a subordinate, will be punished. Those are the facts of life in our society, and psychiatry has traditionally been aimed at getting people to fit into society as it is, not to change it. The clinicians are saying, "Adjust yourself to the stereotypes; only thus can you be normal and healthy." The costs of conforming to the stereotype—low self-esteem, a tendency toward depression and economic dependence—are simply not recognized.

Another finding of the Broverman study shows that women are caught in a non-win situation. The experts were also asked to describe a mature, healthy adult. Their description of a healthy adult—sex unspecified—was very similar to their description of a healthy male and thus very different from their description of a healthy female. If a woman displays the characteristics our society attributes to the healthy adult, she will be considered unfeminine; if she displays the appropriate feminine characteristics, she is not a mature healthy adult.

Since the clinicians seem to define adjusting to society's expectations—however destructive they may be—as healthy, their views must be looked upon with considerable suspicion. Nevertheless, there is a modicum of truth in the description when applied to the average woman. Although there is a great deal of overlapping of the sexes on all such traits, studies

---

[2] Ibid., p. 322.

through the 1960s consistently found that females on the average were more passive-dependent, more fearful and anxious, and less aggressive than males. Differences in self-esteem, in conformity and suggestibility, in need for affiliation and in achievement need were also frequently found.[3]

What accounts for these differences? The popular view and that held by some psychologists attributes them to biological differences. Other psychologists contend that such differences in behavior are learned, that they are the result of the socialization process.

BIOLOGICAL SEX DIFFERENCES

Men are taller, heavier, and stronger than women. Right? Not exactly. Within any given population group, the average male is taller than the average female, but some women are taller than some men. And the average female in some societies is taller than the average male in other societies. Thus secondary sex characteristics such as the male's greater height, higher muscle-to-fat ratio, more massive skeleton, and more abundant body hair distinguish male and female within a given society but not across societies.[4]

Chromosomal, gonadal, and hormonal sex differences are universal. A normal woman has two X chromosomes; a normal man, an X chromosome and a Y chromosome. The internal and external reproductive and sex organs, of course, differ in normal men and woman. The sex hormones secreted and the timing of secretion differ, with the woman exhibiting a cyclical pattern.

These differences have provided the basis for a number of theories concerning psychological sex differences. The more sophisticated argue that since sex hormones, which differ for male and female, enter the brain, different behaviors along sex lines are to be expected. Yet no link between sex hormones and complex behavior patterns has been established. In fact, the relationship between physiological and psychological state

[3] Roberta M. Oetzel, "Annotated Bibliography," in Eleanor E. Maccoby, ed., *The Development of Sex Differences* (Stanford, Calif.: Stanford University Press, 1966), pp. 223–321.

[4] Roy G. D'Andrade, "Sex Differences and Cultural Institutions," in Maccoby, op. cit., p. 175.

seems to depend very much on social context. For example, since adrenaline produces a physiological reaction much like what naturally occurs when a person is very much afraid, one would expect a subject injected with adrenaline to show the psychological symptoms of fear. Yet, when an experimenter put some subjects who were under the influence of adrenaline into a room with someone who was pretending to be euphoric, the subjects became euphoric. When the subjects were put in the presence of someone acting very angry, they became angry.[5] Clearly the subjects' social environment was more important than their physiological state in determining their behavior.

One cannot simply assume that biological differences will result in psychological differences. One *must* provide evidence. This should be kept in mind during the following examination of theories on the origins of psychological sex differences.

ANATOMY IS DESTINY

According to Freud, the normal woman is passive, masochistic, and narcissistic.[6] Woman's inferiority is anatomically based. She is an incomplete—"maimed"—man because she lacks a penis.

Freud saw early childhood development as being similar for both sexes until about age five. Children then enter the phallic stage, which is characterized by great interest in their own genitals and those of the opposite sex and by considerable masturbatory activity.

At this point the boy's Oedipus complex develops. He desires his mother sexually and would like to kill his father, whom he sees as his rival. He realizes, however, that his father is much more powerful than he is. The boy fears that the father will learn of his desires and, in retaliation, cut off the boy's penis, which gives him so much pleasure. The threat of castration leads the boy to abandon the Oedipus complex.

In the process of destroying these strongly held feelings, the

---

[5] Naomi Weisstein, "Psychology Constructs the Female, or the Fantasy Life of the Male Psychologist," in Michele Hoffnung Garskof, ed., *Roles Women Play* (Belmont, Calif.: Brooks/Cole, 1971), pp. 76–77.

[6] For a brief summary of Freud's theory of female psychology, see Janet Shibley Hyde and B. G. Rosenberg, *Half the Human Experience: The Psychology of Women* (Lexington, Mass.: D. C. Heath, 1976), pp. 32–38.

superego develops. The superego includes the conscience and an internal set of standards that are used to evaluate oneself. A man with a strong superego evaluates himself in terms of these internal standards and does not rely heavily on the opinions of others for a feeling of self-worth. In Freud's thought the development of the superego and the development of civilization are closely bound together.

In the girl the process is different and the outcome less satisfactory. From her observation of little boys, she learns that she lacks a penis and concludes that she has been castrated. Lacking "the only proper genital organ,"[7] the girl develops penis envy. In normal development the girl will eventually transfer her desire for a penis into a desire for a child by her father. "The feminine situation is only established . . . if the wish for a penis is replaced by one for a baby. . . . Her happiness is great if later on this wish for a baby finds fulfillment in reality, and quite especially so if the baby is a little boy who brings the longed-for penis with him."[8]

This process has a number of effects on female psychology, according to Freud. Women do not develop strong superegos. "In the absence of fear of castration the chief motive is lacking which leads boys to surmount the Oedipus complex. Girls remain in it for an indeterminate length of time; they demolish it late and, even so, incompletely. In these circumstances the formation of the super-ego must suffer; it cannot attain the strength and independence which give it its cultural significance. . . ."[9]

Because penis envy is never entirely sublimated even in normal women, "envy and jealousy play an even greater part in the mental life of women than of men."[10] "The fact that women must be regarded as having little sense of justice is no doubt related to the predominance of envy in their mental life."[11]

Normal femininity is attained, according to Freud, when the girl represses her own impulses toward activity; that is, when

---

[7] Quoted in Judith M. Bardwick, *Psychology of Women* (New York: Harper & Row, 1971), p. 9.

[8] Sigmund Freud, "Anatomy Is Destiny," in Betty and Theodore Roszak, eds., *Masculine/Feminine* (New York: Harper & Row, 1969), p. 24.

[9] Ibid., p. 25.

[10] Ibid., p. 22.

[11] Ibid., p. 29.

she becomes passive. A woman who is not passive, who wishes to participate in the world outside the home, to pursue an intellectual profession, is neurotic. Such desires in a woman are symptoms of penis envy. Not only must the female give up competitive strivings and desires for achievement in the male world; she must also give up clitoral sexuality. Freud refers to the clitoris as a "penis equivalent"[12] and sees clitoral sexuality as masculine. The clitoris is a protruding organ and does not require a male penis for enjoyment. Thus it does not fit in with Freud's notion of women as passive. A normal female, according to Freud, transfers her erotic sensitivity from clitoris to vagina. Only vaginal orgasms are normal. A woman who has only clitoral orgasms is considered frigid.

According to Freud, then, women are innately inferior owing to their anatomy. More precisely, in Freudian theory the inferiority stems from the female's psychological reaction to her anatomy. Freud leaves little doubt, however, that the female's reaction—her feeling that she has been cheated because she lacks a penis—is realistic and correct. He calls the penis the organ of "power and creativeness";[13] the female's lack of it, an "anatomical tragedy."[14]

One is tempted to dismiss Freud and his theories as a sick joke. One wonders what happened during his childhood to produce such a penis fixation. Anyone who considers half the human race to be "mutilated creatures"[15] on the basis of the characteristics that make the continuation of the species possible has got to be sick. Unfortunately, we cannot dismiss him so easily; he has had too much effect on our thinking. That his theories could have been and, in many quarters, still are taken seriously illustrates the incredible misogyny (hatred of women) prevalent in Western society.

In criticizing Freud, one can point out that his notions are based on his observations of affluent Viennese women during the Victorian era. To generalize to all places and all times is hardly legitimate. His patients were psychologically ill. To generalize from an abnormal to a normal population is also suspect.

One can, however, make an even stronger criticism: Freud

---

[12] Ibid., p. 20.
[13] Quoted in Bardwick, *The Psychology of Women,* op. cit., p. 9.
[14] Quoted in ibid.
[15] Quoted in ibid.

never tested his theories at all. They were based on clinical experience, on insight, not on controlled scientific experiments. Psychologist Naomi Weisstein[16] explains that Freud's "insights" came to him during his psychoanalytic sessions with patients. She notes that this is just as good a way as any other to *formulate* an hypothesis. A scientific hypothesis or theory may be inspired by anything, from God to a table of random numbers. A scientific theory, however, is not confirmed as valid until it has been tested under controlled conditions. Yet Freud never even attempted to put his theories to such a test. His *Sexual Enlightenment of Children* is usually offered as the scientific basis for the existence of the castration complex. In that work, however, the sole empirical evidence is of a secondhand nature, obtained from the boy's father. Moreover, the father was far from an unbiased observer, since he was also in therapy and enthusiastically believed in Freudian theory. Thus, Freud obtains an insight from one patient, constructs a theory on that basis, and then "confirms" the theory by examining other patients in the light of his preconceptions.

Most of Freudian theory has not been scientifically tested. Furthermore, much of it, as now stated, seems to be inherently untestable. Take the notion of penis envy as an example. As we saw earlier, according to Freud all females experience penis envy and most never completely get over it. This would seem to be easily testable. We go out and ask females of various ages if they ever experienced penis envy. Certainly we will find females who deny such an experience. Does this refute the theory? No, according to the Freudians. A female who denies penis envy has simply repressed the experience. In fact, it seems that no evidence that could conceivably exist would refute the theory. If a woman is passive, she has sublimated her penis envy; if she is aggressive, she has also sublimated it but in another way.

In essence, any conceivable sort of female behavior can be explained by Freudian theory. Because that is so, the theory really explains nothing. It is an ideology, not a scientific theory. A theory, to be scientific, must be testable. It predicts that certain things will happen and others will not. If the theory predicts, for example, that certain types of behavior will not

[16] Weisstein, op. cit., pp. 71–72.

occur and they actually do occur, then the theory is shown to be false. If the predicted behaviors do occur, then our confidence in the validity of the theory increases. If the theory does not forbid any sort of occurrence, it cannot be tested, and so there is no way of determining whether it is true or false. Thus it is dogma, not science. People may believe the theory because it makes them feel good, but there is no evidence supporting it.

Some aspects of Freudian theory are testable. One aspect, the notion of the double orgasm, has recently been tested and found to be false. Masters and Johnson have conclusively demonstrated that there is only one type of orgasm and that anatomically it is a clitoral orgasm.[17] Female orgasm may be brought on by different types of stimulation—direct clitoral stimulation, intercourse, or even breast manipulation—but the resulting orgasms are physiologically identical. The clitoris is much more sensitive than the vagina and is physiologically similar to the penis. Yet under the influence of Freud, the vaginal orgasm was held to be the only normal form of sexual pleasure. A woman who required clitoral stimulation for orgasm was considered infantile, unfeminine, and frigid.

WOMAN IS NOT INFERIOR, BUT . . .

A number of psychologists and psychoanalysts agree with Freud that women and men are psychologically very different and that the difference is biologically determined, but they disagree with the notion of penis envy.

According to Erik Erikson, a well-known exponent of this view, woman's psychology is determined not by the missing penis but by the existence of a "productive inner-bodily space."[18] Woman's "somatic design harbors an 'inner space' destined to bear the offspring of chosen men and, with it, a biological, psychological, and ethical commitment to take care of human infancy."[19] For Erikson, woman's psychology is determined by her procreative potential. In this view women are not passive; they are active in nonmale ways—bearing and

---

[17] Susan Lydon, "The Politics of Orgasm," in Garskof, op. cit., p. 64.

[18] Erik H. Erikson, "Inner and Outer Space: Reflections on Womanhood," in Robert Jay Lifton, ed., *The Woman in America* (Boston: Beacon, 1967), p. 6.

[19] Ibid., p. 5.

taking care of babies. They are not masochistic; they have "an ability to stand (and to understand) pain as a meaningful aspect of human experience in general and of the feminine role in particular."[20]

Erikson does not deny that women may have interests and abilities that are unrelated to their procreative role. He states, as a general proposition, that women should be given equal rights and that he would not deny them other experiences by "dooming" them to nothing but motherhood. Yet, he claims that everything a woman may do is limited by the fact that she is a woman and can only do things according to her "natural dispositions."[21] What Erikson so magnanimously concedes in general, he nullifies in particular for women. He concedes that a woman's interests may extend beyond children, but they are still distinctly feminine interests, or that a woman may be capable of competing successfully against men in the masculine sphere, but no "real" woman would want to. Erikson sees the normal woman as an earth mother. She is not inferior to men, but she is very, very different.

On what evidence does he base these conclusions? Erikson conducted an experiment with 150 girls and 150 boys. Within a two-year period he saw each child three times. Each time he put some toys on a table and asked the child to construct some kind of scene with them.[22] He found that boys and girls used space differently. Girls tended to build interior scenes that were surrounded by low walls with the people and animals mostly within the enclosure. Boys tended to build either houses with high walls or exterior scenes. In the boys' scenes most of the people and animals were outside the enclosure. "The girls," Erikson concluded, "emphasized inner and the boys outer space."[23]

To draw from such an experiment conclusions concerning the basic psychology of women would seem to be an Olympic leap of logic. Furthermore, the children involved were from ten to twelve years old. The possibility that they had already learned what is considered appropriate behavior for boys and for girls is very likely, yet it was never considered.

[20] Ibid., p. 13.
[21] Ibid., p. 26.
[22] Ibid., p. 7.
[23] Ibid., p. 9.

Judith Bardwick, in her widely used text *Psychology of Women,*[24] presents another variant on the "woman is different but not necessarily inferior" theme. Like Erikson, she believes that the existence of the female reproductive organs, not the absence of the penis, accounts for the differences. Unlike Erikson, with his rather mystical notion of inner space, Bardwick has a more physiological emphasis. The greater passivity, dependence, and conformity of girls and the greater aggressiveness, independence, and creativity of boys do, according to Bardwick, have a biological origin. Chromosomal, hormonal, and anatomical differences result in different potentialities, which are then emphasized or muted by the socialization process.

The evidence she presents for the genetic origin of these differences is very slim. She admits that "we know astonishingly little about the relationship between particular sex hormones and specific male and female behaviors."[25] She cites a few findings on sex differences in infancy. For example, some studies report that male infants are somewhat more active and girls more sensitive to stimuli at birth.[26] Again she admits that "infant research is just beginning, and little of it has been directed towards sex differences."[27] Primate studies are mentioned, but generalizing from monkeys to humans in the area of personality is questionable. A great deal of evidence on sex differences at later ages is available and is cited. Such studies cannot be used to show the genetic origin of sex differences in personalities, since learning could well account for them.

Although Bardwick does believe in the genetic origin of personality differences, she emphasizes the effect of socialization much more than either Freud or Erikson. Girls are more dependent, less aggressive, and less highly sexed than boys owing to genetic and hormonal differences. Because of these inborn traits, the girl's behavior is more acceptable to her parents, so she is less likely to come into conflict with them at an early age. Furthermore, the normal dependent behavior of small children is considered acceptable in girls, so her parents will not penalize and may even reward such behavior. As a result, the girl finds it easy to win the approval of her parents and

[24] Bardwick, *The Psychology of Women,* op. cit., passim.
[25] Ibid., p. 21.
[26] Ibid., p. 93.
[27] Ibid., p. 90.

of other adults and thus is much less likely to develop internal standards of self-worth and independence, at least at an early age. She will depend much more heavily on the opinions and affection of others for her feeling of self-worth, and this dependence on others leads to conformity.

In contrast, the boy's natural aggressiveness and greater sexuality brings him into conflict with his parents early. He is penalized for overaggressive play and for overt sexual activity. If he shows dependent behavior, he is also penalized because this is considered unmasculine. Because he cannot act as he wishes and still obtain parental approval, he turns inward for approval and develops an independent sense of self-worth. Such independence allows for the development of creativity.

Until puberty there are fewer pressures on the girl than on her brother. After puberty, the pressures to adopt the feminine role intensify. It is made clear that achievement, at least high achievement, is not feminine, that competition is aggressive and therefore masculine. Because such deviance will threaten her relationships with boys, a girl gives up her attempts at achievement. According to Bardwick, the girl finds it relatively easy to do so because of the personality characteristics she has already developed, particularly her dependence on others for a sense of self-worth. Such dependence also results in the female's placing greater value on interpersonal relationships, especially heterosexual ones, and results in her being more empathic, nurturant, and supportive than the male.

Although Bardwick believes these psychological differences have a genetic origin, she feels present socialization practices result in an exaggeration of the differences:

> The sex differences that are present when children enter the school system are most likely to increase until girls and boys are very different. Dependency, affiliation, passivity and conformity versus independence, achievement, activity and aggression are the important variables. The origin of the differences lies in early constitutional proclivities which the culture enhances by reward and punishment along sex-specific lines.[28]

Psychological differences and society's ideas about appropriate male and female behavior result in a sex role system that assigns

[28] Ibid., p. 113.

tasks on the basis of sex. "While the sexes appear to have characteristic qualities which are more or less functional in different activities, traditional role divisions have been far too restrictive for both sexes."[29]

SOCIETY IS DESTINY

Another group of psychologists hold that the psychological characteristics and behaviors that distinguish male and female are the result not of biology but of socialization. Sex-appropriate responses and behaviors are learned.

There are a number of variants of this view, and the theories are often complex.[30] Social-learning theory is probably the most widely accepted. One psychologist summarizes the theory as follows:

> . . . social-learning theory holds that sex-appropriate responses are rewarded (reinforced) by parents and others, and hence are repeated (increased in frequency). Sex-inappropriate behavior, on the other hand, is likely to be punished and hence to diminish in strength and frequency, i.e., to become extinguished.[31]

According to the social-learning theorists, the society's views concerning sex-appropriate behavior are taught to the child through reward and punishment. A little girl is, for example, encouraged and praised for playing with dolls; a little boy is likely to be penalized for such behavior. Of course the child does not try out all possible behaviors and then repeat or not repeat them on the basis of others' responses. Children also learn from the observation of live and symbolic models (e.g., television), and they generalize from one type of experience to a class of similar experiences. Children learn from experience what is socially approved behavior for women and what is approved for men. "This learning can affect the child's sex-typed activities by providing information about probable outcomes for responses before they are actually performed."[32]

---

[29] Ibid., p. 217.
[30] For an overview of such theories, see Paul H. Mussen, "Early Sex-Role Development," in Nancy Reeves, ed., *Womankind, Beyond the Stereotypes* (Chicago: Aldine-Atherton, 1971), pp. 393–418.
[31] Ibid., p. 399.
[32] Walter Mischel, "A Social-Learning View of Sex Differences in Behavior," in Maccoby, op. cit., p. 60.

Walter Mischel, an exponent of this view, points out that aggression and dependence have received special research attention as behaviors differentiating the sexes, and concludes that these differences can be accounted for by social-learning theory.[33] Sex differences in aggression, especially physical aggression, have been documented for three-year-olds. It has also been found that parents make the greatest distinction between the sexes in this area. Furthermore, in an experiment in which children of both sexes were equally rewarded for aggressive behavior, very little difference between the sexes was found.[34]

Mischel reports that "no strong sex differences in dependency are observed at early ages (e.g., nursery school). . . . At older ages (high school and college) girls are consistently higher on dependency measures."[35] This increase with age in the difference between the sexes suggests that dependence too is learned.

Further evidence that sex-appropriate behavior is learned rather than innate is provided by studies of "persons whose original sex assignment was either incorrect or ambiguous because of the appearance of their external genitalia."[36] The sex to which these people were assigned determined their gender identity. That is, a genetic female reared as a male would grow up to think of herself as a male and to act like a male. Furthermore, an attempt to change the sex assignment after very early childhood (18 months to 3 years) is likely to be unsuccessful and to lead to psychological problems. From these studies "the hypothesis has been advanced that gender role is entirely the result of a learning process which is quite independent of chromosomal, gonadal or hormonal sex."[37]

If women are naturally passive and dependent and men naturally aggressive and independent, anthropology should provide evidence of this regularity. If these differences are innate, they should be found in all societies, past and present. In fact, anthropological studies show that sex-appropriate characteristics and behavior vary greatly from one society to another.

---

[33] Ibid., p. 72.
[34] Ibid., pp. 73–74.
[35] Ibid., p. 74.
[36] David A. Hamburg and Donald T. Lunde, "Sex Hormones in the Development of Sex Differences in Human Behavior," in Maccoby, op. cit., p. 15.
[37] Ibid.

Margaret Mead studied three New Guinea tribes and found that our assumptions about the normal female and male psychology simply do not apply. In two of the tribes, male and female are not expected to and in fact do not display different personality traits. All members of Arapesh society are "trained to be co-operative, unaggressive, responsive to the needs and demands of others."[38] Male as well as female are in personality very like our notion of the normal nurturant woman. Among the Mundugumor, in contrast, "both men and women developed as ruthless, aggressive, positively sexed individuals, with the maternal cherishing aspects of personality at a minimum. Both men and women approximated to a personality type that we in our culture would find only in an undisciplined and very violent male."[39]

In the third tribe, the Tchambuli, sex-linked personality differences are found. "The women [are] the dominant, impersonal, managing partner, the man the less responsible and emotionally dependent person."[40] From our perspective Tchambuli men are feminine; Tchambuli women, masculine.

Mead concludes: "Many, if not all, of the personality traits which we have called masculine or feminine are as lightly linked to sex as are the clothing, the manners, and the form of headdress that a society at a given period assigns to either sex."[41]

FEMINIST REEXAMINATION OF SEX DIFFERENCE STUDIES

Psychologists with a feminist orientation have attacked theories such as Freud's which purport to explain psychological sex differences on the basis of biological differences. The multitude of empirical studies of sex differences have also been reexamined and frequently found to be wanting.[42] Too often, complex characteristics such as passive dependency or aggression

---

[38] Margaret Mead, *Sex and Temperament in Three Primitive Societies* (New York: Dell, 1968), p. 259.

[39] Ibid.

[40] Ibid.

[41] Ibid., p. 260.

[42] See Julia A. Sherman, "Some Psychological 'Facts' About Women: Will the Real Ms. Please Stand Up," in Joan I. Roberts. *Beyond Intellectual Sexism* (New York: David McKay, 1976); and Mary Brown Parlee, "Psychology," *Signs*, vol. 1, no. 1 (autumn 1975).

were measured in unitary and simple-minded ways. Researchers who found a significant sex difference on one trait and no difference on ten others would report the difference and not the similarities. Illegitimate conclusions were often drawn from the data. Thus the finding that males are consistently better at spatial tasks was interpreted as indicating that men have superior analytic ability.[43]

Psychologist Julia Sherman, who has reviewed the sex-difference literature exhaustively, finds the evidence does not support the notion that women generally are more dependent and passive than men,[44] that they are generally more emotional than men,[45] or that men are superior in abstract and logical thinking.[46] In aggressiveness, the sex difference seems to be restricted to attack aggression; that is, "the male does have a greater tendency to attack or retaliate in certain interpersonal situations."[47] She concludes: "Increased research, improved conceptual models, and cultural change have revealed many sex differences to be more apparent than real."[48]

These reexaminations do not prove there are no psychological differences between the sexes. In fact, given the sex role socialization process which will be discussed in the next chapter, it would be surprising if there were none. What is clear is that theories such as Freud's assume much greater sex differences than actually seem to exist.

NATURE OR NURTURE?

Are psychological sex differences innate or learned? The evidence indicates that masculinity and femininity are social concepts that refer to a society's ideas about what men and women are supposed to be like. A society will socialize its children according to these ideas and thus produce men and women who are very like what society expects them to be. Ideas about

---

[43] Sherman, op. cit., p. 130.
[44] Ibid., p. 119.
[45] Ibid., p. 129.
[46] Ibid., p. 130.
[47] Eleanor Maccoby and Carol Jacklin, "Sex Differences in Intellectual Functioning." Paper presented at the meeting of the Educational Testing Service Invitational Conference on Testing Problems, October 1972, p. 11.
[48] Sherman, op. cit., p. 119.

what constitutes masculinity and femininity, however, vary from one society to another.

Are there any innate differences between men and women besides the obvious genital ones? We do not know and probably will never know unless the present socialization process is radically changed. So long as boys and girls are brought up to behave very differently, it will be impossible to disentangle the innate from the learned.

But we do know that human beings are extremely malleable. Psychologists have learned that, by and large, people behave very much the way those around them expect them to behave. A number of studies have shown that the expectations of the experimenter affect the outcome of the experiment. If experimenters are told that their rats are especially good at running mazes, even though in fact they are just average, the rats perform better. If teachers are told that certain students are intellectually promising, even though the students were randomly selected, the students dramatically increase their IQs.[49] Social expectations and social context are crucial: So long as society expects women to be different from men, they are likely to be different.

Intellectual performance is one area in which social expectations seem to have an effect. There are few intellectual differences between the sexes until high school; the few that do exist in the early school years mostly favor girls. In high school, girls begin to fall behind in areas defined as masculine—math in particular.[50] Are innate incapacities becoming manifest at this period in a girl's life or are girls learning too well what is expected of them? Naomi Weisstein concludes that, given society's expectations about women, "what is surprising is that little girls don't get the message that they are supposed to be stupid until high school; and what is even more remarkable is that some women resist this message even after high school, college, and graduate school."[51]

---

[49] Weisstein, op. cit., p. 75.

[50] Eleanor E. Maccoby, "Sex Differences in Intellectual Functioning" in Maccoby, op. cit., pp. 25–55.

[51] Weisstein, op. cit., p. 81.

THE SELF-FULFILLING PROPHECY: SEX ROLE SOCIALIZATION

3

Before a newborn baby leaves the delivery room, a bracelet with its family name is put around its wrist. If the baby is a girl, the bracelet is pink; if a boy, the bracelet is blue. These different-colored bracelets indicate the importance our society places on sex differences, and this branding is the first act in a sex role socialization process that will result in adult men and women being almost as different as we think they "naturally" are.

SOCIALIZATION AND SOCIETY

Every society has a set of ideas about what people are supposed to believe and how they should act—about what is natural and right in beliefs and behaviors. Children are taught these norms and expectations by parental instruction, in school, and by example.

Although the extent to which this socialization "takes" will vary, most children will grow up to act pretty much as they are expected to. The child has internalized society's standards—he or she has come to believe that certain types of behavior are natural and right. Furthermore, behavior at odds with society's standards is costly: at best one is considered deviant; at worst, thrown in jail.

All societies have expectations about how people are to behave, but few expect all their members to behave in the same way. What is proper, natural behavior will depend on certain attributes of the person, such as class, age, occupation, or sex. Perhaps because sex is such an obvious differentiating characteristic, almost all societies have sex roles. Women are expected to think and behave differently from men. The societal expectation and belief that women and men are very different tends to be a self-fulfilling prophecy. The socialization process ensures that so long as such beliefs are widely held, girls and boys will grow up to be different from each other in just the way expected. How this process works in the United States is the subject of this chapter.

EARLY CHILDHOOD

The baby is likely to be taken home wrapped in a blanket of the proper color to a nursery decorated in that color—at least if it is the first child of middle-class parents. Although this makes no difference to the baby, it does show the importance the parents attach to its sex. One study of parents' reactions to their newborn infants found that girl babies were described as significantly softer, finer featured, smaller, and more inattentive than boy babies, even though there actually was no sex difference in size or weight.[1] College students' descriptions of a baby were also found to depend upon which sex they were told the child was. If told the baby was a girl, the students described it as "littler," "weaker," or "cuddlier."[2] These studies indicate that, to a considerable extent, people see what they expect to see. Sex role socialization has led us to expect sex differences even in newborns.

These expectations do result in parents treating their male and female children differently. Sex-linked differences in maternal behavior have been observed toward six-month-old infants.[3] Mothers were found to touch, talk to, and handle their daughters more than their sons. Not surprisingly, at thirteen months the girls were more dependent on their mothers. They tended to stay closer to their mothers, to talk to them and touch them more than boys did. Boys tended to show more

---

[1] Jeffrey Rubin, Frank Provenzano, and Zella Luria, "The Eye of the Beholder: Parents' View on Sex of Newborns," *American Journal of Orthopsychiatry,* 44 (1974), pp. 512–519.

[2] Study by Luria and Rubin reported in *Parade,* February 22, 1976.

[3] Susan Goldberg and Michael Lewis, "Play Behavior in the Year-Old Infant: Early Sex Differences," in Judith M. Bardwick, ed., *Readings on the Psychology of Women* (New York: Harper & Row, 1972), pp. 30–33.

independence and exploratory behavior, to be more vigorous, and to run and make more noise in their play. The authors of a study of early childhood behavior hypothesize that "in the first year or two, the parents reinforce those behaviors they consider sex-role appropriate and the child learns these sex role behaviors independent of any internal motives."[4]

The overprotection most little girls receive seems to result in one of the few early intellectual differences between boys and girls.[5] Boys tend to be better at spatial perception, the ability to visualize objects out of context. This is important because it seems to be related to the sort of analytic thinking required in the sciences. Early independence training—that is, allowing a child to explore and solve problems on its own—is conducive to the development of this ability. Girls are much less likely to receive such training. "Overprotected" boys also tend to do less well on spatial perception tests.

Reinforcement of sex-role appropriate behavior takes place in a variety of subtle and not-so-subtle ways. Boys and girls are given different toys from a very young age. Boys' toys are more varied, more likely to encourage activities outside the house, and have a higher "competency-eliciting value."[6] In nursery school, children are strongly encouraged to play with the "appropriate" toys.[7] Girls are more severely reprimanded for noisy and boisterous behavior.[8] Boys are allowed and often encouraged to be aggressive. One study found that a father often takes pride in his son's being a "holy terror" but is worried if his daughter is "bossy."[9] Fathers expect their daughters to be "nice, sweet, pretty, affectionate and well-liked."

These middle-class fathers were much more concerned about the behavior of their sons than that of their daughters. They worried about "lack of responsibility and initiative, inadequate

---

[4] Ibid., p. 33.

[5] Jo Freeman, "The Social Construction of the Second Sex," in Michele Hoffnung Garskof, ed., *Roles Women Play* (Belmont, Calif.: Brooks/Cole, 1971), pp. 129–130.

[6] Reesa M. Vaughter, "Psychology," *Signs* (autumn 1976), pp. 125–126.

[7] Carol Andreas, *Sex and Caste in America* (Englewood Cliffs, N.J.: Prentice-Hall, 1971), p. 28 passim.

[8] Ibid.

[9] David F. Aberle and Kaspar D. Naegele, "Raising Middle-Class Sons," in Alex Inkeles, ed., *Readings in Modern Sociology* (Englewood Cliffs, N.J.: Prentice-Hall, 1966), p. 104.

performance in school, insufficiently aggressive or excessively passive behavior, athletic inadequacies, overconformity, excitability, excessive tearfulness . . . and 'childish' behavior."[10] Such behaviors are considered inappropriate when exhibited by a male child and, presumably, are penalized. When they appear in girls, they are not a source of worry and are not discouraged, at least not to the same extent.

Another study of nursery school children found very much the same patterns.[11] Parents valued malleability, cooperativeness, and willingness to take direction, but disapproved of assertiveness and quarrelsomeness in girls. In boys, independence, assertiveness, and inquisitiveness were valued; timidity and fearfulness disapproved. The teachers' attitudes were similar to those of the parents. They encouraged boys to be daring and aggressive, but discouraged girls. Their behavior toward a child having trouble climbing to the top of a jungle gym, for example, varied with the sex of the child. A girl would be told, "Take it easy, dear—we'll help you down"; a boy, "That's the boy! You can make it if you want to!"

Thus, from birth male and female children are treated differently and are rewarded for displaying differing types of behavior.

By age three, children can label themselves correctly as boy or girl, although they are not clear about the genital differences underlying that distinction. They do know which jobs are performed by men and which by women, and what they report is the traditional, sex-stereotyped division of labor.[12] By age five or six, children are not only clear that there is a distinction between the male and female role but are also aware that the male role is the more highly valued. "Fathers are perceived as more powerful, punitive, aggressive, fearless, instrumentally competent and less nurturant than females. . . . Thus power and prestige appear as one major attribute of children's sex-role stereotypes. . . ."[13] By age six, children consistently attrib-

---

[10] Ibid., p. 103.

[11] Kirsten Amundsen, *The Silenced Majority* (Englewood Cliffs, N.J.: Prentice-Hall, 1971), pp. 116–117.

[12] Judith Bardwick, *Psychology of Women* (New York: Harper & Row, 1971), p. 142.

[13] Lawrence Kohlberg, "A Cognitive-Developmental Analysis of Children's Sex-Role Concepts and Attitudes," in Eleanor Maccoby, ed., *The Development of Sex Differences* (Stanford, Calif.: Stanford University Press, 1966), p. 99.

ute more social power to the father; they consider him smarter than the mother and the boss of the family.[14]

All small children seem to think their own sex is best and to express preferences for others of the same sex. Psychologists explain these findings on the basis of the child's egotism—"what's like me is best." For boys, the same-sex preferences continue throughout childhood. With girls, a decline sets in at the time they learn the greater prestige attributed to the male role. Girls, as they get older, become less and less likely than boys to say their own sex is better.[15] Their opinion of boys and boys' abilities grows better with age, while the boys' opinions of girls grow worse.[16] Girls, then, begin to develop a negative self-image at an early age.

In the child's early years the family is the most important socializing agency, but it is not the only one. Children's books and television programs also influence perceptions of what is normal and appropriate. Until very recently, both presented a rigidly sex-stereotyped view. Most books for young children were about boys; when girls or women appeared, they were restricted to traditional feminine pursuits. One mother reports that when she started reading to her daughter at age two, the little girl would ask questions like "Why aren't the girls fixing their own bikes?" and "Why isn't the little girl riding the horse?" After a few years of such books, the woman found that her daughter was constantly making derogatory remarks about girls—"Girls can't do anything"; "Girls can only do dumb things."[17]

Children's television programs further reinforce the notion that girls are less important and capable than boys. On the highly acclaimed "Sesame Street," females appear less than half as often as males and about one-third as often when the appearance involves any dialogue.[18] The women who do appear are almost always wives and mothers. "Virtually all [the programs] emphasized that there is men's work and then there is women's work—that the men's work is outside the home

---

[14] Ibid., p. 102.
[15] Ibid., p. 120.
[16] Freeman, op. cit., p. 125.
[17] Quoted in Riverside, California, *Daily Enterprise*, May 31, 1973.
[18] Carolyn Calvery, "Sexism on Sesame Street," available from the author at 11541 Hierra Court, Los Altos, California 94022.

and the women's work in the home."[19] Of course children are quite aware of which type of work is valued by society.

GRADE SCHOOL

Grammar school continues the sex role socialization process. One study found that more than half of the teachers questioned admitted that they consciously behave differently toward boys and girls. Several studies have found that boys receive more attention from the teacher than girls. While teachers tended to direct more supportive remarks to girls and more critical ones to boys, they were much more likely to reward creative behavior in boys than in girls. "The message to girls is that one does best by being good and being conformist; creativity is reserved for boys."[20]

Having themselves grown up in a sexist society, most teachers, female as well as male, have internalized sexist attitudes, and such attitudes affect their behavior toward their students. Most teachers probably never say girls are inferior to boys; they convey their feelings through their behavior. An occasional teacher is more blatant. A young woman recalls a discussion of a story concerning a male chef when she was in grammar school. One student commented that only a "sissy" would cook because that's a woman's job.

> The teacher's response surprised us all. She informed us calmly that men make the best cooks, just as they make the best dress designers, singers, and laundry workers. "Yes," she said, "anything a woman can do a man can do better."[21]

The attitudes of parents, teachers, and peers affect the child's view of what is natural and right. So, also, do the schoolbooks from which he or she learns to read. These provide one of the child's first views of the wider world outside the neighborhood. What, then, is "reality" as portrayed by elementary schoolbooks?

---

[19] Jo-Ann Gardner, quoted in Judith Hole and Ellen Levine, *Rebirth of Feminism* (New York: Quadrangle, 1971), pp. 250–251.

[20] Bardwick, op. cit., p. 113.

[21] Quoted in Florence Howe, "Sexual Stereotypes Start Early," in Marie B. Hecht et al., eds., *The Women, Yes!* (New York: Holt, Rinehart and Winston, 1973), pp. 190–191.

An excellent study entitled *Dick and Jane as Victims*[22] answers this question. Because the answer is so disturbing, the results will be presented in detail. One hundred and thirty-four elementary school readers currently being used in three suburban New Jersey towns were examined. Fourteen different national publishers are represented, so these are books used all over the United States.

In the world of elementary readers, there are a lot more boys than girls. There are many more stories about boys. Boys also appear more frequently in illustrations; when girls are shown, they are often just scenery. The ratios speak for themselves.[23]

Boy-centered stories to girl-centered stories	5 : 2
Adult male main character to adult female main character	3 : 1
Male biographies to female biographies	6 : 1
Male animal stories to female animal stories	2 : 1
Male folk or fantasy stories to female folk or fantasy stories	4 : 1

In terms of sheer numbers, these books portray a male-dominated world. The numbers by themselves convey to the child the notion that males are more important and more interesting. The content of the stories leaves no doubt about it.

Most of the stories are about the development and display of ingenuity, creativity, bravery, perseverance, achievement, adventurousness, curiosity, sportsmanship, autonomy, and self-respect.[24] These traits are generally valued in our society, and their development is presumably an important part of growing up. In the school readers, it is the male who displays such traits by a ratio of 4 to 1.

There are 164 stories emphasizing ingenuity and resourcefulness. The main character in these meets a situation with intelligence; he builds things; he uses his wits. In 131, the main character is a boy. The authors of the study comment, "The girl who figures out how to earn bus fare when she finds herself stranded seems like a visitor to these pages."[25]

In stories emphasizing perseverance and initiative, boys out-

---

[22] *Dick and Jane as Victims, Women on Words and Images,* 1972 (P.O. Box 2163, Princeton, New Jersey 68540).
[23] Ibid., p. 6.
[24] Ibid., p. 7.
[25] Ibid.

number girls by 169 to 47. And what sort of obstacles do girls overcome? In one story a girl wins a tennis match despite a dirty tennis dress.

Bravery and heroism are male traits—143 to 36. Typically boys rescue whole towns and save planes and spaceships; the occasional brave girl rescues younger siblings or small animals.

The acquisition of skills and coming-of-age themes are again found predominantly in stories about boys (151 to 53). In one story a boy kills a grizzly while taking care of the ranch in his father's absence. (We wonder what his frontier mother did before her son was old enough to protect her.) Any grown-up skills a girl learns tend to be domestic ones.

Stories in which competitiveness and the use of power play a role mostly concern sports. The boys almost always win; when a girl wins, it's often the result of a fluke.

Not only are boys more frequently involved in exploration and adventure stories (216 to 68); their adventures are a lot more exciting. Boys explore in China and meet bears in Yellowstone; girls watch their first snowstorm from inside the house.

When discussing stories on the theme of autonomy and normal assertiveness, the authors comment, "Stories about girls behaving as complete and independent persons are so rare they seem odd."[26] The traits considered desirable in our society are depicted in these books as male traits.

When one looks more carefully at how girls are portrayed in these stories, one begins to wish there were no stories about girls at all. The traits of passivity, docility, and dependence are displayed by 119 girls and only 19 boys. Girls cry a lot; they depend on boys to help them with things they should be quite capable of doing themselves; they are shown as spectators of life. In both stories and illustrations, girls spend a large part of their lives watching and admiring boys.

A good part of the rest of their lives is spent doing domestic chores—scrubbing floors, washing dishes, baking cookies—and usually enjoying it. "A girl's inborn aptitude for drudgery is presented in the same spirit as a black person's 'natural rhythm.' "[27] A girl who succeeds at anything nondomestic is seen as exceptional. One biographical story insists, "Amelia

---

[26] Ibid., p. 13.
[27] Ibid., p. 19.

Earhart was different from the beginning from other girls."[28]

Girls are not just dependent and domestic ; frequently they are just plain stupid. Both boys and girls have mishaps, but boys' occur because of adventuresomeness, the girls' because of stupidity. If a boy fails at something, he will presevere and finally succeed. Girls give up. Boys are frequently smarter than their mothers, who are, after all, female. The foolish/female, smart/male equation is exemplified "in one amazing story [in which] the author, by some Freudian slip, changes the sex of the stupid *female* kitten in time for 'him' to out-wit the fox!"[29]

If the image of girls is bad, the portrayal of their mothers is even worse. Mother is not really human at all. She is the perfect servant, "a limited, colorless, mindless creature."[30] When a boy is stuck in a tree, he has to wait for his father to come home to rescue him. Mother is evidently incapable of thinking of bringing the ladder. Not only does mother never do anything undomestic; even in this sphere tasks are strictly sex segregated. Father does all the yard work and is the fixer; mother does all the inside work.[31] The notion that tasks might be alternated or even shared appears to be considered heresy. Basically, mother is dull.

Are there any positive role models for girls? Very few. One hundred and forty-seven occupations are shown for men; 26 for women. Mothers, of course, don't work. In the 2760 stories only three working mothers appear, and they work only out of dire necessity. Fathers, of course, work. Men in these stories are everything from airplane builders to zookeepers. Women are mostly in the traditional feminine occupations—babysitter, cashier, dressmaker, librarian, school nurse, teacher. The more exotic female "occupations"—circus fat lady and witch—are hardly viable role models.

Another study,[32] one of California elementary school texts, found a woman scientist. She was the only working woman in a series of descriptions of present-day professionals, and the

---

[28] Quoted in ibid.
[29] Ibid., p. 21.
[30] Ibid., p. 26.
[31] Ibid., p. 27.
[32] Marjorie B. U'Ren, "The Image of Woman in Textbooks," in Vivian Gornick and Barbara K. Moran, eds., *Woman in Sexist Society* (New York: Signet, 1971), p. 324.

text says twice that she is working on an idea not her own. The men scientists are shown as doing work that requires originality.

The biographical stories do offer some worthy female role models, but not many. There were 119 stories about 88 different men, but only 27 stories about 17 women. Boys are offered the full range from Albert Einstein to Mickey Mantle. There is a biography of Alexander the Great, but none of Queen Elizabeth I. Susan B. Anthony and other women's leaders are, of course, not included. The California study found a story about Marie Curie in which she is made to appear as little more than an assistant to her husband.[33]

According to these books, then, the normal girl is dependent, fearful, and incompetent. Girls are not even shown as excelling in schoolwork, as they actually do in grade school. In some cases the point that a girl should not be assertive is made in really gross fashion. In one story an Indian girl who wanted to be tall, brave, and strong like the men is turned into a shadow for her presumption. And what happens when the girl grows up? Not much. She becomes the textbook mother—a household drudge incompetent at anything outside her narrow province. The California study found not one story in which the mother so much as suggests a solution in a family crisis. Textbook mothers don't even drive cars (which, given their IQ, is probably a good thing).

No wonder, then, that textbook boys have such a low opinion of females. The New Jersey study found 67 stories in which one sex demeans the other; girls are victims in 65 cases, boys in 2. Boys attack and ridicule girls as being "foolish, vain, silly, dumb, boring, no good at games and sports, etc., ad nauseam."[34] In one story, "Smart Annabelle" asks a group of boys about the contraption they are building. She is put into her place with the comment, "We are willing to share our great thoughts with mankind. However, you happen to be a girl."[35] Such behavior by boys is never condemned or even commented on. Even worse, in these stories girls agree with boys' low opinions of their sex and frequently put themselves down with remarks

---

[33] Ibid., p. 323.
[34] *Dick and Jane as Victims,* op. cit., p. 21.
[35] Quoted in ibid., p. 2.

like: "I'm just a girl but I know enough not to do that," and "Even I can do it and you know how stupid I am."[36]

The image of females conveyed by these readers is almost wholly negative. Little girls are generally nicer than little boys, but, as is made clear, nice is dull. Girls are also self-sacrificing, an admirable trait in moderation. But the readers portray self-abnegation as a natural component of the female personality, thus clearly implying that if a girl ever puts herself first she is some sort of monster. "The readers present a twisted view that happiness for girls lies chiefly in giving happiness to boys and men. Success, excitement, confidence, and status must be derived from association with the 'powerful' sex."[37]

The image of males, while much more positive, does contain some disturbing elements. Ingenuity, independence, creativity, and bravery are presented as admirable male traits, but excessive aggression and even dishonesty are not clearly condemned. Even when the fantasy and animal stories were excluded, almost 100 stories condoning meanness and cruelty as part of the story line were found. The study concludes that "boys are being given permission to vent a twisted type of aggression and sadism."[38] As far as dishonesty goes, the authors comment: "There is a blurry line drawn between praise-worthy enterprise and rather shady accomplishment in which a bright lad with a head on his shoulders bends the rules to his needs."[39]

Boys are being taught that overt aggressiveness is at least normal, if not praiseworthy, male behavior and that winning is more important than playing by the rules. They are also taught that displaying emotion is unmasculine. Showing emotions is a feminine trait and one that attests to the female's weakness and foolishness. Under the most extreme circumstances boys must keep calm; in contrast, girls become terrified and cry on the slightest provocation. "Only on the pages of a reader does a girl weep non-stop from morning to night over a broken doll. Only on the pages of a reader does a boy remain impassive while his canoe proceeds out of control through the rapids."[40]

---

[36] Quoted in ibid., p. 21.
[37] Ibid., p. 30.
[38] Ibid., p. 22.
[39] Ibid., p. 15.
[40] Ibid., p. 22.

The images the texts present for children to model themselves upon are almost completely negative in the case of girls and contain destructive elements in the case of boys. But do these books really have an effect? They might not have much if these were the only forces pushing children into sex-stereotyped attitudes and behaviors. But in fact the texts present and reinforce society's attitudes toward men and women.

Television carries much the same message as the children's readers. A study of the most-watched prime-time shows during the 1973 viewing season found that 61 percent of the major characters were male.[41] On the adventure shows, 85 percent were male. Thus TV, which takes up so many hours of most children's time, portrays a predominantly male world. The women who do appear tend to be stereotyped occupationally—they are housewives, teachers, secretaries, and waitresses.[42] Only rarely does a professional woman appear. On the adventure shows particularly, women are depicted as incompetent. Forty-six percent of male behaviors but only 14 percent of female behaviors were classified as displaying competence; in contrast, 3 percent of male but 31 percent of female behaviors displayed incompetence.[43]

Sex role stereotyping thus begins at birth and is conveyed by most of the institutions in our society. Family, school, the media in concert teach children to think and act in sex-appropriate ways.

In many ways, until adolescence, the pressures are greater on the boy. Girls are allowed and encouraged to be dependent, but this is normal behavior for a small child. Boys, from a very young age, are told not to cry, not to run to mother but to fight back, to "be a man," not to "act like a girl."

While allowing a child independence is important for intellectual development, pressing a little boy to be physically aggressive and emotionally impassive is likely to leave scars. The child knows he is not really the person his parents expect him to be, even if he outwardly displays the expected behavior. Not surprisingly, many boys grow up with doubts about their masculinity, and many compensate for their doubts through

---

[41] *Channeling Children* (Princeton, N.J.; Women on Words and Images, 1975), p. 19.

[42] Ibid., pp. 19–21.

[43] Ibid., pp. 22–25.

overly "masculine" behavior. A man who values physical strength and aggressiveness above all else, who is convinced that any display of emotion or sensitivity to others' feelings is a feminine characteristic, is likely to find life very difficult. In a complex, industrial society there are very few comfortable niches for the John Waynes of the world.

For little boys the male role is frequently defined as the opposite of the female role. Fathers and mothers often tell a boy, when he is doing something of which they disapprove, that he is acting like a girl. This clearly contributes to the virulent antigirl feelings expressed by many little boys. One woman wrote to ask why girls could not be included in the Tonka Toys slogan, which says, "You can't raise boys without Tonka Toys." The company replied that if little boys know that girls also play with a toy, they will not want it.[44]

Dislike and disparagement of girls is fostered by childrearing practices and by the school texts. The texts seldom show cross-sex friendships, and most organized recreational activities for grade school children are sex segregated. Cub Scouts is for boys only; Brownies and Bluebirds for girls. Such segregation again reinforces the notion that boys and girls are very different.

The idea that males are naturally brave, independent, and resourceful while females are timid and dependent tends to be a self-fulfilling prophecy. Parents base their childrearing practices on this idea. Thus boys are given more independence at an earlier age than girls. They are allowed to play away from home, to walk to school alone, to pick their own activities, movies, and books earlier than their sisters. Boys are also given more personal privacy—to pick friends and girlfriends and to come and go as they please without parental consent being required. Psychologist Mirra Komarovsky concludes, "Parents tend to speed up, most often unwittingly, but also deliberately, the emancipation of the boy from the family, while they retard it in the case of his sister."[45]

That males are physically strong and females weak is another self-fulfilling prophecy. Boys are strongly encouraged and

---

[44] Hole and Levine, op. cit., p. 337.

[45] Mirra Komarovsky, "Functional Analysis of Sex Roles," in Marvin B. Sussman, ed., *Sourcebook in Marriage and the Family* (Boston: Houghton Mifflin, 1968), p. 261.

sometimes forced to participate in athletics from a very early age. Being good at sports is an important element of "masculinity" in our society. A boy who doesn't love baseball and football is considered a sissy, if not an incipient homosexual. A boy learns early that athletic prowess brings prestige with his peers and approval from his parents.

Delicacy and even physical weakness are still components of our notion of femininity. Girls are not encouraged to participate in athletics. Sometimes they are actively discouraged. "Several years ago in California there was a movement trying to say that it's too strenuous for girls to compete in sports," an Indio, California, school principal reports.[46]

Girls who wish to participate often find little opportunity. The Little League, until very recently, admitted only boys, and there was no comparable organization for girls. Although in high school some organized sports are available to girls, the bulk of the money and effort goes into boys' sports. Lucy Komisar reports that "the Syracuse school system spent about $90,000 for boys' extracurricular athletics compared to $200 for girls."[47] Until recently women coaches generally got no coaching pay. Girls' teams did not get special equipment; they had to make do with equipment used in gym classes, which was often in poor shape. If the girls wanted new equipment, uniforms, or travel money, they had to raise it themselves through bake sales and the like.[48]

The low value put on women's athletics will discourage many girls. They will grow up just about as they are expected to—not delicate or weak, but much less strong and physically fit than they could be.

ADOLESCENCE

When children enter adolescence, they are aware of and have to a large extent internalized society's views of sex-appropriate attitudes and behavior. Good girls are sweet, obedient, and docile; they grow up to be mommies. Good boys are "little men"—daring and aggressive; they grow up to be presidents

---

[46] Quoted in Riverside, California, *Press Enterprise,* May 27, 1973.
[47] Lucy Komisar, *The New Feminism* (New York: Warner Paperback Library, 1972), p. 32.
[48] Riverside, California, *Press Enterprise,* May 27, 1973.

or at least firefighters. Until this point, overt socialization pressures have been directed more at the boy than the girl. After all, turning a child into John Wayne is no easy task. Girls have been allowed and encouraged to remain childish—that is, dependent. They have also been encouraged to be little ladies, although most parents will condone a certain amount of tomboyishness in a preadolescent girl.

At adolescence the situation changes. The pressure on the boy to achieve academically and athletically continues. The pressure on the girl to be feminine increases enormously. Mothers particularly are terribly concerned that their daughters be feminine and popular and may push them into absurdly early dating. Padded bras for ten-year-olds are sold, and it's not the little girls who pay for them. Peer pressures become tremendously important in adolescence. Being popular becomes crucial, and for a girl that means being popular with boys as a female. In grade school, the tomboy or girl clown may be popular, and this sort of popularity may continue. But everyone knows that it's not the right sort of popularity. It doesn't get you dates.

Being popular in high school means living up to boys' expectations of what a girl is supposed to be like. She should be pretty; she should not be too smart or talk in class much; she should be supportive and admiring of the boy she is with. In one study, 40 percent of the girls interviewed admitted to "playing dumb" on dates, at least occasionally.[49] And of course not all girls need to *play* dumb. The really popular, successful high school girl is not a "brain" or even an athlete; she is the cheerleader. She embodies the supportive and admiring role assigned to girls. She is defined in terms of her relationship to boys.

Because of their early upbringing, girls are less likely to have developed an independent sense of self-worth, are more likely to depend on the opinions of others for a feeling of worth and thus to define themselves in terms of their relationships with others. Unlike the boy, the girl is not encouraged to be independent, to explore and solve problems for herself. The girl remains more dependent and relies on the family for her

---

[49] Mirra Komarovsky, "Cultural Contradictions and Sex Roles," in Bardwick, *Readings on the Psychology of Women,* op. cit., p. 60.

feeling of self-worth. Now, in adolescence, she is encouraged to define herself in relation to boys. She is successful not if she accomplishes something intellectually, artistically, or athletically, but only if boys like her.

Dating, which can honestly be labeled one of the barbaric rituals of our society, intensifies this process. Awakening sexual drives and the societal prohibition against their expression would make adolescence a difficult time in any case. The dating ritual makes it acutely painful for the great majority. Because boys and girls have been segregated in play activities, they find it very difficult to talk together, much less be real friends. The accepted dating procedure reinforces the female/passive, male/aggressive stereotype. The boy must call the girl; she must passively sit and wait. The boy who has managed to get by and hide the fact that he's not really John Wayne is now expected to be James Bond. If not enough boys call, the girl is a failure as a woman. The fact that the boy is expected to pay for both himself and his date not only places a financial burden on him but encourages in both parties the notion of woman as passive object. "I always feel like I'm being rented for the evening," one girl commented. "I have to be nice and charming and do what he wants to do because he's paying."[50]

The dating ritual reinforces the tendency already instilled in the girl to see herself as passive and to define herself in terms of her relationships with men. It engenders conflicts among girls because they are in competition for the attentions of the same set of boys. The canard that women cannot be true friends contains a grain of truth. Many women do go through life regarding other women as competitors. This is not a healthy sort of competition in which winning depends on the development and expression of skills and abilities. It is, rather, an expression of the slave mentality. Winning depends not on what you can do but on the capricious choice of the master.

The dating ritual also places a tremendous premium on good looks. No girl growing up in America can escape the conclusion that being feminine depends not only on appropriate behavior but also on being pretty. From television, movies, and women's magazines she may well conclude that without beauty happi-

---

[50] Quoted in Komisar, op. cit., p. 39.

ness is impossible, and her experiences with peers are likely to confirm that conclusion. Boys, too, have been socialized into regarding appearance as a girl's most important characteristic. Dating a plain girl, however interesting she may be, means loss of social prestige.

Who determines the standard of beauty? The media, including Hollywood, decree the ideal. The ideal allows for little variety and individuality and, of course, excludes the vast majority of women.

All girls, not just the real plain ones, suffer from this inordinate emphasis on looks. Is there a girl who, during her teen years, was not convinced that some aspect of her looks was just awful? She is too short or too tall, too fat or too thin; her breasts are too small or too big; she has a mole on her face; her nose is too big or crooked; her ears stick out. When beauty becomes the one and only passport to happiness, a morbid sort of self-consciousness results. A girl becomes sure that a flaw so minor no one notices it completely ruins her looks and thus her life. A pimple becomes a cosmic disaster.

Such a preoccupation with looks, while destructive for the girl, is good for the economy. She is willing to believe the wildest advertising claims and will spend any money she has on clothes and cosmetics. Perhaps this product will finally make her look like Raquel Welch or whoever is the latest sex symbol. The girl begins to regard herself as a product that must be adorned and properly displayed so as to command the highest possible price.

The media, of course, encourage such a view. Advertising, with its insistence that you aren't a real woman and will never catch a man unless you use a certain eyeshadow or vaginal spray or whatever, is a major offender. The features in women's magazines are just as bad. *Seventeen,* which is aimed at high school girls, devotes most of its space to fashions, makeup, and hair styling. The message is clear: Success for a girl means attracting boys, and that requires making the best of your physical resources. (Behavioral tips are also given: Be sweet and charming, a little helpless, and not too smart. And don't be domineering—that is, don't show that you have a mind of your own.)

Given these preoccupations, it's remarkable that girls do as well as they do academically. Throughout grade school, girls are ahead of boys academically. In high school, their grades are on the average as good as boys', and more girls graduate than boys. But girls do begin to slip in some areas—those that are defined as masculine. Thus on college entrance exams the sexes do equally well on the verbal aptitude section, but the boys score significantly higher on math. If the problems are reworded so that they deal with "typically" feminine pursuits (cooking, for example), the girls' performances improve.[51] "It's around the eighth or ninth grade that this kind of thing begins to occur," one teacher said. "Girls don't like to answer in class; they don't volunteer very often. If you call on a girl, she'll much more likely give you a blank stare while boys will try to think of an answer or make one up. Often, even if girls know the answer, they giggle and act stupid. They're always putting themselves down. . . . Even if girls don't have trouble with math, they say they do. They think math is somehow for boys."[52] If an occasional girl does not catch on, the teacher may well set her straight. A New York high school student explains:

> Well, within my physics class last year, our teacher asked if there was anyone interested in being a lab assistant, in the physics lab, and when I raised my hand, he told all the girls to put their hands down because he was only interested in working with boys.[53]

The expectations of a girl with respect to academic performance are ambivalent. She is aware that achievement is a societal value. Particularly if they are middle class, her parents will expect her to do well at school. At the same time her mother, especially, is likely to warn her not to do too well. "Let him think he's smarter," she'll be told. Not surprisingly, many girls feel resentment. One high school girl complained that her family told her to work hard at school in order to get into a top university. Simultaneously, however, they compared her to her friend next door who was "pretty and sweet" and very popular. So they also hounded her to work on her appearance and have a "successful" social life. "They were overlooking the fact that this carefree friend of mine had little time left for school work and had failed several subjects. It seemed that my family had

---

[51] Sandra L. and Daryl J. Bem, "Training the Woman to Know Her Place: The Power of a Nonconscious Ideology," in Garskof, op. cit., pp. 87–88.
[52] Quoted in Komisar, op. cit., p. 34.
[53] Quoted in Howe, op. cit., p. 194.

expected me to become Eve Curie and Hedy Lamarr wrapped up in one."[54]

Expectations about careers for girls are considerably less ambivalent. Boys are encouraged to think about growing up to be something from a very early age; in high school the pressure seriously to consider career plans intensifies. If the boy is middle class and not obviously mentally deficient, it is assumed that he will go into a profession or into business. Girls may be encouraged to prepare for a job but seldom for a career. They have been taught from earliest childhood that their most important adult role will be that of wife and mother. This is never presented to girls as a matter of choice. You're either normal or not. A girl who didn't want to grow up and have babies would be some kind of freak, if not a downright monster.

Typically it is the mother who impresses the importance of marriage on her daughters. But fathers are in complete agreement. A study of middle-class fathers found that the men interviewed expected their daughters to get married and preferred marriage over a career for them.[55] Half were willing to accept the possibility of a career for their daughters; the rest completely rejected the idea. Only two wanted their daughters to know how to earn a living.

The schools do little to make up this deficit. The career education materials used at the primary and secondary school level tend to perpetuate sex stereotypes. One careful study found that most occupations were, through the text or the illustrations, presented as being either male or female; few were clearly shown as appropriate for both sexes.[56] At both grade and high school level, many more male occupations were presented, and the female occupations were, by and large, traditional.[57]

Girls but not boys are told that good grooming is important to job success. "Good posture, attractive glasses, manicured hands, smooth arms and legs, proper girdles to firm buttocks—all enhance the physical qualities we have inherited. The secretary who does not make the most of her physical attributes

---

[54] Komarovsky, "Cultural Contradictions and Sex Roles," op. cit., p. 59.
[55] Aberle and Naegele, op. cit., p. 102.
[56] *Help Wanted: Sexism in Career Education Materials* (Princeton, N.J.: Women on Words and Images, 1975), p. 7.
[57] Ibid., p. 7, p. 9 passim.

is not doing herself justice."[58] Combining family responsibility with those of the job are seen as a female problem. Women are frequently portrayed as quitting jobs to get married.[59] Even those materials prepared under the impetus of the women's movement to combat sex stereotyping sometimes assume that the family is the woman's responsibility and that she should make her career choice with this in mind. Thus girls are advised that "a dental practice can often be adapted to the schedule of a woman who wants to have a family. An office can be established in her home, and a part-time practice can be maintained."[60] The girl who would like to be a successful doctor as well as a wife and mother is told that, among other things, she'd better have "the constitution of an ox."[61]

Boys are not only encouraged to begin career planning early; they are also provided with a wealth of role models. In textbooks, television, and films and in their everyday life, they see men in a variety of careers. In contrast, the role models to which girls are exposed are very limited. Betty Friedan remarks that, aside from women who were full-time wives and mothers, "the only other kind of women I knew growing up were the old maid high-school teachers; the librarian; and the one woman doctor in our town, who cut her hair like a man."[62] A younger woman recalls that at an early age she was already sure she did not want to be like her mother. But the only women she knew who were not full-time mothers were teachers, librarians, secretaries, and waitresses, whom she considered dull.[63]

Schoolbooks, as we saw earlier, present an even more restricted set of female role models. In one American history text, for example, only 26 of the 643 people mentioned are women. "If we are to accept the view of our society presented by our history text," several girls using the book wrote, "ours is a society without women."[64] In six richly illustrated high

---

[58] Ibid., p. 17.
[59] Ibid., pp. 16–17.
[60] Ibid., p. 23.
[61] Ibid., p. 23.
[62] Quoted in Cynthia Epstein, *Woman's Place* (Berkeley: University of California Press, 1971), p. 55.
[63] Roberta Salper, *Female Liberation* (New York: Knopf, 1972), p. 14.
[64] Quoted in Hole and Levine, op. cit., p. 333.

school science texts, Florence Howe reports that the only women in illustrations she found were one doctor, one scientist, one lab assistant, and Rachel Carson.[65] A high school text entitled *Representative Men: Heroes of Our Time* featured two women—Elizabeth Taylor and Jacqueline Onassis.[66]

The image of women in the media is largely a restricted, stereotyped one and frequently just plain insulting. Television commercials are a major offender with their presentation of women as either housewife-mothers or sex kittens. The former are always shallow—their major concern is having the whitest laundry in the neighborhood—and often stupid. The latter are always dumb and sometimes masochistic. For both, pleasing a man is their primary purpose in life.

On television programs one does find an occasional career girl. But what do these "girls" actually do? Taking the highly acclaimed "Mary Tyler Moore Show" as an example, one reviewer asked, "Why can't the writers find something for Mary to do other than waiting on the men in her office, or worrying about the flowers on her desk, or solving the mini-crises of her friends?"[67] Surveying evening television programs, the reviewer found only one truly liberated woman—Miss Kitty, the nineteenth-century saloonkeeper on "Gunsmoke." "She is the only woman character on nighttime television who is her own woman, who is successful in her own right and who doesn't bask in the reflection of some man." The reviewer concludes that the vast majority of women on prime-time television are "unliberated ding-a-lings, sex kittens, kooky housewives, lovable widows, crimefighters' secretaries and nosy nurses."

Many young girls never see, much less get to know, even one intelligent, dedicated professional woman who could serve as a role model. And role models are important. Daughters of working mothers are more likely to expect to hold a job themselves. They consider working normal rather than extraordinary for a woman.[68] One study found that 66 percent of career-oriented college women were daughters of working

---

[65] Howe, op. cit., p. 194.

[66] Ibid., p. 197.

[67] Judy Klemesrud, in Riverside, California, *Press Enterprise*, May 31, 1973.

[68] Ruth E. Hartley, "American Core Culture: Changes and Continuities," in Georgene Seward and Robert Williamson, eds., *Sex Roles in Changing Society* (New York: Random House, 1970), p. 129.

women.[69] In contrast, only 22 percent of women not oriented toward a career had working mothers.

The educational system itself encourages girls to live up to sex stereotypes in their career planning or lack of it. Girls are encouraged to take home economics, boys to take shop. Until it became illegal, in many schools more than encouragement was involved; girls were not allowed to take shop courses. A few high schools required girls to take home economics in order to graduate. Of course by the time high school age is reached, such rules usually are not necessary. A social studies teacher reports: "I've heard girls say they want to take auto mechanics, and the guidance counselors and the mothers threw fits and absolutely shamed those girls out of wanting to take those courses."[70] Career day is a common event in many high schools. Doctors, lawyers, and engineers are brought in to talk to the boys; nurses and airline stewardesses, to talk to the girls.

In some areas public sex-segregated high schools remain. Until recently all but one of New York City's special scientific high schools for especially capable students restricted admission to boys.

But what if, after all this, a girl is still interested in a career? What sort of advice is she likely to receive from the counselor? "They ask girls whether the careers they have in mind would 'fit in' with marriage and a family."[71] Again, it is simply assumed that every girl's primary adult role is that of wife and mother and that she will, of course, subordinate all else to that role. Sometimes the message is conveyed in a blunter fashion. A bright female college student who wanted to be a doctor was told by her adviser that the only reason women go to medical school is to catch a husband. "Why don't you do something more appropriate, dear?"[72]

When a girl receives her high school diploma, what has she learned? Probably some English, math, and history; her proper

[69] Elizabeth Almquist and Shirley Angrist, "Role Model Influences on College Women's Career Aspirations," in Athena Theodore, ed., *The Professional Woman* (Cambridge, Mass.: Schenkman, 1971), p. 301.

[70] Quoted in Komisar, op. cit., p. 33.

[71] Ibid., p. 36.

[72] Quoted in Joan Flannigan, "Women in the Professions," in New York City Commission on Human Rights, *Women's Role in Contemporary Society* (New York: Avon, 1972), p. 358.

place in the scheme of things almost certainly. She has learned that men and women are very different. Males are physically strong and emotionally impassive; they are good at math and science and in mechanical matters; they are natural leaders. Women, in contrast, are designed by nature to play the supportive role whether in a job as nurse or secretary or in the family. Women are not good at math or science or matters mechanical; they are emotional rather than logical. A woman can find personal fulfillment only by marrying the right man and bearing his children. And this is enough for any normal woman: She does not need a career for personal fulfillment. Interest in a demanding career is, in fact, a sign of selfishness in a woman. Furthermore, given her intellectual and emotional traits, she is not likely to succeed at one if she tries. Thus the girl learns not only that men and women are different but that men are better. The traits attributed to men are those generally valued by our society.

More boys than girls go to college. For young people of both sexes, their chance of going beyond high school is related to the income of their parents. But at all income levels girls are less likely than their brothers to continue their education. In working-class families, if there is enough money to send one of the children to college it will be the boy. His sister may be expected to help send him through. Mrs. Danielli, a working-class housewife, said that she is considered something of a "women's libber" for insisting that her daughters also go to college.

> Everyone in the family thought our three girls would go to work to help put my son Johnny through. . . . I told my husband, "Joe, if one of our kids is going to college, all of them are. Your girls aren't gonna have 10 children like your mama—they've gotta do something with their lives just like our boy." Both of our families were shocked when our oldest girl went off to college—Joe's papa kept asking if we didn't need the extra money she could bring in working as a typist. We needed the money, all right, but I never gave in. . . .[73]

In middle-class families where money is less of a problem, girls are more likely to go to college, but still not as likely as their brothers. Of the top 40 percent of high school graduates,

---

[73] Quoted in Susan Jacoby in Riverside, California, *Press Enterprise,* June 17, 1973.

about half go to college; two-thirds of those who do not are female.[74]

What happens to the young woman who ends her education with high school? She may marry immediately, get a job, or both. In any case, her chance of ever breaking out of the rigidly stereotyped female role is slim. Any job she can get will almost certainly be a typical female job—low-paid, dull, and dead-end. After a few years at such a job, marriage, motherhood, and full-time housewifery may seem like a welcome change. But when the children are small, she will have little time for self-development; when they enter school, she will probably have to go back to work to help make ends meet.

All the bright promises about the fulfillment inherent in being a "real" woman, a wife and mother, do not materialize. With a dull job, in or out of the home, and little in inner resources, she is likely to take out her frustrations on her husband and children. They must succeed in order to make up for her empty life. Never aware of why she is not content and feeling guilty about it, she will raise her son to be the aggressive, successful, supermasculine man that her husband probably isn't, her daughter to be the "real" woman who finds the fulfillment in the traditional role she herself has never found.

COLLEGE

The young woman who goes to college has another chance to break out of the stereotyped role society has decreed for her. The college years may be a period of intensified social pressures toward appropriate feminine role behavior, or they may be a period of widening horizons and newly perceived possibilities.

It is often assumed that the only reason the young woman goes to college is to catch a husband. Sometimes it's true. After all, that's what she has been taught is her main purpose in life. One study found that the association between college freshmen's desire to please their parents and their desire to attend graduate or professional school was +.47 for men and −.37 for women.[75] That is, men who want to please their parents

---

[74] Epstein, op. cit., p. 59.

[75] Walter L. Wallace, "The Perspective of College Women," in Theodore, op. cit., p. 385.

are interested in further career-oriented education, but women concerned about pleasing their parents are not.

The young woman's college experience may either reinforce or begin to erode previous socialization. A sorority type of college, with its emphasis on football and beauty queens, will act as reinforcement. For many girls, going away to college offers them their first taste of independence. As we have seen, girls are kept more dependent on the family than their brothers. Being away from home when she is at college allows and even forces the young woman to make her own decisions, to develop a certain amount of self-reliance. But sororities act as family surrogates. The social pressures operating within a sorority encourage conformity and discourage independence. Generally they also institutionalize husband catching.

This sort of college life seems to be on its way out or at least is becoming much less prevalent. The new style in college life emphasizes informality and doing your own thing. Young women now have greater freedom from conventional social pressures, but neither they nor their male fellow students can completely escape their previous socialization. Girls may wear tee shirts and blue jeans rather than pleated skirts and bobby socks. Beauty parlor curls have given way to long, straight hair. Young men and women sleep together pretty much whenever they want to and frequently set up housekeeping together.

Under the surface, however, the traditional assumptions about the male and female persist. Men are expected to be the leaders in academic and social life. In class, male students are much more likely to speak up than women. Men tend to dominate college politics. The division of labor when male and female students live together again tends to be highly traditional. She does the cooking and cleaning and shopping; he does the yard work if there's any to be done. And what about the image of women as sex objects? Under pressure from the growing women's movement, the present generation of college men may be more likely than their fathers to regard women as people first. But the circulation of *Playboy* doesn't seem to be decreasing, and its readership is heavily young, male, and college educated.

During the college years, the results of early sex role socialization become starkly obvious. Most young women have developed very clearly negative self-images. A 1968 study asked college students to rate the typical adult male, the typical adult female, and themselves on 122 bipolar items describing personal characteristics.[76] Male and female students agreed closely on their descriptions of the typical adult male and female—and both judged the typically male traits as more socially desirable. Furthermore, the women students attributed to themselves the typically feminine but socially less desirable traits. These women saw themselves as not at all resourceful or intellectual or competent or intelligent or realistic, as very immature, very subjective, very submissive, and very easily influenced.

Given these negative self-images, it's not surprising that women lack self-confidence. Numerous studies have found that, on a wide variety of tasks, women's expectations about their performance are lower than men's expectations.[77] Generally, in these experiments a task will be described and the subject asked to predict his or her performance. On tasks as widely divergent as solving anagrams, taking tests of verbal intelligence and arithmetic abilities, and a marble-dropping game, males consistently expect to do better. Explicitly labeling the task to be performed as feminine raises women's expectations to about the level of the men's.

Women, then, generally do not expect to succeed. When they do, does this raise their self-confidence and lead to higher expectations in the future? In fact, on most of the tasks used in these experiments, men and women perform about the same. Yet men and women explain their performance differently. Women attribute their success to luck while men attribute their success to ability. Women are more likely to explain their failure as due to lack of ability while men seldom do.[78] If success is seen as the result of luck not of competence, it is unlikely to build self-confidence.

If men and women are asked to explain other people's success, the same attribution pattern is found. Both men and women explain a woman's success as being due to luck; a man's, as due to skill.[79] What if the success is one that can't possibly be due to luck? In an experiment, subjects were asked to ex-

---

[76] Hartley, op. cit., p. 138.
[77] Kay Deaux, *The Behavior of Women and Men* (Belmont, Calif.: Brooks/Cole, 1976), pp. 38–39.
[78] Ibid., p. 41.
[79] Ibid., p. 30.

plain the success of a surgeon identified as either Dr. Marcia Greer or Dr. Mark Greer.[80] The male subjects attributed greater ability to Mark; Marcia was seen as having worked harder and having an easier task. The women subjects also thought Marcia had worked harder but did not see her task as easier. A similar study in which the subjects were high school girls found female failure attributed to lack of ability; female success was ascribed to luck, easy courses, and even cheating on exams.[81]

A study by Philip Goldberg further demonstrates the extent to which women have a negative image of women in general.[82] Female college students were asked to evaluate short articles on art history, dietetics, education, city planning, linguistics, and law. Two sets of booklets containing the articles had been prepared, with the only difference being the authors' names. In one set, a given article was attributed to a male author, for example, John T. McKay; in the other set, the same article was attributed to a female author, Joan T. McKay. Each booklet contained articles by three "male" and three "female" authors.

The women students consistently rated "male" authors higher than "female" authors, even in traditionally feminine fields such as elementary school teaching and dietetics. The author concludes that the belief in women's inferiority, particularly in the intellectual and professional sphere, distorted these student's perceptions.[83] Facts are interpreted in such a way as to support the belief. The same experiment was run using male students as subjects, and the results were similar. The male students also consistently rated the "male" authors higher.[84]

Since many young women have internalized the assumption that women are intellectually inferior to men, it is hardly surprising that few strive for professional achievement. Still, many college women are academically successful, and career opportunities for women are expanding. Given the high premium our society places on achievement, why is the number of

[80] Ibid., pp. 31–32.
[81] Ibid., p. 32.
[82] Philip Goldberg, "Are Women Prejudiced Against Women?" in Theodore, op. cit., pp. 167–172.
[83] Ibid., p. 168.
[84] Bem, op. cit., p. 85.

women going into the professions not increasing more quickly?

Psychologist Matina Horner has suggested the presence of "the motive to avoid success" as a psychological barrier to success in women. She says that the motive to avoid success "exists and receives its impetus from the expectancy held by most women that success, especially in competitive achievement situations, will be followed by negative consequences for them. Among these are social rejection and feelings of being unfeminine or inadequate as women."[85]

Horner asked students to write a short story, the first sentence of which was "At the end of first term finals Anne/John finds herself/himself at the top of her/his medical school class." From the content of the stories it was determined whether fear of success imagery was present. Although only 10 percent of the male stories showed fear of success, 65 percent of the female stories did.

Many of the female stories showed fear of social rejection as a result of academic success. In a number, Anne is faced with losing her boyfriend; in others she doesn't have one because she's too smart. In another group of stories, Anne's success makes her worry about her normality or femininity. One story says explicitly that Anne is no longer certain about a medical career because she wonders if it's "normal" for a woman to be a doctor. Another account, which says that Anne starts to feel guilty, supplies a classic conclusion: "She will finally have a nervous breakdown and quit med school and marry a successful young doctor."[86] In their stories, some of the women students simply denied the situation in the lead line. One such story claims that Anne doesn't really exist but that a group of medical students created her as a code name to play a joke on their professors. In another, medical school is taken to mean nursing school. A few stories were truly bizarre. In one, Anne's classmates "jump on her in a body and beat her. She is maimed for life."[87]

In a variant on the basic experiment, students at an outstand-

---

[85] Matina Horner, "The Motive to Avoid Success and Changing Aspirations of College Women," in Bardwick, *Readings on the Psychology of Women*, op. cit., p. 62.

[86] Matina Horner, "Femininity and Successful Achievement: A Basic Inconsistency," in Garskof, op. cit., pp. 111–113.

[87] Ibid., p. 114.

ing eastern women's college were asked to describe Anne. More than 70 percent said she was unattractive in face, figure, or manners: "Wears long skirts. Not feminine; masculine looking. Has short hair."

Horner's study has been criticized on a number of grounds.[88] Because she did not provide a detailed manual for scoring fear of success imagery, a good deal of subjectivity may creep into the scoring. This may explain the contradictory results found by other researchers using the same technique. She has not adequately shown, some claim, that fear of success is actually a motive and that it does predict behavior.

The results of further studies using Horner's technique suggest that some of the subjects may not be displaying their internalized motives in the stories they write. Rather, as psychologist Kay Deaux points out, they may be "responding to a stereotype and writing what they think an average male or an average female might do in that particular situation."[89] In one experiment men and women were asked to write about both Anne and John. Regardless of the sex of the writer, the stories about Anne showed more fear of success imagery than those about John.[90] In another experiment, nursing school was substituted for medical school for some of the subjects. Both men and women displayed more fear of success imagery for Anne in medical school and John in nursing school than for the situations in which sex and occupation were linked in the stereotyped manner.[91]

Taken together, these experiments show that both men and women expect negative consequences when a member of either sex succeeds in a situation considered non-sex-appropriate. Since the occupations sex-typed as male are more highly valued in our society, women are placed in a non-win situation.

THE COSTS OF SEX ROLE STEREOTYPING

In this chapter, we have seen how society molds the child along sex-specific lines. That this process is costly for women

---

[88] David Tresemer, "Fear of Success: Popular But Unproven," *Psychology Today,* 7 (March 1974).

[89] Deaux, op. cit., p. 51.

[90] Ibid., p. 52.

[91] Ibid., pp. 52–53.

hardly needs to be argued. The costs of sex role socialization to men are perhaps less obvious but nevertheless very real.[92] The stereotypical masculine male is aggressive, emotionally impassive, self-sufficient, athletic, brave in the face of danger, a natural leader, and competent at any task defined as masculine. Living up to this image is expecting a lot of any human being, and feeling that one should is likely to produce anxiety and insecurity. Furthermore, in the complex world in which we live, some of these traits are counterproductive. Physical aggressiveness is more likely to lead to jail than to success; a definition of bravery that extends to foolhardiness may get you killed. The male who learns to be emotionally impassive, to hide his feelings from others and often from himself, denies himself a valuable outlet and cuts himself off from an important aspect of human experience.

Sex role stereotyping also limits the options open to men. The male child is frequently expected to be good at athletics whether or not he has the slightest interest or aptitude. In many families, an interest in music, art, or dance is discouraged if displayed by a boy. A male who desires to enter a "female" field—nursing or kindergarten teaching, for example—is considered even more deviant than a woman in a "male" field.

Not only is the male expected to enter an appropriate field, he is expected to be a success. Whatever other attributes he may have, he will be largely judged by his career success. While to many men women are sex objects, men are frequently success objects to women. Because career success is defined as central to masculinity in our society, men often sacrifice all other values in pursuing it.

If masculinity and femininity as defined by our society are destructive of human individuality, what is the alternative? A reassessment of the value of "feminine" and "masculine" traits and an attempt to inculcate those considered valuable in both boys and girls would seem to be the answer. Studies have found that high-achieving and highly creative children are much less sex-stereotyped in behavior than their less outstanding peers.[93] Androgynous people—those who display both masculine and feminine characteristics—have higher self-

[92] Warren Farrell, *The Liberated Man* (New York: Random House, 1974).
[93] Ibid., pp. 34–35.

esteem, achieve more in school, and seem to be more adaptable.[94] There *are* alternatives better than assigning traits and behaviors on the basis of sex. Society has constructed the feminine female and the masculine male; our task is to see that, in the future, society constructs the full human being.

[94] Deaux, op. cit., pp. 139–140.

THE FAMILY: REFUGE OR PRISON?

4

They stare at you from the television screen, the pages of magazines, the billboards—the pretty, smiling woman; the tall, competent-looking man; the cute, clean children. No labeling is necessary for us to recognize them as the typical American family. Ask any man or woman on the street and they will tell you that the family consisting of husband, wife, and children is not just typical but natural and universal—decreed by God or determined by biology. An occasional fun-loving bachelor may have escaped marriage; a few women are simply too ugly to catch any man; some couples are unable to have children, poor things. These cases are exceptions and are abnormal. The proper, accepted, normal state for an adult is marriage and parenthood. Furthermore, the closer one comes to the typical family of advertising fame, the happier and certainly the more normal one will be. The pretty wife stays home taking care of her house, her gadgets, and cute children; the husband goes out to work to make the gadgets and a college education for the children possible. This division of labor is not just typical; it is natural, universal, and good.

Popular stereotypes can hardly be considered scientific knowledge. What do social scientists have to tell us about the family? Sociologists of the structural-functional school agree to a remarkable extent with the popular stereotypes, although of course their language is much more impressive. These sociologists say that the nuclear family, consisting of a man, a woman, and their children, is universal. It is universal because it performs certain functions that are necessary if the society is to survive. Some functions that used to be performed within the family (economic production, for example) are now performed elsewhere. The family still acts as the "primary agent of socialization of the child" and is the "primary basis of security for the normal adult."[1] For the family to function effectively, a division of labor is required: the husband's function is instrumental (i.e., task oriented); the wife's, expressive (i.e., she provides emotional support). In concrete terms, the husband works outside the home to support the family financially; the wife is housekeeper, mother, and binder of psychic wounds for both husband and children.

The structural-functional theorists essentially agree with the popular view that the nuclear family and the present division of labor within it is both natural and good. They do not provide evidence that the functions the family performs cannot be performed by other institutions. They do not explain why the woman should invariably perform the expressive function and the man the instrumental. More basically, they do not ask whether the maintenance of society as it now is should be the overriding goal. Certainly the abolition of the nuclear family would result in major societal changes, but would these changes be for the better or for the worse? The answer depends to a large extent on how one evaluates the present situation. Instead of asking whether the nuclear family is functional for society, we should ask if it is functional for its component units—for the woman, the man, and the children.

Surprisingly, the popular view recognizes more ambiguity concerning the benefits of marriage and family life than the structural functionalists do. According to the stereotype, women want to get married and men do not. This is natural because women get the greatest benefits out of marriage—someone to support them and children to fulfill their natural maternal instincts. Men, in contrast, must work in order to support their often spendthrift wives and, since men are not naturally monogamous, must restrain their natural sexuality. Why men get married at all in this age of easily available sex, and how this view fits with the simultaneously held view that family life is natural, is never explained. Inconsistencies, however, have never destroyed a stereotype. In the popular view

---

[1] Talcott Parsons, "The Normal American Family," in Arlene and Jerome Skolnick, eds., *Family in Transition* (Boston: Little, Brown, 1971), p. 402.

it is clearly the woman who benefits most from marriage.

The sociologists don't seem to be interested in who benefits and how much. They seem to think that if everyone performs his or her proper function, everyone benefits.

In examining the empirical evidence on the modern American family, we will ask who benefits, or (in the jargon) for whom the institution is functional.

THE MYTH

What does a young woman expect of marriage, and what does she actually get? She has been taught that the choice of a marriage partner is the most important decision she will ever make. In marriage she expects to fulfill her true nature as loving wife and mother. This, she has been taught, is the most creative career possible for a woman. She is, in effect, promised instant and complete happiness.

Especially if she is quite young, the bride's image of marriage is likely to come straight from the pages of popular magazines and the TV screen. She sees herself as the glamorous, creative homemaker decorating her house à la *House Beautiful* and cooking gourmet meals. Beautifully dressed, she greets her smiling husband when he comes home from work. They spend a peaceful, intimate hour discussing the events of the day. She, of course, is an interested and sympathetic listener; he, of course, wants to share all aspects of his life with her and values her advice. Some evenings they entertain couples as beautiful and smiling as themselves; other evenings they go out.

Did the young woman have dreams or plans for doing something more with her life? She will, she is sure, manage to keep up in some way. If she has artistic talent, she can write or paint at home. Otherwise, she can at least read good books. This will provide intellectual stimulation for her and keep her interesting to her husband.

Not long after marriage she will become pregnant. Having a baby—an act that she has been told is more creative than painting the *Last Supper*—will complete her happiness. She sees a cute, smiling baby that she can play with, take for walks, and show off to her friends. She may look a few years further into the future and see herself, still vivacious and pretty, as the mother of several clean, attractive grammar school children. Throughout, she is happy and fulfilled as wife, mother, and homemaker. She has lived the American dream.

REALITY: THE MIDDLE-CLASS VERSION

The middle-class, like the working-class, woman is increasingly likely to work until she is pregnant with her first child. During the time she is working outside the home, she finds she has two jobs. She is expected to do most of the housework. It is, after all, woman's work. Her husband may help out, but it is clearly understood that the inside housework is her responsibility.

Whether she is working or not, the first part of the myth crumbles quickly. Housework is neither interesting nor creative; in the expressive phrase of the women's movement, it is "shit work." For those with the talent and interest, decorating and gourmet cooking are creative and fun. But most housework consists of mopping floors, washing dishes, and cleaning toilet bowls. Not only is it boring, it is repetitive and never-ending. Housework does not stay done; a chore done today must be done again tomorrow or, at best, next week. Thus it provides no real feeling of accomplishment. Studies have found that doing housework is a perfect job for the feeble-minded.[2]

When the first baby is born, the young woman is likely to become a full-time housewife and mother. The media tend to present a baby as a wonderful toy—gurgling, smiling, and doing cute things. While babies are wonderful and lovable, they are also a great deal of trouble. They cry as well as smile. Changing a dirty diaper is not a fulfilling experience.

A baby increases the amount of housework that must be done. More serious, with the arrival of the child the young woman loses control over her own schedule. As one young mother explained, "Suddenly I had to devote myself to the child totally. I was under the illusion that the baby was going to fit into my life, and I found I had to switch my life and my schedule to fit *him*."[3] A baby is not a toy that can be put away when one is tired of it. The young mother is always on duty. She cannot take time off to read or rest. When the child becomes mobile, the problem becomes especially acute. A toddler must be watched. The housework must still be done. Neither of these tasks require the woman's full attention, but they require enough of it so that she cannot do anything else. "In industry the most fatiguing jobs are those which only partially

---

[2] Betty Friedan, *The Feminine Mystique* (New York: Dell, 1964), p. 244.
[3] Quoted in Betty Rollin, "Motherhood: Who Needs It?" in Skolnick, op. cit., p. 351.

occupy the worker's attention, but at the same time prevent him from concentrating on anything else. Many young wives say that this mental gray-out is what bothers them most in caring for home and children. 'After a while, your mind becomes a blank,' they say. 'You can't concentrate on anything. It's like sleep-walking.' "[4]

The child also severely restricts the woman's mobility. Isolated in her own home in suburbia, she spends most of her time with people under six years old. She is progressively cut off from participation in the world outside the home. There is, of course, the television set, but as Myrdal and Klein point out,

> The isolated woman at home may well be kept "in touch" with events, but she feels that the events are not in touch with her, that they happen without her participation. The wealth of information which is brought to her without any effort on her part does not lose its vicariousness. It increases rather than allays her sense of isolation and of being left out.[5]

The lack of adult conversation is a universal complaint among young American housewives. In the past housework was much more physically taxing, but at least the woman had other adults around for help and companionship. "The idea of imprisoning each woman alone in a small, self-contained, and architecturally isolated dwelling is a modern invention dependent upon an advanced technology," Philip Slater says. "In Muslim societies, for example, the wife may be a prisoner, but she is at least not in solitary confinement. In our society the housewife may move about freely, but since she has nowhere in particular to go and is not a part of anything, her prison needs no walls. . . . Most of her social and emotional needs must be satisfied by her children, who are hardly adequate to the task."[6]

The young woman's good intentions about staying intellectually or artistically active dissipate. One cannot read a serious book, much less write a novel, in ten-minute snatches. Connected, uninterrupted time is needed, and this the young mother does not have.

---

[4] Quoted in Friedan, op. cit., p. 240.

[5] A. Myrdal and V. Klein, *Women's Two Roles* (London: Routledge and Kegan Paul, 1968), p. 148.

[6] Quoted in Jessie Bernard, *The Future of Marriage* (New York: Bantam, 1973), p. 50.

Progressively she becomes more and more dependent on her husband as her only link with the outside world. Yet the couple find they have less and less to talk about. Their experiences are too divergent. She becomes boring because her experiences are boring. Small household catastrophies and a few cute stories about the children do not make for stimulating conversation. One of the results is the sort of sex segregation one sees at suburban parties—the men in one part of the room discussing business and politics, the women in the other talking about children and home.

Eventually, of course, all the kids are in school. For the average American woman this occurs when she is thirty-four years old.[7] There is still housework to do, and school-age children do require care, but finally the woman has some uninterrupted time. What can she do with it?

At this point she could return to work. Some women are prevented by the strong disapproval of their husbands. Such men have so strongly internalized the notion that the provider role defines masculinity that their whole sex identity is threatened by a working wife. Even if the husband is supportive, the return to work is not easy. The middle-class woman may well have completed college, but usually she has not been trained for a career. Too often the only jobs she can get are not commensurate with her education. A clerical job is frequently the best she can do. Many women find that even such jobs are better than staying home. Working at all may provide a feeling of independence as well as social stimulation. The financial costs of holding a job—transportation, new clothes, and especially babysitters—may, however, be greater than what she earns. If the husband prefers that she not work, he can use this as an argument.

For the professionally trained woman, the return to work may be even more difficult. Her training is likely to be out of date, and she has probably found it impossible to keep up with the professional literature. In order to become competitive with recent graduates she will have to retool, and she may very much fear that she is no longer capable of the analytic thinking and sustained concentration required. Assuming that she survives the retooling process, she will still have difficulty finding a good position. In addition to the prejudice against

---

[7] Mirra Komarovsky, in New York City Commission on Human Rights, *Women's Role in Contemporary Society* (New York: Avon, 1972), p. 64.

women, she will face prejudice on the basis of her age. As the prestige professions require extremely long hours, she may want a part-time job, but such jobs are often difficult to find and are marginal in pay and prestige. Even with a Harvard Ph.D., she may well end up teaching at Podunk Community College.

There are alternative ways of filling one's day. Volunteer work has long been considered an appropriate outlet for middle-class female energies. More and more, however, such work is becoming professionalized. The tasks for which unpaid volunteers are used are busywork jobs that are neither stimulating nor creative. Especially in the suburbs, the volunteer is likely to end up stuffing envelopes and answering phones.

Artistic endeavors would seem to be easier than any sort of outside work for the woman to fit in with her still considerable responsibilities in the home. Most women, however, like most men, do not have real talent for writing or painting. Furthermore, a serious talent requires a strong commitment in time and energy if it is to be developed. The housewife's artistic endeavors tend to degenerate into dilettantism. For a month she will attempt to write a novel; then she will take up painting, followed perhaps by potting and then weaving.

Some women do manage to develop a full and interesting life of their own without taking a paid job. A few seriously develop an artistic talent; others become deeply involved in community affairs or in politics. Such involvement requires considerable chunks of connected time at regular intervals. Finding this time takes *more* organization and determination for the woman who is "only" a housewife than for the woman holding a paid job. A working woman's family understands that she must go to work regularly. Even so, in two-job families, the woman and not the man is expected to stay home with a sick child. Nevertheless, the family recognizes that the woman will be away from the home during her working hours and should not be disturbed unless a real emergency arises. The woman who does not hold a paid job continuously has to justify and protect her time from encroachments. As she is not getting paid for her efforts, her family is unlikely to take them seriously and thus will expect her to change her schedule to suit them. She will need a great deal of determination and sense of her own rights as an individual if she is seriously to pursue her non-family-related interests.

Whether she works at a paid job or pursues another interest, the woman is expected to keep it from interfering with her principal functions in the family. Working just because she enjoys doing so is suspect. Women are expected to be service oriented, not achievement oriented. A woman who feels that achievement is necessary for her self-realization is considered selfish. A working woman married to a man making quite a large salary often claims she works because the family needs the money. Working in order to help her family is considered legitimate; working because she enjoys it is not.

For the married woman, her husband and children must always come first; her own needs and desires, last. When the children reach school age, they no longer require constant attention. The emotional-expressive function assigned to the woman is still required of her. Called the "stroking function" by sociologist Jessie Bernard, it consists of showing solidarity, raising the status of others, giving help, rewarding, agreeing, concurring, complying, understanding, and passively accepting.[8] The woman is expected to give emotional support and comfort to other family members, to make them feel they are good and worthwhile human beings.

The stroking function is a vitally important one; everyone needs stroking at least occasionally. Here precisely is the problem of specializing the function in the wife. Who raises her status? Who agrees with and passively accepts her? Despite its glamorization in the media, housework is not highly valued in our society. Nor does it provide intrinsic satisfaction. For many women childrearing does provide such satisfaction, but intermittently and interspersed with a great deal of frustration. Thus, the woman needs emotional support and assurance that she is a worthwhile human being at least as much as the man. But the stroking function is seen as her responsibility, so she is not likely to receive much of it. Boys are brought up to believe that the characteristics associated with emotional support—empathy, sympathy, and showing tender emotions—are female traits. Men feel uncomfortable and unmasculine displaying such traits and thus are not very good at doing so. Yet they expect women—not only, but especially, their wives—

[8] Jessie Bernard, *Women and the Public Interest* (Chicago: Aldine, 1971), p. 88.

to always provide such support with little or no reciprocation on their part.

A man generally expects his wife to center her life around him. She should not need anything but a husband who is a good provider and healthy children to make her happy. After all, both he and she have been taught that a normal woman finds total fulfillment in this way. He is surprised and upset if the pretty, admiring girl he married turns into a nagging shrew. Being barred from achieving on her own, the wife may put all her excess energy into her husband's career. He may be satisfied with his present position; she demands greater and greater success. Aware of his weak spots, she may question his masculinity if he does not live up to her expectations. He will be hurt and angry; he may seek out other female companionship to provide the stroking his wife withholds. He probably considers his wife overly money hungry and status conscious. He is unlikely to realize that she is trying to live his life because she does not have one of her own.

The traditional American family structure does not seem to be good for the wife and can also be pretty hard on the husband. What about the children? Surely the children must benefit from having a loving mother always around. Child psychologists have found that the answer is often no. Children can be overmothered. Such children are overly dependent on their mothers; they tend to be passive and remain infantile. Overmothering stunts a child's emotional and intellectual development. Small children who are not given independence to explore and solve problems on their own are unlikely to develop the ability to think analytically.[9] Such children often do not develop an independent sense of self-worth.

The woman may be overmothering her children because she believes this is the proper mother's role. Child care books and popular Freudian psychology convey the impression that, by sins of omission or commission, she can easily scar her child for life. Her full-time loving presence is said to be essential for the child's healthy development. She is never told that she can scar her children as well as herself by paying too much attention to them.

---

[9] Eleanor E. Maccoby, "Sex Differences in Intellectual Functioning," in Eleanor E. Maccoby, ed., *The Development of Sex Differences* (Stanford, Calif.: Stanford University Press, 1966), pp. 25–55.

Excessive mothering is often a result of the woman's lack of a life of her own. She may attempt to live vicariously through her children. Through them she will experience all the things she has missed. Her daughter must be the prettiest and most popular girl in her class; her son, the smartest and most athletically proficient. She may push her daughter into absurdly early dating so that she can relive the most exciting part of her life. She will give up anything and everything for her children. Nothing is too good for them. They need not help around the house or get part-time jobs. The only thing she will not give them is their independence.

When their children leave home, such supermothers find adjustment especially difficult. Depression severe enough to require hospitalization is a not-infrequent problem.[10] For most full-time housewives, the children's leaving home means a loss of function and, often, of identity. The woman frequently feels that no one needs her any more, and because she has based her life on satisfying others' needs, she now sees herself as superfluous. She has nothing to live for, nothing to do. All the extra time is seen as a curse, not a benefit. Because over the years her interests have been so narrowly centered on her family, wider interests have atrophied. Now she has no idea what to do with the 20 or 30 years of life left to her.

Even if her husband understands her problem, there is often little he can do to help. If he is successful, his career may well require increasing amounts of time. Even if he does have time to spend with his wife, they may find they have so little in common that neither finds much satisfaction in their being together.

The middle-class American ideal is the companionate marriage in which husband and wife are friends. The typical division of labor in the family along sex lines makes the ideal almost impossible to achieve. Friendship requires common interests. The very different lives that husband and wife lead tend to erode any common interests they may have had and does not encourage the development of new ones. Friendship also requires equality. Even if the couple consciously try to attain an egalitarian marriage, so long as the traditional division of

---

[10] Pauline Bart, "Depression in Middle-Aged Women," in Judith Bardwick, ed., *Readings on the Psychology of Women* (New York: Harper & Row, 1972), pp. 134–142.

labor is maintained, the husband will be "more equal." He is the provider not only of money but of status. Especially if he is successful, society values what he does; she is just a housewife. Their friends are likely to be his friends and co-workers; in their company, she is just his wife. Because his provider function is essential for the family's survival, major family decisions are made in terms of how they affect his career. He need not and usually does not act like the authoritarian *paterfamilius* of the Victorian age. His power and status are derived from his function in the family and are secure so long as the traditional division of labor is maintained.

REALITY: THE WORKING-CLASS VERSION

While the middle class pays lip service to the ideal of egalitarian marriage, in the working class older, more traditional values prevail. In her recent study of blue-collar families, Lillian Rubin found that both men and women believe that the man should be the ultimate authority in the family.[11] Thus, in discussing something she wanted to do—such as going back to school—the blue-collar wife will frequently conclude, "He won't let me."[12] In contrast, middle-class wives do not speak in terms of getting *permission* from their husbands.

The difference may be one of style and language rather than of substance. The working-class man simply tells his wife she cannot do certain things; the middle-class husband, with his greater verbal skills, uses a subtler form of coercion. Thus one middle-class husband told his wife that whether or not to get an abortion was her decision. However, if she did, he would never consent to having another child.[13]

The differing economic circumstances of middle- and working-class families also have an effect. The blue-collar families Lillian Rubin interviewed were not poor according to U.S. government standards; their median income was $12,300.[14] Nevertheless, they were economically insecure; for almost all, paying the bills was a continuous struggle. In most families, regardless

---

[11] Lillian Breslow Rubin, *Worlds of Pain: Life in the Working Class Family* (New York: Basic Books, 1976), p. 96.
[12] Ibid.
[13] Ibid., p. 97.
[14] Ibid., p. 106.

of class, men have the ultimate decision-making power in important spending decisions.[15] In blue-collar families where money is tighter, the husband's power may have a greater effect on the wife's life because harder choices have to be made. Conflicts about spending priorities can seldom be resolved by saying "Let's buy both."

On housework, a highly traditional division of labor prevailed in these blue-collar families. All agree that housework is the woman's job; her husband may help her, but it is her responsibility. As one man said:

> That's just the way life is. It's her job to keep the house and children and my job to earn the money. My wife couldn't do my job and I couldn't be as good a cook and housekeeper as she is. So we just ought to do what we do best.[16]

If the wife works outside the home, as over half the women interviewed do, the burden is especially great. These families lack the money to hire any outside help as middle-class families often can. Asked "whose life is easier, a man's or a woman's?" the wives often expressed their frustration:

> I get mad sometimes and wish I could change places with him. It would be a relief to worry only about one thing. It feels like I drag around such a heavy load.[17]

Despite the double burden these working wives carry, most enjoy holding a job.[18] The jobs these women have—salesclerk, waitress, factory worker—are by no means glamorous, yet they do provide satisfactions not available at home. As a factory worker said:

> I really love going to work. I guess it's because it gets me away from the home. It's not that I don't love my home; I do, but you get awfully tired of just keeping house and doing those housewifely things.[19]

Another working woman said about her job, "I'm good at it, and I like that feeling. It's good to feel like you're competent."[20]

---

[15] Ibid., p. 108.
[16] Ibid., p. 100.
[17] Ibid., p. 106.
[18] Ibid., pp. 168–169.
[19] Ibid., p. 170.
[20] Ibid., p. 172.

Thus, although most of these women work out of economic necessity, they do find other satisfactions in holding a job. Getting out of the house, a sense of competence, some feeling of independence are the less tangible rewards. There are, however, costs involved beyond those of the double burden. In a society in which men so heavily define their masculinity in terms of the provider role, the wife's working may be seen as a threat. As one woman said, "I guess it's a matter of pride with him. It makes him feel bad, like he's not supporting us good enough."[21] A number of the husbands of working women feel that their wives have become too independent, that their authority is threatened:

> I'd like to feel like I wear the pants in the family. Once my decision is made, it should be made, and that's it. She should just carry it out. But it doesn't work that way around here. Because she's working and making money, she thinks she can argue back whenever she feels like it.[22]

In her study of blue-collar marriage in the late 1950s, sociologist Mirra Komarovsky found that many of the couples she interviewed did not expect friendship in marriage.[23] Men and women were seen as having sufficiently different interests that cross-sex friendship was not really possible. Thus, husband and wife had few mutual friends. The wife had female friends whom she saw during the day; the husband, male friends whom he saw on his night or nights out.

Lillian Rubin's study indicates that expectations are changing. The wife especially does expect marriage to be more than an economic and sexual arrangement. Though she often cannot express her desires clearly, she wants communication and companionship.

> I keep talking to him about communication, and he says, "Okay so we're talking, now what do you want?" And I don't know what to say then, but I know it's not what I mean.[24]

The men, not knowing what is expected of them, feel confused and threatened. The socialization process, which is more

---

[21] Ibid., p. 173.
[22] Ibid., p. 177.
[23] Mirra Komarovsky, *Blue-Collar Marriage* (New York: Vintage Books, 1967), p. 112 passim.
[24] Rubin, op. cit., p. 120.

sex-stereotyped in working-class than in middle-class families,[25] has produced in the man a "trained incapacity to share."[26] "The ideal of masculinity into which they were socialized inhibits expressiveness both directly, with its emphasis on reserve, and indirectly by identifying personal exchange with the feminine role."[27] She wants to talk about their inner feelings, to establish a truly intimate relationship. He may try but he literally does not know how. As one man said:

> I sometimes think I'm selfish. She's the support—the moral support—in the family. But when she needs support, I just don't give it to her. Maybe it's not just selfishness, it's that I don't know what she wants and I don't know how.[28]

Many of the wives, while dissatisfied and yearning for a deeper relationship, for something more out of life, also feel guilty about the new demands they are making on their husbands.

> What do I have to complain about? Jim's a steady worker; he doesn't drink; he doesn't hit me.[29]

Some even question whether they are normal.

> . . . I worry sometimes that maybe there's something the matter with me that I'm not satisfied with what I've got.[30]

Lillian Rubin concludes that for most of the couples interviewed, "despite the yearning for more, relations between husband and wife are benumbed, filled with silence; life seems empty and meaningless."[31]

MARRIAGE AND THE FAMILY—IS IT GOOD FOR HUMAN BEINGS?

If the description of the family presented here is correct, the traditional family structure is not good for human beings. The woman in particular is trapped in a situation that provides little opportunity for intellectual growth or the satisfactions of achievement. The man at least gets a maid.

---

[25] Ibid., pp. 125–127.
[26] Komarovsky, op. cit., p. 156.
[27] Ibid.
[28] Rubin, op. cit., p. 129.
[29] Ibid., p. 19.
[30] Ibid., p. 132.
[31] Ibid., p. 123.

Certainly there must be women content with the traditional female role of housewife and mother. Available evidence indicates that the happy housewife may indeed be relatively rare.[32] A number of studies have found that women of all social classes express more dissatisfaction with marriage than do men.[33] "More wives than husbands report marital frustration and dissatisfaction; more report negative feelings; more wives than husbands report marital problems; more wives than husbands consider their marriages unhappy, have considered separation or divorce, have regretted their marriages; and fewer report positive companionship."[34]

Many widows do not want to remarry. A study by the Department of Health, Education and Welfare of 390 Chicago widows found that only one-fifth said they would like to marry again. The other 80 percent said no and gave as their reason, "I'm free and independent now."[35] A study of people over sixty-five found that the wives envied the widows for their freedom, independence, and fun in life. The wives felt "they were unfortunate, in contrast with the widows, in being stuck in the house at the beck and call of a usually temperamental and demanding retired husband."[36]

More disturbing are the figures on mental health. According to Jessie Bernard, "being a housewife makes women sick."[37] When married men and married women are compared, the men show up much better on various indexes of mental health. "More married women than married men show phobic reactions, depression and passivity; greater than expected frequency of symptoms of psychological distress; and mental-health impairment."[38]

Perhaps women are simply psychologically less stable than men. No; the poorer mental health of married women is not due to a general sex difference. On the same measures, unmarried women show up as mentally healthier than both married women and unmarried men. "Many symptoms of psychological

[32] Friedan, op. cit., p. 227.
[33] Komarovsky, op. cit., p. 199.
[34] Bernard, *The Future of Marriage,* op. cit., p. 28.
[35] Riverside, California, *Press Enterprise,* October 11, 1973.
[36] Barbara Seaman, *Free and Female* (Greenwich, Conn.: Fawcett, 1973), p. 224n.
[37] Bernard, *The Future of Marriage,* op. cit., p. 53.
[38] Ibid., p. 30.

distress show up more frequently than expected among married women: nervous breakdowns, nervousness, inertia, insomnia, trembling hands, nightmares, perspiring hands, fainting, headaches, dizziness and heart palpitations. They show up less frequently than expected among unmarried women."[39] Unmarried women's mental health also compares very favorably with that of unmarried men. "Single women show far less than expected frequency of symptoms of psychological distress as compared with single men. . . . Single women suffer far less than single men from neurotic and antisocial tendencies. More single men than single women are depressed and passive."[40] When unmarried women and married men are compared, little overall mental health difference is found, although the women show a markedly smaller incidence of psychological distress symptoms such as nervousness and insomnia.[41]

The data would seem to show that marriage is good for men and bad for women. Perhaps, however, some of these differences are due to selective factors. That is, maybe mentally healthy men and mentally sick women tend to marry more frequently than mentally sick men and mentally healthy women. Bernard believes that such selection may account for some but far from all the difference. "In our society, the husband is assigned superior status. It helps if he actually *is* somewhat superior in ways—in height, for example, or age or education or occupation—for such superiority, however slight, makes it easier for both partners to conform to the structural imperatives."[42]

Men may tend to marry women to whom they can feel superior; women to marry men they can look up to. If women tend to marry up and men to marry down, then "bottom-of-the-barrel" men and "cream-of-the-crop" women are least likely to marry.

The selective process cannot, however, completely explain the poor mental health of wives because almost everyone does eventually get married. Something about the woman's marriage must account for the problem. A comparison between working women, many of whom are married, and housewives is illuminating. Working women, whatever their marital status,

[39] Ibid., p. 32.
[40] Ibid., p. 33.
[41] Ibid., p. 35; also see Table 23, p. 343.
[42] Ibid., p. 35.

are on the average far healthier mentally than housewives. "Far fewer than expected of the working women and more than expected of the housewives, for example, had actually had a nervous breakdown. Fewer than expected of the working women and more than expected of the housewives suffered from nervousness, inertia, insomnia, trembling hands, nightmares, perspiring hands, fainting, headaches, dizziness, and heart palpitations."[43] Clearly being only a housewife is the problem: It literally makes many women sick.

The nuclear family structure, with its strict division of labor along sex lines and the resulting isolation of wives in the home, is not functional for women. For men, the balance between costs and benefits is less clear. In mental health and reported happiness, married men far surpass single men. On the other hand, if there is strict adherence to the traditional division of labor, the husband is solely responsible for the support of his wife and children. This may mean very long working hours, considerable anxiety, and little freedom to change the type of work he does if he should desire to do so. Furthermore, as his wife becomes more and more unhappy with her lot she is likely to take it out on him.

The family as presently constituted presents some serious problems for children, too. Living their first six years of life almost exclusively in the company of a woman who is harried, often depressed and unhappy and, not infrequently, on the brink of serious mental illness, must have a deleterious effect on children. As one young mother said,

> I feel it should be more widely recognized that it is in the very nature of a mother's position in our society, to avenge her own frustrations on a small, helpless child; whether this takes the form of tyranny, or of a smothering affection that asks the child to be a substitute for all she has missed.[44]

THE AMERICAN FAMILY AND MYTH AS SOCIAL SCIENCE

A critique of the nuclear family is useful only if better alternatives can be found. Many people, social scientists as well as

---

[43] Ibid., p. 52.

[44] Quoted in Rochelle Wortis, "Acceptance of the Concept of the Maternal Role by Behavioral Scientists," in Helen Wortis and Clara Rabinowitz, eds., *The Women's Movement* (New York: Wiley, 1972), pp. 41–42.

ordinary people, contend this is not possible. The nuclear family is universal and is based on our biological nature. Women must have babies for their own good, not just for the continuation of the species. Motherhood is a biological imperative; no woman can find true fulfillment without having children. The division of labor within the family is decreed by nature; since women have the babies, they must stay home and take care of them. Any absence of the mother will have disastrous psychological and intellectual effects on the child. The father performs the instrumental function; he is the provider, a role for which (the biological determinists contend) he is well fitted by virtue of his natural aggressiveness, innovativeness, and independence. According to the sociologists, however, the male cannot effectively perform his function unless the female performs her expressive function. That is, the husband is dependent on his wife for emotional support or, in Bernard's term, stroking. The female's effective performance of the stroking function is dependent on her being in a position that the male sees as not competitive with his own. If a woman has a career in the cruel, competitive world outside the home, she is unlikely to be effective at stroking, since her husband will see her as a competitor and not as a quiet port in a stormy world. According to Talcott Parsons, if both husband and wife have careers, the resulting competition between them is likely to have a disruptive effect on the solidarity of the marriage.[45]

If we are to determine whether alternatives to the nuclear family are possible and desirable, each of these tenets must be examined.

George Murdock, a well-known anthropologist, contends that the nuclear family is universal.[46] When one examines his much-reprinted article on the topic, one finds that his definition of the term is very broad. So long as a man, a woman, and their children live together, no matter who else lives with them, this is, according to Murdock, a nuclear family. Under this definition Murdock includes both polygamous and extended fami-

---

[45] Talcott Parsons, "The Kinship System of the Contemporary United States," in Talcott Parsons, ed., *Essays in Sociological Theory,* rev. ed. (New York: Free Press, 1954), p. 192.

[46] George Peter Murdock, "The Universality of the Nuclear Family," in Norman Bell and Ezra Vogel, eds., *A Modern Introduction to the Family* (New York: Free Press, 1960), pp. 37–44.

lies, since in these forms of the family a man, a woman, and their children also live together. In common usage the term *nuclear family* refers to the isolated nuclear family, composed solely of a man, a woman, and their children. Of the 192 societies on which Murdock had data, 42 had isolated nuclear families, 53 had polygamous families, and 92 some form of extended family.[47] Obviously the isolated nuclear family is atypical. Furthermore, a few cases of "visit" marriages, in which a man does not live with his wife and children, have since been discovered.[48] An extended discussion of different forms of the family will be undertaken in a later chapter. Data so far presented show clearly that the nuclear family consisting solely of a man, a woman, and their children is far from universal and thus cannot be biologically determined.

Is motherhood natural? This question really consists of two parts. Do women need to be mothers in order to find fulfillment? Does mothering, that is, taking care of children, come naturally to women?

There is no evidence that women have a biological need for children. "Women don't need to be mothers any more than they need spaghetti," says Dr. Richard Rabkin, a New York psychiatrist. "But if you're in a world where everyone is eating spaghetti, thinking they need it and want it, you will think so too."[49]

If there were such a biological need, the motherhood-is-bliss myth and all the social pressures on women to become mothers would be unnecessary. As sociologist William Goode says, "There is no innate drive for children. Otherwise, the enormous cultural pressures that there are to reproduce wouldn't exist. There are no cultural pressures to sell you on getting your hand out of the fire."[50]

A woman's desire to have children is due to her psychological, not her biological, state. Do women, then, have a psychological need for children? To the extent that they do, the need is a socially developed one. Nevertheless, despite the motherhood-is-bliss myth, many women find it more frustrating than blissful. As one young mother said, "In the abstract sense, I'd have

---

[47] Ibid., p. 38.
[48] Clyde Kluckhohn, "Variations in the Human Family," in ibid., p. 45.
[49] Quoted in Rollin, op. cit., p. 346.
[50] Quoted in ibid.

several (children). . . . In the non-abstract, I would not have any. . . ."[51] A number of studies have found that childless marriages are happier.[52]

A look through the newspaper should suffice to convince anyone that women are not naturally good mothers. Cases of child neglect and physical abuse are far from rare. The complex behavioral pattern we call mothering is learned, not innate. Even among the apes, mothering does not come naturally. A female primate reared in isolation where she has no opportunity to learn from others of her species will often reject her baby. She will not care for it properly and may kill it or let it die from neglect.[53]

If women have no biological need or special aptitude for motherhood, why should society expect all women to become mothers? As long as population growth was considered desirable and pregnancy could not be prevented, such expectations made some sense. In an already overpopulated world, to push women into motherhood no matter how unprepared and unfit they are is not only foolish but dangerous.

> One of the most absurd aspects of the Myth is the underlying assumption that, since most women are biologically equipped to bear children, they are psychologically, mentally, emotionally, and technically equipped (or interested) to rear them. . . ."[54]

If a woman does have children, should she necessarily be expected to assume sole responsibility for their care? Many women would like to escape the isolation and monotony of suburbia by working at least part-time when their children are small. Some have been deterred by the experts, who warn them about the effects on the child of "maternal deprivation."[55] Women have been told that any separation of mother and child during the child's first few years will have serious deleterious effects on the child.

The evidence supporting the notion of maternal deprivation is far from convincing. Studies of children in hospitals and or-

---

[51] Quoted in ibid., p. 351.
[52] Ibid., p. 352.
[53] Sally Linton, "Primate Studies and Sex Differences," in Skolnick, op. cit., p. 194.
[54] Rollin, op. cit., p. 352.
[55] Wortis, op. cit., pp. 35–36.

phanages show that such institutionalization frequently does have negative effects. But, such a traumatic separation of the child from its home and family cannot be equated with the routinized and shorter separation that occurs if the mother works. Studies of children of working mothers find no deleterious effects.[56]

Anthropological evidence shows that the American child-rearing pattern is atypical:

> There is no known primitive society where mothers spend as much time with their children as they do in America today. . . . in the primitive cultures child care is much less the exclusive responsibility of the mother. In less complex societies the job is shared by father, mother, grandmother, aunt, big sister and women "too old for heavy work" who perform as general babysitters.[57]

Placing upon the mother the sole responsibility of child care is bad for her and bad for the child. According to Margaret Mead,

> At present the specific biological situation of the continuing relationship of the child to its biological mother and its need for care by human beings are being hopelessly confused in the growing insistence that child and biological mother, or mother surrogate, must never be separated, that all separation, even for a few days is inevitably damaging, and that if long enough it does irreversible damage. This . . . is a new and subtle form of antifeminism in which men—under the guise of exalting the importance of maternity—are tying women more tightly to their children than has been thought necessary since the invention of bottle feeding and baby carriages. Actually, anthropological evidence gives no support at present to the value of such an accentuation of the tie between mother and child. . . . On the contrary, cross-cultural studies suggest that adjustment is most facilitated if the child is cared for by many warm friendly people.[58]

Children do not need and are better off without a mother who spends every waking moment with them. What they do need is "consistent care; sensitivity of the care-taking adult(s) in responding to the infant's needs; a stable environment the characteristics of which the growing infant can learn to iden-

---

[56] Seaman, op. cit., pp. 290–291.
[57] Ibid., p. 222.
[58] Margaret Mead, "A Cultural Anthropologist's Approach to Maternal Deprivation," in *Deprivation of Maternal Care: A Reassessment of Its Effects,* Public Health Papers, No. 14 (Geneva: World Health Organization, 1962).

tify; continuity of experience within the infant's environment; and physical and intellectual stimulation, love, and affection."[59] The caretaking adult need not be the child's mother and, in fact, need not be female. A recent study found that children can become just as attached to a male as to a female if the man spends sufficient time with them.[60]

Margaret Mead's contention that children are best off if cared for by many warm, friendly people is gaining increasing recognition. Urie Bronfenbrenner says "the young child does not require care by the same person all the time, and indeed profits from the intercession of others, notably his father."[61] Some social scientists go a good deal further. "A number of recent theories of schizophrenia have argued that the isolated nuclear family provides a fertile setting for driving children crazy. In the isolation of the nuclear family, the parent can easily deny some aspect of reality, usually the parents' behavior or motives, thus causing the child to doubt his own perceptions. For example, the parent may act very angry or sexy, yet deny he or she is doing so."[62]

If the child does not need the constant presence of its mother, then one of the major arguments for the present division of labor in the family is destroyed. According to the second argument, a strict division of labor along sex lines is necessary to prevent competition between husband and wife that would threaten the solidarity of the family.

Lynda Holmstrom's study of two career families shows that feelings of competitiveness are far from inevitable in such families. Sixty-five percent of the couples she studied reported no such feeling and gave no indication during their interviews that they actually felt competitive.[63] Whether two people feel that they are in competition is not simply a function of the situation; it depends on their perception of the situation. As one wife said, "We identify very much with each other. . . . We will be in competition *together* against some other person, not in competition with each other."[64] Feelings of competitive-

---

[59] Wortis, op. cit., p. 40.
[60] Seaman, op. cit., p. 295.
[61] Quoted in ibid., p. 282.
[62] Skolnick and Skolnick, *Family in Transition,* op. cit., p. 306.
[63] Lynda Lytle Holmstrom, *The Two-Career Family* (Cambridge, Mass.: Schenkman, 1972), p. 105.
[64] Ibid., p. 103.

ness were not related to whether the couple were in the same field. Such feelings, "especially among the men, were associated with other feelings such as lack of self-assurance, feeling threatened, not feeling competent in a given area, feeling inadequate, or 'pride of the male ego.' "[65]

According to Parsons, "So long as lines of achievement are segregated and not directly comparable, there is less opportunity for jealousy, a sense of inferiority, etc., to develop."[66] Holmstrom found that the sex-linked division of labor is not sufficient to prevent jealousy and a sense of inferiority. Several wives who had given up their careers to play the traditional female role were clearly resentful.

> I think that I do occasionally feel just a little resentment as to my role as opposed to my husband's role. After all, I made things as easy for him so that he has all the time he can available for his work. . . . I sometimes wonder a bit now (laughter) . . . is this fair (laughter) that I should be doing all the work?

> I am intensely envious of the prerogative of a man to devote himself to a career without giving up the family. It is grossly unfair that he should have both. I feel that I can't. I have moments of bitterness about this.[67]

The traditional division of labor relegates women to an inferior status and thus frequently breeds jealously and resentment.

A final argument for maintaining the traditional division of labor is based on the fragility of the male ego. Having to compete against women and possibly even coming out second best will undermine the man's sense of masculinity. Mental illness and even impotence may result. So long as males are taught that they are superior to all females, a competent woman will be seen as a threat. But to argue that women should stay in their place to avoid damaging the ego of the superordinant male is similar to arguing that southern blacks should have stayed in their place to avoid damaging the fragile egos of southern whites.

None of the arguments for maintaining the status quo are persuasive. As so often happens, social scientists have at-

---

[65] Ibid., p. 109.
[66] Parsons, "The Kinship System of the Contemporary United States," op. cit., p. 192.
[67] Holmstrom, op. cit., p. 116.

tempted "to justify a particular, local and almost certainly, temporary, economic and cultural pattern as an eternal biological law."[68]

What is needed now is more serious consideration of alternatives. Restructuring the professions to allow both men and women to work part-time and thus share child care would be a first step. High-quality child care centers staffed by both men and women are needed. Experiments in communal living should be encouraged. Perhaps most important is recognition that no one life-style will meet the needs of everyone. We do not expect everyone to do the same work or have the same interests and hobbies. Why should we expect everyone to have the same kind of family life?

---

[68] Quoted in Wortis, op. cit., p. 38.

THE EXPLOITATION OF WORKING WOMEN

5

"Everyone knows that women don't work for the same reasons as men. They work for other reasons, for self-gratification, so they really can't be counted the same."[1] This statement, attributed to a high official in the Ford administration, reflects one of the many myths about working women. In this chapter, myth and reality will be explored.

MYTHS ABOUT WORKING WOMEN

Many people still believe that the working woman is atypical. Yet according to 1977 data, for every 6 men workers there are now 4 women workers; that is, women account for 40.8 percent of the civilian labor force.[2] In fact, 55 percent of all women between 18 and 64 now work. Almost 39 million women hold paid jobs. Of all American males age 16 and over, 76 percent are in the labor force. Of all American females age 16 and over, 47 percent are in the labor force. Over 90 percent of all women now do paid work at some time in their lives; and, of course, almost all women also do unpaid work in the home.

The myth implies that only young, single women work outside the home, and then only for a short time before getting married. This was partially true a quarter of a century ago.

---

[1] Statement of William Seidman, quoted by Walter Mondale. *Los Angeles Times,* October 23, 1976.

[2] Data in this paragraph from U.S. Department of Labor, *Employment and Earnings,* 24 (February 1977).

Now, however, 58 percent of all working women are married.[3] To put it another way, 44 percent of all wives work outside the home as well as inside.[4] According to the myth, these women must be childless. But on the contrary, 52 percent of mothers in two-parent families with children between 6 and 17 have jobs. Even among mothers with children under 6, 37 percent work.[5]

Figure 5.1 shows how the pattern of labor-force participation by women of different ages has changed over the years. In 1890 most working women were young; after their early twenties, most dropped out of the labor force. By 1940, there were many more women working, but the pattern had not really changed; women still tended to quit working during the child-rearing years and not return. The 1960 pattern is dramatically different; women still left the labor force during their late twenties, but when their children reached school age, many returned. The 1975 curve again shows a major change; the tendency for women to drop out of the labor force during their late twenties and early thirties is much less pronounced. Fewer

[3] U.S. Department of Labor, Women's Bureau, *1975 Handbook on Women Workers,* p. 124.
[4] U.S. Department of Labor, *Handbook on Labor Statistics 1976,* p. 53.
[5] Ibid., p. 53.

FIGURE 5.1
Patterns of labor force participation by women of different ages, 1890–1975

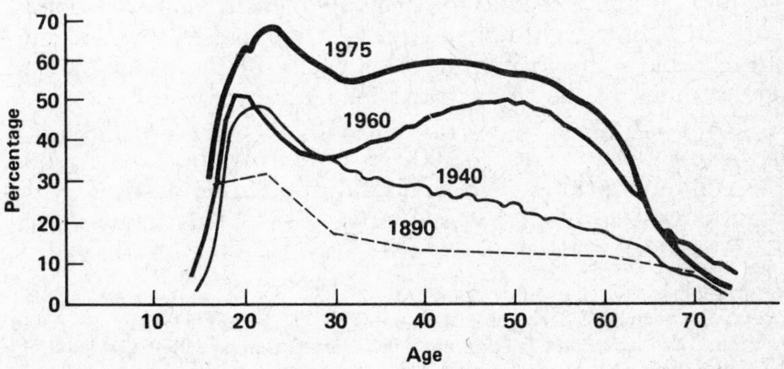

Source: U.S. Department of Labor, *Employment and Training Report of the President,* 1976, p. 143.

women leave during the childrearing years; and of those who do, most return. The working woman is no longer the exception; she is the norm.

It is a waste to educate women, it has frequently been claimed; they will only get married and not use their training. The evidence presented so far casts doubt on that statement, and Table 5.1 shows it just is not so. The more education a woman has, the more likely she is to hold a job. Over 90 percent of women with Ph.D.s work outside the home. Women with very little education don't work because they cannot find jobs.

TABLE 5.1

Education and labor force participation, 1975

Education	Percentage of all women working
Less than high school graduate	31.6%
High school graduate	52.5
One to three years of college	53.5
Four or more years college	64.1

Source: U.S. Department of Commerce, *A Statistical Portrait of Women in the United States* (April 1976), p. 29.

Sexist mythology would lead us to believe that women at least work at physically easy jobs. Yet 5 million women work in factories.[6] According to a woman factory worker, the only kind of job women are allowed to do in the factories is "the fast, picky shitwork."[7] She also testified that promotion was almost unheard of for the factory women. Moreover, these women all had a second job at home. This meant that before and after their eight-hour workday, they had to care for children, cook, and clean the house. Many of them also had to spend much of their paychecks for babysitters.

One million women work as domestic servants, 211,000 work as farm laborers, and 352,000 as nonfarm laborers.[8] Among the women working year-round, full-time in domestic service, the median yearly wage was $2,676 in 1974.[9] This below-starva-

[6] *Employment and Earnings,* op. cit., p. 39.

[7] Jean Tepperman, "Two Jobs: Women Who Work in Factories," in Robin Morgan, ed., *Sisterhood Is Powerful* (New York: Vintage, 1970), p. 118.

[8] *Employment and Earnings,* op. cit., p. 39.

[9] U.S. Department of Commerce, *A Statistical Portrait of Women in the United States* (April 1976), p. 49.

tion wage is partly the result of domestic workers not being covered by federal minimum wage laws, by equal pay laws, workmen's compensation laws, or most state protective laws. It is also partly due to their being unorganized and thus easily exploited by unscrupulous hiring agencies. For example, Homemaker's, Inc., of Southern California rents cleaning women; in 1976, of the total hourly wage of $3.25, the women received $2, the agency $1.25. Similar agencies rent temporary secretaries for one-third of their pay.

Almost all women, whether they "work" or not, do housework. It has been estimated—in 1918, 1928, and again in 1968—that the housework labor done by women equals *one-fourth of the U.S. gross national product.*[10] Why is it not included in the calculation of the GNP? One reason is the sexist attitude that housework is easy, that women sit in pampered leisure. The other reason is the more general attitude of capitalist society that a product or service is only really "worth" something if it is bought and sold for money in the market.

In addition to unpaid home labor, about 13 million women do volunteer work. It has been estimated that the monetary worth of volunteer work in 1965 was $14.2 *billion.*[11] Women are hooked on this unpaid volunteer work largely on the basis of sexist ideology and discrimination. Husbands, friends, and women's own social conditioning are all elements that discourage careers. Volunteer work is seen not as a permanent career, but as proper, temporary charity work. Moreover, our capitalist system does not guarantee full employment, and older women have a hard time getting any job. Most of the volunteers are women over forty with grown children.[12] No other interesting work (or no work at all) is available to them.

Why do women work?

According to the popular stereotype, women work for fun or for "pin money"—and can therefore be paid less, hired last, and fired first. In 1950, acting on this stereotype, a Detroit labor union voted that all women should be fired so that unem-

---

[10] Juanita Kreps, *Sex in the Marketplace* (Baltimore: Johns Hopkins Press, 1971), p. 67.

[11] Doris Gold, "Women and Voluntarism," in Vivian Gornick and Barbara Moran, eds., *Women in Sexist Society* (New York: Signet, 1972), p. 534.

[12] Ibid.

ployed men could be hired. When Congresswoman Martha Griffiths mentioned this injustice to the Detroit head of the National Labor Relations Board, he said: "Well, I think it is wrong to permit a woman with top seniority to remain on a job and lay off a man supporting a wife and five kids when all the woman is doing with her money is buying good clothes, Cadillacs, and going to Florida."[13]

Here is a man—who should know better—accepting the extreme stereotype. What woman (or man) working in a factory buys Cadillacs or Florida vacations? Not only do 39 million women have jobs, but most of them *must* work. Of all women workers, 42 percent are heads of families because they are single, divorced, separated, or widowed; and most have children. An additional 16 percent of all working women are married to men who make less than $7,000 a year, so they obviously must work to stay out of poverty.[14] Together, these two groups of women who absolutely must work to support their families comprise 58 percent of all working women.

Many middle-class families are middle class only because the wife works. In 1974, working wives contributed 26.5 percent on the average to family income.[15] Median income for husband-wife families in which the wife did not work was $12,082—$544 below what the U.S. government considers necessary for an urban family of four to enjoy a moderate standard of living. The median income of husband-wife families in which the wife worked was $16,461.[16]

Do women get equal pay?

There is a myth that, in this country, people get paid what they are worth. Unfortunately, it is only a myth. One evidence of this is the fact that under the Equal Pay Act of 1963, the courts have found extensive wage discrimination and have forced companies to give back pay of $18.7 million to 54,000 women from 1963 to 1970.[17] This legally determined discrimination is only the tip of the iceberg. In 1974, women who

---

[13] Quoted by Martha Griffiths in Mary Thompson, ed., *Voices of the New Feminism* (Boston: Beacon, 1970), p. 107.
[14] *1975 Handbook,* op. cit., p. 124.
[15] *Statistical Portrait,* op. cit., p. 52.
[16] Ibid., p. 52 and *1975 Handbook,* op. cit., p. 137.
[17] Kreps, op. cit., p. 92.

worked full-time, year-round were paid on the average only 57 percent of men's wages. The average male worker made $97 more a *week* than the average woman worker. The gap between men and women's wages has been increasing. In 1960, for example, women made 61 percent as much as men. By race and sex, the pecking order is very clear (see Table 5.2).

TABLE 5.2

Median wage or salary income of full-time, year-round workers, 1974

Group	Wage	Wage as percentage of white male's wage
White men	$12,343	100%
Black men	9,082	74
White women	7,025	57
Black women	6,611	54

Source: U.S. Department of Labor, Women's Bureau, *The Earnings Gap between Women and Men* (1976), p. 12.

Even the median white male wage is under what the Bureau of Labor Statistics considers "moderate, but adequate," which is why so many wives must work. But the black man's wage is much lower, which is why even more black wives must work. Still lower is the white woman's wage, showing even greater economic discrimination. And lowest of all, reflecting the double burden of racist and sexist discrimination, is the wage of the black woman. And remember, these are all full-time, year-round workers.

The same dreary picture shows up in the figures on poverty (see Table 5.3). Women head 12 percent of all families; yet women-headed families constitute 45 percent of all poverty

TABLE 5.3

Poverty, 1974, by race and sex

Family "head"	Percentage under official poverty level
Man	6%
White woman	25
Black woman	53

Source: U.S. Department of Commerce, *A Statistical Portrait of Women in the United States* (April 1976), pp. 53, 75.

families.[18] In 1974, 26 percent of all female year-round full-time workers earned less than $5,000 and 53 percent earned less than $7,000; the comparable figures for men were 9.3 percent and 18.3 percent. On the other end of the scale, 28.9 percent of men but only 3.5 percent of women earned $15,000 or more.[19]

Are women paid according to their education?

Perhaps women have lower wages because of less training and education. No; in spite of discrimination in higher education, the woman worker has exactly the same educational level as the male worker. The median level for both in 1974 was 12.5 years—yet as we have seen, her wages are only 57 percent of his. When we compare income by sex at different levels of schooling, we find that a woman with a high school education gets lower wages than a man with less than eight years of elementary school education (see Table 5.4). A woman with some college education is paid far less than a man with only some high school education, and a woman with a college diploma less than a man with a high school diploma.

[18] *1975 Handbook,* op. cit., p. 141.

[19] U.S. Department of Labor, Women's Bureau, *The Earnings Gap Between Women and Men* (1976), p. 7.

TABLE 5.4

Median income by sex and education, 1974 (full-time, year-round workers, 25 years and over)

Education	Women's median wage	Men's median wage	Difference
Less than eight years elementary	$ 5,022	$ 7,912	$2,890
Eight years elementary	5,606	9,891	5,606
One to three years high school	5,919	11,225	5,306
Four years high school	7,150	12,642	5,492
One to three years college	8,072	13,718	5,646
Four or more years college	10,357	17,188	6,831

Source: U.S. Department of Commerce, *A Statistical Portrait of Women in the United States* (April 1976), p. 48.

When we compare the earnings of men and women with the same education working at similar jobs, we get the same depressing results (see Table 5.5). Women white-collar workers with four years of high school make only 56.6 percent as much as male white-collar workers with the same education; women managers and administrators with at least a college degree make 59.9 percent of what a man with a comparable job makes. The smallest percentage difference is for professional and technical workers with one to three years of college, and even in that category, women make less than 70 percent of what men do.

TABLE 5.5

Women's median earnings as a percentage of men's by education and occupation, 1973 (full-time, year-round workers, 18 years and over)

Occupation	Total	Elementary, 8 years or less	High school: 1 to 3 years	High school: 4 years	College: 1 to 3 years	College: 4 years or more
Total	58.5%	56.8%	56.3%	57.3%	59.0%	60.9%
White-collar workers	54.9	58.0	56.8	56.6	55.8	59.8
Professional and technical workers	66.1	62.5	58.1	65.4	68.9	63.9
Managers and administrators (except farm)	54.3	62.4	56.0	55.1	59.2	59.9
Clerical and sales workers	57.7	59.8	58.5	59.8	58.2	53.9
Blue-collar workers	54.0	55.4	56.3	54.0	54.4	54.2
Service workers	55.2	60.2	58.1	52.1	56.9	58.4

Source: U.S. Department of Labor, Women's Bureau, *1975 Handbook on Women Workers,* p. 195.

A Bureau of Labor Statistics study found that "in each of eight occupations studied for men and women in the same jobs, men always were paid more than women."[20] Thus female class A accounting clerks received on the average 82 percent as much as males doing the same work. Women payroll clerks were paid 77 percent of what male payroll clerks received.[21]

[20] *1975 Handbook,* op. cit., p. 145.
[21] Ibid., p. 147.

Are women promoted equally with men?
In each area of the economy there is evidence that women receive lower-level jobs to start with and are less likely to be promoted than men of equal training and experience. Look at almost any company or educational institution, or at government employment, and you will find large numbers of poorly paid women (and minority males) in the bottom ranks and a few highly paid white males at the top.

Thus American Telephone and Telegraph, which is the single largest employer of women in the United States, systematically excluded women from both higher-level management jobs and from better-paying craft jobs. Table 5.6 shows the situation at New York Bell. In 1970, only 1.1 percent of all craft jobs were held by women in the entire Bell System. Telephone operators were 99.9 percent female.[22] AT&T was sued for sex and race discrimination and in 1973 was ordered to rectify its hiring practices. Although there seems to be some improvement, it has been slow. At Pacific Telephone, one of the AT&T operating companies, 2.5 percent of the top supervisors were women in 1977.[23]

Banks have also been major offenders. A recent survey of 24 major banks found that women were 63 percent of all workers but only 13 percent of bank officers. Even this small percent-

[22] Barbara Allan Babcock, Ann E. Freedman, Eleanor Holmes Norton, Susan C. Ross, *Sex Discrimination and the Law* (Boston: Little, Brown, 1975), p. 292.
[23] *Los Angeles Times*, February 6, 1977.

TABLE 5.6
Women at New York Bell Telephone, 1970

Job	Percentage of women to total
Top-level managers (18 men)	0%
4th-level managers (80 men)	0
3d-level managers	0
2d-level managers	23
1st-level managers	95
Supervisors (2,000 women)	100
Operators (21,000 women)	100

Source: James Horris, Assistant Vice President, Bell Telephone, in New York Commission on Human Rights, *Women's Role in Contemporary Society,* hearings (New York: Discus Books, 1972), pp. 232–255.

age is an increase over 1971, when only 6.4 percent of the officers were women.[24] The same pyramid of pay and prestige is found in education. About 88 percent of elementary school teachers are women; yet elementary school principals and administrators are 78 percent male. Approximately half of high school teachers are women, but 96.5 percent of high school principals are men.[25]

One way many companies pay women less—without appearing to discriminate—is to create a new job title for women to do a job previously done by men under another name (the men getting higher pay). "Men and women often do exactly the same thing in all but name and pay. . . . Management consultants frequently turn up men and women doing the same job under differing titles when they analyze what each employee really does."[26]

In fact, until recently, when the law made it illegal, most private employers openly admitted sexist discrimination. As late as 1961 a questionnaire on sex discrimination was answered by the 1900 employers in the National Office Managers Association. A third of them admitted quite honestly that they always paid women less than men.[27]

Surely, however, women are treated equally in public employment. False! Look at the example set by the federal government (see Table 5.7). The U.S. Civil Service is another pyramid

[24] Ibid.
[25] Carol A. Whitehurst, *Women in America: The Oppressed Majority* (Santa Monica, Calif.: Goodyear, 1977), p. 61.
[26] Caroline Bird, *Born Female* (New York: Pocket Books, 1969), p. 63.
[27] Ibid., p. 62.

TABLE 5.7

Full-time federal white-collar employment by grade, 1973

Grade groups	Percentage of women to total grade group
17 and above	1.8%
13–16	4.6
9–12	17.1
5–8	35.1
1–4	75.7

Source: U.S. Department of Labor, Women's Bureau, *1975 Handbook on Women Workers,* p. 117.

with thousands of women at the bottom and a small number of well-paid men at the top. Even in the public agencies of the enlightened city of New York, women in 1970 held 54 percent of the jobs with salaries under $10,000 (mostly secretaries, teachers, nurses, social workers), but only 24 percent of all jobs with salaries over $15,700. Of the 300 top jobs in the New York City administration, only 24 were held by women.[28]

How can such discrimination continue in government jobs, in which selection is supposedly by written or oral civil service examinations? Ersa Postan, president of the New York State Department of Civil Service, explains that in New York civil service oral promotion exams, the examining boards are predominantly male. She states that such boards often rate men above women simply because of their preconception that women are not qualified.[29] If both a man and a woman pass an exam with equal grades, it often happens that the man rather than the woman is actually appointed. Moreover, heads of agencies still worry over whether employees wouldn't feel "more comfortable" with a male supervisor.

Are women more often absent? do they quit more often?

The first sexist apologia for lower pay, low-level jobs and no promotion for women is that women are inherently inferior. This can no longer be said in public, however, so the second sexist apologia is that men "need more money to support their families." But we know that this is utterly false for most working women; women are the sole or a main support of most of the neediest families. The third sexist apologia is that women are absent more often because they have to care for their families, and that women quit their jobs more often because they get pregnant.

Now it is true that women are forced, often involuntarily, to drop out to have families, and it is true that they bear the burden of a second job at home. It is also true that they are given precious little help with these burdens by employers, husbands, or government; maternity leaves and child care facil-

---

[28] John Lindsay, Mayor, New York City, in New York Commission on Human Rights, *Women's Role in Contemporary Society* (New York: Discus Books, 1972), p. 53.

[29] Ersa Postan, in ibid., p. 344.

ities are mostly nonexistent. Astoundingly, however, in spite of these extra burdens, women in general are *not* absent more often, and women do *not* quit jobs more often.

A very extensive Labor Department study concludes from all the earlier studies and from its own statistics: "Women workers have favorable records of attendance and labor turnover when compared with men employed at similar job levels and under similar circumstances." One can predict absenteeism and turnover much better from (1) the skill level of the job, (2) the age of the worker, and (3) the length of service with the employer than from "the mere fact that the worker is a man or a woman."[30]

True, some studies find very slightly higher *aggregate* rates of absence or turnover for women. A 1967 study found the average woman worker lost 5.6 days a year from illness or injury, while the average male worker lost 5.3 days. But this overlooks the fact that discrimination forces most women into miserable jobs in which *all* workers are ill or injured more often—and men in these jobs are absent more often than women. Similarly, a 1968 study found that 2.6 women per 100 voluntarily quit their jobs that year, while 2.2 men voluntarily quit. Again, this overlooks the fact that most women are pushed into jobs everyone tries to quit at the first opportunity—and in which men quit more often.[31] In fact, as another study shows, from January 1965 to January 1966 only 7 percent of women but 10 percent of men workers changed occupations. Moreover, from 1957 to 1960 an average of only 6 percent of women workers but 8 percent of men changed the region of their main job.[32] Women workers may be less likely to change jobs than men because, as a result of discrimination, they have fewer options.

Particularly at higher job levels, there are no differences between labor turnover for men and women workers. Thus, turnover was reported "about the same" for men and women at the same grades in a study of 65 large chemical and pharmaceutical laboratories.[33] Notions that a woman worker on any

---

[30] U.S. Department of Labor, Women's Bureau, *Facts About Women's Absenteeism and Labor Turnover* (1969), p. 1.

[31] Ibid., p. 2.

[32] Ibid., pp. 3, 5.

[33] Ibid., p. 7.

particular job is more likely to be absent or quit than a man are quite wrong; the opposite is more often true in lower-level jobs. Such notions are pure sexist myths—and are used, consciously or unconsciously, to pay women lower wages, not promote them, or not to hire them at all.

DISCRIMINATION BY SEGREGATION

Although many women are paid less for doing the same jobs as men, the major cause of the wage gap between men and women is employment segregation. Employer prejudice and women's own internalized sex role socialization keep most women out of better-paying "men's" jobs and herd them into low-paying, dead-end "women's" jobs.

Even in the most general classifications used by the Census Bureau, the pattern of segregation is apparent (see Table 5.8). Men dominate in the better-paying occupations: managers and administrators, and craft workers. Of course not all male jobs are well paid; nonfarm laborers are mostly men. Clerical work, domestic service, and other service occupations, which are less prestigious and less well-paying, are predominantly female. Of all women at work, 36 percent are clerical workers and another

TABLE 5.8

Occupation by sex, 1977

Occupation	Women as percentage of total in occupation
Mainly male occupations	
Craft and kindred workers	5.0%
Nonfarm laborers	9.4
Managers and administrators, except farm	21.7
Mixed occupations	
Factory operatives, except transport	39.1
Professional and technical workers	42.9
Salespeople	42.1
Mainly female occupations	
Service (other than domestic)	57.4
Clerical workers	78.6
Domestic service	95.5

Source: U.S. Department of Labor, *Employment and Earnings,* 24 (February 1977), p. 39.

20 percent are in domestic and "other" service (e.g., waitresses, dental assistants, hairdressers).[34]

More detailed occupational classifications show that there are few truly mixed occupations. Almost all jobs are predominantly male or predominantly female. In 1973, more than 40 percent of all women workers were employed in ten occupations: secretary, retail trade sales worker, bookkeeper, private household worker, elementary school teacher, waitress, typist, cashier, sewer and stitcher, and registered nurse.[35] Very few men are employed in any of these jobs. With the exception of retail sales workers, of which 69 percent are women, in all the other occupations over 80 percent are women. Men are much less occupationally concentrated. Less than 20 percent of male workers are employed in the ten largest occupations for men.

One interesting study presents an index of segregation for blacks and for women based on the more than 500 detailed occupations listed by the Census Bureau. The author constructed an "index of segregation" from the differences in the numbers of men and women (or whites and blacks) in each occupation, given in percentages and averaged. In 1960, the index of segregation for black and white employment was 47 percent; the index of segregation for male and female employment was a much higher 68 percent.[36]

Because the jobs into which women are segregated are low in status, low in pay, and dead-end in that experience brings little or no reward, the total loss of developmental possibilities to women, plus the loss of talent to society, is astronomical. One Swedish study estimates that Swedish GNP could be 50 percent higher if there were no sex discrimination. In the United States, the losses to women (and to society) can be seen in the fact that 47 percent of all employed women with one to three years of college have clerical jobs; 13.5 percent of all employed women with four years of college or more have clerical jobs.[37] What a waste!

---

[34] *Employment and Earnings,* op. cit., p. 39.

[35] *1975 Handbook,* op. cit., p. 91.

[36] Edward Gross, "Plus Ca Change . . . ? The Sexual Structure of Occupations over Time," in Athena Theodore, ed., *The Professional Woman* (Cambridge, Mass.: Schenkman, 1971), pp. 39–51.

[37] *Statistical Portrait,* op. cit., p. 36.

Under pressure from the women's movement, some previously all-male preserves are being breached. Progress in the professions, which will be discussed in the next chapter, has gotten most of the media attention, but just as important are the inroads women have made into the skilled trades. Between 1960 and 1970, the number of women carpenters rose from 3,300 to 11,000; electricians from 2,500 to 8,700; plumbers from 1,000 to 4,000; auto mechanics from 2,300 to 11,000; and tool and die makers from 1,100 to 4,200.[38] These increases are important because such jobs pay a great deal more than "women's" jobs which require comparable education. For the woman who does not have the opportunity to train for a profession, the skilled trades offer a chance to escape from near poverty-level wages. But although the figures offer hope for the future, they do not mean that sex segregation is ended. Women still constitute only a tiny proportion of skilled trade workers.

Rationalizations for segregation

Segregation in employment is frequently defended as natural; biological and psychological differences supposedly determine that some jobs are "obviously" women's jobs and others just as "obviously" suited only for men. Our earlier discussion of psychological sex differences showed that there simply is no evidence to support such views. For a very few jobs, biological differences may disqualify most women. Few women are large enough and strong enough to be professional football players—but the same is true of men. About the only jobs for which the sex of the worker is crucial are semen donor and wet nurse.

If the present division of labor were "natural," it should be worldwide. But a study of 324 primitive societies by anthropologist G. P. Murdock found that every occupation done by men in one was done by women in another, and vice versa. Even child care was not invariably women's work. The only exception was metal working, which was always done by men. Yet during World War II, when a labor shortage forced U.S. employers to hire women, they suddenly discovered that women were good at metal working. Rosie the Riveter became a na-

---

[38] Mary Dublin Keyserling, "The Economic Status of Women in the United States," *American Economic Review*, 66 (May 1975), p. 210.

tional heroine. Today, almost all jobs done mostly by men or mostly by women in one country are done by the other sex elsewhere. For example, in the United States being a doctor is considered too unpleasant or difficult for women, but it is considered a "nurturing" or "woman's job" in the Soviet Union. In the United States, women are told to go into nursing because it is a "nurturing, woman's job." But why not become a doctor? There's no heavy lifting and the pay is a lot better.

The sexist defense of segregation, including "explanations" by some sociologists, often rests on the notion that women's jobs are mostly natural extensions of women's family role. But the largest number of employed women are typists; when do they type at home? What women do at home does include cooking and child care, yet men have the top posts in restaurant cooking and in academic child study programs. Moreover, the housewife may gain expertise in dressmaking and in the use of cosmetics, but men hold the top positions both in the cosmetics industry and in the dress designing and manufacturing industries.

In terms of tasks performed, the argument is nonsense. It is true, however, that in the world of work, as in the home, women are cast in the role of auxiliaries. Women are the support troops; men, the decision makers. Thus a good secretary is expected to do more than type and take dictation. She is expected to take care of all the picky details—getting coffee, reminding him of his appointments, shielding him from people he does not want to see, sometimes even buying birthday presents for his family. She is expected to do all this so that he can concentrate on the really important tasks. In general, women's jobs are those considered too boring and not sufficiently important to occupy the time of men. It is the notion that women are naturally subordinate to men that is carried over from the home to the employment world. Only when we realize this can we understand the seeming inconsistency in the sex stereotyping of particular jobs.

Women supposedly are physically weaker than men, but nurses and waitresses carry heavy loads, while doctors and chefs do the "women's jobs" of nurturing and cooking. And this is not a matter of choice! There are many obstacles in the way of a woman who wants to be a doctor. And becoming a chef is just as hard. In New York City a woman went through a 40-week union training program in culinary art to be a chef or cook. She was turned down for hundreds of such jobs. The union said not to worry: "It is very easy, we will just switch you to a waitress local."[39] So a woman can cook at home but not in an expensive restaurant. There was a case in which a man was denied a job as an electronic circuit assembler "because women are better at this work," since women have more "finger dexterity."[40] Yet some medical schools have said that women can't be brain surgeons because it "takes a steady hand." Similarly, well-paid accountants are mostly men "because women have no head for figures," but the poorly paid bookkeepers—who do much more arithmetic—are mostly women. Finally, we note that employers give many reasons for preferring men to women but usually can't say or write anything coherent when pushed to justify them. "In 1962 a Presidential order requesting all Federal appointing officers to give reasons for requesting a man or a woman for a job opening cut down requests for candidates of a certain sex to one percent of their former volume."[41]

Before examining the reasons for sex segregation, it must be emphasized that one result is low wages and little prestige in all "women's occupations." Waitresses are paid and respected less than chefs, bookkeepers less than accountants, nurses less than doctors, and electronic assemblers less than brain surgeons. Most economists now agree that one reason for the low wages is that the overcrowding by women in these segregated occupations raises the supply above the demand. Since the 1950s, the number of women in the labor market has rapidly increased. But most of the increase was in these occupations, so the oversupply forced women's wages relatively down further. Another reason for low wages is weak unionization, which we will investigate later. The resulting lower wages are, of course, welcomed by employers.

The obstacle course

Juanita Kreps, a liberal Establishment economist and now secretary of commerce, examined "women's jobs" and commented: "It is not difficult to explain, in simple demand and supply terms, why the wages in these over-supplied fields re-

---

[39] Carol Jacobson, in New York Commission, op. cit., p. 447.
[40] See Kreps, op. cit., p. 95, and Bird, op. cit., p. 69.
[41] Bird, op. cit., p. 68.

main low; but why is a service offered when the wage is so low?"[42] It is indeed a mystery to the neoclassical economist who pictures the worker making a perfectly rational choice with no constraints on the basis of perfect knowledge of all the possibilities. The mystery is deepened because the question is misstated. The woman does not voluntarily "offer" her services (nor "prefer" nor "have a taste for") but is pushed into these fields by extreme social pressure—some of which is internalized.

Getting into the women's jobs is like sliding down a greased incline, while getting into men's jobs is like running an obstacle course. The first obstacle is the socialization of men and women from birth; Johnny gets a toy stethoscope while Jeanie gets a nurse's cap. Throughout her development, the "proper role" is instilled into a woman by family, school, church, and the media. This brainwashing means that women (and men) internalize a conception of male and female jobs. So most women never even think of trying for the higher-status, higher-paying "male jobs."

Suppose a brilliant and independent young woman does overcome the brainwashing that sex-types jobs and decides to become a lawyer rather than a secretary. The second obstacle on the course is marriage under the present sexist social conditions. If she marries a typical middle-class man, it is assumed when they have children she (but not he) will drop out of school to take care of the children and the house (and sometimes get a secretarial job to help him finish). If she somehow manages to finish college and then law school, circumstances still hinder her chances of getting a job. Because the husband's career comes first, she can look for a job only in the same geographic area. Because children and housework are her sole responsibility, she can work only at limited times. Because of the same brainwashing, no one considers the possibility that husband and society should share these burdens.

Suppose the woman is not only brilliant but also ingenious enough to manage all this. The third and cruelest obstacle is discrimination. She may face discrimination in getting admitted to law school. If she gets in, she may be awarded fewer fellowships than she deserves and lower grades than she deserves

[42] Kreps, op. cit., p. ix.

because many law professors are prejudiced against women. And if she graduates, many law offices won't hire her. The same discrimination exists in many nonprofessional jobs: discrimination prevents her from being an airline pilot rather than a stewardess, or a chef rather than a waitress. It was also noted earlier that most women who work do so out of necessity. Therefore if she can't get a job as a pilot but is offered one as a stewardess, she must take it. The combination of socialization, marital constraints, and discrimination in other areas amply explains the "mystery" of why millions of women "prefer" boring, dead-end jobs with low wages.

The question may be asked, *why* do some jobs become "women's" and others "men's"? U.S. history shows that the key to sex-typed jobs for women is low wages and low status. Before 1880, almost all clerical and sales workers were men, who had decent pay and prestige. Then there was a demand for many more cheap but competent clerks and sales workers, so women were substituted at low wages. Similarly, the earliest public school teachers were men; after the Civil War, women were recruited for about one-fourth of the pay, and the status of teaching naturally dropped. Similarly, women became nurses when the work was mostly unpaid volunteer work done under miserable conditions.

Being a bank teller was considered a good-status, well-paid, man's job until World War II, when—of necessity—banks substituted women. Then the job lost status, partially because of routinization and the new "supermarket" atmosphere, but also because women were doing it. As a result, women were kept on at low wages; now every sexist knows that it is a "woman's job" by "nature."

By contrast, in 1940 librarians were low paid and low status, 90 percent female, a "woman's job." After World War II, however, many men on the GI Bill found that they could get to be librarians in just one year of graduate work; jobs were plentiful, and veterans were not worried about being called "sissies." At the same time, libraries started to be more important. The war showed the importance of knowledge, and computers were soon introduced. Now men hold most of the top library jobs, and sexists among them are saying the job of head librarian is too important to be trusted to a woman. Most of the lowest-paying library jobs, however, still belong to women.

One important mechanism for maintaining the segregated

status quo is the procedure used by employment agencies. The law says they can no longer keep separate male and female files, but they get around the law by using pink and blue cards, separate interviewers, and other devices. For example, Susan Sands, who has a B.A. in applied science and nine years of experience in technical publishing, asked several employment agencies in New York State to help her get work. One agency tried to get her to take a secretary's job in a "lovely office" where she could "get the knack" of technical publishing. Another sent her to a typing/bookkeeping/phone-answering job. She says the employment agencies "should call themselves what they are—slave peddlers."[43]

In a similar case, Gloria Greenberg went to the employment agencies with 8 years experience in the New York State Department of Labor, including 1½ years at the executive level. They asked her: "What about typing and stenographic skills?" "Would your husband approve of your doing such and such a job?" "Why is an attractive girl like you not satisfied to raise a family?"[44]

Recruiters and colleagues still ask women, even executive and professional women: "Can you type?" A woman engineer in a West Coast space research company was pushed into acting as secretary for a conference of engineers. She says: "They tried it only once. They asked me to take notes at a conference—and I did." But she didn't take down the very long-winded discussion; she just summarized it, and added her own sarcastic comments: "Target Date: None" and "Action Required: Policy Definition." They never tried that again.[45]

Men often say they would hire women if they were "qualified," usually meaning superwomen. One management expert said any woman could get a job with no discrimination if she had a Harvard Master of Business Administration degree. This idea was tested by a study of the recruiting experiences of a group of women who did graduate with the M.B.A. from Harvard. It was found that they received fewer job offers than equivalent men, and they were poorer jobs. They were offered jobs in research or testing, not jobs handling accounts. One recruiter said bluntly: "We don't feel our clients will accept

---

[43] Susan Sands, in New York Commission on Human Rights, op. cit., p. 405.
[44] Gloria Greenberg in ibid., p. 414.
[45] Bird, op. cit., p. 46.

a woman account executive."[46] Strange that a woman's face is necessary as a low-paid receptionist for men, but impossible as a high-paid account executive for men.

DISCRIMINATION BY UNEMPLOYMENT

There is a myth that all women without paid jobs are voluntarily staying at home. Not true. Women are much more likely to be unemployed than men. Because of sexism, they are the last hired and first fired (see Table 5.9). Racial discrimination is also shown in the greater unemployment of black men. Double discrimination, because of racism and sexism, is revealed in the even higher unemployment of black women.

TABLE 5.9

Unemployment rates, February 1977

	Men	Women
White	7.6	8.0
Black	13.9	14.1

Source: U.S. Department of Labor, *Employment and Earnings,* 24 (March 1977), p. 39.

Many employers have admitted sex discrimination in hiring and firing, excusing it on the basis of the myth that all men need money to support families, whereas all women work just for pin money. We have seen that the reality is quite different; most women also work from necessity.

In addition to direct discrimination in employment, a second reason for the higher unemployment of women is the segregation of jobs, which very much narrows the range of their job opportunities. Furthermore, and not by coincidence, the jobs considered women's jobs are mostly in areas with extreme fluctuation of demand, such as clerical work. Thus women form a convenient reserve army of workers for business, available for low wages in wartime expansions and other temporary booms, but easily (employers hope) sent back to the home in every recession.

In addition to those who are actually unemployed, many

[46] Ibid.

women can find only part-time employment; they form a cheap, marginal work force. In 1973, almost 70 percent of women workers had full-time jobs sometime during the year, but only a little over 40 percent of working women were employed full-time during the entire year.[47] This temporary or part-time work results in another very important discrimination against women who are forced to accept it. The U.S. government reports that 24 percent of all wages (somewhat less in factory work) come in the form of fringe benefits.[48] But these fringe benefits are given only to full-time workers and/or to someone who has worked a certain length of time. Women who work part-time or part-year are often not eligible.

It must also be emphasized that "unemployment" is officially defined in such a way that the official figures seriously understate it, particularly among women. In the first place, part-time workers, even those working only one hour a week, are considered "employed." Second, if a woman can't get a job for a long time and finally gives up, she is not considered unemployed but is just not part of the labor force. Even the Women's Bureau of the U.S. Department of Labor admits, with regard to unemployment data on women: "Since no account is taken of the many who have given up job hunting because it seemed hopeless, these figures may be deceptively low."

Table 5.10 shows the official unemployment rate and a corrected rate that takes into account discouraged workers and part-time workers who would like to work full time. Clearly,

---

[47] *1975 Handbook,* op. cit., p. 52.
[48] Bird, op. cit., p. 66.

TABLE 5.10

Corrected and official unemployment rates by race and sex (June 1975)

Category	Official Unemployment	Minimum corrected unemployment*
White men	7.6	9.9
White women	9.4	13.3
Black men	15.4	20.1
Black women	15.5	22.9

* The more conservative of two ways of correcting is given.
Source: Howard J. Sherman, *Stagflation* (New York: Harper & Row, 1976), p. 16.

actual unemployment is much higher than official unemployment for all workers. Furthermore, when the figures are corrected, the gap between men and women increases.

To add insult to injury, recent Republican administrations have not seen women's unemployment as a serious problem. Several spokesmen for the Nixon and Ford administrations have claimed that the unemployment situation is not as bad as the official figures make it look because there are now so many women and young people in the labor force. The implication is that women and young people do not really need to work and thus their unemployment is not really important.

IS DISCRIMINATION AN IRRATIONAL PREFERENCE?

There is a myth that only irrational males want sexual discrimination and that it's just a matter of their inexplicable tastes or preferences. The economist Gary Becker, whose work is considered definitive by conservatives, says: "Discrimination and prejudice are not usually said to occur when someone prefers looking at a glamorous Hollywood actress rather than at some other woman; yet they are said to occur when he prefers living next to whites rather than next to Negroes. At best calling just one of these actions 'discrimination' requires making subtle and rather secondary distinctions."[49] Note that he thinks discrimination against blacks is as trivial as preferring apples to oranges, and that he uses a sexist example to make his point.

Ray Franklin and Solomon Resnick point out that Becker is wrong to consider discrimination trivial, "just" a preference: "Becker errs because his analysis ignores the distribution of power and the use of the double standard."[50] First, employers, union leaders, and military and government leaders are white males who have power to discriminate. Second, employers choose by a double standard—they assume that white males are good, qualified workers, while blacks and women are not; and the burden of proof is on blacks and women to show themselves qualified. Even where there are laws against discrimination, control of the power structure means the laws are fre-

[49] Gary Becker, *The Economics of Discrimination* (Chicago: University of Chicago Press, 1957), p. 5.
[50] Ray Franklin and Solomon Resnick, *The Political Economy of Racism* (New York: Holt, Rinehart & Winston, 1973), p. 16.

quently not enforced. Prejudiced propaganda is continued through the media, church, and schools; and blacks and women continue to get inferior training.

Conservatives such as Milton Friedman emphasize that discrimination by business is irrational because (so they claim) business loses profits by it. The theory is this: Suppose there are equally qualified male and female workers. Suppose only males are hired because of prejudice. Female workers, because of discrimination against them elsewhere, could be hired more cheaply. Therefore the capitalist who hires only males must be paying higher wages. Under competition there is no way to pass on this higher cost, so business must pay the price of the irrational exclusion of women. In Friedman's opinion, there is a high degree of competition in most of the U.S. economy; thus, capitalists who discriminate pay for it in much higher costs.[51] He argues that, since discrimination loses money for capitalists who discriminate, the prejudiced capitalists who are so irrational as not to hire qualified women will be bankrupted by the competition of those who do hire women at lower wages. Therefore, he claims there is very little discrimination now and the little that does remain will disappear in long-run equilibrium under capitalism.

Some extreme conservatives use this argument to prove the inferiority of women. Since women still receive lower pay and poorer jobs, and since this is not due to discrimination by employers (assuming the economy is in competitive equilibrium), therefore the woman worker is inferior. Some conservatives say the inferiority is due to past discrimination, but true sexists claim that the inferiority is inherent. One economist, Angus Black, says bluntly: "If a woman were more like a man, she'd be treated as such."[52]

Liberals like Martin Bronfenbrenner[53] agree with Friedman on the high cost of discrimination under competition but emphasize the facts of monopoly and monopoly power. Given pervasive monopoly power, business *can* discriminate in long-

---

[51] Milton Friedman, *Capitalism and Freedom* (Chicago: University of Chicago Press, 1957), pp. 108 ff.

[52] Angus Black, *A Radical's Guide to Economic Reality* (New York: Holt, Rinehart & Winston, 1970), p. 37.

[53] Martin Bronfenbrenner, "Potential Monopsony in Labor Markets," *Industrial and Labor Relations Review* 9 (April 1956): 577–588.

run equilibrium with less loss. All traditional economists, both conservative and liberal, thus agree on the main points and differ only in emphasis: (1) Discrimination by employers reflects an inexplicable "preference" (like apples instead of oranges); (2) capitalists must pay a cost, heavy or light, for it; (3) so more competition will tend to eliminate those capitalists and automatically end discrimination.

The only major difference between liberals and conservatives is the fact that the liberals realize there is a great amount of discrimination, while the conservatives deny it. Thus, the liberal economists advocate reforms, while the conservatives believe reforms are unnecessary. Both agree that the radicals are totally incorrect in saying that capitalists benefit from sex discrimination. For example, liberal economist Barbara Bergmann ridicules the idea (which no one has ever suggested) that capitalists conspire together in a Watergate-like plot to discriminate against women in order to make more profits. She says that the status quo of large-scale discrimination against women only helps male workers, not male capitalists. She admits that the capitalist employers are the ones who do the actual discriminating, but denies that they profit from it: "The employers actually tend to lose financially, since profits are lowered when cheap female help is spurned in favor of high-priced male help."[54] Thus, she accepts Milton Friedman's basic argument.

If capitalists are in business to make profit, why do they systematically choose to lose money? This is not a problem for Friedman, because he simply denies that there is much discrimination. It is a problem for Bergmann, however, because she shows the vast extent of discrimination against women, while continuing to argue that capitalists lose money from it. Her answer to the riddle is that capitalists lose financially, but they gain psychological utility: "It feels so good to have women in their 'place.' "[55] She does not seem to find it astounding that such irrational behavior has persisted for many decades under capitalism.

This split over whether sex discrimination is due to an irrational response by all men or to a desire for profit by the capital-

---

[54] Barbara Bergmann, "Economics of Women's Liberation," *Challenge* 16 (May–June 1973): 14.
[55] Ibid.

ist class is not limited to professional economists; it is also a very controversial issue within the women's movement. Some feminists claim that all men benefit from sexist discrimination. Like the traditional economists, they do not claim that the benefits are material in most cases, but that all men benefit psychologically from the oppression of women. It follows from this, as June Safer of the New York Feminists asserts, that all "men are enemies," not just capitalist men.[56] On the contrary, Frances Beale of the Third World Women's Alliance argues that "male chauvinism and racism is economically profitable" to the capitalist system.[57] She says explicitly that men do not merely get a vicarious pleasure out of sex discrimination, but exploit women workers in order to make more profits.

It is important to distinguish between the whole system of labor-capital relations and the attitudes of individual capitalists and workers. Radicals claim only that the whole system makes profits and benefits from sex discrimination, so that it is "rational" from the viewpoint of the system as a whole. Certainly, many men hold irrational sexist prejudices—including workers, who lose from discrimination in the aggregate—and these prejudices are the immediate causes of discrimination. Because of their own sexist prejudices, many employers *perceive* all male workers as better than all female workers, so they often do not even seriously consider a woman who is equally or better qualified than a man for a good job. This is the case in many businesses, in government, and in most universities. A large number of studies have shown that employers, having very imperfect knowledge about workers, just take the easy way out by classifying all black and/or female workers as inferior to white male applicants.[58]

Not only do employers exhibit this prejudice (some even in the face of evidence to the contrary), but foremen add their own racist and/or sexist prejudices to increase the discrimination. Over 20 percent of all white males with jobs in the economy are foremen (or kindred workers); less than 14 percent

---

[56] June Safer, in New York Commission on Human Rights, op. cit., p. 135.
[57] Frances Beale, in ibid., p. 134. See also Marilyn Goldberg, "Economic Exploitation of Women," *Review of Radical Political Economics* 2 (Spring 1970): 3.
[58] Michael Spence, *Market Signalling, Discussion Paper, Public Policy Program,* no. 4 (Cambridge, Mass.: Harvard University, Kennedy School of Government, 1972).

of black males are foremen, and only 1 percent of white women and much less than 1 percent of black women are "foremen."[59]

It is also true that many male workers perceive women as inferior and/or as rivals. Male workers have this perception because of their own sexist upbringing in this society. Certainly employers do sometimes respond to the prejudices of male workers, but they also use some alleged (and nonexistent) workers' prejudices as convenient excuses for their own actions. Finally, it is true that many male clients, industrial purchasers, and advertisers perceive women as inferior. Certainly capitalists do pander to the prejudices of these buyers, but again they also use buyers' prejudices as convenient justifications for their own behavior.

Can we believe, however, that such prejudices would have been allowed to influence corporate behavior for so many decades if it were not profitable? Can we conceivably believe, as some economists contend, that these prejudices continue unabated even though they cause large losses to the capitalist system? In fact, it is possible to present an impressive list of the ways in which sexism is very profitable to U.S. capitalists.

IS SEXIST PREJUDICE PROFITABLE?

It will be shown here that sex discrimination and prejudices are profitable in dollars and cents, after which the question of noneconomic benefits to the ruling elite will also be investigated.

Segregation and lower wages

First, it is important to review one crucial point concerning the reality of women at work. Women and men are mostly segregated at work, so that half of all women workers are in occupations that are over 70 percent female. On the other side of the segregated job world, most males are in occupations that are far over 70 percent male. There are some mixed occupations, but they are so few that they may be ignored here in order to simplify the analysis.

What is the situation in the mostly female occupations? The evidence shows that in areas where most of the labor force is female, the pay for *both* men and women is lower, even

[59] Franklin and Resnick, op. cit., p. 46.

though workers in many of those areas have higher qualifications (shown in more education) than the average worker. This may be shown for all the clerical occupations in which women predominate (see Table 5.11). The table reveals that, in every clerical occupation where women are in the majority, women's wages are much lower than the average American male's wage, although the women's education is above the average American male worker's education. The women's wages are also very considerably below those of men in the same occupation, yet their education is almost the same as the men's. But these four facts only tell us what we knew already, that women suffer from job segregation and discrimination. More interesting is the fact that men in these occupations had much lower wages than the average American male worker, even though these men had more education than the average American male worker. Therefore, *sexist discrimination not only hurts women workers, it also hurts men workers*—and the lower wages produce higher profits.

TABLE 5.11

Education and income of clerical workers, 1970*

	Percentage by which median education is above or below median of all U.S. male workers		Percentage by which median earnings are above or below median of all U.S. male workers	
Occupation	**Men**	**Women**	**Men**	**Women**
Bank teller	+4%	+2%	−25%	−45%
Bookkeeper	+4	+2	−3	−41
Cashier	0	−2	−59	−68
File clerk	+2	+1	−35	−55
Library attendant and assistant	+13	+7	−80	−73
Key punch operator	+2	+2	−2	−40
Payroll & time-keeping clerk	+2	+2	+3	−32
Receptionist	+5	+2	−44	−56
Secretary	+5	+3	−1	−37
Telephone operator	+2	+1	−15	−44
Typist	+2	+2	−21	−47

* In all occupations listed, women are a majority of the total.
Source: Department of Commerce, *1970 Census of Population,* Subject Report PC(2)–7A, Occupational Characteristics, Table 1.

To understand the much lower wages of all workers in the mostly female sectors, it is necessary to understand that these sectors differ systematically in several other characteristics from the mostly male sectors. Most important, one careful study shows that the industries into which women are largely segregated, such as the service areas and the garment industry, are small and relatively competitive, whereas the mostly male dominated industries are large and highly concentrated.[60] Because of the competitive nature of the mostly female industries, they have low rates of profit. On the other hand, the more concentrated male industries use their monopoly power to restrict competition and achieve a higher rate of profit.[61]

The mostly female, more competitive sector also has much lower wages for all employees than does the mostly male sector.[62] Finally, the female industries and occupations mostly have much weaker unions than the mostly male industries. Of course, these are generalizations and do not hold true in every case. Nevertheless, the attributes of a high percentage of female employees, competition, low profits, low wages, and weak unions do tend to be found together.

Now, several questions may be asked and answered. The first is why the average wage of women is much lower than that of men. A large part of the answer is that women are mainly in the low-wage areas. Why are they in the low-wage areas? Partly this is because they are discriminated against in the other areas; furthermore their own sexist conditioning tells them these low-wage areas are the proper places for them to be. Thus they are in these areas because it is much, much harder for them to move into the better paying areas. Discrimination, sexist conditioning, and family circumstances all work to keep women in traditional female jobs.

A related question is: Why do employers segregate women into these particular areas? The key to answering this is to recognize that, in the competitive sectors, employers are forced by low profits to economize in every way. Even though they

---

[60] See the discussion and data in Mary Stevenson, "Women's Wages and Job Segregation," *Politics and Society* 4 (Fall 1973): 92–93.

[61] See Howard Sherman, *Profits in the United States* (Ithaca: Cornell University Press, 1972), p. 89 ff.

[62] See Barry Bluestone, "Economic Crisis and the Law of Uneven Development," *Politics and Society* 3 (Fall 1973): 65–82.

may be as prejudiced as employers in the monopoly sector, they must still hire women if they can pay them lower wages. In fact, when they discover out of necessity that women can do the jobs as well as men but will work for lower wages, they scramble to hire women in order that they can make higher profits.

If higher profits are to be made by hiring women at lower wages, why don't employers in the monopoly sphere do this as well? One could refer to their biased perceptions, but it was shown that these could be overcome. One could refer to the biases of strong male unions, but these have also been overcome, when it was important for employers' profits. The key point is that they have less reason to resist high wages in this sector. The monopoly power of these capitalists can be used to pass on to the consumer all of the higher wages. In fact, a small increase in wages is often used by the monopolists as the excuse for a major price increase.

Finally, it may be asked why wages are kept much lower for *all* workers in the mostly female industries. As was shown earlier, both discrimination and socialization push women into these areas, so there is great overcrowding of labor into this sector. The excess supply is one reason for lower wages. Furthermore, the fact that competitive employers cannot simply pass on wage increases means that they fight against them and are more likely to run sweat shops. And, because of weak unions, workers in this area are greatly handicapped in fighting for higher wages.

Why are the unions much weaker in the mostly female, more competitive sector? One reason is that the oversupply of labor decreases bargaining power, while the competitive employers are forced to protect their own limited profits by tough bargaining. Moreover, many of these industries and occupations are quite spread out in physical terms. It is much easier to organize one enormous factory in the monopoly sector than it is to organize a thousand smaller ones in the competitive sector. Many of the women and much of the competition are found particularly in the service industries, which are also spread out and harder to organize. Yet another important factor is that some of these areas have significant numbers of men as well as a majority of women, so the situation is ideal for the working of sexist prejudice to divide the workers, weaken their unions, and make them easy to rule.

Divide and rule

For the entire country, one out of every four male workers is unionized, but only one out of every seven female workers.[63] One reason for the lower proportion of women in unions is that the areas in which most of them work are harder to organize. The other reason is the hostility or indifference of union men and union leaders, an attitude fostered by their own prejudices. The degree of union sexism may be observed by the fact that most union executive boards are exclusively male, even though women do average about 20 percent of all union members. Even in unions such as the International Ladies Garment Workers Union, where women constitute over three-fourths of the members, only a few token women are on the executive board.

Jean Tepperman reports that women in the factories where she worked were very angry and would have liked a militant union to act on their grievances, but never even dreamed of having such a union. They thought of unions as run by men who were selling them something like car insurance. The women joined the union because they were forced to and because they thought that, without it, their situation might be even worse. Tepperman says: "The way most people chose between the unions was to compare prices (union dues) against the product (the list of union promises), adjusted by how much you felt they were lying."[64] The unions did very little, if anything, for the women's specific grievances.

Union men often pay for their prejudices in broken unions and lower wages. In a strike by Standard Oil workers in San Francisco, the union was beaten because of its own prejudices against women. "Women at Standard Oil have the least chance for advancement and decent pay, and the union has done little to fight this. Not surprisingly, women formed the core of the back to work move that eventually broke the strike."[65]

The liberal economist Morris Silver finds that prejudice between black and white workers makes unions more difficult and thus may lower the total wage bill. Therefore, "far from being indifferent to the existence of discriminatory attitudes

---

[63] Kirsten Amundsen, *The Silenced Majority* (Englewood Cliffs, N.J.: Prentice-Hall, 1971), p. 96.

[64] Tepperman, op. cit., p. 120.

[65] Kathy McAfee and Myrna Wood, "Bread and Roses," in Roberta Salper, ed., *Female Liberation* (New York: Knopf, 1972), p. 155.

on the part of workers, the capitalist gains from them and may find it profitable to invest in their creation."[66] The same conclusion obviously holds for sexist attitudes against women.

A good example of male employees' attitudes—the kind that make it easy for employers to divide and rule employees—comes from a book by Harmon Ziegler, a "social scientist" who expresses the sexist views of male high school teachers.[67] In 1950, men represented 40 percent of all high school teachers; by 1960, men were a majority in this field. Ziegler boasts that this change was not an accident, but the result of a concerted campaign to reduce "female dominance" by giving elaborate inducements to males to enter high school teaching. He defends this discrimination in favor of male high school teachers because "the identification problems of girls are not very severe. However, if a boy establishes an emotional contact primarily with women teachers, . . . the school can offer him little help in learning a male role. . . ."[68] Here is sexism in the scientific verbiage of educational psychology. Ziegler presents no evidence that girls have less severe identification problems—whereas it was shown earlier that high school is where women develop the "will to fail." He presents no evidence that boys' egos are more fragile, that they have more identity problems. Finally, he merely assumes that males and females should learn sex-stereotyped roles.

Ziegler complains that, because of the stereotype of high school teachers, a U.S. Supreme Court case involving male high school teachers always referred to them as "she." He says this is just one example of how males must struggle to overcome the female stereotype of high school teaching. Somehow the picture of these courageous sexists fighting a stereotype—in the one case where the shoe pinches the other foot—arouses more amusement than sympathy.

Then, Ziegler gets to his main argument. He claims that male teachers suffer financial discrimination in their pay both with reference to males in other occupations and with reference to female teachers. Yet, he admits that male and female teachers at the same levels are paid *the same salary!* He even

---

[66] Quoted in Franklin and Resnick, op. cit., p. 23.

[67] Harmon Ziegler, *The Political Life of American Teachers* (Englewood Cliffs, N.J.: Prentice-Hall, 1967), a section of which is reprinted in Athena Theodore, *The Professional Woman* (Cambridge, Mass.: Schenkman, 1971), pp. 74–92.

[68] Ibid., p. 75.

admits that male teachers receive "various under-the-table inducements."[69] If men get equal or more pay, where is the discrimination? He argues that men are discriminated against because they are not paid a lot *more* than female teachers. To support this, he assumes implicitly that all teachers are married. Then, he claims that the married female just works for pin money, whereas the married male must support a family with his salary. This excuse was exploded in previous sections of this book. Moreover, since when does capitalism consider need? Would he pay more to all the female black domestic servants who make less than $2000 a year and most of whom head families? Would he pay more to single female teachers? Would he pay more to married ones with husbands who earn little or nothing? Ziegler concludes: ". . . not only are male teachers doing women's work, they are only getting paid women's wages for doing it"[70] and he cries that it is damaging to the male ego to be paid the same as women. Again, we find a sexist talking about the fragile male ego when it suits him. If men are so fragile and inferior in this respect, perhaps they should be paid less.

Ziegler particularly tries to divide men from women in their associations and unions. He is worried because elementary and high school teachers may be in one union and elementary teachers are mostly female. Therefore, he fears that women will outnumber men in the union and will dominate all the conferences. Must males dominate every meeting? It is attitudes like these that have retarded the development of strong unions and have kept wages low for all workers in the "female" occupations.

Other functions of sex discrimination

In addition to lower wages and weaker unions, sex discrimination helps provide a handy but disposable labor force. The process has been well described by Franklin and Resnick in the case of racism. If an employer has 10 black and 10 white workers, and must fire half for a couple of months, which will he fire? "If he is rational and seeks to minimize his labor turnover costs, he will lay off his ten black workers on the assumption that they will be unlikely to get permanent or better jobs

---

[69] Ibid., p. 78.
[70] Ibid.

elsewhere because of the discriminatory practices of other employers."[71] Obviously women workers are treated the same way by "rational" employers.

Another reason sexism is profitable to capitalists is the closely related savings on fringe benefits. It is now common for employers to keep a permanent crew of skilled white males plus a large number of temporary women (and black) workers. The temporary workers are usually fired in less than 90 days. Under most laws this is soon enough so that they have no legal rights to fringe benefits; this includes no vacation pay, no sick leave, no extra medical benefits, and no employer contributions to pension plans.

Sexism is also profitable because it instills the desire to consume in women. The sexist image of the good woman shows her in her kitchen surrounded by the very latest gadgets, made up with miracle cosmetics, and using the latest thing in laundry detergent, dishwasher soap, and wall cleaner. This image helps business sell billions of dollars of useless (or even harmful) goods.

Still another reason sexism is profitable is that women's unpaid work in the home is crucial to the provision of the needed supply of labor. In other words, women raise children to be workers, and they cook and clean and take care of adult male workers. These valuable services are unpaid. Such housework is valued at about one-fourth GNP, though it is not counted in official GNP. If business had to pay women *in full* to raise and clean and cook for the labor force, profits would be much, much lower.

Women in the family are not only profitable to capitalism because of their unpaid material labor, but perhaps even more for the psychological jobs they perform in the family. The woman in the sexist family must play a certain role as wife and mother. That role includes keeping the family safe and stable, which sometimes means "adjusting" it to harsh realities. As a mother, she is expected to tell her children to behave docilely in school. Later, she is the one who must train her children to be "good" workers, that is, to be quiet and disciplined, but enterprising and competitive with other workers.[72]

---

[71] Franklin and Resnick, op. cit., p. 20.

[72] See Peggy Morton, "A Woman's Work Is Never Done," in Edith Altback, ed., *From Feminism to Liberation* (Cambridge, Mass.: Schenkman, 1971), pp. 211–228.

As a wife, she is often the one to caution her husband not to involve himself in a strike lest he lose his job. Both the wife's influence and the family responsibilities then join to reduce the husband's mobility, his resistance to low wages, and his ability to strike.[73] At the same time, wives act as lightning rods for the reactions of men to the system. If he is angered by the boss on the job, a husband can come home and act as a petty dictator over his wife and children. He can let out his frustrations within the family, rather than against the system. He also enforces the child's acceptance of authority and belief in a hierarchical view of all social relations, a view which is very helpful to factory management.[74]

As a result of their dependent role in the sexist family, women are socialized to be passive, submissive, and docile as workers. Employers can also more easily exploit wives as cheap labor because women are socialized to believe the myth that they work for pin money or just "supplementary" income; that their work is only temporary; and that they must only work close to their homes for limited hours. Yet this "supplementary" income is now massive enough so that many husbands may be more willing to settle for lower wages. The mother also trains her daughter to be a good mother, and the process begins again.

The last, but not the least important, profit to capitalism from sexism comes in its increased support for political stability. On the one hand, women's psychological role in the sexist family has the same effects politically as economically. It tends to make her more fearful and conservative; she tends to influence her husband in this direction and to pass it on to her son and especially to her daughter. Sexism is used for political "divide and rule" in many of the same ways as racism. Some white politicians blame all urban problems on blacks. Hitler blamed unemployment on Jewish capitalists and agitation on Jewish communists. Secretary of the Treasury Schultz blamed unemployment (and accompanying pressure for low wages) on the competition of women workers. Thus women provide a scapegoat for men's problems rather than becoming an ally against the system.

---

[73] See Margaret Benson, "Political Economy of Women's Liberation," in ibid., p. 199–210.

[74] See McAfee and Wood, op. cit., p. 156.

The effects of divide and rule by sexism are also evident in radical movements. Many examples can be found in U.S. history. In the late 1960s, the Students for Democratic Society and other New Left organizations wasted women's talents and were weakened by the resulting male-female struggles. It should also be noted that the Establishment sociologist Daniel Moynihan helped divide and weaken the black movement with his "theory" that black women are domineering matriarchs who psychologically castrate their men. Finally, it is saddest to note how universities and corporations can sometimes play women against blacks and other minority males in awarding scarce jobs.

In conclusion, sexism yields profits for capitalists by splitting unions and radical organizations, getting cheaper labor from women *and* men, obtaining a flexible reserve army of unemployed, saving on fringe benefits, giving an outlet to men's frustrations, providing unpaid maintenance for the labor force, and socializing women to economic and political conservatism. On the other hand, sexism is costly to society, which loses many of the potential talents of women. It is costly to women themselves, in low wages and unemployment, the stifling of their creativity and personality development, and their subordinate, miserably unhappy home life. It is also costly to male workers in lower wages, weaker unions, less political strength, and a miserably unhappy home life. So why does it persist?

HOW IS SEXISM CREATED AND MAINTAINED?

There is a myth that sexist discrimination is natural and eternal, has always existed and always will, and that men are born with this irrational prejudice. Yet anthropology shows that sexism had no functional role in primitive societies for one or two million years, or about 99 percent of our existence. It would have been harmful to social survival because women had to be strong and independent. Sexism seems to have arisen with class-divided societies, reaching its awful peak in slavery and feudalism. Furthermore, many contemporary societies, such as China and Sweden, have reduced sexism.

Even in U.S. history there have been times when this "eternal" prejudice could suddenly be changed. For example, in World War II women were badly needed by the government and capitalist employers. Suddenly it was discovered that women were perfectly competent to do all sorts of industrial jobs, that it was "natural" for them to do so.

Prejudice is not eternal or innate but is learned through propaganda, respected examples, and pressure. Men and women are shaped by society to believe in sexism and to conform to sexist roles. The mechanisms of sexist socialization include the family, media, schools, churches, the work situation, and overt political statements by leaders.

Why is there sexist socialization? The most honest answer is that it is "functional" for those who have social-economic-political power in our present system. It is functional in the sense that it allows them to maintain and extend their profits and power. This statement must be qualified to note that the sexist ideology originated in and was inherited from slave and feudal societies, where it also played the function of support for the status quo.

How do the powers that be control the direction of socialization in our society? The answer is that those who benefit from sexism control the media, jobs, schools, churches, and political power. There are few women in top media positions. There are few in top church positions. There are also few women in top educational positions, and very few in top corporate or political positions. This explanation, however, must not be understood in a simplistic fashion. Barbara Bergmann claims that radicals think sexist oppression is a plot or conspiracy by capitalists. Sexism is not a conspiracy, but rather the result of the normal functioning of our society. And it is hard to imagine this society operating differently, because all the parts must fit together. Suppose women suddenly got the top positions in the media, churches, politics, and the economy. They would quickly revolutionize our ideology by ridding it of sexism, or else they would just as quickly be pushed out again by a counterrevolution. Or suppose that somehow, even with males in all power positions, sexist brainwashing ended and was replaced by an ideology of male-female equality: Then women would have to be given half the top positions, or a revolutionary situation would occur—or else the ideology would revert to sexism. The society's ideology and power structure *must* conform to each other (except in revolutionary situations).

Perhaps the normal operation of our sexist society can best be seen as a circular process repeating itself over time. If we cut into the process at an arbitrary point, here is what the sequence looks like:

1. Children are socialized into sexist views by the family, education, religion, the media (books, radio, TV, magazines, newspapers, advertising), corporations, and politicians.
2. As a result of their sexist upbringing (and further sexist discriminations)
   a. Women accept subordinate positions in the family, economy, churches, schools, media, and politics.
   b. Women pass on the sexist ideology to their children.
3. As a result of their sexist upbringing
   a. Men aspire to top positions of income, status, and power in all areas.
   b. Men get these positions as a result of the sexist views of and discrimination by the men of the previous generation who held these positions.
   c. Men use their positions of power to reinforce sexist ideology (and promote other men) in the schools, churches, economy, media, politics, and family—both because they believe it and because it is in their interest.
4. The next generation repeats process 1.
5. The next generation repeats process 2.
6. The next generation repeats process 3.

And so forth.

This vicious circle—from sexist socialization to sexist power to sexist socialization, and so forth—is sometimes misread in a defeatist way. The defeatist notion is that the circle has always existed and always will, and nothing can be done about it. The grain of truth is that it *is* a self-reinforcing circle, and it is difficult to change. But there have been societies without sexism. Moreover, the process is not totally automatic but is aided by overt discrimination and propaganda at each level. Therefore reforms can also begin by ending overt discrimination and propaganda at each level. Finally, it is not impossible that a socioeconomic revolution could lay the foundation for reversing the whole process.

PROFESSIONAL WOMEN: THE OBSTACLE COURSE

6

"The nature and proper timidity and delicacy which belongs to the female sex evidently unfits it for many of the occupations of civil life." So wrote the justices of the Supreme Court when, in 1872, they denied Myra Bradwell the right to practice law. Although the legal barriers have now been abolished, most women are still effectively excluded from the prestige professions.

The data reveal a systematic pattern in which women are heavily represented in some professions but hardly visible in others. There are very few in the prestige professions, such as law and medicine; but some low-paid and low-prestige "professions" such as nursing and elementary school teaching are almost wholly female. Women are segregated within the professions quite as much as blacks are segregated in housing.

PATTERNS OF SEGREGATION IN THE PROFESSIONS

In 1977, women accounted for 43 percent of what the census calls "professional and technical workers."[1] This percentage has declined from its high point of 45 percent in 1940. Yet even the 43 percent figure is misleading. The category of "professional and technical worker" is very wide, and over half of all women in this category are nurses or noncollege teachers, low-pay and low-prestige professions.

In the high-paying and high-prestige professions, the situa-

[1] U.S. Department of Labor, Bureau of Labor Statistics, *Employment and Earnings,* 24 (February 1977), p. 39.

tion is very different. According to 1974 data, women were only 7 percent of lawyers and judges, 9.8 percent of physicians, 16.5 percent of pharmacists, 24 percent of accountants, and 9.4 percent of scientists and engineers.[2] Yet these very low figures are an improvement over 1960, when only 3.5 percent of lawyers and 6.8 percent of doctors were women. In the academic world the picture is a little better, but not much. Women are 31 percent of university and college teachers but, as we will see later, they are mostly found in the less prestigious schools and in the lower ranks. The university is still predominately a male preserve.

The picture is quite different in the lower-paying professions into which women are segregated. According to 1974 data, women account for 98 percent of all nurses, 61 percent of all social workers, 82 percent of all librarians, and 85 percent of all elementary school teachers.[3] An interesting area in transition is high school teaching; formerly almost all female, it is now only 47 percent female. Its relative pay and prestige have risen somewhat, so, as we have seen, men have invaded the area—and have taken most of the better positions with higher pay.

WAGES IN THE "FEMALE" PROFESSIONS

In those professions where women predominate, *both* men and women receive lower wages even though they have higher educational qualifications than the average worker (see Table 6.1 and compare it with Table 5.11). In every single professional area with a majority of women, the male professionals' wages are far below what their education would ordinarily get for them, and the female professionals' wages are much farther below what their education should earn them. In a few areas the men's wages are slightly above the average (though their education merits more); in no area do the women's wages even near the average. These low wages are due to overcrowding as a result of segregation of women professionals. Weakened

[2] Stuart H. Garfinkle, "Occupations of Women and Black Workers, 1962–74," *Monthly Labor Review,* 98 (November 1975), p. 28. National Science Foundation, *Characteristics of the National Sample of Scientists & Engineers 1974,* p. 11.

[3] Garfinkle, op. cit., p. 11.

bargaining power, disunity, and lack of unions due to men's sexist attitudes, women's socialization, and successful "divide and rule" tactics by employers are further contributing factors.

TABLE 6.1
*Education and income in selected "female" professions, 1970**

	Percentage by which median education is above median of all U.S. male workers		Percentage by which median earnings are above or below median of all U.S. male workers	
Profession	**Male**	**Female**	**Male**	**Female**
Librarian	+38%	+35%	+1%	−19%
Dietician	+3	+5	−21	−41
Registered nurse	+10	+8	−8	−26
Therapist	+30	+33	+3	−29
Clinical lab technician	+20	+19	−5	−27
Therapy assistant	+5	+2	−9	−50
Religious worker	+34	+20	−21	−68
Social and recreational worker	+34	+33	+4	−19
Elementary teacher	+37	+35	+7	−14
Kindergarten teacher	+31	+29	−31	−60

* In all professions listed, women are a majority of the total.
Source: Department of Commerce, *1970 Census of Population,* Subject Report PC(2)-7A, Occupational Characteristics, Table 1.

Why then have women not invaded the men's professions in greater numbers? For a woman to achieve success in a prestige profession means overcoming an enormous number of barriers. These obstacles to success may be divided, somewhat arbitrarily, into three major categories: the sexist socialization of women, discrimination against women by men who are sexist because of their socialization, and the traditional structure of the professions and the family.

THE SOCIALIZATION OF WOMEN

Women are socialized from infancy to accept certain roles and to reject others as "unfeminine." These roles are taught them in the family, churches, schools, and media. Thus for Christmas a girl gets either a doll house so she can learn to be a "mommy," or at best a nurse's outfit; a boy gets a doctor's kit or an astronaut's helmet. Advisers, including parents and professional counselors, tell girls to go to college only to get a husband. In high school and college most girls get the message to act dumb because boys won't date smart girls. Girls are supposed to be passive. The creativeness and independence needed for professional work are considered unfeminine traits.

Women are socialized to be "helpmates" and mothers, not creative individuals. Moreover, most women have no professional role models to follow. The professionals shown in the media are almost exclusively men, particularly those in the high-paying and/or high-prestige areas of law, medicine, architecture, science, and university teaching. At college, most of their professors are men. Most have nonprofessional or even nonworking mothers. Role models are important. Many studies have shown that a woman whose mother works in a professional field is much more likely to become a professional herself.

Through the socialization process and even by explicit counseling, the college girl is encouraged to plan to get married and not to make long-range career plans. Indeed, she is told that marriage is the key to eternal bliss and that a career will hurt or prevent marriage. If she does go to college, counselors reinforce segregation by encouraging girls to major in decorative arts, humanities, nursing, and teaching while pushing boys to major in science, math, prelaw, and premed.

This socialization makes the average woman less apt to try to enter a profession and less apt to be successful in the attempt than a man, but this internal barrier is not the most important obstacle a woman faces. It is strongly reinforced by sex discrimination at all levels and by external structural barriers.

DISCRIMINATION IN THE PRESTIGE PROFESSIONS

The immediate cause of sex discrimination is the sexist attitude of male professionals, attributable both to their own sexist socialization and to their selfish interests (the latter being usually much less important and often unconscious). For example, a New York professor of art says "art is male, . . . aesthetic values are in masculine terms."[4] How can he act equally toward male and female students?

[4] Quoted in Judith Hole and Ellen Levine, *Rebirth of Feminism* (New York: Quadrangle, 1971), p. 366.

Following are other sexist comments made by male faculty members to women graduate students and even to women faculty.[5]

"A pretty girl like you will certainly get married; why don't you stop with an M.A.?"

"You're so cute. I can't see you as a professor of anything."

"Women are intrinsically inferior."

"Any woman who has got this far has got to be a kook."

Another man said to a prospective female faculty member that the department already had "too many" women. Still another told a candidate that he could not take women seriously in his profession. Another looked at a woman who was being interviewed for a job and asked her age; then, he said she probably couldn't handle the job because she didn't look like the "academic" type. A dean told a woman who was trying to enter graduate school that they would take any man, but that a woman should have at least an A– average from Bryn Mawr. Another dean told a young widow (with a five-year-old child) that she didn't need to go to graduate school because she was quite attractive and could easily find a man to marry her. And, he added, he wouldn't give her a fellowship because men needed aid more than she did. Finally, over 50 percent of 3000 academic men replied to a questionnaire[6] that the prime responsibility of a woman is to be a mother and wife, that women don't have as much need to achieve as men, and that women do have an equal opportunity to achieve their full potential (presumably while staying at home). A majority also believed the myth that women have higher job turnover and sick-leave rates; and most believed that women cannot deal with men who are their subordinates.

Such sexist attitudes on the part of academic men are not merely curiosities; they distort their judgments of women as students and as colleagues. As one careful study in educational psychology puts it, "the expectations and prejudices of those who judge the performance of anything from white rats to

---

[5] Quoted in Ann Harris, in New York Commission on Human Rights, *Women's Role in Contemporary Society* (New York: Avon, 1972), pp. 587–588.
[6] Ibid., p. 584.

human beings are reflected in the judgments they make."[7] Thus sexist prejudices affect judgments on admission, grading, hiring, and promotion of women. There is even evidence that they negatively affect the performance of women students.

The beliefs of prejudiced people bias the way in which they perceive women, furnishing distorted "facts" to confirm their prejudices. The John McKay/Joan McKay experiment described in Chapter 3 shows that both male and female students tend to be antifeminist in just this way.[8] Their biases do distort their perceptions of women. Does this mean that students and colleagues and reviewers evaluate books and articles by women differently from those by men? Does it mean that student evaluations of teaching are biased against women? It probably does.

A paper called "The Clash between Beautiful Women and Science,"[9] which was presented at the American Psychological Association meetings in 1968, is a classic example of antifeminist bias. The charitable interpretation is that the author's thesis—beauty and science are mutually exclusive in women—is a joke, but the author (a man) presents it seriously. He uses a questionnaire asking women their interests. He finds that women Ph.D.s in chemistry and mathematicians are less interested in being actresses, artists, fashion models, or dancers, or in being the first to wear the very latest fashions than are top fashion models, airline stewardesses, or TV entertainers! He concludes that scientific interests and beauty in women are antagonistic, though he magnanimously concedes there must be exceptions. "In research laboratories across the country, there must be a few attractive women who enjoy zesty activities."[10] One reason that women scientists are ugly and dull, he assumes, "is that scientific training . . . may dampen one's livelier instincts." Another reason, he asserts, is that all the pretty women students get married, leaving only the ugly one to go for Ph.D.s. He also gives as "evidence" this informa-

---

[7] R. Rosenthal and L. Jacobson, *Pygmalion in the Classroom: Teacher Expectation and Pupils' Intellectual Development* (New York: Holt, Rinehart and Winston, 1968).

[8] Philip Goldberg, "Are Women Prejudiced Against Women?" in Athena Theodore, ed., *The Professional Woman* (Cambridge, Mass.: Schenkman, 1971), p. 168.

[9] David Campbell, "The Clash between Beautiful Women and Science," reprinted in Theodore, op. cit., pp. 135–141.

[10] Ibid., p. 139.

tion: "Of the last 78 Playmates (in *Playboy*) only three of these spectacularly displayed women have expressed any interest in scientific activities."[11]

This strange stereotype of women scientists as ugly, uninterested in beauty, and usually also uninterested in sex and unable to attract men has been used against every group of women who attempted to step out of their "proper place." In the mid-nineteenth century, women college students were always portrayed as ugly and sexless. Of course now that it is "proper" to go to college, women coeds are assumed to be the apex of beauty and sex, but brainless. Since it is still not considered feminine to be a serious graduate student, the stereotype persists against women graduate students, even though they are a cross-section in terms of appearance, and many are married.

If women graduate students are said to be ugly and sexless, the stereotype is even more intense against faculty women. Several attractive women have testified that men faculty stood agape when meeting them at an airport for job interviews. Usually it took a perceptible time interval for the man to believe this really was an applicant for a professional job ("but you don't look like a professor"). All of the prejudice translates into discrimination.

Similar stereotypes work against women in other professional areas. For example, one survey of attitudes of male lawyers found about half saying that women are too "weak and feminine," that they go to law school only to catch a man. The other half characterized all women lawyers as "tough and masculine."[12] Naturally such biases result in discrimination against women.

Admission

In this era of equality it is still true that "girls need higher grades for admission to many institutions."[13] For example, in 1970 the University of North Carolina at Chapel Hill still said openly: "Admission of women on the freshman level will be restricted to those who are especially well-qualified." Maximum

---

[11] Ibid.

[12] See James White, "Women in the Law," *Michigan Law Review,* 65 (April 1967): 1052.

[13] Bernice Sandler, in U.S. Congress, House Committee on the Judiciary, *Hearings on Equal Rights for Men and Women* (1971), p. 267.

quotas for women graduate students have been exposed in departments of art, genetics, and journalism, and in law and medical schools.

A 1969 survey[14] asked deans of medical schools about their policies for admitting women. Selected answers: Dean A, "We have refused to admit women with children." Dean B, "We would not admit a married student unless she was quite outstanding." Dean C, "I have enough trouble understanding my wife and daughters without attempting to explain the questions in this paragraph." Dean D (orally to a woman applicant, a Phi Beta Kappa in chemistry), "I cannot accept you this year because I have my quota of women. . . . My God, I don't know what I am going to do with all these female over-achievers who keep applying." In medical school some male doctors and students continue these sexist attitudes. A male medical student to a female: "You don't belong here, sweetie, you took the place of some guy who could make a more significant contribution than you will."

In 1968, the chairman of a political science department said: "We don't discriminate against women. We just put all the applications from women at the bottom of the stack; when we run out of qualified men, we consider women."[15] In the debate on the Civil Rights Act of 1964, a congressman pointed out that in Virginia "21,000 women were turned down for college entrance during a period when not one male applicant was rejected."[16] As a result of such discrimination, women college freshmen have higher high school grades than men. Entering women graduate students also have higher college grades than men.

Partly as a result of socialization and partly as a result of biased admissions policies, the ratio of women to all students declines at higher levels. In 1970, women received 51 percent of the high school diplomas but only 42 percent of the B.A.s, 40 percent of M.A.s, and 13 percent of Ph.D. degrees.[17] In

---

[14] Reported by Joan Flannigan, in New York Commission on Human Rights, op. cit., p. 359.

[15] Reported in Lucy Komisar, *The New Feminism* (New York: Warner, 1972), p. 137.

[16] Doris Pullen, "The Educational Establishment," in Mary Thompson, ed., *Voices of the New Feminism* (Boston: Beacon, 1970), p. 133.

[17] Rudolph Blitz, "Women in the Professions," *Monthly Labor Review,* 97 (May 1974), p. 38.

the last few years, the situation has improved some. In 1974 women received 19 percent of the Ph.D.s; and in 1976 women earned almost half the bachelor's degrees.[18] Even taking these improvements into account, sexist discrimination still results in a lower level of education for women than for men.

Financial aid

Many of the best scholarships were until recently limited to men. This was the case, for instance, at New York University Law School before a major protest by women forced a change in policy. Even without formal limitations, most male-dominated faculty committees award more financial aid to male than female graduate students on the stereotyped grounds that "the men need the money more" and "the men are the more devoted students."

One woman graduate student reported that both she and her husband had applied for fellowships.[19] Even though she had the higher grades, he received a fellowship and she did not. Why? He was married and had a child; thus he needed the money and was considered a good risk because he had settled down. She was told that because she was married and had a child, she was a poor risk. Not only do institutions give less aid to women; families also reveal the usual sexist attitude by giving financial aid to men but often not to women students.

A comprehensive study of all college faculty in Minnesota found that women more often than men financed their graduate training out of their own personal savings: ". . . men far exceeded women in the use of scholarships and fellowships, staff appointments as teaching research assistants, GI aids and 'earnings of a spouse'."[20] Yet remember that the average graduate woman has better college grades than the average graduate man.

In a careful study of all departments of political science, it was found that all four groups questioned—female and male graduate students, female and male faculty—put bias in finan-

---

[18] Mary Keyserling, "The Economic Status of Women in the United States," *American Economic Review,* 66 (May 1976), p. 209, and *Los Angeles Times,* February 14, 1977.

[19] Riverside, California, *Daily Enterprise,* May 15, 1974.

[20] Ruth Eckert and John Stecklein, "Academic Women," in Theodore, op. cit., p. 349.

cial assistance and scholarships near the top of their lists of types of discrimination against women graduate students.[21] In fact, in 1970, female graduate students in political science, *who had top honors in college,* were supported 50 percent by fellowships but only 17 percent by assistantships, and 33 percent were forced to support themselves on their own resources. Among male graduate students with similar top honors, 50 percent were supported by fellowships; but 47 percent received assistantships and only 3 percent were forced to use their own resources.[22] There is more discretion (and hence more room for prejudice) in awarding teaching assistantships than in awarding fellowships, since the latter are awarded almost exclusively on the basis of grades. Whatever the reason, almost all men with top honors got support, while one-third of the women did not.

Training

Most of the objectively proved discrimination in training is the discrimination in financial aid mentioned before. In addition, however, the sexist attitudes of faculty obviously prejudice their handling and evaluation of women students. This is most evident in the areas of medicine and law. A recent graduate of Harvard Law School reports that as late as 1970, several professors still had "ladies days," when they asked female law students cute questions about supposedly female areas of the law. On all other days they were ignored.[23] No women were admitted to Harvard Law School until 1950, and only about 3 percent of its students have been female since then. Until 1970, the only eating place in the law school, Lincoln's Inn, did not admit women. Women couldn't play on the squash courts at Harvard until 1971. There were no women faculty at Harvard Law School; this not only is an instance of discrimination but also deprives female students of successful role models to emulate.

Women law school graduates in Indiana were even subjected to blatant sexism on the 1973 bar examination. One of the

[21] Jean and Philip Converse, "Status of Women as Students and Professionals in Political Science," *PS,* 4 (Summer 1971), p. 342.
[22] Ibid., p. 339.
[23] See Brenda Easteau, "Law and Women," in Jonathan Black, *Radical Lawyers* (New York: Avon, 1971), p. 240.

major questions ridiculed women involved in the women's movement. The hypothetical case the students were to analyze concerned an article written by a mythical movement activist named Ms. Clytemnestra Toris, editor-publisher of *The Daily Dildo.* The article was described as "infantile, sophomoric and freshmanic . . . poorly reasoned, unresearched and written with her usual strident and shrill hysteria."[24] The question was not just offensive and tasteless; it very likely had a negative impact on women's performance on the exam. The response it deserved would not have received a passing grade.

Entry and hiring

In medicine and law, women were simply prohibited for much of the nineteenth century. As late as 1872, the United States Supreme Court agreed that the State of Illinois could refuse to admit a woman (Myra Bradwell) to practice law.

Discrimination in academic hiring is still bad enough so that in 1970 the Women's Equity Action League filed charges of sex discrimination in the courts against over 100 colleges and universities. As late as March 1970, the psychology department of Lehman College (of City University of New York) advertised for a faculty vacancy: "prefer male, but will consider either."[25] Theodore Lowi, a well-known political scientist, reported that "a very high proportion of my graduate students were women, and collectively they were in every respect the equal of the male candidates. Yet, I had tremendous difficulty getting interviews for them."[26]

Women lawyers meet similar problems. Many have been told by employment agencies: "Well, we don't have anything for a woman lawyer, but we have some openings for legal secretaries."[27] The password among women lawyers—and all women professionals—is: "Don't ever let them know you can type."

A female law student at Harvard reported that when she graduated in 1970, she was refused four separate law jobs on

---

[24] *Women's Rights Law Reporter,* 2 (April 1974), p. 38. The entire question is reproduced on pages 37–39.

[25] Bernice Sandler, "Patterns of Discrimination and Discouragement in Higher Education," in New York Commission on Human Rights, op. cit., p. 575.

[26] Women's Caucus for Political Science, *Newsletter,* fall 1973.

[27] Sue Caplan, in New York Commission on Human Rights, op. cit., p. 408.

the simple ground that she was a woman. In the 1970 Harvard class 99 percent of the men, but only 44 percent of the women, received two or more job offers. Moreover, 72 percent of the men, but only 52 percent of the women, got jobs with law firms.[28] In 1967, in a study of 1300 women law graduates, the women reported 1963 separate cases in which they were told "we do not hire women" by law firms, banks, unions, corporations, and government agencies.[29] The same survey asked the women lawyers if they had suffered sex discrimination in hiring or other ways: 50 percent said yes with "certainty"; another 18 percent said "probably."

One need not rely upon such reports for proof; a number of careful studies provide more evidence. In one, the subjects were 30 male undergraduate industrial management students and 30 male professional interviewers representing a wide range of companies. Each was given twelve resumes and asked to rate and rank the applicants as to suitability for a management position. Both groups rated male applicants higher than female applicants, and 72 percent chose a male for the first-rank position. Since the resumes were identical except for the sex of the applicant, this study provides clear evidence of discrimination on the basis of sex.[30]

In another study, chairmen of psychology departments were sent descriptions of ten hypothetical young psychology Ph.D.s.[31] They were asked to rank the candidates and to indicate at what level the candidate should be offered a position. The sex of the hypothetical candidates was systematically varied. Male candidates were consistently deemed worthy of higher level positions than identical female candidates and were generally ranked higher in terms of desirability. When a description indicated the candidate was female, the modal position considered appropriate was that of assistant professor; for males, associate professor was the modal position. None

---

[28] Easteau, op. cit., p. 245.

[29] White, op. cit., p. 1053.

[30] Robert Dipboye, Howard Franklin, Kent Wilback, "Relative Importance of Applicant Sex, Attractiveness, and Scholastic Standing in Evaluation of Job Applicant Resumés," *Journal of Applied Psychology,* 60 (February 1975), pp. 39–43.

[31] L. S. Fidell, "Empirical Verification of Sex Discrimination in Hiring Practices in Psychology," *American Psychologist,* 25 (December 1970), pp. 1094–98.

of the respondents considered any of the women candidates ready for a full professorship, although some did consider identical men candidates for that position. These studies show that women per se tend to be perceived as less qualified even when there is no supporting evidence.

As a result of hiring discrimination in academia, women faculty are more often found in the smaller colleges. In 1963, 82 percent of all women faculty, but only 74 percent of men faculty, taught in colleges with less than 200 faculty members.[32] Very few women teach in the big, prestigious universities, even though the men and women get their Ph.D.s from schools of about the same quality. One careful study found that 38 percent of academic men, but only 22 percent of academic women, teach at universities of high academic rank.[33] The survey of political science found that sex discrimination in hiring was considered the most extensive form of sex discrimination by both male and female political scientists.[34]

The fact that a higher percentage of women must take jobs in the smallest colleges (and at the lowest levels) not only lowers their average pay but handicaps them in other ways: "Being burdened with the heavier teaching and service loads characteristic of junior-level positions, they . . . had little opportunity to do research and scholarly writing."[35]

Since most women are in small colleges with big teaching loads, Kreps talks about "apparent preference for teaching"![36] She quotes Jessie Bernard in saying that women follow this teaching pattern where men follow the research pattern: "Women tend to serve in institutions which emphasize different functions, and they themselves are attracted to different kinds of functions." Nonsense! This is not primarily a preference; it is due mainly to discrimination. Kreps and Bernard admit some discrimination, but this pattern must be due *mostly* to discrimination. Certainly undergraduate socialization might lead some women to emphasize teaching, since they are told

---

[32] Cynthia Epstein, *Woman's Place* (Berkeley: University of California Press, 1971), p. 180.

[33] Jessie Bernard, *Academic Women* (University Park: Pennsylvania State University Press, 1964), p. 93.

[34] Converse, op. cit., p. 334.

[35] Eckert and Stecklein, op. cit., p. 352.

[36] Juanita Kreps, *Sex in the Marketplace* (Baltimore: Johns Hopkins Press, 1971), p. 59.

that teaching is "more feminine" than research. Kreps admits, however, that most women receive Ph.D.s from the same universities as men—and graduate socialization is fiercely in favor of research. The difference in job patterns must therefore be due primarily to discrimination.

There is also segregation of academic women by area; most women are in history, English, sociology, and Romance languages. Because of the oversupply of women, these areas have lower than average salaries. They are, however, also considered "women's areas" *because* of the low wages. Kreps again makes the mistake of thinking women simply prefer or are solely interested in these areas: "What we do not know is the extent of women's interests in the future in areas other than the humanities."[37] Academic women are not born with interests in these specialties; they are herded into them by sexist socialization in their past upbringing and training and by present discrimination in other areas.

Another problem of discrimination in hiring is the existence of antinepotism rules at many U.S. colleges and universities. The antinepotism rules merely specify that two related individuals cannot be hired in the same academic unit. The rules have the worthy purpose of preventing favoritism due to family ties in hiring and promotion, and they sound fair. The problem arises because a large percentage of all academic women marry men in the same field. In 1967, 55 percent of married women with professional and engineering degrees were married to men with the same degrees.[38] In practice, therefore, the rules discriminate against many academic women because no one ever suggests hiring the wife and letting the husband stay home. The rules are also inconsistent: A professor can—and sometimes does—hire and promote an old friend. Moreover, a man and woman living together without being married do not violate the nepotism rules.

The dimensions of the problem are apparent in a study of 18 of the most creative U.S. women mathematicians, each selected as being far above the average by mostly male mathematicians in their specialized fields.[39] The main point of the study

---

[37] Ibid., p. 60.

[38] Jessie Bernard, *Women and the Public Interest* (Chicago: Aldine, 1971), p. 190.

[39] See Ravena Helson, "Woman Mathematicians," in Judith Bardwick, *Readings on the Psychology of Women* (New York: Harper & Row, 1972), pp. 93–100.

is that their personalities are very similar to those of all other women (surely not surprising), but that they have more of the qualities found in most creative people, such as independence, flexibility, and pleasure in research. The study then mentions, almost casually, that the most creative *male* mathematicians "held important positions" at prestigious universities. In contrast, only two or three of the creative women taught graduate students, and one-third, including some of the highest rated, had no regular position at all. Several had young children. Most of the married ones were married to mathematicians, so that nepotism was a constant problem.[40]

Working conditions

Women do not have as much access to colleagues for serious discussions and information. Yet this access is crucial in the professions, because so much important information is still unpublished and because one needs the stimulation. Some men simply won't hold a serious discussion with any woman. Some important meetings are routinely held in explicitly men-only clubs or men's associations or implicitly men-only golf courses or luncheons. An amusing illustration of this problem appeared in the late 1960s in the political profession. At a Washington party given by Perle Mesta, one of the guests was a woman senator. After dinner the men retired to another room to discuss politics, while the women were supposed to engage in "women's talk." After consideration, the woman senator joined the men. Although this tale had a happy ending for the senator if not for the wives, how many times are women professionals (and all women) hopelessly segregated at parties?

In most professions it is important for a student to be the protégé of some prominent member, but men will seldom accept women as protégés and won't push for their employment even when they do. The famous anthropologist Ruth Benedict was the protégé of Franz Boas, but he thought she didn't need much money because her husband supported her, and that she would never work hard. He helped get her an assistant professorship only after she separated from her husband.[41] Another particularly unpleasant but well-documented problem of professional women is that secretaries (and other staff) are

[40] Ibid., p. 97.
[41] Epstein, op. cit., p. 170.

far more willing to carry out important tasks for males than for females. This results, of course, from the sexist socialization of the secretaries, even though most are women.

Journalism is male-dominated and has all the problems mentioned earlier, but there are also some additional ones with the "personalities" women must interview. While at a public bill-signing ceremony in the White House, then President Nixon had some sexist "fun" with reporter Helen Thomas. He said, "Helen, are you still wearing slacks? Do you prefer them actually? . . . Slacks can do something for some people and some it can't. I think you do very well—turn around. . . . Do they cost less than a gown?" "No," she replied. " 'Then change,' the President suggested, and everyone in the room laughed."[42]

Promotion

The preceding sections show the poorer working conditions of women professionals, biases in evaluations by colleagues and outside reviewers, and poorer initial jobs. It follows that promotion is more difficult and less frequent for women. Obviously, if a woman is perfect, a superwoman, she can get promoted. Obviously too, the average woman is promoted less than the average man. In 1960 the National Academy of Sciences studied a group of men and women, all of whom received Ph.D.s in 1935. The study found that women took two to five years longer to become full professors in the natural sciences and five to ten years longer in the social sciences.[43] In fact, only 50 percent of women with a Ph.D. and twenty years' teaching experience are full professors, but 90 percent of men Ph.D.s with the same teaching experience are full professors.[44]

The pyramid effect

Discrimination in hiring and promotion boxes women into the lower levels of each profession. Women account for 85 percent of elementary school teachers but only 22 percent of elementary school principals. Women constitute 47 percent of high school teachers but only 4 percent of high school principals. Similarly, most librarians are women, but most chief librarians

---

[42] Washington *Post,* August 7, 1973.
[43] Kreps, op. cit., p. 53.
[44] Sandler, "Patterns of Discrimination and Discouragement in Higher Education," op. cit., p. 569.

and library administrators are men. In social work, most caseworkers are women, but most supervisors are men. Most nurses are women, but most doctors are men. Most legal secretaries are women, but most lawyers are men. In advertising and journalism, most researchers are women, but the more prestigious job of writing is mainly reserved for men.

In the academic world, there is a very definite prestige and pay pyramid from the many lowly instructors to the few full professors. Fewer women hold positions on the higher rungs of the ladder (see Table 6.2). Almost half the instructors, who are poorly paid, often part-time, and frequently not on the promotion ladder, are women. The well-paid and prestigious full professorships are held predominantly by men. A 1973 study by the National Center for Educational Statistics found that women held only 22 percent of the full-time faculty jobs.[45]

TABLE 6.2

Women faculty at all colleges and universities, 1974

Rank	Percentage of women
Professor	9%
Associate professor	15
Assistant professor	24
Instructor	45

Source: Mary Keyserling, "The Economic Status of Women in the United States," *American Economic Review,* 66 (May 1976).

As Table 6.3 shows, women teach at the less prestigious schools. Almost one-third of the full-time faculty in public two-year colleges was female; women were less than one in five faculty members at universities. At each type of school, women are concentrated in the lower ranks. The most prestigious schools are the least likely to hire and promote women. In the academic year 1969–70, there were no women among the 350 associate and full professors in the Faculty of Arts and Sciences at Harvard.[46] Five years later, after a great deal of pressure on academic institutions by the women's movement, there were thirteen. During the 1974–75 academic year, fifty-

[45] Reported in Leigh Beinen, Alicia Ostriker, and J. P. Ostriker, "Sex Discrimination in the Universities: Faculty Problems and No Solutions," *Women's Rights Law Reporter,* 2 (March 1975), p. 5.
[46] Ibid., pp. 5–6.

five women held associate or full professorships at Princeton, Yale, Harvard, and Columbia. These women constituted 2.7 percent of the total faculty in those ranks—a very modest increase over the 1.0 percent that women held in 1969–70.

TABLE 6.3

Women's share of full-time faculty positions at public colleges and universities

Institution	All ranks	Professor	Associate professor	Assistant professor	Instructor
All public institutions	22.7	10.0	15.8	23.7	39.2
Universities	17.1	6.7	12.3	20.0	44.4
Other four-year	23.2	12.7	17.4	24.7	44.0
Two-year	32.3	21.2	24.3	31.3	35.1

Source: National Center for Educational Statistics, reported in *Women's Rights Law Reporter,* 2 (March 1975), p. 5.

The pattern of women being relegated to the lower ranks and the less prestigious schools is found with monotonous regularity in each discipline. Taking political science as an example, we see that, during the 1975–76 academic year, only 2.5 percent of the full professors in Ph.D.-granting departments were women (see Table 6.4). Granting Ph.D.s is a minimum definition of a prestigious department, and these are, of course, the schools to which aspiring women scholars will go for training. Yet there are only 26 women full professors and 37 women associate professors at all these schools combined. The role model problem for women graduate students is obvious. In departments that grant masters degrees but not Ph.D.s, the

TABLE 6.4

Women as full-time tenure-track faculty in Ph.D.-granting departments of political science, 1975–1976

Rank	Percentage of women
Professor	2.5%
Associate professor	5.8
Assistant professor	16.4
Instructor	27.5

Source: Report by Committee on the Status of Women in the Profession, *PS,* 9 (spring 1976), pp. 189–190.

situation is better only in comparison. There, 5.5 percent of full professors and 8.9 percent of associate professors are women.[47] The most prestigious departments are again the worst offenders. Yale has no woman at either the associate or full professor level; Michigan and Berkeley have one each; Harvard and MIT, two each.

Academic men have an interesting use of the word *qualified.* Department chairmen often say: "I would be glad to hire a *qualified* woman if I could find one." But they define qualified very differently for women than for men. When applied to women, *qualified* really means "best in field." A University of Chicago history professor said "his department would be happy to hire more women, but there were only three good women historians in the country, and none of them were available."[48]

The pyramid also appears across the board in most universities, including publicly funded ones. The enormous University of California illustrates this very well (see Table 6.5). Even at the women's colleges, the percentage of women faculty has been declining, and the pyramid is present (see Table 6.6). Moreover, in the late 1960s men replaced women as presidents of Vassar, Bryn Mawr, Sarah Lawrence, Smith, Mt. Holyoke, and Kirkland women's colleges.[49]

Other professions are just as guilty of relegating women to

[47] Report by Committee on the Status of Women in the Profession, *PS,* 9 (spring 1976), pp. 189–193.
[48] Sandler, "Patterns of Discrimination and Discouragement in Higher Education," op. cit., p. 570.
[49] Patricia Grahame, "Women in Academe," in Theodore, op. cit., p. 722.

TABLE 6.5
Women at the University of California, 1973

Rank	Percentage of women
Professors	4%
Associate professors	7
Assistant professors	11
Librarians	46
Associate librarians	70
Assistant librarians	79
Office and clerical workers	88

Source: University Bulletin (issued by University of California administration), 21 (May 28, 1973), p. 152.

lower-paying and less prestigious positions. Among lawyers, there is segregation by subfield. For example, the field of matrimonial law is low paying and low prestige. In New York City only 1 percent of male lawyers, but 13 percent of women lawyers are in matrimonial law.[50] Another low-paying area mainly inhabited by women lawyers is the law of trusts and estates. Similarly, in medicine, where women account for only a small proportion to begin with, they are further segregated into the fields of lowest pay and prestige (see Table 6.7). Men are dominant even in obstetrics and gynecology.

TABLE 6.6

Women Faculty at Barnard College, 1970

Rank	Percentage of women
Professors	22%
Associate professors	54
Assistant professors	64
Instructors	82

Source: Patricia Grahame, "Women in Academe," in Athena Theodore, ed., *The Professional Woman* (Cambridge, Mass.: Schenkman, 1971), p. 722.

TABLE 6.7

Women in medicine, 1969

Field	Rank of field (out of 10) in pay and prestige	Percentage of women in field
Surgery	1st	1%
Psychiatry	7th	11
Pediatrics	9th	19

Source: Cynthia Epstein, *Woman's Place* (Berkeley: University of California Press, 1971), p. 163.

Earnings

In all the professions, women on the average are paid less than men. Table 6.8 presents data on selected professions taken from the 1970 census. In each profession, women are paid substantially less. An apologist might argue that women's lower earnings merely reflect less training or experience. Such differences do not account for anywhere near all the differences in earnings. In academia, for example, women at each rank earn less than men, the difference for all ranks combined aver-

[50] See Epstein, op. cit., p. 164.

aging 18 percent.[51] Women engineers with 11 years of experience earned $2500 a year less than men with the same amount of experience.[52] When both education and type of employer are held constant, women chemists consistently make less than comparable males (see Table 6.9). Furthermore, women with a master's degree make less than men with only a bachelor's, and women Ph.D.s make only slightly more than men with only the master's.

Perhaps the most careful research survey of all was done by James White on salaries of women lawyers.[53] Using a sample

[51] Keyserling, op. cit., p. 208.
[52] U.S. Department of Labor, Women's Bureau, *1975 Handbook on Women Workers*, p. 158.
[53] White, op. cit.

TABLE 6.8
Median earnings in selected professions, 1970

Profession	Men	Women	Women's earnings as a percentage of men's
Physician	$25,000+	$9788	less than 39%
Lawyer	18,749	8980	48
Engineer	13,151	9648	73
Life and physical scientist	12,025	7518	63
Social scientist	13,280	7687	58
College and university teacher	11,248	6220	55

Source: Department of Commerce, *1970 Census of Population*, Subject Reports, Occupational Characteristics, PC(2)-7A, Table 1.

TABLE 6.9
Average salaries (in thousands of dollars) of chemists who were members of the American Chemical Society, March 1974

Type of employer	B.A.		M.A.		Ph.D.	
	Women	Men	Women	Men	Women	Men
Industry	$13.3	$18.0	$14.0	$20.0	$21.0	$23.4
Educational institution	9.0	11.5	11.0	14.0	15.0	17.5
Government	15.2	18.7	15.0	19.5	20.9	24.0

Source: U.S. Department of Labor, Women's Bureau, *1975 Handbook on Women Workers*, p. 158.

of 1300 female and 1300 male law graduates, he found that the median salary of the women was $1500 less than the men's in the first year after graduation. Ten years later, the median salary of the men was $8300 higher than that of the women. Of course it could always be said that these enormous differences were due to factors other than discrimination. The nice thing about White's survey is that every conceivable factor was taken into consideration.

First, perhaps the men graduated from better or more prestigious law schools. White used all the women graduates from a list of schools and asked the schools to select at random an equal number of men graduates, so there were the same percentages by sex from low- and high-prestige schools. Second, perhaps the men had more experience. White's sample took men and women from the same graduating classes. Third, perhaps more men worked full-time than the women. White used only women who worked full-time at law. Fourth, perhaps the men happened to be brighter than the women. There was no significant difference in law class standing nor in law review participation. Fifth, perhaps relatively more women than men worked for low-paying employers. Yes, women were more likely to work for the government, where pay is relatively low, rather than for private firms. But they were paid less (in similar proportions) in *both* areas, so the employer segregation was an additional cause but not the only cause of lower wages. Sixth, perhaps relatively more women worked in low-paying specialties. Yes, women were forced to work relatively more in the low-paying areas—trusts and estates and domestic relations. But they were paid less (in similar proportions) in all fields, so the segregation by field also explained some but not all of the lower wages. Eliminating all these excuses, White concludes that sex discrimination as well as segregation accounts for the lower wages.

Another study of matched graduates from the classes of 1953–59 of Harvard Law School found that in 1970, some 70 percent of the full-time women lawyers were making less than $20,000, whereas only 16 percent of the men lawyers were making less than $20,000.[54]

In political science, a survey by the American Political Sci-

[54] See Easteau, op. cit., p. 246.

ence Association found that in 1970 men faculty averaged $17,000 a year, but women faculty only $10,500.[55] Careful corrections for possession of Ph.D. training, quality of graduate school, and amount of professional work experience still found women with the same training and experience making $3750 a year less than comparable males.[56] The survey then corrected for every other conceivable factor, including productivity, and still found that "as far as we can carry inquiry there remains significant differentials by sex in annual incomes after a wide variety of extenuating circumstances are dutifully taken into account."[57]

Fringe benefits

The biggest problem in the area of fringe benefits comes with pregnancy, which is generally not included under possible sicknesses, either for sick leave or for free medical care. Yet even counting pregnancy, men have longer absences from work than women. At a California college, a woman faculty member was refused a two-week sick leave to have a baby. Yet the same college allows "sick leave" for a male faculty member to help at home when his wife has a baby! Furthermore, until recently, at many colleges and most elementary and high schools, a woman could not get a short, paid sick leave for pregnancy, but she was *required* to take an *unpaid* leave of up to a year's length.

OBSTACLES OF TRADITIONAL FAMILY STRUCTURE

A woman is expected to do the housework regardless of her job, so the average American woman Ph.D. spends 28 hours a week on household tasks.[58] A number of studies have shown that when the wife goes to work, the husband does not increase the amount of housework he does. It is also expected by traditional sexists that a woman will follow her husband wherever he decides to go. This traditional family folkway restricts the geographic mobility of professional women, so their choice of jobs is much more limited than for other professionals.

---

[55] Converse, op. cit., p. 342.
[56] Ibid., p. 343.
[57] Ibid., p. 345.
[58] See Grahame, op. cit., p. 729.

Because of child care and housework duties in traditional families, about half of all professional women interrupt their careers for family purposes. These interruptions have drastic negative effects. A study of 300 professional women shows that "the achievement level of women with interrupted work histories was far below that of women with uninterrupted work histories, fewer than a third as many showing a high achievement level [7 percent to 23 percent] and five times as many showing a low achievement level [36 percent to only 7 percent]."[59] Dropping out and then going back to a career also presents more difficult problems of adjustment for her and her family.

Women in our society are forced to interrupt careers for children because society does not provide decent child care; nor does it provide maternity leaves. If women were given one- or two-month maternity leaves with pay, as in some countries, plus more unpaid leave if necessary, plus publicly run high-quality child care, they would not have to interrupt their careers—assuming that the husband is also willing to do his share of housework and child care. This alternative is actually cheaper for society because more professional women would continue to work full-time and would achieve more.

In our society women have long faced a cruel dilemma: career *or* marriage. As a result, professional women were more likely to remain unmarried than other women. As late as 1950, only 59 percent of women with Ph.D.s were married.[60] There has been some change; a 1966 study found 72 percent of women Ph.D.s married, and some live with men without being married. It is important to note that these lower percentages of married professional women do not represent inherent psychological preferences for a life without love or sex. Some were driven to "choose" a career instead of marriage because of the rigid and sexist structure of the professions and of the traditional family, which made it impossible to have both. Furthermore, there was and is discrimination against married women. In elementary teaching in the nineteenth century and in some colleges as late as the 1930s, there were rules firing women who got married! Discrimination, combined with lack

---

[59] *1975 Handbook*, op. cit., p. 174.
[60] Ibid., p. 187.

of child care facilities and unsympathetic husbands, forced women into a cruel choice, and the situation is changing only slowly.

EXCUSES FOR DISCRIMINATION

The first excuse is that education (and jobs) are wasted on women because they drop out. A study based on a large sample[61] of women Ph.D.s in 1966 found that 96 percent of the unmarried ones worked full-time! Where the obstacle of marriage is added, 91 percent of the married women Ph.D.s without children work (87 percent full-time and 4 percent part-time). Even when the obstacle of children is added, most highly educated women still do professional work. The percentage of all married women Ph.D.s with children working professionally is astonishing—85 percent, including 60 percent full-time and 25 percent part-time.[62]

Thus the notion that women Ph.D.s drop out is pure myth. It is true that earlier studies showed about 40 percent of all professional women interrupting their careers at some time, mostly to raise small children. Giving birth is not what causes the problem (unless women are not given a brief sick leave). What causes the interruption is the socially determined fact that women alone are responsible for child care. If there were decent child-care facilities and the husband did his half, there need be no interruption. Furthermore, an almost identical number of men, about 50 percent, also interrupt their careers, mostly for military service. It is surely a "curious paradox of human values" that "men have been only slightly criticized for career interruptions in which their task was to kill off other members of the human race; but women have been severely criticized for taking time away from their profession in order to raise the next generation."[63]

Despite the burden of child care, more recent women Ph.D.s seem less likely to interrupt their careers than older professional women were. A study of women who received the Ph.D. in 1957–58 found that 91 percent were working, 81 percent

---

[61] See Rita Simon et al., "The Woman Ph.D.," in Bardwick, op. cit., p. 83.
[62] Data from ibid., p. 84. Also see Helen Astin, "Participation of Women Doctorates in the Labor Force," in Theodore, op. cit., p. 445.
[63] Lynda Holmstrom, "Career Patterns," in Theodore, op. cit., p. 525.

full-time; 79 percent had not interrupted their careers in the ten years after receiving their doctorate.[64] It need only be added that professional women, in spite of emergency family problems, show no more tardiness or absenteeism than professional men—which is very little in both cases.

The second major excuse for discrimination is that women are less productive; in academia it is claimed that they publish less. Some early studies did find that women faculty were less productive than men in producing books and articles, and in the number of grants they obtained. These studies, however, were unscientific in that they ignored the variables of location and rank. We have seen that women are located disproportionately in the smaller departments of poorer colleges at the lower academic ranks, all of which means heavier teaching loads and less time to do research. In spite of poorer working conditions and in spite of the sexist structure of most families, *women faculty produce identically with men in the same locations and ranks.*[65] The most recent study found that the average woman Ph.D. produced as many books and articles as the average man (without consideration of rank or location!), with slightly less for unmarried women, equal for married women with children, and slightly more for married women without children.[66] The differences are so slight that they could easily be due to sampling biases.

The silliest excuse for wage or financial aid discrimination is that women don't need the money as much as men. If they are married, their husbands can support them. If they are unmarried, they don't need much money because they have no family. Of course many professional women are unmarried heads of households; many more are equal contributors to a household. At any rate the excuse is feeble; a capitalist society does not pay people on the basis of their needs.

AFFIRMATIVE ACTION AND "REVERSE DISCRIMINATION"

The women's movement has brought some changes. Women are entering professional training in greater numbers than ever before. In 1960, only 6 percent of medical students were

[64] Bienen, et al., op. cit., p. 9.
[65] See Bernard, *Academic Women,* op. cit., pp. 160–170.
[66] Simon, op. cit., p. 90.

women; by 1974, women were 18 percent.[67] In 1977, 22.4 percent of all medical students and almost one quarter of first-year medical students were women.[68] Women were 4 percent of all law students in 1960; in 1974, they were 19 percent. As Table 6.10 shows, similar increases in women's enrollment are occurring in a variety of professions. The proportion of Ph.D.s earned by women has also increased from 15.3 percent of the total for 1969–72 to 21.4 percent for 1972–75.[69]

TABLE 6.10

Enrollment in professional training, 1960–1974

Field	Women as a percentage of total enrollment		Percentage of women, first year enrollment, 1974
	1960	1974	
Architecture	5%	9%	10%
Dentistry	1	7	11
Engineering	1	6	6
Law	4	19	23
Medicine	6	18	22
Optometry	1	10	13
Pharmacy	12	32	31
Veterinary medicine	4	21	25

Source: John B. Parrish, "Women in Professional Training—An Update," *Monthly Labor Review,* 98 (November 1975), pp. 49–50.

That these figures are encouraging shows how far from equality we still are. To give women and minority members a truly equal chance, affirmative action is needed on every campus and in every profession. Yet, as soon as anything is done, cries of "reverse discrimination" favoring minorities and women become deafening. The U.S. Department of Health, Education and Welfare (HEW) reported in 1973 that women faculty working full-time at the nation's universities earned $3500 less on

[67] John B. Parrish, "Women in Professional Training—An Update," *Monthly Labor Review,* 198 (November 1975), pp. 49–50.

[68] *Los Angeles Times,* February 6, 1977.

[69] Carol Whitehurst, *Women in America: The Oppressed Majority* (Santa Monica, Calif.: Goodyear, 1977), p. 50.

the average than male faculty. Yet a government employee, Samuel Solomon of HEW, when sent out to help fight discrimination, reported: "I've been out on the campus trail in recent weeks and I'm getting the impression that most institutions are engaged in some form of discrimination against white males."[70]

Did he talk to any blacks and women? Most HEW people speak to white male administrators and senior white male professors, who do indeed relate many horror stories about reverse discrimination. Yet there seems to be no single well-documented case of reverse discrimination. The Labor Department and HEW itself have found thousands of cases of discrimination against blacks and women.

The "reverse discrimination" cry has been raised as part of a major counterattack to preserve discrimination. There has been a flood of media articles worrying over reverse discrimination (in universities, in industry, and at the Democratic party convention). For example, an Associated Press writer, John Wheeler, wrote an article claiming that militant women want unqualified women hired and promoted.[71] Corporations say they are worried that these unqualified women will reduce productivity and produce unreliable and unsafe products (since when do corporations worry about such consumer interests?). He also notes that universities claim to be worried that scholastic standards will drop. Of course corporations and universities are really worried about preserving cheap female wages and keeping women at the bottom of the prestige pyramid.

Wheeler's article relies on the combined opinion of big business, big labor, and government "leaders" to "prove" reverse discrimination. In talking about goals for hiring women and minorities, he writes: "Both big business and big labor say the goals are just quotas by a different name and in rare agreement are fighting hard to make things more flexible." But without such goals or "quotas," things will be so "flexible" that nothing will happen. For decades big labor and big business have said they would get rid of discrimination by voluntary action, but the situation has only gotten worse. In fact, rather than trying

[70] *Parade,* June 3, 1973.

[71] John Wheeler, reprinted in Riverside, California, *Press Enterprise,* June 10, 1973.

to end discrimination, Wheeler mentions that "businessmen have developed their own stratagems for circumventing their goals in many cases."

From the minimal progress which has been made on university faculties, one may guess the university administrators too have "developed their own stratagems." It is in academia that the most virulent attack on affirmative action has taken place. Defenders of the status quo claim that standards will be lowered and faculty quality undermined. Their usually unstated assumption is that white males are always more qualified, so that whenever a woman or a minority male is hired, reverse discrimination has taken place. In a book which received a great deal of media attention, Richard Lester explicitly argued that the "pool" of women and minority candidates is inferior in quality to the pool of white males.[72] What is the evidence for this contention? Women and minority males teach at less prestigious schools and tend to be concentrated in the lower ranks. Since, according to Lester, universities are pure meritocracies and of course do not discriminate, this proves women and minorities are less qualified.

Because of attitudes such as these, which are still too prevalent, affirmative action must be pursued with vigor. Opponents speak of the injustice of passing over better-qualified white males in favor of less-qualified women and minority men. Given the level of prejudice, there seems little danger of that occurring. The real purpose of affirmative action is to ensure that an effective search for women and minority men is made and that women and minority males are evaluated on the basis of their qualifications and not on the basis of prejudiced assumptions such as those expressed by Lester.

---

[72] Richard Lester, *Antibias Regulation of Universities: Faculty Problems and Their Solutions* (New York: McGraw-Hill, 1974). Good critical discussions of the book can be found in Bienen, et al., op. cit., and *Women's Studies Newsletter,* 2 (fall 1974, winter 1975).

WOMEN AND THE LAW

7

A society's standards as to what is natural and right are reflected in its laws. An examination of the differential treatment of men and women in U.S. federal and state law will reveal more than inequalities. It will provide another perspective on society's image of women. Under the impetus of the women's movement, that image is beginning to change, and this too is reflected in recent developments in the law.

THE DOUBLE STANDARD INSTITUTIONALIZED: WOMEN, SEX, AND THE LAW

When it comes to sexual matters, the American woman, according to the law, is a delicate and pure creature who must be protected. To effect such protection, even free speech is not too much to give up. Many states have laws prohibiting obscene or vulgar language in the presence of women. An Arizona statute provides that a person who "in the presence of or hearing of any woman or child, or in a public place, uses vulgar, abusive or obscene language, is guilty of a misdemeanor. . . ."[1] In at least 12 states, impugning the chastity of a woman is a criminal offense.[2] Many states used to require only the male to get a venereal disease test before issuing him a marriage license.

---

[1] Quoted in Leo Kanowitz, *Women and the Law* (Albuquerque: University of New Mexico Press, 1969), p. 175.

[2] Lois J. Frankel, "Sex Discrimination in the Criminal Law: The Effect of the Equal Rights Amendment," *American Criminal Law Review*, 2 (winter 1973), p. 485.

In Washington as late as 1969 the requirement still applied only to men.[3] Obviously the pure, delicate female would not need such a test.

In most states, if an adult male has sexual intercourse with a female who is below a certain age, he is committing the crime of statutory rape. These laws are based on the incapacity of the underage female to give meaningful consent, a principle on which many laws treating minors differently from adults are based. But why is it assumed that, in the sexual realm, underage males can give meaningful consent? In very few states can an adult female be guilty of statutory rape; and in states where the crime is defined without regard to the sex of the adult, women are not prosecuted. Professor Kanowitz was told in an interview with a California prosecuting attorney that "a district attorney would 'feel silly' if he were to prosecute a 22 year old girl . . . for having sexual relations with a 17 year old boy. No such compunction would arise, however, in prosecuting a 22 year old male for statutory rape because he had engaged in sexual intercourse with a 17 year old girl."[4] The law and the way it is enforced obviously reflect the double standard. Tennessee carries the protection of the female "child" to an absurd point; there the age of meaningful consent is twenty-one.[5] In most states, a female can get married without her parents' consent before that.

Although the laws against forcible rape are intended to protect women, the manner of their enforcement reveals the other side of the double standard. In many states, the maximum penalty for rape is as severe as that for murder—indicating, perhaps, that a violated woman might as well be dead. If a rape victim attempts to bring charges under these laws, however, she frequently suffers more than the rapist. Her character will be attacked, her past sex life scrutinized. Until recently, any and all questions about her sex life were permissible. A common defense tactic is to attempt to discredit the woman by questioning her about her sex life in excruciating and insulting detail. If the jury can be convinced she is promiscuous, they are likely to decide that she consented or, if not, that she deserved being raped.

---

[3] Kanowitz, op. cit., p. 13.
[4] Quoted in ibid., p. 246.
[5] Ibid., p. 21.

The notion that a sexually active woman cannot really be raped is very strong; in some places, it is enshrined in the law. Thus, in California, the judge was required to read this "unchastity instruction" to the jury:

> Evidence was received for the purpose of showing that the female person named in the information was a woman of unchaste character. A woman of unchaste character can be the victim of forcible rape but it may be inferred that a woman who has previously consented to sexual intercourse would be more likely to consent again. Such evidence may be considered by you only for such bearing as it may have on the question of whether or not she gave her consent to the alleged sexual act and in judging her credibility.[6]

The attitude expressed in this instruction lends credence to the claims of some lawyers that rape laws are really property laws. Rather than being intended to protect the women, their purpose is to protect a man's private property—his wife or daughters. As an "unchaste" woman is neither valuable nor private property, she is not worth protecting.

The rape laws are further premised on the assumption that women are liars, for much stricter standards of proof are required than in crimes of comparable seriousness. The woman's word must be corroborated by other testimony.[7] In other crimes, the victim's testimony is sufficient. In California, the judge was required to read the following cautionary instruction to the jury:

> A charge such as that made against the defendant in this case is one which is easily made and, once made, difficult to defend against, even if the person accused is innocent. Therefore the law requires that you examine the testimony of the female person named in the information with caution.[8]

Too many judges and lawyers seem to subscribe to the notion that women frequently make false charges of rape. The author of a 1970 law review article states, "Women often falsely accuse men of sexual attacks to extort money, to force marriage, to satisfy a childish desire for notoriety, to attain personal

---

[6] CALJIC 10.06 (1970 Rev.).
[7] Susan C. Ross, *The Rights of Women* (New York: Avon, 1973), p. 181.
[8] Quoted in American Civil Liberties Union of Southern California news release, May 2, 1974.

revenge."[9] Although there is no evidence to support these charges, it has been suggested that all women who bring rape accusations be forced to submit to psychiatric examination.[10]

In some states, a woman must physically resist the rapist; otherwise she is considered to have consented.[11] A typical judge's instruction on nonconsent reads: "Mere verbal protestations and a pretense of resistance are not sufficient to show want of consent. If the female fails to take such measures to frustrate the execution of the male's design as she is able to make and are called for under the circumstances, the inference may be drawn that she did in fact consent."[12] Lack of resistance to a robbery, a mugging, or any other violent crime is not taken as implying consent. Whatever the law, if the woman cannot show considerable visible injury, the jury will frequently assume that she actually consented.

Given the severity of the penalties for rape, strict standards of proof must be maintained. But justice for the accused rapist does not require the sort of brutal treatment to which the victim is often subjected. The abuse heaped upon the victim reflects society's view that there are two types of women—the pure and the evil. For women, evil is associated with sexuality. It seems to be assumed that good women don't let such things happen to them, that any woman who really wants to resist can do so successfully. The fact that this contradicts a major tenet of the male mystique—the vastly superior strength of the male—and ignores the existence of guns and knives is simply overlooked.

Under pressure from the women's movement, some states have changed their rape laws. In 1974, California, Florida, Iowa, and Michigan passed laws prohibiting introduction of evidence about the victim's previous sexual conduct unless the defendent first demonstrates to the judge that the evidence is relevant to a fact at issue in the case.[13] Some states have repealed laws requiring the more offensive cautionary instruc-

---

[9] Quoted in Barbara Allen Babcock, Ann E. Freedman, Eleanor Holmes Norton, and Susan C. Ross, *Sex Discrimination and the Law: Causes and Remedies* (Boston: Little, Brown, 1975) p. 855.

[10] Ibid., p. 860.

[11] Ross, op. cit., p. 183.

[12] Babcock, op. cit., pp. 826–827.

[13] *Women's Rights Law Reporter,* March 1975, p. 38.

tions. On the matter of resistance, progress is also evident. A number of courts have rejected the contention that anything less than resistance to the point of serious physical injury implies consent.[14]

The double standard is also reflected in elements of divorce law. A number of states provided that a wife's having had intercourse with another man before marriage was ground for divorce. A husband's similar behavior was not.[15] In some states, a single act of adultery was ground against the wife but not against the husband. This is still the case in Kentucky.[16] The "unwritten law" defense is actually in the legal code in several states, including New Mexico, Texas, and Utah.[17] It provides that a husband may kill his wife's lover without penalty if he catches them in the act. If the wife should kill her husband's lover, it would be considered murder.

That it is much worse for women than men to have intercourse outside the bonds of marriage and that if a woman does so she must be made to pay for it are pervasive notions in our society that are only beginning to be cast aside. The "man in the house" rule, applied by many states to female welfare recipients until recently struck down by the Supreme Court, is a particularly vicious example of these notions.[18] The rule specified that if a man spent the night in her house, the woman could lose her welfare benefits. The public justification for the rule was that if a man lived with her, he could support her and her children. The actual purpose was punitive.

Pregnant girls are routinely expelled from high school, frequently even if they are married. A federal district court has declared the practice of excluding unwed mothers from the public schools unconstitutional. "The fact that a girl has one child out of wedlock does not forever brand her as a scarlet woman undeserving of any chance for rehabilitation or the opportunity for further education,"[19] the court said. Thus the court clearly recognized the punitive intention of such rules

---

[14] Ibid., p. 38.
[15] Kanowitz, op. cit., p. 14.
[16] Ibid., p. 96.
[17] Ibid., p. 92.
[18] See Babcock, op. cit., pp. 761–770.
[19] Quoted by Martha Griffiths, in U.S. Congress, House Committee on the Judiciary, *Hearings on Equal Rights for Men and Women* (1971), p. 38.

and their basis in the notion that good girls are sexually pure and bad girls must be made to pay for their behavior. The question is far from legally settled; more cases are being brought.

The same notion seems to account for a good deal of the opposition to abortion on request. If a woman gets herself into a position in which she may get pregnant, well she's just got to take the consequences. Actually, the right to abortion on request before quickening (about four months) had been recognized in common law. Laws prohibiting abortion except to save the life of the mother were adopted by the states during the second half of the nineteenth century—a time of general sexual repression.

A number of states did pass reform laws during the period from 1967 to 1970, but even these laws were still highly restrictive. Abortions could now be obtained if pregnancy would gravely impair the woman's physical or mental health, if the baby was likely to be deformed, or if pregnancy was the result of rape or incest. In 1970, three states—Hawaii, Alaska, and New York—passed much more liberal laws. These came close to abortion on request, although some restrictions on how late in pregnancy an abortion could be performed were maintained. By 1972, a large number of cases had been brought, and some state abortion laws had been declared unconstitutional by lower courts. In early 1973, the Supreme Court, in the landmark decisions of *Roe* v. *Wade* and *Doe* v. *Bolton,* upheld a woman's constitutional right to abortion.[20] The Court declared that during the first three months of pregnancy, the decision on abortion should be left to the woman and her doctor. During the second three months, a state may regulate abortion if the regulations are reasonably necessary to protect the woman's health. During the last three months, the state may, but need not, ban abortion except to save the mother's life. In *Doe* v. *Bolton,* the Court struck down the requirement of approval by a three-doctor committee and a requirement for special accreditation for hospitals performing abortions.

Attempts to circumvent the decision began immediately. Laws passed in Rhode Island and Utah which, in effect, ignored the decision, were struck down immediately.[21] Laws requiring the consent of the woman's husband were declared unconstitu-

---

[20] *Congressional Quarterly Weekly Report,* 31, 4 (January 27, 1973), p. 142.
[21] Babcock, op. cit., p. 380.

tional by the Supreme Court.[22] The Court further ruled that the states may not impose "blanket" restrictions requiring all minor females to get the consent of a parent.[23]

The U.S. Congress has passed a provision allowing hospitals, even if they receive federal money, to refuse to perform abortions on the basis of "religious beliefs and moral convictions."[24] Several federal district courts, on the other hand, have ruled that public hospitals may not refuse to perform abortions.[25] This is an area in which law and practice are still in a state of flux.

Ensuring that poor women have access to abortion has been another problem area. A number of states have refused Medicaid payments for elective abortions.[26] The courts generally struck down such provisions. In 1976, the U.S. Congress passed the Hyde amendment, a similar provision denying Medicaid reimbursements for elective abortions. A federal district court declared it unconstitutional and ordered the Department of Health, Education and Welfare to continue Medicaid funding.

In June 1977, the Supreme Court ruled that neither the Constitution nor federal Medicaid law requires state governments to pay for elective abortions. While the Hyde amendment prohibiting the federal government from paying for elective abortions was not at issue, the Court's decision made it unlikely that such provisions would be struck down, and the injunction against its enforcement was lifted.

The ruling set the stage for a bitter struggle on abortion funding. The House of Representatives again added the Hyde amendment to the Labor-Health, Education and Welfare appropriations bill. When the bill went to conference, the Senate refused to accept the extremely restrictive House language. After almost five months of deadlock, a compromise was reached in December 1977. Under the compromise, poor women covered by Medicaid can have a government-paid abortion if (1) the woman's life is in danger because of the pregnancy (2) the woman has been the victim of rape or incest and the incident was promptly reported to the police or to a public

---

[22] Riverside, California, *Daily Enterprise,* July 2, 1976.
[23] Ibid.
[24] Babcock, op. cit., p. 983.
[25] U.S. Department of Labor, Women's Bureau, *1975 Handbook on Women Workers,* p. 381.
[26] Ibid., pp. 380–381.

health service agency or (3) two doctors determine that the woman would suffer "severe and long-lasting physical health damage" if the pregnancy continued.[27]

While an improvement over the House version, the compromise is still very restrictive. States may still pay for elective abortions, but since they will have to finance the full cost, the pressure to cease such funding will increase. Only seventeen states now do pay for elective abortions. Many poor women again face the choice of a back-alley butcher or forced motherhood.

Laws concerning contraceptives are another institutionalized expression of American puritanism. As late as 1968, 60 percent of the states had laws placing restrictions of some sort on the dispersal and use of contraceptives.[28] Frequently the restrictions take the form of denying contraceptives to the young or unmarried. Legally, these prohibitions apply to both sexes equally, but since it is the female who gets pregnant, she is the major victim.

In 1965, in the Griswold decision, the Supreme Court threw out a Connecticut law against *using* contraceptives. The decision was based on the law's hampering doctors in the practice of medicine and on the violation of marital privacy.[29] A Massachusetts law banning contraceptives for unmarried people was struck down by the Supreme Court in 1971.[30]

When women do not live up to society's image of them as good and pure, the law punishes them. The prostitute is the antithesis of society's ideal woman and is treated as such. She and her customer are treated very differently. He is seldom prosecuted, even if there is a law against patronizing a prostitute.[31] In New York State, the prostitute faces a maximum sentence of three months; the maximum for the customer is 15 days.[32] She can be convicted on the uncorroborated testi-

---

[27] *Congressional Quarterly Weekly Report,* 32 (December 10, 1977), pp. 2547–49.

[28] Lucinda Cisier, "Unfinished Business: Birth Control and Women's Liberation," in Robin Morgan, ed., *Sisterhood Is Powerful* (New York: Vintage, 1970), p. 249.

[29] Ibid., p. 250.

[30] *Eisenstadt* v. *Baird, Women's Rights Law Reporter,* 1 (spring 1972), p. 39.

[31] Kanowitz, op. cit., p. 16.

[32] New York City Commission on Human Rights, *Women's Role in Contemporary Society* (New York: Avon, 1972), p. 43.

mony of a policeman posing as a customer. The pimp cannot be convicted on her uncorroborated testimony.[33]

WHEN SHE IS BAD SHE IS HORRID: CRIMINAL PENALTIES FOR WOMEN

The proposition that women are by nature good and pure has a corollary: Bad women, perhaps because they are unnatural, are a lot worse than bad men.

Law and practice with respect to juveniles presents a good example of this principle. The New York State Family Court Act relating to "persons in need of supervision" provides that youths who are "habitually truant, incorrigible, ungovernable or habitually disobedient and beyond lawful control of a parent or guardian" may be imprisoned.[34] The law applies to boys up to age sixteen; if a boy is imprisoned before he is sixteen, he may be kept until he is eighteen. For a girl, however, the age of applicability is eighteen, and she may be kept until she is twenty. This law applies only to noncriminal conduct and, for girls, is used primarily for sexual misconduct.

Sally Gold, a member of the legal staff of the New York City Department of Consumer Affairs, made a study[35] of juvenile delinquents in jails and "homes" across the country. She found that over half of the girls incarcerated were in for noncriminal conduct such as sexual activity, while only one-fifth of the boys were in for noncriminal matters. The crimes that girls did commit tended to be minor—shoplifting rather than car theft or burglary—yet girls served significantly longer terms than boys. Even though their crimes or conduct were usually less serious than those of boys, girls were no more frequently let off with a warning. They were sent to reform schools as frequently as boys.

State statutes requiring that women be more severely sentenced than men for committing the same crime have recently come under attack. A lower court upheld, but the Pennsylvania Supreme Court struck down, the Muncy Act, which provided that "women sentenced for offenses punishable by imprisonment for more than one year *must* be sentenced to the maxi-

---

[33] Norman Dorsen, in ibid., p. 507.
[34] Quoted by Sally Gold, in ibid., pp. 512–513.
[35] Ibid., p. 515.

mum permissible term. Men, on the other hand, *may* be sentenced to lesser terms."[36] In 1968, a federal district court struck down a similar Connecticut law.[37] Several other states have such laws, but after these decisions they seemed vulnerable to attack. On October 27, 1971, however, the New Jersey Supreme Court upheld a sentencing law similar to the Muncy Act.[38]

CITIZENSHIP SECOND CLASS: WOMEN'S POLITICAL RIGHTS

In 1851, Ernestine Rose, an early feminist, summed up the political position of women in the United States thus: "In the laws of the land she has no rights; in the government she has no voice."[39] The voice was a long time in coming. Despite the work of women's groups, women were not included in the Fourteenth and Fifteenth Amendments to the Constitution, which granted blacks the rights of citizenship, including the right to vote.

Some hoped that the Supreme Court might interpret the Fourteenth Amendment so as to give women the vote. But in 1875, in the case of *Minor* v. *Happersett,* the court ruled that while women were citizens, suffrage was not one of the privileges and immunities of citizenship protected by the Fourteenth Amendment. The battle would have to be won in the political arena where women, lacking the vote, had very little power. Starting in 1890 with Wyoming, women did gain the vote in a number of states, but only after the ratification of the Nineteenth Amendment in August 1920 were all American women enfranchised. The winning of the vote did not bring about equality. Until 1933 an American woman lost her citizenship if she married an alien. An American man did not.

Equal rights and responsibilities in jury service still have not been established. In 1880, the Supreme Court held that

---

[36] Kanowitz, op. cit., p. 168.

[37] Ibid., p. 197.

[38] *State* v. *Costello.* For a discussion of this and similar statutes and cases, see Carolyn Engel Temin, "Discriminatory Sentencing of Women Offenders: The Argument for the ERA in a Nutshell," *American Criminal Law Review,* 2, 2 (winter 1973), pp. 357–361.

[39] Ernestine Rose, "On Legal Discrimination," in Aileen S. Kraditor, ed., *Up from the Pedestal* (New York: Quadrangle, 1968), p. 224.

a West Virginia law barring blacks from jury service was unconstitutional but that it was not unconstitutional to bar women.[40] Not until 1966 did a federal district court rule that the exclusion of women from juries was a violation of the Fourteenth Amendment's equal protection clause. In *White* v. *Crook,* the courts struck down an Alabama law, and the ruling also applies to similar laws in Mississippi and South Carolina, the other two states that completely excluded women from juries.[41] Despite this ruling, during the late 1960s women served on juries on the same basis as men in only 32 states. In others, women were granted special exemptions not available to men; in 15, sex alone was a valid exemption. Three states required a woman to register with a clerk of the court if she wished to be considered for jury service.

These special "privileges" were based on the stereotyped notion that women's place is in the home. The Supreme Court, upholding Florida's registration law in 1960, said:

> Woman is still regarded as the center of home and family life. We cannot say that it is constitutionally impermissible for a State, acting in pursuit of the general welfare, to conclude that a woman should be relieved from the civic duty of jury service unless she herself determines that such service is consistent with her own special responsibilities.[42]

Leo Kanowitz, a professor of law, concludes that such special exemptions "freeze the position of women as second-class citizens in the field of political rights. . . . They also express present day vestiges of male supremacy doctrines."[43] Furthermore, if a woman wishes to perform her civic duty, such laws can result in a real hardship. New York State allowed women to refuse jury service on the basis of sex alone. As a result, New York City would not pay the salary of a female employee if she chose to serve. Male employees' salaries were paid during jury service. In 1968, this practice was tested in the courts and upheld.[44]

Finally, in 1975 the Supreme Court declared unconstitu-

---

[40] *Strauder* v. *West Virginia,* 100 U.S. 303.
[41] Kanowitz, op. cit., pp. 28–29.
[42] *Hoyt* v. *Florida,* quoted in ibid., p. 30.
[43] Ibid., p. 31.
[44] Rose Aronoff, in New York City Commission on Human Rights, op. cit., p. 562.

tional a Louisiana law that automatically exempted women from jury service unless they volunteered to serve.[45] By that time, only seven states still provided an unqualified exemption for women and only Louisiana required women to volunteer before they would be eligible.[46] Under *Taylor* v. *Louisiana,* states may still grant exemptions to men and women on different grounds so long as the result is a "reasonably representative" jury.[47]

A SLOW RESURRECTION FROM CIVIL DEATH: MARRIED WOMEN'S RIGHTS

"By marriage, the husband and wife are one person in law; that is, the very being or legal existence of the woman is suspended during the marriage, or at least is incorporated and consolidated."[48] This is the doctrine of coverture as described by Blackstone. A basic principle of English common law, its result was that upon marriage a woman lost even the rights she possessed when single. Much of her property became her husband's, and all fell under his complete control. He did not even have to account to her. She could not transfer her property, enter into contracts, or sue or be sued. Marriage meant, in effect, civil death.[49]

Coverture in America

English common law was somewhat less stringently applied in America. Colonial courts had recognized some rights of the wife: to live with her husband in house and bed, to receive support from him even if he abandoned her, to be protected from violence at his hands.[50] None of these really minimal rights had been recognized in England. The wife was also entitled to inherit the life use of one-third of her husband's estate.

The rich protected their daughters' property through marriage contracts and trusts. Without such an arrangement, if

[45] *Women's Rights Law Reporter,* March 1975, p. 33.
[46] Ibid., p. 34.
[47] Ibid., p. 36.
[48] Quoted in Kanowitz, op. cit., p. 35.
[49] Ibid., p. 36.
[50] Andrew Sinclair, *The Emancipation of the American Woman* (New York: Harper & Row, 1965), p. 84.

the marriage ended in separation or divorce the husband was entitled to everything—even the wife's clothes.

Starting in 1839, a series of Married Women's Property Acts were passed in a number of states. The earlier laws gave women a right to the property they brought to marriage; later ones gave her a right to the wages she earned. The New York Married Women's Property Act of 1848 provided that the real and personal property that a woman brings with her to marriage "shall not be subject to the disposal of her husband nor be liable for his debts and shall continue her sole and separate property as if she were a single female."[51] This law was passed after a twelve year campaign by feminists. Success was, however, probably due largely to the interest of the wealthy in protecting their daughters' property rights. Ernestine Rose, a feminist leader in the campaign, said the act was "not much . . . only for the favored few and not for the suffering many. But it was a beginning and an important step."[52]

The New York Married Women's Property Act of 1860 was of more importance to the average woman. It gave her the right to her earnings and declared her "to be the joint guardian of her children, with her husband, with equal powers, rights and duties. . . ."[53]

Property rights

At present, a married woman's property rights depend on the state in which she lives. In the 42 common law states, the property each spouse brings to marriage and that which each earns is his or her separate property. A wife thus has no present interest in or control over any of her husband's earnings, although upon his death she is entitled to receive a specific share of his property—usually one-third or one-half. A wife who does not work is dependent on her husband's generosity for anything beyond basic support. One New York husband refused to give his wife money for tuition when she wished to complete her education.[54] Under the law, this was his right.

---

[51] Married Women's Property Act, New York, 1848, in Miriam Schneir, ed., *Feminism: The Essential Historical Writings* (New York: Vintage, 1972), p. 73.

[52] Rose, quoted in ibid.

[53] Married Women's Property Act 1860, in ibid., p. 123.

[54] A housewife, in New York City Commission on Human Rights, op. cit., pp. 792–793.

In the eight community property states, marriage is seen as a type of partnership, and the couple's earnings are considered community property. However, until recently the husband had the exclusive right to manage and control that property. In California, for example, the husband was declared by law to be the "head of the family." Until changed in the mid-1970s, his control of community property, while no longer absolute, was extensive. He had to obtain his wife's signature to give away, sell, or mortgage real community property; and a 1951 law gave the wife the right to manage and control community property earned by her.[55] The husband could still dispose of community property like cars and furniture without his wife's consent, but she could not do likewise. Furthermore, lawyer Roberta Ralph pointed out that "since a woman doesn't have management and control, she has no say in investments her husband makes. He can go and buy a diamond mine in Alaska. She can say, 'No dear, I don't think so.' And he can say, 'Shut up, dear, I make the decisions.' "[56]

Even after the death of one spouse, the inequality continued. If the wife died first and if she had left her share of the community property to her husband, he did not have to go through probate court. If the husband died first, however, the wife had to probate everything, including her own share. Probate is expensive and inconvenient. The estate could be tied up for months or even years, during which time the woman had no money. She could get support money to tide her over by court action, but again, this costs money and inconvenience.

Under pressure from feminists, bills to equalize the positions of men and women were recently passed by the California state legislature. A bill giving wives equal control with their husbands over community property was signed into law on October 2, 1973, and became effective on January 1, 1975.[57] A bill equalizing procedures for inheriting community property was approved in early 1974 and became effective at the beginning of 1975.

Despite the nineteenth-century Married Women's Property

---

[55] Kanowitz, op. cit., p. 65.

[56] Quoted by Barbara Fryer in Riverside, California, *Daily Enterprise,* June 25, 1973.

[57] Press Release of California State Senator Mervyn M. Dymally, October 5, 1973.

Acts, a number of states still restrict a woman's right to make contracts and her right to engage in business on her own.[58] In Kentucky a woman cannot by herself be surety of (i.e., guarantee) anyone's debt except her husband's. In Georgia, on the other hand, she may not use her separate estate to pay her husband's debts. Some states will not let a woman mortgage or lease her real property unless her husband is involved in the transaction. Maryland places limits on a woman's right to sue and be sued in her own name. Utah places limitations on her right to serve in a position of trust. An Idaho statute providing that "the court is to prefer male over female when persons otherwise entitled to a selection apply to be named an administrator of a descendant's estate" was recently ruled unconstitutional by the Supreme Court.[59]

In five states, a wife must get court approval to engage in an independent business. In Florida, for example, she must present a petition setting forth her name, age, "and her character, habits, education and mental capacity for business, and briefly set out the reasons why such disabilities [to engage in her own business] should be removed."[60] In New York State, a woman applying for a liquor license must submit a personal history from her husband or nearest male relative.[61]

Domicile

A married woman's domicile (roughly, her legal residence) follows her husband's. Some states make certain exceptions, but this is the general rule. Domicile is important because it determines such matters as where one can obtain a divorce, where probate will take place, where one has the right to vote and hold public office or receive welfare benefits, and where one qualifies for residence tuition at state schools.

A husband can choose any reasonable domicile, and his wife is legally bound to abide by his choice. Of course at present a real and serious conflict on where to live would most likely result in divorce. The law cannot be used to force a woman to live in a place she considers totally unacceptable. The exis-

---

[58] Kanowitz, op. cit., p. 56.

[59] Association of the Bar of the City of New York, Committee on Federal Legislation, "Amending the Constitution to Prohibit State Discrimination Based on Sex," in U.S. Congress, op. cit., p. 633.

[60] Quoted in Kanowitz, op. cit., p. 57.

[61] *Ms.*, 5 (May 1977), p. 20.

tence of the law does mean that if a couple, for financial or other reasons, want to maintain separate domiciles, they may not. It is another enshrinement in the law of the second-class citizenship of women.

In several domicile cases decided in 1971, the courts ruled in favor of the women plaintiffs.[62] The University of Arizona defined resident women married to nonresident men as nonresidents and thus required them to pay the higher out-of-state tuition. The judge did not rule on the broader issue of domicile but simply held the rule to be unreasonable. In a similar Colorado case, the judge ruled that the law that read "the domicile of a married woman is normally that of her husband" did not apply for the purpose of tuition at state schools.[63] In a Florida case, a woman married to a foreigner who had never provided a home was allowed to retain her own domicile. "*Normally* and perhaps *presumptively,* but not *inevitably,* a wife acquires the husband's domicile upon marriage," the court said.[64]

These cases show the problems that domicile laws create for married women. Although the women plaintiffs won these cases, all were decided on very narrow grounds and did not change the basic law on domicile.

A married woman's name

By custom, a woman has taken the name of her husband upon marriage. The common law would indicate that this is an option and not a requirement, some lawyers contend.[65] Under the common law any person may adopt any name he or she likes so long as fraud is not intended. Only one state, Hawaii, specifically requires by law that a woman take her husband's name.

Many lawyers say that by common law rule a wife must assume her husband's surname. A great many state laws are based on this presumption. Statutes relating to the issuance of drivers' licenses often require a woman to notify a state agency of a change in name upon marriage. Voter registration

---

[62] *Women's Rights Law Reporter,* 1 (spring 1972), p. 25 passim.
[63] Quoted in ibid., p. 25.
[64] Quoted in ibid.
[65] See Priscilla Ruth MacDougall, "Married Women's Common Law Right to Their Own Surnames," *Women's Rights Law Reporter,* 1 (fall–winter 1972–1973).

laws frequently require that a woman reregister in her married name. Administrative rules at the state and local levels also frequently require a married woman to use her husband's name. When such laws and rules have been tested in court, the results have been varied.[66] In the 1971 case of *Forbuse* v. *Wallace,* an Alabama requirement that women use their married names in applying for drivers' licenses was upheld by the Supreme Court. Maryland's requirement that a woman must use her husband's name in registering to vote was struck down by the state court of appeals in 1972.

With the growth of the women's movement, more cases can be expected. Women contend that having to take their husbands' names is a submergence of their personality and another example of the demeaning doctrine of coverture. The requirement also has practical consequences. *Newsweek* reports that "in Lowell, Massachusetts, counselor Gail Dunfey was marked absent from city-council meetings because she insisted upon using her own name—under which she had been elected—and not her husband's."[67]

Many states do have formal procedures for changing one's name, but married women are frequently excluded from these provisions. In Iowa, for example, a married woman cannot change her name, but if her husband changes his, the new name automatically becomes her legal surname.[68] Even if state law allows her to change her name, she is frequently harassed if she attempts to do so. "In Indiana, where a woman recently sought to restore her maiden name, State Attorney General Theodore Sendak suggested that her 'need was not for a change of name but for a competent psychiatrist.' "[69]

Recently several state court decisions and rulings by state attorneys general have held the women need not assume their husbands' names upon marriage.[70] The Hawaii statute requiring a woman to take her husband's name has been struck down as contrary to the state constitution.[71] There have also been several contrary rulings, so the law is still unclear in this area.[72]

---

[66] Ibid., pp. 2–3.
[67] *Newsweek,* August 20, 1973.
[68] Kanowitz, op. cit., p. 43.
[69] *Newsweek,* August 20, 1973.
[70] *1975 Handbook,* op. cit., pp. 387–388.
[71] Ibid., p. 386.
[72] Ibid., p. 388.

The law of support

If a woman loses many rights upon marriage, she does, it is claimed, gain security. The husband is responsible for supporting his wife and children. In some states, a wife is legally responsible for supporting her husband under certain circumstances—if he is disabled, for example. Nevertheless, the main burden of support falls upon the husband.

These laws are based, some legal scholars contend, on the notion that a wife is her husband's property.[73] He owns her and therefore must take care of her. Certainly the laws are an expression of rigid sex-role stereotyping. The husband's obligation applies whether or not the wife can support herself. The law is not based on functional relationships within the family—on whether, in fact, the wife stays home and takes care of the children while the husband is the major breadwinner. It is based simply on sex.

While women are more likely to stay home and take care of children and thus require support from their husbands than vice versa, support laws need not be based on sexist premises. The National Commission on Uniform State Laws has drafted a Uniform Marriage and Divorce Act that completely avoids mention of sex. "It provides for alimony for either spouse (called 'maintenance'), child support obligations for both spouses in accordance with their means, and custody of children based upon the welfare of the child."[74] The act bases support obligations on the circumstances of a given case and not on sex per se. It avoids the offensive assumption that all women are incapable of taking care of themselves and makes the law a great deal fairer for both husband and wife.

In actual practice, the support laws do not offer a woman much protection. While she is living with her husband, there is very little she can do to ensure enforcement.[75] If he is a gambler, an alcoholic, or just doesn't want to work, it's too bad for her. Contrary to public opinion, the divorced wife usually ends up with the short end of the stick. An American Bar Association study found that temporary alimony is awarded in less than 10 percent of the cases; permanent alimony, in

---

[73] Kanowitz, op. cit., p. 71.

[74] Citizen's Advisory Council on the Status of Women, "The Equal Rights Amendment—What It Will and Won't Do," in U.S. Congress, op. cit., p. 564.

[75] Lisa Cronin Wohl, "The Sweetheart of the Silent Majority," *Ms.*, 2 (March 1974), p. 56.

about 2 percent.[76] In general, the ex-husband's child support payments cover less than half of the cost of actually supporting the children. Furthermore, alimony and child support are difficult to collect. A study found that ten years after divorce, 87 percent of the husbands were no longer meeting such court ordered payments.[77]

The assumption that the man is the primary breadwinner has been used to deny women employee benefits extended to men. Army rules formerly stipulated that male armed forces members could claim their wives as dependents, whether or not the wife was in fact financially dependent. The dependency status entitled them to a supplementary housing allowance and various medical and dental benefits. A female member of the armed forces could claim her husband as a dependent only if she could show that she provided over half of his support. First Lieutenant Frontiero brought suit against the army. In January 1973, the Supreme Court ruled in her favor and threw out the discriminatory statutes as violating the Fourteenth Amendment's equal protection clause.[78]

In private employment similar discrimination in fringe benefits frequently takes place. A number of such cases have been taken to the Equal Employment Opportunity Commission, and the EEOC has ruled that "the assumption that any working female is dependent upon her husband for her support, regardless of the extent to which she contributes to the actual support and maintenance of her family, is plainly indefensible."[79] In one such case, the employer financed health insurance for the dependents of married men but not for those of married women on the basis that men were heads of household or primary breadwinners, but women were not.

Many provisions of the social security law are also based on the assumption that the family is dependent on the male breadwinner. In a series of recent decisions, the Supreme Court has struck down a number of the discriminatory aspects. Until declared unconstitutional in 1975, a nonemployed widow with children received benefits based on her deceased husband's earnings, but a comparably placed widower did not.[80] Under

[76] Cited in ibid.
[77] Cited in ibid., p. 57.
[78] *Women's Rights Law Reporter,* spring–summer 1973, pp. 82–83.
[79] Quoted in ibid., p. 89.
[80] *Women's Rights Law Reporter,* September 1975, p. 13.

social security law, a husband, to be eligible for dependency benefits when his wife dies, retires, or becomes disabled, had to prove that he was dependent on his wife for at least half of his support. There was no such requirement for wives.[81] In two decisions handed down in March 1977, the Supreme Court declared these provisions unconstitutional.[82] Interestingly, the justices could not agree on whether the law discriminated against men or women. One can argue that either way, but the result of the provisions was that a woman paid as much social security tax as a comparably placed man, yet she and her husband received smaller payments when she retired.

Credit

Prior to passage of the Equal Credit Opportunity Act, practices in the area of home mortgage financing were dominated by the same stereotyped assumptions. The amount one can borrow for buying a home depends on one's income, but most lending institutions would not give full credit for the wife's income. The assumption was that the husband was the main breadwinner and the wife a temporary worker. One survey of lending practices found that in general, if the wife was not a professional, no allowance was made for her income if she was under thirty-five; half was counted if she was from thirty-five to forty-two; and only thereafter was her full income counted.[83]

Such practices were not restricted to private lending institutions; the Veterans Administration had the same type of policy.[84] For example, a twenty-nine-year-old woman and her husband wished to buy a home for which they would be eligible only if her income were counted. This woman had worked full-time since graduating from high school. The most she had ever taken off from work was two months, when she had her only child eight years previously. She had also completed two years of college in night school and was working for her degree, which would increase her earning potential. She had, in fact, owned a house in another state, and her payment record was good. When they applied for the loan, she and her husband

---

[81] Ibid.

[82] *Los Angeles Times,* March 22, 1977.

[83] Dennis Kendig, "Discrimination against Women in Home Mortgage Financing," *Yale Review of Law and Social Action,* 3 (winter 1973), p. 164.

[84] Ibid., pp. 168–169.

were renting an apartment that cost $50 per month more than what their mortgage payments would be, and they had never had difficulty paying their rent.

What was the VA's response to their request? She is a woman of childbearing age, the VA said, so her income cannot be counted. However, her income could be counted if her doctor would specify that she was incapable of having more children or if she would sign an affidavit saying she was using birth control and intended to continue and not have more children. The woman considered this an invasion of her rights and refused to sign.

The 1974 Equal Credit Opportunity Act outlaws discrimination on the basis of sex or marital status in any aspect of a credit transaction.[85] Creditors may not discount income from part-time work, they may not ask about a woman's childbearing intentions, and they must, if requested, give reasons for denying credit.

The act is a big step forward but it is far from perfect. Feminists had hoped that creditors would have to give an explanation for all denials of credit, but business opposition resulted in weakening that provision. Creditors are required to record family accounts in the names of both spouses only if requested. This enables a woman to establish her own credit identity—but many woman may not be aware that this is important and may not take advantage of the provision. As in the past, many women will find, upon divorce or widowhood, that in the eyes of potential lenders they are nonpersons. Penalties for discrimination under the act are rather mild, and enforcement authority is dispersed among a number of federal agencies. The act, then, is no panacea; it is a useful weapon in the fight for equal rights. Women themselves will have to take on the major burden of seeing that it is enforced.

SINGLE WOMEN: THERE OUGHT TO BE A LAW

Problems specific to the single woman stem from the lack of antidiscrimination laws rather than from the existence of discriminatory law. Under the common law, even at a time when

[85] The following discussion is based on Lisa Cronin Wohl, "Equal Credit Opportunity Act: Some Good News, Some Not So Good," *Ms.*, March 1977.

married women had almost no rights, single women's property and contract rights were the same as those of men. But even at present, the single woman who is not rich finds that in practice her rights in financial transactions are limited.

Getting credit of any sort is frequently difficult, if not impossible, for the single woman. She is often refused a credit card. If she wishes to buy a home, she will have great difficulty getting financing, even if her financial status is clearly adequate.[86] A twenty-eight-year-old woman attempted to get mortgage financing for a $34,500 townhouse she wished to buy. This woman had a master's degree, an annual salary of $12,000, $9,000 in cash, and no debts. Yet no bank was willing to give her a loan. She had not even been able to get a credit card. Until passage of the Equal Credit Opportunities Act, such discrimination was not illegal.

Until recently, most areas had no laws prohibiting discrimination against women in housing or in public accommodations. In New York City, for example, a number of landlords would not rent to single women, claiming that the financial risk was too high.[87] Such policies were prevalent in the most desirable areas. Thus it was estimated that in 1970 there were about 1000 buildings in New York City's Upper East Side that refused to rent to single women. Even public housing authorities discriminated. Carter Burden, a member of the New York City Council, reported that a single woman who had applied for nearly every middle-income housing development over the past 15 years had consistently been turned down because she was single.[88]

Nightclubs, cocktail lounges, and even some restaurants will not admit unescorted women. The policy has frequently been justified as necessary to discourage prostitutes.[89] That in itself says a great deal about how women are viewed.

From 1970 on, a number of states passed laws prohibiting discrimination on the basis of sex in places of public accommodation.[90] Such discrimination is still not prohibited by

---

[86] Ibid., p. 171.
[87] Carol Greitzer, in New York City Commission on Human Rights, op. cit., p. 146.
[88] Carter Burden, in ibid., p. 151.
[89] Babcock, op. cit., p. 1059.
[90] Ibid., p. 1057.

federal law, although discrimination against minority males is illegal under Title II of the 1964 Civil Rights Act.

WOMEN AS WORKERS: LAWS ON EMPLOYMENT

Laws affecting women as workers again reflect society's sexist image of women. Women have been relegated to low-paid, low-prestige, dead-end jobs, and employment laws often seemed designed to keep women from bettering their position. Recently, however, legislation to end sex discrimination in employment has been passed, and women have been going to court to force compliance with these laws. The picture, then, is a mixed one: continuing discrimination and considerable progress.

Women need not apply

In 1872, the Supreme Court upheld an Illinois law prohibiting women from practicing law. Myra Bradwell, the plaintiff, claimed that the law was an abridgement of the privileges and immunities of citizenship guaranteed by the Fourteenth Amendment and thus unconstitutional. The court disagreed, basing its decision on the "nature" of women.

> . . . the civil law, as well as nature herself, has always recognized a wide difference in the respective spheres and destinies of man and woman. Man is, or should be, woman's protector and defender. The natural and proper timidity and delicacy which belongs to the female sex evidently unfits it for many of the occupations of civil life. The constitution of the family organization, which is founded in the divine ordinance, as well as in the nature of things, indicates the domestic sphere as that which properly belongs to the domain and functions of womanhood. The harmony, not to say identity, of interests and views which belong, or should belong to the family institution is repugnant to the idea of a woman adopting a distinct and independent career from that of her husband. So firmly fixed was this sentiment in the founders of the common law that it became a maxim of that system of jurisprudence that a woman had no legal existence separate from her husband, who was regarded as her head and representative in the social state; and notwithstanding some recent modifications of this civil status, many of the special rules of law flowing from and dependent upon this cardinal principle still exist in full force in most states. One of these is, that a married woman is incapable, without her husband's consent, of making contracts which shall be binding on her or him. This very incapacity was one circumstance which the

Supreme Court of Illinois deemed important in rendering a married woman incompetent fully to perform the duties and trusts that belong to the office of an attorney and counselor.

It is true that many women are unmarried and not affected by any of the duties, complications, and incapacities arising out of the married state, but these are exceptions to the general rule. *The paramount destiny and mission of woman are to fulfill the noble and benign offices of wife and mother.* This is the law of the Creator. And the rule of civil society must be adapted to the general constitution of things, and cannot be based upon exceptional cases.

. . . in my opinion, in view of the peculiar characteristics, destiny, and mission of woman, it is within the province of the legislature to ordain what offices, positions, and callings shall be filled and discharged by men, and shall receive the benefit of those energies and responsibilities, and that decision and firmness which are presumed to predominate in the sterner sex.

For these reasons I think that the laws of Illinois now complained of are not obnoxious to the charge of abridging any of the privileges and immunities of citizens of the United States.[91]

Over 20 years later, the court upheld a similar Virginia law. Not until 1921 did women gain the right to practice law in all states. The right was won not through court action but by changes in state legislation.

Many states bar women from such occupations as mining, wrestling, and bartending. In 1948, in *Goesart* v. *Cleary,* the Supreme Court upheld a Michigan bartending prohibition saying "Bartending by women may, in the allowable legislative judgment, give rise to moral and social problems. . . ."[92]

These laws as well as the judicial decisions upholding them are based on sexist premises. But more than the notion that women are weak, incompetent creatures who need protection is involved. The Michigan law exempts the wives and daughters of bar owners from the bartending prohibition. Michigan law does not prohibit women from working as waitresses in a bar. In the Goesart decision, Justice Frankfurter wrote, "Since the line [the legislators] have drawn is not without a basis in reason, we cannot give ear to the suggestion that the real impulse behind this legislation was an unchivalrous desire of male bar-

---

[91] *Bradwell* v. *Illinois,* quoted by Diane B. Schulder, "Does the Law Oppress Women?" in Morgan, op. cit., pp. 147–148.

[92] Quoted in Kanowitz, op. cit., p. 33.

tenders to monopolize the calling."[93] Given the difference in pay between the jobs of bartender and waitress, that in fact seems a reasonable conclusion.

The Court, however, in this and other cases, has decided that the grossest stereotypes about women provide a reasonable reason for discrimination. "The 14th Amendment has never yet been applied by the Supreme Court to guarantee to an individual female citizen the right to work at any lawful occupation of her choice, although the Court has applied its 'equal protection' clause to insure the right to work to Chinese laundrymen, Japanese fishermen, a train conductor, and an Austrian cook."[94]

Protective laws

Most states have protective labor laws that apply to women only. Laws establishing maximum hours, minimum wages, weight-lifting ceilings, mandatory rest periods, or lunch breaks and prohibiting certain types of night work are considered protective laws. The states vary greatly both in terms of which types of protections are included and in the specific standards set.

In the late nineteenth and early twentieth centuries, many states passed non-sex-based protective laws. Working conditions in industry were abominable; many people were forced to work 12 to 14 hours a day, often 7 days a week, for starvation wages. In 1905 the Supreme Court declared a maximum hours law for bakers unconstitutional (*Lochner* v. *New York*).[95] The states realized that other such laws would not survive a judicial challenge. Then, in 1908, the Court upheld an Oregon maximum hours law for women only.[96] Many of the early protective laws, then, were restricted to women because only thus would they survive the Court. Half a loaf was considered better than none.

The Court based its decision in *Muller* v. *Oregon* on the biological differences between the sexes: "The two sexes differ in structure of body, in the functions to be performed by each,

---

[93] Quoted in ibid., p. 180.
[94] Marguerite Rawalt, in U.S. Congress, op. cit., p. 195.
[95] *Lochner* v. *New York*, 198 U.S. 45 (1905).
[96] *Muller* v. *Oregon*, 208 U.S. 412 (1908).

in the amount of physical strength. . . ."[97] Woman's inferior physical strength, the court asserted, means she is incapable of taking care of herself and must look to men for protection:

> History discloses the fact that woman has always been dependent upon man. . . . As minors, though not to the same extent, she has been looked upon in the courts as needing especial care that her rights may be preserved. . . . Differentiated by these matters from the other sex, she is properly placed in a class by herself and the legislation designed for her protection may be sustained, even when like legislation is not necessary for men, and could not be sustained. It is impossible to close one's eyes to the fact that she still looks to her brother and depends upon him.[98]

According to Kanowitz, this language provided the basis for the principle that

> . . . sex is a valid basis for classification . . . a principle that is often repeated mechanically without regard to the purposes of the statute in question or the reasonableness of the relationship between that purpose and the sex-based classification. The subsequent reliance in judicial decisions upon the Muller language is a classic example of the misuse of precedent. . . .[99]

While the early sex-specific protective laws were a way of circumventing a conservative Court, later ones sprang from less noble motives. In the early 1930s, there was a movement to bar women from night work in a number of industries, including wool manufacturing and textiles. Its purpose was "to solve the unemployment situation by throwing women out of work."[100] Until revised in 1969, the New York State labor laws specified maximum hours for women but made exceptions for women working in restaurants in rural places of 1500 or less or in factory jobs in the canning of fruit or sauerkraut.[101] The law further specified that no woman could work after midnight in a factory or in a dining room or kitchen unless she obtained a special permit. Hat check girls, cigarette girls, and ladies

---

[97] Quoted in Kanowitz, op. cit., p. 153.
[98] Quoted in ibid., pp. 153–154.
[99] Ibid., p. 152.
[100] Burnita Sheldon Matthews, statement during Senate hearings on the Equal Rights Amendment, in Kraditor, op. cit., p. 295.
[101] Mary Ann Krupsak, Assemblywoman, New York State Assembly, in New York City Commission on Human Rights, op. cit., pp. 330–331.

room attendants did not require a permit. Generally, the maximum hours and no night work laws do not cover domestics and cleaning women. *Thus jobs have been covered or exempted depending on the convenience of employers and of competing males.*

"Most of the so-called protective legislation has really been to protect men's rights in better paying jobs," Congresswoman Martha Griffiths states.[102] Both maximum hours and weight-lifting laws have been used to deny women promotion. To give just one example, Southern Bell refused to promote a woman to switchman because of Georgia weight-lifting laws. Her salary was $78 per week; as a switchman she would have made $135 per week.[103]

The 1963 Equal Pay Act and Title VII of the 1964 Civil Rights Act

In 1963 and 1964, the first federal laws prohibiting sex discrimination in employment were passed. The 1963 act specifies that men and women must receive equal pay "on jobs the performance of which requires equal skill, effort and responsibility and which are performed under similar working conditions. . . ."[104] The act was passed as an amendment to the Fair Labor Standards Act and thus covers the same employees. Executive, professional, and administrative jobs were not included until June 1972, when the Equal Pay Act was extended to cover such jobs.[105]

In *Shultz* v. *Wheaton Glass Company* (1970), the first circuit court decision on the Equal Pay Act, the court ruled that jobs meriting equal pay need not be identical but only substantially equal.[106] Following this decision, most courts have ruled that different pay rates are justified only if there is a substantial difference in the effort, skill, or responsibility required. In *Shultz* v. *Hayes Industries, Inc.*, for example, the company

---

[102] U.S. Congress, op. cit., p. 176.
[103] Faith A. Seidenberg, "The Submissive Majority: Modern Trends in the Law Concerning Women's Rights," in Jonathan Black, ed., *Radical Lawyers* (New York: Avon, 1971), p. 236.
[104] Quoted in Kanowitz, op. cit., p. 138.
[105] Judith Hole and Ellen Levine, *Rebirth of Feminism* (New York: Quadrangle, 1971), p. 428.
[106] Babcock, op. cit., p. 445.

argued that only men helped in changing the die in the machines and that this justified the pay differential. The court disagreed, saying the infrequency of the extra task did not justify the men's receiving 40 cents per hour more.[107]

Title VII of the Civil Rights Act states that it "shall be an unlawful employment practice" for a covered employer, because of race, color, religion, sex, or national origin

> (1) to fail or refuse to hire or to discharge any individual or otherwise to discriminate against any individual with respect to his compensation, terms, conditions, or privileges of employment . . . or
> (2) to limit, segregate or classify his employees in any way which would deprive or tend to deprive any individual of employment opportunities or adversely affect his status as an employee. . . .[108]

The act covers employers and labor unions having 25 or more employees or members and employment agencies that deal with such employers. Educational institutions and government as an employer were exempted.

The Equal Employment Opportunity Commission (EEOC) established by the act may investigate complaints and attempt to conciliate the matter. If conciliation fails, the person injured may bring suit in federal court. The U.S. Attorney General may intervene in cases of "general public importance." Upon finding an intentional unlawful employment practice, the federal courts may enjoin the defendant from engaging in it and order reinstatement or hiring of employees with or without back pay. If there is a pattern of intentional violations, the attorney general may also bring a civil action in a federal district court. Under the original act, the EEOC could initiate a court proceeding on its own only to compel compliance with a previously issued order under the provisions just stated.

In 1972, the commission's powers were extended. It was given the power directly to sue an employer in federal court for violation of the civil rights laws. It was not, however, given the power to issue cease and desist orders. The EEOC's authority was also extended to educational institutions and to government employment.[109]

Title VII states that it is legal to discriminate on the basis

---

[107] *Women's Rights Law Reporter,* 2 (spring–summer 1973), p. 72.
[108] Quoted in Kanowitz, op. cit., p. 108.
[109] *Congressional Quarterly Weekly Report,* 30, 9 (February 26, 1972), p. 456.

of sex, religion, or national origin, but not race, where these characteristics are a "bona fide occupational qualification reasonably necessary to the normal operation of that particular business or enterprise."[110] This provision is potentially a major loophole, and much of the litigation under the act has centered on what are bona fide occupational qualifications (bfoqs).

EEOC guidelines specified that the bfoq provision was to be interpreted narrowly. According to Commissioner Jerolyn Lyle, "sex is a bona fide occupational qualification only when necessary for authenticity or genuineness of job performance such as acting or modeling."[111] The following are violations of Title VII:

(1) Refusing to hire women on the basis of assumed comparative employment characteristics of women in general.
(2) Refusing to hire women on the basis of stereotyped characteristics of the sexes.
(3) Refusing to hire women because of real or assumed negative preferences of persons who would become their co-workers.
(4) Refusing to hire women because separate facilities would have to be provided, unless clearly unreasonably high expenses would be incurred thereby.[112]

In *Diaz* v. *Pan American Airways, Inc.*, the airline contended that sex is a bfoq for the position of cabin attendent.[113] Passengers prefer female stewardesses because they are more comforting, the company claimed. The Fifth Circuit Court found for the male plaintiff, saying that customer prejudice does not justify discrimination.

Denying a woman promotion on the assumption that women resent taking orders from another woman is a violation of Title VII, the EEOC has decided. The case was brought by a bank employee who had been refused promotion to trust officer. A memo from a vice president to the woman's supervisor said, "My observation is that [charging party] is a most capable employee, but long experience in personnel work makes me question the advisability of having a woman supervise all female employees. . . ."[114]

---

[110] Quoted in Kanowitz, op. cit., p. 109.
[111] Jerolyn Lyle, in New York City Commission on Human Rights, op. cit., p. 293.
[112] Quoted in ibid.
[113] *Women's Rights Law Reporter,* 1 (fall–winter 1972–1973), pp. 52–53.
[114] Quoted in ibid., p. 56.

The relationship between the bfoq provision and state protective laws has presented especially troublesome questions. If state protective laws were interpreted as making sex a bfoq for jobs covered by such laws, the sex provision of Title VII would, to a large extent, be nullified.

The EEOC's position on this question has vacillated. In December 1965, the EEOC's first guidelines did allow state protective laws to be interpreted as a bfoq exception to Title VII so long as the laws actually protected rather than discriminated against women. It did not, however, specify how this distinction was to be determined. In its next set of guidelines, issued in August 1966, the EEOC claimed it did not have the authority to determine the relationship between the protective laws and Title VII. This was up to the courts to decide. Reversing itself in February 1968, the EEOC said it would decide on a case-by-case basis whether state laws were discriminatory and thus superseded by Title VII. Finally, in August 1969, the EEOC declared that state laws were in general no longer protective and were superseded by Title VII.

There have been a number of court cases in which the relationship between Title VII and state protective laws was at issue. The courts have held that state protective laws may not be used to deny women jobs and promotions. Title VII as federal law supersedes the state protective laws.

In 1968, in *Rosenfeld* v. *Southern Pacific Co.,* the court held California's maximum hours and weight-lifting laws invalid.[115] Ms. Rosenfeld had been rejected for the job of agent-telegrapher without any evaluation of her ability to do the job, even though she was the senior employee applying. The court ordered that she be considered for any future job without regard to sex.

Ms. Weeks was refused a job as a switchman because of a state 30-pound weight-lifting limit. The court of appeals in 1969 found for Weeks and said, "An employer has the burden of proving that he had reasonable cause to believe, that is, a factual basis for believing, that all or substantially all women would be unable to perform safely and efficiently the duties of the job involved."[116]

---

[115] Ibid., p. 36.

[116] *Weeks* v. *Southern Bell Telephone and Telegraph Co.,* quoted in ibid., p. 37.

In *Bowe* v. *Colgate-Palmolive Co.*, the court of appeals struck down a company weight-lifting limit, saying the Title VII prohibits "stereotyped characterization of the sexes [which precludes] consideration of individual capacities as to physical strength and particular job requirements."[117]

These three cases, all decided in 1968 and 1969, are considered particularly important as trend setters. The principles established—that state protective laws cannot be used to deny women jobs or promotion, that the burden of proof regarding bfoq falls upon the employer, that stereotyped notions about women may not be used to establish bfoq—have been used in a large number of subsequent decisions.

Cases challenging somewhat subtler forms of discrimination have also been brought. In *Griggs* v. *Duke Power Co.* (1971), the Supreme Court ruled that aptitude tests must be job related, saying that the employer has "the burden of showing that any given requirement has a manifest relationship to the employment in question."[118] In that case, plaintiff charged that the non-job-related aptitude test used discriminated against him on the basis of race, but the ruling is also applicable to sex.

The New York State Division of Human Rights found the New York City Department of Parks and Recreation's height and weight requirements (5 feet 7 inches and 135 pounds) for lifeguards discriminatory, since the department had not shown that meeting the requirements was essential to the job.[119] In a similar case, the EEOC struck down a minimum height requirement of 5 feet 7 inches for bus drivers, saying that it had a "substantially disproportionate effect" on women as a class and that "business convenience may not be equated with business necessity."[120] In a very important 1976 decision, a three-judge federal court invalidated Alabama's height and weight requirements for police personnel.[121] The court found that the requirements had a disproportionate effect on women applicants; for state troopers, the minimums were 5 feet 8 inches and 160 pounds. It concluded that the requirements

---

[117] Quoted in ibid.

[118] Quoted in ibid., p. 45.

[119] Ibid., p. 58.

[120] Quoted in ibid., p. 39.

[121] *Poverty Law Report*, 4 (September–October 1976), p. 3.

had not been shown to be sufficiently job-related so as to further the legitimate interests of the state. The judges said: "One lesson the women's rights movement has taught us is that many long-hailed conceptions concerning the sexes have been found to be erroneous when exposed to the light of empirical data and objectivity."[122] Since 97 percent of the nation's police jobs have some minimum height and weight requirements, this decision is likely to set an important precedent.

In a number of cases, employers have claimed that their decision was based not on the sex of the employee or potential employee but on some other characteristic such as marital state or parenthood. The complainants have charged sex discrimination because males with the given characteristic were treated differently from females. The argument in these cases centers on whether sex plus some other characteristic is a legal ground for discrimination. If such an argument were allowed to stand, Title VII would lose much of its usefulness.

Ida Phillips, who was making $45 a week as a waitress, applied for the position of assembly line trainee at $2.25 an hour. Martin Marietta Corporation turned her down, saying that the company did not hire women with preschool children. She brought suit, and the case was decided by the Supreme Court in 1971. The Court held that the company could not automatically preclude mothers of preschool children from consideration when it did not do the same with fathers. But it added that "the existence of such conflicting family obligations, if demonstrably more relevant to job performance for a woman than for a man, could arguably be a basis for distinction under [the bfoq provision]."[123] The Court thus left the door open to a sex-plus argument.

In a concurring opinion, Justice Marshall wrote, "I fear that in this case . . . the Court has fallen into the trap of assuming that the Act permits ancient canards about the proper role of women to be a basis for discrimination. Congress, however, sought just the opposite result."[124] Martin Marietta did not attempt to show that the bfoq provision applied in its case. Following the *Phillips* decision, a number of lower courts have ruled on the airline's no-marriage and under-thirty-two rules

---

[122] Quoted in ibid., p. 3.
[123] Quoted in *Women's Rights Law Reporter* (fall–winter 1972–1973) p. 59.
[124] Quoted in ibid.

for female but not male cabin attendants. The airlines lost all these cases, and the sex-plus defense has fallen into disuse.[125]

Many employers force women to take an unpaid maternity leave of several months or more, and some fire a pregnant woman outright. EEOC guidelines declare that firing or refusing to hire a pregnant woman is a violation of Title VII. According to 1972 EEOC guidelines, pregnancy must be treated like any other temporary disability.[126]

A number of cases challenging enforced maternity leave have been brought.[127] The Supreme Court agreed to hear two such cases during its 1973 term. One involved two junior high school teachers. The school board's policy required that they quit work after the fourth month of pregnancy and not return until the school term on the first day of which the child is at least three months old. For the two women bringing the suit, the rule would have resulted in almost a year of unemployment. The attorneys for the employers in the two cases, the Cleveland Board of Education and the Chesterfield County School Board, based their arguments on pregnant women's inability to do the job efficiently. In oral arguments before the Court, they claimed that "pregnant women are subject to 'certain medical conditions,' urinate more frequently, lose their sense of balance and become prone to falling down. . . . Moreover, they are forced to miss class in order to see their obstetricians as many as 13 times in the last three months of pregnancy."[128] On January 21, 1974, the Supreme Court struck down mandatory maternity leave policies, declaring such rules to be a violation of the teachers' constitutional right to due process.

In two subsequent pregnancy-related decisions, the Supreme Court decided against the women plaintiffs. The Court upheld the California temporary disability insurance program which denies benefits for pregnancy-related disabilities (*Geduldig* v. *Aiello*).[129] Dissenting, Justice Brennan wrote:

> . . . the economic effects caused by pregnancy related disabilities are functionally indistinguishable from the effects caused by any other disability: wages are lost due to a physical inability to work, and medi-

---

[125] *Signs,* September 1976, Part 2, p. 70, and Babcock, op. cit., p. 246.
[126] *Women's Rights Law Reporter,* 2 (spring–summer 1972), p. 90.
[127] Ibid., p. 65.
[128] Riverside, California, *Daily Enterprise,* October 17, 1973.
[129] Babcock, op. cit., p. 318.

cal expenses are incurred for the delivery of the child and for post-partum care. In my view, by singling out for less favorable treatment a gender-linked disability peculiar to women, the State has created a double standard for disability compensation: a limitation is imposed upon the disabilities for which women workers may recover, while men receive full compensation for all disabilities suffered, including those that affect only or primarily their sex, such as prostatectomies, circumcision, hemophilia and gout. In effect, one set of rules is applied to females and another to males. Such dissimilar treatment of men and women, on the basis of physical characteristics inextricably linked to one sex, inevitably constitutes sex discrimination.[130]

An even more serious setback for women occurred when the Supreme Court, on December 7, 1976, handed down its decision on *General Electric Co.* v. *Gilbert.*[131] GE's disability insurance covers almost every possible disability—including recovery from hair transplants and plastic surgery—but excludes pregnancy. Ms. Gilbert sued under Title VII. Despite the plan's covering disabilities unique to men (prostatectomies, vasectomies, and circumcisions, for example), a majority of the justices ruled that the exclusion of pregnancy is not sex discrimination. Writing for the majority, Justice Rehnquist states: "Gender based discrimination does not result simply because an employer's disability benefits program is less than all inclusive."[132] Justice Brennan, in dissent, called the majority's assumption that the GE plan was sex-neutral "purely fanciful."[133] According to Columbia law professor Ruth Bader Ginsburg, the decision takes "pregnancy out of Title VII. It means that an employer can say when you're pregnant, 'Go, I don't want you any more.' It gives an employer carte blanche to treat a woman as if she were a temporary member of the labor force."[134]

The Equal Pay Act and Title VII have had a favorable impact on employment equality for women, but much still needs to be done. Legislation to counteract the pregnancy decisions must be sought. Pressure on the EEOC for strict enforcement must be maintained, and cases must continue to be brought.

---

[130] Quoted in ibid., p. 130.
[131] *Los Angeles Times,* December 8, 1976.
[132] Quoted in ibid.
[133] Quoted in ibid.
[134] Quoted in *Newsweek,* December 26, 1976.

The acts have, however, provided a powerful weapon in the struggle for equality in employment.

THE EQUAL RIGHTS AMENDMENT

The proposed federal Equal Rights Amendment reads: "Equality of rights under the law shall not be denied or abridged by the United States or by any State on account of sex." Approved by the United States Congress on March 22, 1972, it now awaits ratification by the needed 38 states.

Opposing arguments take two forms: first, that the amendment is unnecessary to secure equality and, second, that it will have harmful effects. A number of lawyers, including some who are profeminist, have argued that earlier constitutional amendments already provide the basis for sexual equality under the law. They contend that the Fifth and Fourteenth Amendments, which guarantee due process and equal protection of the law, can and should be interpreted by the Supreme Court to outlaw sex discrimination. ERA supporters answer that the Court can and should have so interpreted the Constitution but that it has not. The Senate Judiciary Committee report on the ERA states: "If the Supreme Court were to hold that discrimination based on sex, like discrimination based on race, is inherently 'suspect' and cannot be justified in the absence of a 'compelling and overriding state interest,' then part of the reason for the Amendment would disappear. But the Court has persistently refused so to hold."[135]

Until 1971, the Supreme Court had never ruled favorably in a sex discrimination case. Its recent decisions striking down state laws as discriminatory have been based on narrow grounds. In *Reed* v. *Reed,* the Court used the standard of "reasonableness," which puts the burden of proof that a discriminatory law is unreasonable on the woman plaintiff.[136] Under this standard, a law distinguishing between men and women will be upheld so long as it bears a "reasonable relationship" to a permissible legislative objective. In *Frontiero* v. *Richardson,* the Court used a somewhat stricter standard, and a plurality

---

[135] U.S. Congress, Senate Committee on the Judiciary, *Equal Rights for Men and Women,* March 14, 1972, p. 10.
[136] Ibid.

but not a majority declared "classifications based upon sex, like classifications based on race, alienage or national origin . . . are inherently suspect" and therefore subject to "close judicial scrutiny."[137] Three other justices, however, specifically said that it is "unnecessary for the Court in this case to characterize sex as a suspect classification, with all of the far-reaching implications of such a holding."[138] This and cases decided subsequently suggest that, unless the Equal Rights Amendment is passed, a majority is unlikely to declare sex a suspect classification—a ruling which would shift the burden of proof from the woman plaintiff to the state.[139]

Another group of opponents base their opposition on the potentially "terrifying consequences" of the ERA. According to Dr. Pincus, who is quoted with approval by Senator Sam Ervin, "the Equal Rights Amendment and many of the other goals of its proponents will bring social disruption, unhappiness and increasing rates of divorce and desertion. Weakening of family ties may also lead to increased rates of alcoholism, suicide, and possible sexual deviation."[140]

Laws that protect married women will be struck down, the opponents contend. A husband will no longer be required to support his wife and children. If the marriage ends in divorce, the woman will have no right to alimony and child support nor a special right to child custody. A marriage law basing rights and obligations not on sex but on circumstances has already been written and recommended to the states. As pointed out earlier, such a law is a great deal fairer to both husband and wife and would not be unconstitutional. Actually, the ERA may well give the nonemployed wife greater protection than she now has. According to Common Cause, the ERA "will require state law to recognize the contribution of the homemaker who takes care of home and family . . . [it] would entitle the homemaker to financial support in compensation for her services as homemaker."[141]

A recent study of the effect of state ERAs supports this posi-

---

[137] Quoted in *Women's Rights Law Reporter,* summer 1973, p. 3.
[138] Ibid., p. 4.
[139] Babcock, op. cit., pp. 122–125.
[140] Minority Views of Mr. Ervin, in U.S. Congress, op. cit., p. 48.
[141] Quoted in Wohl, op. cit., p. 57.

tion. "Fairer decisions on divorce to homemakers, to children and the husbands are resulting,"[142] according to the report. The director of the Pennsylvania state commission for women says that the state ERA has substantially improved the status of homemakers and mothers: "In child support cases the court said a homemaker's care of the children must be considered an economic contribution in assessing support obligations. For the first time, a woman's work in the home is legally recognized."[143]

A number of unions based their opposition on the conflict between the ERA and state protective laws. The ERA would make sex-specific protective laws unconstitutional. Since the courts have been striking down protective laws as in conflict with Title VII, this argument is of little relevance. Many such laws did not, in fact, protect women. Protective laws that really do protect can be extended to men and thus escape constitutional challenge. Some lawyers contend that, when such laws are challenged, the courts have the power to extend the truly protective provisions to cover men, and in some cases this had been done.[144]

Women would be drafted into the armed services, ERA opponents say with horror. There is no draft in effect now, but if it were reinstated, women would be eligible on the same basis as men. Although many people, men as well as women, would consider army service an unwelcome interruption in their lives, it is difficult to understand opponents' horror. Women serve as volunteers in the armed services now. During peacetime, the tasks performed by most recruits are of the office work variety. Whether, in time of war, women would be required to serve in combat depends on whether they are judged physically capable of such duty. If having women killing and being killed in the front lines seems so much worse than placing men in the same position, perhaps we had better work harder at avoiding wars.

The clinching argument against the amendment, according to opponents, is that it would force desegregation of restrooms,

---

[142] Quoted in Riverside, California, *Daily Enterprise,* July 9, 1976.
[143] Quoted in ibid.
[144] *Hayes* v. *Potlatch Forests, Inc.,* 1972. See Babcock, op. cit., pp. 283–285.

prisons, and the like. Representative Abner Mikva has called this the "toilet training trauma."[145] The Supreme Court has recognized a right to privacy, which ERA supporters say would be applied in such cases. At last resort, restrooms providing for individual privacy could be built. Restrooms on airplanes and in private homes are not sex-segregated now.

The arguments against the amendment are unconvincing. Wives and children would not be left without financial support; men and women would not be forced to use restrooms together.

What would the amendment do? All state and federal laws and practices that treat men and women unequally would be rendered unconstitutional. The vestiges of the doctrine of coverture that remain in some state property laws would be swept away. For example, laws that require the husband's signature when the wife sells some of her property but do not require her signature when he is the seller would no longer be valid. A number of states would be required to change their laws on jury service. Men and women would be eligible for such service on the same basis; grounds for exemption could not differ for the sexes.

The ERA would have important consequences in the area of public education. That a state university may not deny admission on the basis of race was established by the Supreme Court in 1938.[146] In 1960, a Texas court upheld the exclusion of women from Texas State University's Agricultural and Mechanical College, even though some majors are available at no other state school. The United States Supreme Court refused to review the case, thus letting the state court's decision stand. In 1971, the Supreme Court again refused to review the state court's decision upholding the exclusion of one sex, this time male, from a state school.

The ERA would prohibit sex-segregated public schools and universities. Discrimination in admissions policies would also be outlawed.

Title IX of the Educational Amendments of 1972 does prohibit some forms of sex discrimination by schools receiving federal funds. It does not, however, outlaw single-sex under-

---

[145] Abner Mikva, in U.S. Congress, House, op. cit., p. 86.

[146] Rawalt, in U.S. Congress, House, op. cit., p. 202.

graduate colleges and contains a number of other glaring loopholes.[147] In April 1977, the Supreme Court upheld a lower court decision approving sex-segregated public high schools for academically superior students.[148] This would not have been possible if the ERA had been ratified.

The ERA would prohibit government at all levels from discriminating against women in public employment and in job training programs. Since teachers and professors in public schools and universities are, of course, public employees, a large number of people are involved. The armed services would be required to enlist women on the same basis as men. Military service is usually regarded as a burden by those debating the ERA. Some supporters have, however, pointed out that such service offers advantages as well. For the poor, the armed services have offered upward mobility. Job training is often available, and the GI Bill makes further education possible after leaving the military. Veteran status also carries with it numerous benefits, such as eligibility for VA loans. Until recently women were limited by law to 2 percent of the total military forces, and there are still informal limits in effect.[149] Women must also meet higher requirements in order to enlist. To become officers, women compete only against one another for a very limited number of openings. The ERA would make such unequal treatment unconstitutional.

The ERA is no panacea. Purely private discriminatory practices are not covered. Suits to enforce the amendment will have to be brought. Still, ratification would declare equality of the sexes a national policy and would provide a sound constitutional basis for challenging sexual discrimination.

---

[147] Ross, op. cit., pp. 132–133.

[148] *Los Angeles Times,* April 20, 1977.

[149] Mariclaire Hale, "Equal Rights Amendment—Women and the Selective Service," in U.S. Congress, House, op. cit., p. 369.

Part two

WOMEN'S PLACE THROUGHOUT HISTORY

WOMEN IN PRIMITIVE, SLAVE, AND FEUDAL SOCIETIES

8

Among anthropologists and historians there are two conflicting approaches to the position of women in earlier societies. A few still cling to the old approach, which claims that nothing ever has or ever will change because the status and role of women and men are determined by biology. In contrast, most anthropologists agree that a tremendous variety of social and sexual relationships, attitudes, and behavior is found in various societies. With regard to the forms of the family, the typical personality characteristics of male and female, and the status and occupations of women and men, almost anything found in one society can be found to be exactly opposite in some other society.

WOMEN IN PRIMITIVE SOCIETIES

Margaret Mead's[1] classic anthropological study of the relationship between sex and personality, or temperament, was discussed in Chapter 2. Of the three New Guinea tribes she investigated, among the Arapesh the personalities of both sexes are, according to our notions, "feminine"; among the Mundugumor, in contrast, both sexes have personalities stereotyped in our society as "masculine." In neither society do the people believe that personality should vary with sex and, in fact, it does not. The Tchambuli do show a relationship between sex and personality, but in this tribe, the normal male shows "feminine" per-

[1] Margaret Mead, *Sex and Temperament in Three Primitive Societies* (New York: Dell, 1935, 1971).

sonality traits and the normal female, "masculine" traits. Mead concludes that social conditioning, not biology, accounts for these differences. The average Arapesh is gentle and cooperative because he or she has been brought up in a society where that is the expected behavior. The average Mundugumor is violent and aggressive not by nature, but because of the society's socialization process. A child born into one of these tribes and reared in the other would grow up to display the personality and behavior characteristic of the tribe in which it was socialized.

Not merely attitudes but the actual relations and status of men and women differ in various societies. In hunting and gathering societies, which were the predominant form for 99 percent of human history, men and women were roughly equal.[2] Slave societies, in contrast, were characterized by female subordination. Moreover, family organization and forms of marriage differ drastically in various periods and societies. The nuclear family, with husband and wife and their children living in an isolated household, is not eternal, omnipresent, or "natural." In fact, in most primitive societies the band or clan had much more social importance than the family.

Most clan societies are "patrilineal," meaning that descent and inheritance are calculated through the father, the wife usually goes to live with her husband's family, and in some cases, if a man dies his brother must support and may marry his widow. All the kin terms relate the husband, wife, and children to the man's clan relatives. Many, but not all, patrilineal societies are also "patriarchal"; that is, male dominated. Yet there are also many clan societies that are "matrilineal," with descent and inheritance through the mother, kinship calculated to the mother's clan, and usually the husband moving to live with the wife's clan—and in some cases, if a man is widowed he may marry his wife's sister. Matrilineal societies still exist among American and Canadian Indians, in some areas of Africa, and among the Dravidians of India.[3] In most matrilineal societies the status of women is high. There is, however,

---

[2] Ruby Rohrlicht-Lequitl, "Gatherer-Hunters," in Barbara Bellow Watson, ed., *Women's Studies: The Social Realities* (New York: Harper's College Press, 1976), pp. 181–201.

[3] Jacquetta Hawkes and Sir Leonard Woolley, *Prehistory and the Beginning of Civilization* (New York: Harper & Row, 1963), p. 122.

very little evidence of "matriarchy"; that is, clear female dominance.

Marriages of one man and many women are also not uncommon. Polygyny is allowed in most Muslim societies and was practiced among the Mormons in nineteenth-century Utah. In practice, however, only the very wealthy man can afford many wives, so it has never been common among the working classes. On the other hand, there are a few societies in which one woman marries several men. Among the Todas of India, a woman marries a man and all his brothers, and no one cares who the biological father of her children is.

There are no undisputed cases of group marriage in primitive societies, but societies differ greatly in their views on sex. Among many Eskimo tribes, the wife would normally offer sexual hospitality to each visitor from afar. Among the fifty people of the Emerillon tribe of French Guiana, "marriages" are so short-lived that almost everybody marries everyone else of the opposite sex at some time.[4] In the Muria tribe of India, all adolescent boys and girls live together in communal huts with a high degree of sexual freedom, although adolescent lovers are not later permitted to marry.[5]

THE SEXUAL DIVISION OF LABOR

So far, it can be observed that the attitudes and status of women and men, as well as the forms of marriage and family, differ drastically in various societies. How and why?

Some argue that the biology of sex itself determines that women are limited to home and children and must play an inferior role in the economy, in public affairs, and even in the home. According to this view, all social forms everywhere can be explained by biological determinism. Strangely, some radical feminists, like Shulamith Firestone, also take this approach. She argues that male domination is, at origin, due to women's reproductive role.[6] She therefore advocates test-tube babies as the only solution; she seems to forget that childbearing

---

[4] Claude Levi-Strauss, "The Family," in Arlene and Jerome Skolnick, *Family in Transition* (Boston: Little, Brown, 1971), p. 60.

[5] Ibid., p. 62.

[6] See, e.g., Shulamith Firestone, *The Dialectic of Sex* (New York: Bantam, 1970), passim.

by itself is not very time consuming, and there is no biological reason, given baby bottles, to leave childrearing exclusively to women.

The problem with this approach is that the biology of sex is a constant throughout history and a constant cannot be used to explain changes in societies. For example, French geography cannot be used to explain the French revolution because it was the same before and after. Similarly, sex cannot be used to explain changes in marriage forms or the status of women because sex has remained constant. Neither can the biology of sex be used to explain differences between societies because it is the same in each society; the biology of American men and women is no different from that of the Tchambuli of New Guinea.

What we do find is that the status of women and the form of marriage are closely related to the division of labor between the sexes and the occupational roles of women and men. An anthropologist writes: "The most important clue to woman's status anywhere is her degree of participation in economic life and her control over property and the products she produces. . . ."[7]

Because it is more efficient and aids survival, every known society divides and specializes labor tasks to some degree. In every known society, women and men do somewhat different tasks (though some still unknown, very primitive societies may have no such division of labor). But the division of labor by sex is totally different in different societies. Whatever one sex does in one society, the other sex does in some other one.

Only 6 percent of all U.S. doctors are women, but Soviet doctors are about 75 percent female. American men seldom take responsibility for child care, but in the Nambikwara tribe fathers take care of babies and clean them when they soil themselves, while many young Nambikwara women disdain domestic activities and prefer hunting and even war expeditions.[8] Most Americans think it is "natural" for men to do the heavy work in society, but women carry all the heavy burdens in about four times as many societies as men do.[9] Likewise, it is

---

[7] Ruby Leavitt, in Vivian Gornick and Barbara Moran, *Women in Sexist Society* (New York: Signet Books, 1971), p. 396.

[8] Levi-Strauss, op. cit., p. 62.

[9] Lucy Komisar, *The New Feminism* (New York: Warner Paperback Library, 1972), p. 159.

"natural" for men to be the providers, but there are many societies, such as the Alorese of Eastern Indonesia or the Otomi Indians of Mexico, where women do all the heavy labor while their husbands lie in the shade and gossip.

In most primitive societies the group doing the labor and providing the food has a high status, while the opposite is often true in more advanced societies. We saw that among the Tchambuli of New Guinea, women tend to be aggressive and dominant, men passive and responsive. This is closely related to the fact that Tchambuli women fish and sell their catch in the market; Tchambuli men do the shopping, wear jewelry, love to dance and paint. Thus male and female personalities and status are intimately connected in each society to their economic role. Moreover, just as Mead shows how society conditions each sex to a particular personality and status, so also she shows how they are conditioned to accept a certain economic role, a certain part in the division of labor.

Why is the ideology and the whole conditioning process what it is in each society? The basic answer is that in the long run an ideology develops which conditions people to accept what is necessary for the operation and survival of the society under existing power relationships. Different economic conditions require different divisions of labor, and the society will socialize people to think of that division as natural. One archeologist writes: ". . . in the long run an ideology can survive only if it facilitates the smooth and efficient functioning of the economy. If it hampers that, the society—and with it the ideology—must perish in the end."[10] Of course one should emphasize "in the long run." Evolution, even social evolution, takes a long time to eliminate the losers and declare the fittest to be winners. Thus in the short run—which may be a very long time—an ideology may hamper the most efficient working of the society. The ideology may come into being when it is useful and necessary for survival. But each division of labor implies the equality or, often, the dominance of some group. Once a group has power, whether slave owners in Rome or white males in American society, that group makes every effort to defend and propagate the existing ideology to maintain its position.

We shall see in following sections that the sexist ideology of male supremacy grew out of a division of labor by sex which

---

[10] Gordon Childe, *What Happened in History* (Baltimore: Penguin, 1954, 1971), p. 24.

was very useful to efficient social development *when it first arose.* Now it hampers further development, but it is promoted, consciously or unconsciously, by males with great power in our society—and by all of us unconsciously, since that is the way we have been conditioned.

HUNTING AND GATHERING SOCIETIES (OLD STONE AGE)

For one to two million years, humans lived in societies based on hunting animals and gathering wild food. The available evidence indicates that the men did most of the hunting, while the women gathered fruits, vegetables, and grains. So this first division of labor was along sexual lines. In this very limited sense, Firestone and the male sexists are correct: It appears that the biological facts of childbirth and nursing did limit women's mobility, so it made more sense for men to do the wide-ranging hunting.

This does not mean that women played an inferior role. On the contrary, everything indicates that they worked just as long and hard as the men, their economic contribution was at least as important and more stable, and their status roughly equal. One should not think of "status" in its complex modern forms. These were small groups, all relatives, of 20 to 200 people. There was little private property except one's immediate tools or weapons, and really very little wealth or property of any kind. There was no government. People worked as a collective unit and shared collectively by tradition and out of the necessity for survival. "The large collective household *was* the community, and within it both sexes worked to produce the goods necessary for livelihood. . . . Women usually furnished a large share—often the major share—of the food."[11] Many hunter-gatherers, such as the Bushmen of the Kalahari Desert, depended primarily on the fruits and vegetables gathered by women; the meat provided by men was a luxury.

When Europeans from capitalist societies first came into contact with some of these primitive hunting-gathering societies, they were both shocked and confused by the high status of women and the role of the extended family or collective community. For example, in the seventeenth century, Jesuit mis-

[11] Eleanor Leacock, anthropologist, in Introduction to Frederick Engels, *The Origin of the Family, Private Property, and the State* (New York: New World Paperbacks, 1972), pp. 33–34.

sionaries encountered the Naskapi tribe of Canada. The Jesuits were shocked at the great power women possessed to decide where to live and what projects to undertake; they scolded the men for not being masters in their own homes "as in France." They were particularly worried about the degree of sexual freedom women enjoyed; men often didn't know who their biological children were. The Naskapi, however, thought that this objection was nonsensical and that the French were immoral to love only their own children. The Naskapi said: "You French people love only your own children; but we love all the children of our tribe."[12]

AGRICULTURAL VERSUS HERDING SOCIETIES (NEW STONE AGE)

For hundreds of thousands of years, women and men slowly improved their tools and weapons without major changes in social structure. Eventually enough progress was made in improving implements and methods of work to affect social conditions. This change from the Old to the New Stone Age is called the Neolithic Revolution. It occurred 10,000 to 12,000 years ago in the Middle East, somewhat later in other areas, and not at all in a few still-existing primitive tribes.

Two different "discoveries" occurred in the Neolithic Revolution. One was agriculture, the domestication of plants; the other was herding, the domestication of animals. Most societies discovered or emphasized one or the other long before they could do both. In a majority of cases agriculture probably came first.

What does this have to do with the relations of men and women? Everything. There was no change in human biology, but a major social change depending on which sex discovered what. Since men had been hunting, men were the inventors of systematic herding. Since women had been gathering plants, women were the inventors of systematic agriculture.

> It is generally accepted that owing to her ancient role as the gatherer of vegetable foods, woman was responsible for the invention and development of agriculture. Modern analogies indicate that so long as the ground was prepared by hoeing and not by ploughing woman remained the cultivator.[13]

---

[12] Quoted in ibid., p. 38.
[13] Hawkes and Woolley, op. cit., p. 265.

The business of learning agriculture, selection, planting, weeding, and so forth was an extended process that took place over many hundreds of thousands of years. To accomplish it, women had to invent many other things besides methods of cultivation and better hoes. They learned enough chemistry to make pottery that would hold water and could be cooked in. "It has never been doubted that . . . pottery was both shaped and decorated by women."[14] Women learned enough mechanics to construct looms for spinning textiles, as well as better ways of home building (which is a purely feminine occupation in some neolithic tribes). They also learned—and shaped tools for—grinding wheat, constructing ovens, and using the biochemistry of yeast to make bread.

In mainly agricultural societies of the primitive hoe type, women were the most important food providers. The meat provided by male hunters was much less in quantity and more unstable in supply. As a result, women had a very high status: "The earliest Neolithic societies throughout their range in time and space gave woman the highest status she had ever known."[15] Of course, in class-divided societies the fact that a group does a lot of work does not mean it has high status—quite the contrary. But these societies were still communal, doing work collectively without rulers or bosses. The group that performed a task made all the decisions concerning it. Therefore, the fact that women were often the main food-providing group meant that they made many of the most important social decisions.[16]

Just as the high status of women is strongly correlated with primitive agriculture, so too is the existence of matrilineal clans. When the number of people in a tribe grew to 300 or 400, the old anarchical family structure was no longer possible. The denser population that resulted from agricultural productivity required a new form of organization. The anarchical family was replaced, at a very early date in many places, by the clan system. The evidence from contemporary primitive tribes indicates that they are composed of groups of clans, with the family being of little social importance. Everyone in the clan is supposed to be descended from some mythical ancestor. This an-

[14] Ibid., p. 331.
[15] Ibid., p. 264.
[16] Leacock, op. cit., p. 34.

cestor is their symbol or "totem," which may be a plant or animal important in the economic life of the tribe.[17] The clan system lasted through the Neolithic Revolution. The clan, not the family, normally held the land in common. An individual "family" might be allocated a plot, but only for immediate use and usually for one year only. Pastures were always held in common by the whole clan, as is still the case in many primitive agricultural societies.

Where a society is almost totally dependent on agriculture and women do most of this work, descent and kinship are usually calculated from the female—that is, the clan is matrilineal. Where a society is primarily based on animal herding and men do most of this work, descent and kinship are usually calculated from the male—that is, the clan is patrilineal.[18] Matriliny, early agriculture, and female influence are highly but not perfectly correlated, as are patriliny, herding, and male influence.

Many good examples of matrilineal societies in which women have a high status are found among American Indian cultures. The Hopi technology is similar to the technologies of the New Stone Age, as are their social relations. The Hopi have a matrilineal clan, the leadership of which is mainly in the hands of the older active women.[19] The family group includes the woman's brothers, but not the women who marry them. The whole clan owns the land together and there is no privileged class. The group of men collectively owns the livestock, but the group of women owns the houses, the furnishings, and all the vegetable food. Since vegetables provide most of the food supply, the women are socially and economically secure regardless of whether they are married or not.[20] A woman is always elected clan leader, though her brother leads all ceremonies.

Predominantly livestock-raising tribes were most likely to develop patrilineal clans, since male hunters first tamed animals. Men also invented new weapons and other implements needed for animal herding. In such clans, the family group is organized around and related to an older male. This man is usually, but not always, the dominant personality in the ex-

---

[17] Childe, op. cit., p. 53.
[18] Ibid., p. 73.
[19] Leavitt, op. cit., p. 398.
[20] Ibid.

tended family. Yet even where the man is dominant, there is not the demeaning subordination of women found in later class-divided and exploitive societies. So although no Neolithic community shows matriarchy, or all-out female dominance, neither does any Neolithic community show all-out male domination. Each sex continues to do its own important jobs in its own area; there is no oppression.

In a Neolithic community combining some agriculture and animal herding, the men probably cleared the land, built most of the homes, herded the animals, hunted, and manufactured weapons and some tools. The women did all the other agricultural work on the land, made the clothing, made all the pottery, ground the grains, and cooked the food.[21] In these communities men and women had a rough equality of status.

THE ADVENT OF SLAVERY

The Neolithic life was a hard life for all, but the relationship between men and women tended to be characterized by "dignity, freedom and mutual respect."[22] The clan had a collective economy and no slaves. How did all this change in a few thousand years?

Men provided milk and meat from cows, while women hoed the fields. Then great progress was made in lifting the burden of hoeing from women; animal power would be used instead. "The first step, perhaps, was to make a pair of oxen drag over a field a variant on the hoe that women had hitherto wielded—a plough."[23] Since men had tamed and herded the cattle and oxen, it was the man who followed the plough and thus took over the main agricultural duties. Agriculture was totally changed by the use of the plough from a female to a male occupation. This ended some of the hardest labor for women, but it also ended their control of the food supply and reduced their socioeconomic status.[24]

Women's shoulders, the oldest means of transport, were re-

---

[21] Childe, op. cit., p. 67.

[22] Kathleen Gough, "The Origin of the Family," in Rayna R. Reither, ed., *Toward An Anthropology of Women* (New York: Monthly Review Press, 1975), p. 75.

[23] Ibid., p. 88.

[24] Ibid., p. 89.

placed by animals pulling wheeled vehicles. Along with the animals came male drivers. Besides the wheel for vehicles, men also invented the potter's wheel; henceforth pottery was done by men. These male inventions helped women live better, but reduced their status. When women no longer carried the heaviest burdens, did most of the agriculture, and made the pottery, the new situation removed the economic bases of women's equal status. After men took over agriculture, transport, and pottery, as well as cattle raising, most societies became patriarchal. The male dominated the family or household, which included married sons and their families.

Yet even male economic dominance did not automatically mean the total subordination of women—any more than it did in the predominantly herding societies. What sealed the doom of women was the coming of slavery and/or serfdom, which ended both collective ownership and the matrilineal clan system. The clan system slowly gave way to individual families based on private property, beginning with the cattle owned by the male.[25] The process by which the patriarchal family replaced the matrilineal clan as the basic economic unit was always long and usually painful.

The new inventions utilizing animal power greatly increased human productivity. When, in addition, bronze was substituted for wood and stone, a worker could for the first time produce more than his or her own subsistence. This meant that a surplus of food and other wealth could be accumulated. It meant that specialists could concentrate on one task, such as metalworking, while others could produce food. It meant, above all, that it became profitable to keep slaves or serfs. Before a worker could produce a surplus, war prisoners were adopted or killed or eaten. When they could produce a surplus, however, they were made into slaves or serfs to be exploited for their master's benefit.

As some men accumulated wealth in goods or cattle or slaves, they gained the power to oppose the democratic and collective clan structure. The ancient commune was poisoned by class division, private property became the rule, and internal government and armed forces were formed to support the rule of the wealthy owners over the slaves and serfs. The formerly temporarily elected war chief could consolidate his position

[25] Leacock, op. cit., pp. 40–41.

as ruler with this new wealth. Moreover, the male chief found ways to give his sons not only his private wealth but also his authority, and this ruling line of wealth and power finally became hereditary.[26]

In such societies, even ruling-class women came to be treated as property, the same as slaves and serfs, sometimes more valuable, sometimes less so. Woman's value declined both because slaves could do the productive work and because slave women could be used for sexual pleasure. The double standard was instituted whereby a husband could have sex with any woman but the wife was to be strictly monogamous. The reason for the strict control and seclusion of wives was to ensure that only legitimate sons inherited the private wealth.

Ancient slavery

In ancient Greece, slave women sometimes worked in the fields, but most did household drudgery. They were completely the property of the patriarch, who could enjoy them sexually at will. Some of the women were allowed slave husbands, but they were still at the master's pleasure—and their children could be taken and sold at any time. Yet it was a crime for any women of the household to have sex with a stranger. In Homer's *Odyssey,* when Odysseus returns home, he first kills his wife's suitors. Then he discovers that 12 of his servant women have had sex (he was gone ten years), so he orders his son Telemachus: "Take the women out of the hall . . . and use your long swords on them, till none are left alive to remember their lover and the hours they stole in these young gallants' arms."[27] Thus, he punishes his property.

Later, in Athenian Greece, 80 percent of all women were slave women; that is, property. The slave owner's wife was to be seen, not heard. She was well-off materially, but even in so-called democratic fifth-century Athens, she was not to leave the house. Women were completely secluded—as in some Islamic countries today—and were prohibited from any role in the active political life of the city.[28] She was secluded not because of romantic love (a modern concept), but to ensure legitimate heirs. In ancient Greece, even in the ruling-class

---

[26] Childe, op. cit., p. 95.
[27] Quoted in Julia O'Faolain and Lauro Martines, eds., *Not in God's Image* (New York: Harper & Row, 1973), p. 4.
[28] Childe, op. cit., p. 216.

woman's own home, she could not be present at her own dinner parties unless everyone present was a family member. Moreover, she was required to spend most of her day in the "gynaeceum," an isolated area of the house that was off limits to any stranger.[29]

Woman's place was in the home with children. Demosthenes said: "Mistresses we keep for our pleasure, concubines for daily attendance upon our person, wives to bear us legitimate children and be our faithful housekeepers."[30] While women were secluded to bear "legitimate children," men were out on the town having sex where they pleased. Euripides has Medea say: "If a man grows tired of the company at home, he can go out, and find a cure for tediousness. We wives are forced to look to one man only."[31] This was the double standard with a vengeance. For lower-class and slave women, life was very different. Many, often against their will or from dire necessity, were forced to become prostitutes, mistresses, or concubines.

The ruling-class man did not stay at home with his wife. Concern with household matters was considered demeaning. He spent his time in the market or the forum or the public baths, talking about economics and politics with other men. Women had no political rights in "democratic" Greece. They could not make contracts for more than a bushel of barley. They must always have a legal guardian, father or husband or someone appointed. The guardian could give a woman in marriage and could even will her to someone else at his death. Moreover, a man could easily divorce a wife, provided only that he returned her dowry to her father or other guardian. A woman could get a divorce only on rare occasions under extreme provocation. The husband owned all the property and slaves, and his sons inherited most of it. Ruling-class women usually learned to read and write, but higher education was reserved for boys. Slaves were never educated, except where their job necessitated it.

FEUDALISM

In Western Europe, slavery was followed by feudalism. Under feudalism, human beings were no longer owned by other hu-

---

[29] Cornelius Nepos, quoted in O'Faolain and Martines, op. cit., p. 16.
[30] Quoted in ibid., p. 9.
[31] Quoted in ibid., p. 15.

man beings; rather, serfdom prevailed. Serfs were slightly better off than slaves in that they were not owned, but merely bound to the landlord's land. Serf men and women had to labor a certain number of days a year for the landlord; in return, he was supposed to "protect" them. In the earliest period, serfs did need protection from wandering barbarian tribes, but later they needed protection only from the economic and sexual exploitation of the landlords. The landlords, in turn, held their land at the pleasure of the feudal nobility, to whom they owed military support. The same hierarchy of obligations continued through the lesser nobility, to the greater nobility, and thence to the king, who owed allegiance only to God.

The nobility was divided into the secular and the religious nobles. The Church was the largest single landowner, the holder of most accumulated knowledge, and the greatest power in Europe during this period. The Church had a very low opinion of women. In the first century, St. Paul said: "The head of the woman is the man. . . . For a man . . . is the image and glory of God. . . . I suffer not a woman to teach, nor to usurp authority over the man, but to be in silence."[32] A few hundred years later, St. Augustine repeated the notion: "The woman herself is not the image of God; whereas the man alone is the image of God. . . ."[33] Finally, in the thirteenth century, St. Thomas Aquinas could still write: "As regards the individual nature, woman is defective and misbegotten, for the active force in the male seed tends to the production of a perfect likeness in the masculine sex; while the production of woman comes from a defect in the active force. . . ."[34]

Although the Church stated clearly that women were the weaker and inferior sex, that did not stop either secular or religious landlords from working their serf women in the fields the same as the men. Women did every kind of agricultural labor except heavy plowing. In England, in 1265, a serf's widow had the following obligations to the lord of the manor: ". . . From Michaelmas to the Feast of St. Peter in Chains she must plow half an acre every week. . . . And from the Feast of St. John the Baptist until August she must perform manual service 3 days every week. . . ."[35] She was also required one day a

---

[32] Quoted in ibid., p. 128.
[33] Quoted in ibid., p. xi.
[34] Quoted in ibid., p. 131.
[35] An old manual, quoted in ibid., pp. 160–161.

week to transport goods on her back anywhere the bailiff told her to go. In addition, she must find four days in the spring to mow the landlord's meadow, four more days to gather hay for him, and two more days for weeding his land. In some places, female serfs were exempted from work on the lord's land, but that only meant they did most of the work on the serf's own plot.

Female serfs were also used in the lords' homes. Their lot was described by an English Franciscan monk in the thirteenth century. He stated that the domestic serf or chambermaid had to do the heaviest and foulest jobs, was given the poorest food and clothing, had to marry whomever the lord told her to marry, and had to give her children to the lord as serfs. The monk stated matter-of-factly: "Chambermaids are frequently beaten, . . . they rebel against their masters and mistresses and get out of hand if they are not kept down. . . . Serfs and that sort are kept in place only through fear."[36]

During the early feudal era even free women and the wives and daughters of lords had little freedom. One important outlet for women was the nunnery. There, serf women still did all the hardest work but were protected from male exploitation. Upper-class women had the opportunity to get an education, which they were otherwise denied. Furthermore, they could live their own lives, practice management and business, and assume leadership roles respected by the whole community. From the sixth to the twelfth centuries, nuns were treated on an equal basis with male monks. In fact, the women who headed the larger nunneries often were the representatives of the king or the pope in that area. They had judicial powers to try and to sentence people, and they sometimes even raised armies. Education and scholarship were highly regarded, so there were some famous women scholars at a time when most people lived in total ignorance.

In later periods, the Protestant Reformation closed many nunneries, but by this time increased urbanization and the spread of commerce and industry had opened up new opportunities for upper-class women. The wives of some of the powerful lords themselves grasped power when their husbands were frequently away fighting wars. Some of the crafts in the cities were opened to women. However, in most of the guilds, which

[36] Quoted in ibid., p. 163.

were a sort of combined monopoly and trade union organization of small craftsmen, women were not admitted to full status—and everywhere women were paid lower wages. Yet in Paris, by 1300, five different crafts were completely dominated by women, some of whom accumulated considerable fortunes. Women monopolized weaving and spinning in most of Europe—hence the name "spinster" for older unmarried women. Women in England were also barbers, apothecaries, armorers, shipwrights, and tailors.[37] By the late medieval period, a few bourgeois women were in business for themselves as wholesale and retail merchants.

As early as the thirteenth century, the rise of embryonic capitalist relations caused some improvements in the lives of well-to-do bourgeois women, due to their greater economic strength. They were still treated, however, as inferiors. There were legal changes that allowed a married woman who was engaged in trade to be considered legally as a *femme sole* or single woman.[38] In other words, feudal law gave married women no rights, so when women began to go into business they were treated as if they were single. As women went into commerce on a wider scale, both the legal and the social position of women began to rise, although very slowly. Even the non-businesswoman who was married to a bourgeois husband had a wide range of duties, including acting as a doctor for her family and taking over the family business when necessary. Under these conditions, some increased respect between husband and wife began to appear.

Although women played a greater economic role in the feudal period than stereotypes would grant, they continued to be fettered legally and prohibited from participating in public life, as they had been under slavery. Married women had no power over property and no power to make contracts. Men managed and had complete power over all the family property. A late sixteenth-century English lawyer wrote:

> Every Feme Covert [married woman] is a sort of infant. . . . It is seldom, almost never that a married woman can have any action to

---

[37] See A. Abram, "Women Traders in Medieval London," in Susan Bell, ed., *Women: From the Greeks to the French Revolution* (Belmont, Calif.: Wadsworth, 1973), p. 153.

[38] Eileen Power, "The Position of Women," in ibid., p. 163. Ms. Power has written a great deal on medieval women in other books and articles.

use her wit only in her own name: her husband is her stern, her prime mover, without whom she cannot do much at home, and less abroad. . . . It is a miracle that a wife should commit any suit without her husband.[39]

The only exception, even in the late feudal period, was the right of a married woman engaged in trade to make certain binding contracts. Acts making this possible were not passed till the fifteenth century. Only in the seventeenth century did the equity courts of England devise ways for rich women to hold separate property while married. In most areas, in the feudal period, even widows did not usually have ownership of family property but could use it only in their lifetimes as trustees for their male children. The only woman who regained full rights to property and contractual rights was the childless widow.

Among the feudal lords, all marriages were arranged by the parents, often while the children were still in their cradles. The important criteria for a good marriage were the joining of another family's land and military power. Love had nothing to do with it. In the late feudal period, when bourgeois families first emerged into riches and power, the same custom prevailed. Marriages were arranged on the basis of the relative fortunes of different families. Again, love had nothing to do with it.

The feudal lords also generally had the right to decide whom their underlords and ladies should marry. They even had the right to decide whom a widow should marry—though she had to be given a year to herself. The lesser lords, in turn, might decide whom their serfs should marry. On the whole, though, no one cared whom a serf married because no land or power was involved. The father of a serf sometimes decided whom the son or daughter would marry but sometimes didn't pay any attention. In fact, many serfs lived together without marriage. Thus at least a few serfs may have married or lived together for love (though there is no evidence one way or the other).

Since marriage was not founded on "love," even in theory, divorces were never granted for incompatibility, nor in fact were divorces granted for any reason under Church law. A

---

[39] Quoted in O'Faolain and Martines, op. cit., p. 145.

marriage might be annulled for very specific reasons: fraud in the marriage contract, nonconsummation of marriage, or the parties' being too close relatives. A legal separation might be granted for adultery or leprosy, but not much else. Only in very rare cases in which the woman's family was very powerful would a legal separation be granted for extreme brutality and cruelty. A "normal" amount of violence against the wife was expected. A writer in late thirteenth-century France said: "In a number of cases men may be excused for the injuries they inflict on their wives, nor should the law intervene. Provided he neither kills or maims her, it is legal for a man to beat his wife when she wrongs him—for instance, when she is about to surrender her body to another man, when she contradicts or abuses him, or when she refuses, like a decent woman, to obey his reasonable commands."[40] Her husband was her lord, so if she attacked him she was a traitor. She could be burned at the stake if she killed him for any reason; he could kill her for adultery.

Changing attitudes toward love and sex

Since almost all marriages were marriages of convenience, arranged by the parents, it was assumed that they involved no romantic love. Thus the concept of romantic love in literature first arises for the extramarital liaisons of wandering knights or troubadours with the love- and sex-starved wives of lords. It is this image of medieval love that comes down to us. It includes knights chivalrously saving ladies from ogres, eternal but unsatisfied devotion, and serenades.

As we have seen, this image bore no relation to the usual marriage under feudalism. It might be added that the religious lords were supposed to be celibate, so their sexual activity was an even greater transgression of God's law. The songs of chivalrous love seem to reflect only the frustrations of the ruling-class women and the illegal desires (and activities) of some of the men. Of course such extramarital sex was mostly condoned for men but not for women.

The view of romantic love mixed with marriage began to have a little more substance only when a middle class grew common in the cities of the late feudal period:

---

[40] Quoted in ibid., p. 175.

> The aristocracy and the upper classes of the towns tended to regard sex with the greedy cynicism and tolerant amusement we find in Boccaccio's stories. . . . On the other hand, the artisan class in the towns followed a life-pattern that gave new meaning to marriage. The growth of craft production established a mutuality of interest within the family. The master of a trade performed his tasks at home, assisted by his wife and children.[41]

In these circumstances, the woman assumed a more important role in the family, ensuring its survival if the man died. In such families the woman was treated somewhat more equally, and marriage for love or at least the development of love within marriage became a little more common.

Nevertheless, the double standard carried over from feudalism to modern capitalism; the following description of sexist views of women might characterize the early twentieth century as well as it characterized the thirteenth century in Western European society: "The degradation of women is based on class distinctions, and is exhibited in the treatment of the upper-class woman as a prized sexual object as well as the assumption that women of the less privileged classes are available to the conquering male for casual gratification."[42] The only difference was that some of this was institutionalized in the feudal period. For example, the feudal lord had the right of the first night, the right to have the first sexual intercourse with the new bride of a serf—though it was often bought off by a monetary tribute in the later feudal period.

Witches

Partly because of their double oppression, serf women generally played a major role in the peasant rebellions and protest movements. In some areas where heretics tried to found more egalitarian communities, there were much more equal relationships between men and women. As a consequence, the first charge against them was always "free love." Similarly, when the peasants organized nocturnal assemblies pledged to rebellion against lay and clerical lords, the leading role of women in them allowed their enemies often to describe them as "witches' sabbaths." Women were the main doctors and healers

[41] John Howard Lawson, *The Hidden Heritage* (New York: Citadel, 1968), p. 57.
[42] Ibid., p. 60.

for several centuries, and this also gave those in power a chance to persecute them as witches. Because of the ignorance of the times, all medical cures were ascribed to magic. "The idea of the woman as a witch—which led to such brutal persecutions over the centuries—is in part a superstitious acknowledgement of her special medical skill. But the more profound reason for accusations of sorcery lay in the fear of the woman's social influence, her role in organizing protest against oppression, and the necessity of *keeping her in her place.*"[43]

[43] Ibid., p. 61.

WOMEN IN CAPITALIST AND SOCIALIST SOCIETIES

9

In the last chapter, we saw that women's status underwent great changes from prehistoric times to the end of the feudal era. In this chapter, the changes from the end of feudalism to the present will be traced and the position of women in some contemporary societies will then be surveyed.

THE TRANSITION TO CAPITALISM

In the fourteenth and fifteenth centuries, some of the forms of commercial capitalism began to appear in Northern Italy and Flanders (Holland and Belgium). In the towns of these areas, the new socioeconomic conditions gave rise to that whirlwind of change in ideas known as the Renaissance. One major strain of the Renaissance was the humanist ideas expressed by scholars like Erasmus. The humanists particularly emphasized that the widest possible education leads to the greatest virtue. For the first time a large number of writers argued for educating women as well as men, both for their own sakes and for the further education of their children. In 1516 Thomas More wrote in his *Utopia* that women must be educated equally with men, though some books were more appropriate to one sex and some to the other.[1]

The humanist prescriptions were actually put into effect for most upper-class Western European women. This education and new appreciation for women's minds resulted in a large

---

[1] See excerpts of humanist writers in Susan Bell, ed., *Women: From the Greeks to the French Revolution* (Belmont, Calif.: Wadsworth, 1973), part 5.

number of famous women scholars and doers in this period. In Italy Beatrice d'Este (1475–1497) showed considerable political skill. Her sister Isabella (1474–1539) brought order and affluence to her husband's impoverished estate and used the new wealth to become the patron of many great poets and artists. In Spain, Queen Isabella (1451–1504) successfully unified Spain, founded new universities, subsidized scholars, and funded Columbus's expedition. Princess Marguerite of Angoulême in France (1492–1549) encouraged and protected many humanist scholars as well as some of the persecuted Protestant reformers. She was a writer of note, including in her works both lofty poems of mystical religious beauty and a book of lewd stories, the *Heptameron*, which has been compared with Boccaccio's *Decameron*. Yet she also found time to deal carefully with statesmen and ambassadors on behalf of her brother, the king of France.

Another woman who played a very important political role was Catherine de Medici (1519–1589), the niece of a powerful pope and herself regent of France. Still another worthy of mention was Elizabeth I of England (1533–1603), whose education was of the highest caliber. Her tutor gave her the sexist compliment that "the constitution of her mind is exempt from female weakness, and she is endowed with a masculine power of application. No apprehension can be quicker than hers, no memory more retentive."[2] There was much more than flattery. She kept peace between the warring English factions, actively led England to a successful defense against the Spanish Armada, and encouraged the great artists and writers of what we call the Elizabethan period.

Unfortunately, this early rise in the status of women was cut short by the increasing religious bigotry during the wars accompanying the Protestant Reformation. The Protestant preachers gave thunderous sermons against sinful wives. Their very practical advice told husbands how to keep their wives meek and subservient.[3] Thus much of the feminine advance, but not all of it, was set back in the sixteenth and seventeenth centuries. The Protestant sects particularly saw the husband as the secular ruler and religious head of his household, charged with making sure that the whole household was obedient to

[2] Quoted in ibid., p. 215.
[3] Ibid., p. 200.

the desires of king and church. Women could still own no property, were expected to be silent, and were required to obey their husbands and God.

Yet at the same time the Reformation led to greater political participation by some women—those who participated in the most radical religious sects. At this time the political spectrum was represented in the spectrum of religious sects. The more radical sects—the Brownists, the Baptists, the Quakers, for example—did strive for socioeconomic as well as religious change. All agreed that women should have spiritual equality, though none argued for social equality. As a result, many women joined these sects and played a prominent role in their struggles. In them women could express themselves publicly; they learned more about the world, and many emancipated themselves from the restrictions of the family—though those who were married still had to render obedience to their husbands.

St. Paul had prohibited women from preaching. Yet by the 1630s and 1640s, women were preachers in the radical sects in Holland, England, and Massachusetts. There were so many women among the Quakers that it was first thought the sect was limited to women.[4] Women were important among the Quakers even in the universities, and in the 1670s they started to hold their own women's meetings and to send delegates to take part in the church's governing bodies.

Women also played a major role in the Revolution of 1640 to 1666 that ended feudalism in England. Upper-class women took over estates when their husbands were exiled and directly helped them escape. Many working-class women joined the radical Levellers. In 1649 their leader, Lilbourne, and three other leaders were arrested: "When the men durst not any more petition in behalf of Lilbourne and his associates, the women took it up."[5]

During the sixteenth and seventeenth centuries, capitalism was spreading throughout Western Europe. Many bourgeois women became involved in business in town and country. Willy-nilly, education—at least the learning of arithmetic—spread to these women. In Holland, women learned accounting and kept the books in most businesses.

---

[4] Ibid., p. 226.

[5] Quoted in Julia O'Faolain and Lauro Martines, eds., *Not in God's Image* (New York: Harper & Row, 1973), p. 268.

Still, there was plenty of resistance to the education of women; many men insisted they should be kept in their place in the home. Molière satirized these sentiments when he had a man in his play *Les Femmes Savantes* (1672) say:

> I'm speaking to you, sister. . . . I don't like all these useless books of yours. Apart from that big Plutarch that keeps my neckbands pressed, you should burn them all. . . . It's not decent . . . for a woman to study and know so much. Teaching her children good principles, running her household, keeping an eye on her servants, and managing her budget thriftily are all the study and philosophy she needs.[6]

Meanwhile, working-class women of town and country were kept too busy to even entertain the possibility of an education. In 1555, Sir Anthony Fitzherbert explained carefully the chores a good country wife should do:

> First set all things in good order within thy house, milk the kine, suckle thy calves, strain up thy milk . . . get corn and malt ready for the mill to make and brew. . . . Thou must make butter and cheese when thou may, serve thy swine both morning and evening . . . take heed how thy hens, ducks, and geese do lay. . . . In the beginning of March is time for a wife to make her garden and to get as many good seeds and herbs as she can. . . . March is time to sow flax and hemp . . . to help her husband to fill the muck wain or dung cart, drive the plow, to load hay, corn and such other.[7]

THE ENLIGHTENMENT AND THE FRENCH REVOLUTION

The English Revolution of 1648 ended feudalism in one country, helped raise the status of women, and produced several philosophers, like John Locke, who were dedicated to equality and freedom. The American Revolution of 1776 ended colonial control in another country, spread revolutionary ideas of liberty and the pursuit of happiness for all, and encouraged some people to raise the question of women's rights (see the next chapter). But the French Revolution—which was influenced directly and indirectly by the English and American revolutions—had a much wider and more profound impact on all of Europe and the United States. It ended feudalism and encouraged capitalism and parliamentarianism over a wide part of Europe.

[6] Quoted in ibid., pp. 244–245.
[7] Quoted in ibid., p. 253.

More important, perhaps, its philosophers, like Voltaire and Rousseau, put on everyone's tongue the ideas of liberty, equality, and *fraternité,* or brotherhood.

These philosophers of enlightenment spoke only of brotherhood, not sisterhood. Some of them, like Condorcet, did speak in favor of women's rights, but they were in the minority. Many spoke of liberty and equality for all *men* but continued to hold an utterly reactionary position on women. This position was stated baldly by Jean-Jacques Rousseau in *Emile,* his manual on education:

> Men and women are made for each other, but their mutual dependence is not equal. . . . We could survive without them better than they could without us. . . . Thus women's entire education should be planned in relation to men. To please men, to be useful to them, to win their love and respect, to raise them as children, care for them as adults, counsel and console them, make their lives sweet and pleasant; these are women's duties in all ages and these are what they should be taught from childhood.[8]

In spite of such male attitudes, women did play a role in the French Revolution. Upper-class women held "salons," meeting places for the elite and the intelligentsia, in which a vast amount of criticism was voiced and digested. Much of the critical discussion of the seventeenth century was literary and artistic, but by the eighteenth century many of the salons turned to religious, philosophical, and finally political criticism. Many of the ideas of the Enlightenment and the Revolution were first discussed in these salons, which played the role the news media play today. Many of the initial contacts necessary for the Revolution were made in these salon gatherings. The salon of Madame Roland, for example, became the intellectual center of the Girondin party.

During the Revolution itself, working-class women played a very important part. Since feeding the family was seen as a feminine role, they were the leaders in the bread riots that formed the background of the Revolution. And many women took part in storming the Bastille and liberating its prisoners.

Moreover, women finally found voice to speak for themselves. In 1789, the French Assembly proclaimed the Rights

---

[8] Quoted in ibid., pp. 246–247.

of Man. In 1791, Olympe de Gouges replied with a *Declaration of the Rights of Woman:*

> Woman is born free and her rights are the same as those of man. . . . The law must be an expression of the general will; all citizens, men and women alike, must participate in making it. . . . Women have the right to go to the scaffold; they must also have the right to go to parliament. . . .[9]

One of the most remarkable people of her time was Mary Wollstonecraft, an English writer and activist. At a time when most women stayed in the home and were uneducated, she made a living by writing novels, critical essays, and book reviews. She lived an independent life, despite the economic and social constraints on women; she lived with a man without marriage for some time; participated in an artistic and liberal discussion circle on an equal basis; married a leading anarchist philosopher (William Godwin); and was the mother of Mary Shelley (author of *Frankenstein* and wife of the poet Percy Bysshe Shelley). When married, she continued to live in a separate residence and to act and write independently.

When the French Revolution broke out, its liberal philosophy and actions were attacked by the conservative Edmund Burke. Wollstonecraft wrote *A Vindication of the Rights of Men* which was the first reply to Burke. She even went to France in order to live in a freer country. Most important of all, in 1792, Wollstonecraft wrote *A Vindication of the Rights of Woman.* This book reflected the liberal ideas of Locke and Voltaire and Rousseau, but argued that they must now be applied equally to women. It was the first full-scale book favoring women's liberation, and nineteenth-century leaders of the women's movement in Europe and the United States read it and were much affected by it. Wollstonecraft argued that human limitations are given not by nature but by social environment, that men *and* women can learn anything if they are given the opportunity. She described the average woman as totally subordinate and dehumanized by social constraints and lack of education. She speaks of the constraints and limitations on women's education and opportunities in very personal terms, as she suffered most of them in her early years. Women, she claimed, had been reduced to sex objects: "the toy of man, his rattle, and

[9] Quoted in ibid., p. 307.

it must jingle in his ears whenever, dismissing reason, he chooses to be amused."[10]

Although Wollstonecraft accepted Rousseau's liberal philosophy, she wrote a detailed critique of his views on women's education, tearing them to shreds as a piece of sexist nonsense. As a substitute, she expressed some of the earliest ideas on progressive education for both male and female, rich and poor. Her earlier works argued for the fullest education possible for middle-class and upper-class women. She later became aware of and exposed the crimes against working-class women, their miseries, and their need for liberation. In her *Rights of Women* she wrote: "It is time to effect a revolution in female manners—time to restore to them their lost dignity—and make them, as part of the human species, labour by reforming themselves, to reform the world."[11]

WOMEN UNDER FRENCH CAPITALISM

In 1787, on the eve of the French Revolution, an economic study in France showed that working women in manufacturing made only 15 sous a day. The cost of a day's food was at least 14 or 15 sous, so they had no money for anything but food. The average wage for men was twice as much, or 30 sous, so women were dependent on men for survival. A petition to the king in 1789 by women described their lot: "If nature has not granted them good looks, they get married . . . to unfortunate artisans and drag out a grueling existence in the depths of the provinces, producing children whom they are unable to bring up. If . . . they are pretty, . . . they fall prey to the first seducer, make one slip, come to Paris to conceal it, . . . and end up dying as victims of debauchery."[12]

After the Revolution, there were three interrelated changes. First, the feudal nobility were destroyed and the political balance swung to the bourgeoisie. Second, feudal economic relations were replaced by capitalist ones; that is, serf labor was replaced by "free" labor. Capitalists hired, if it looked profit-

---

[10] Quoted from Wollstonecraft, "Vindication," in Eleanor Flexner, *Mary Wollstonecraft* (Baltimore: Penguin, 1973). Flexner's is an excellent, moving biography, a delightful experience to read.
[11] Ibid., p. 151.
[12] Quoted in O'Faolain and Martines, op. cit., p. 305.

able, free men and women; the workers were free to work for what the capitalists offered, or starve. Third, the Industrial Revolution meant a vast increase in all of Western Europe (though less in France than in England) of jobs in industry and commerce and resulted in a great population movement from rural to urban areas.

These changes did eventually affect women, but for a long time the effects were hardly noticeable. A study in 1840 found that women still worked 15 hours a day; they were still paid about the same 15 sous a day; and men still earned about twice as much. "Generally speaking, a man can earn enough to save, but a woman scarcely makes enough to subsist on and a child of less than twelve years hardly earns the price of his food."[13] Since machinery required less physical strength, employers hired more women and children, who could be paid very little for very long hours. Yet since the whole family could survive if all its members worked, capitalists were able to reduce the wages of men accordingly.

In 1793, there were still many women active in political clubs (the main driving force of the Revolution), such as the club of Revolutionary Republican Women, but in that year all the women's clubs were suppressed. Women's participation in politics was violently opposed during the whole nineteenth century. In government employment, women were only allowed to be schoolmasters and postmasters. The Napoleonic Code gave all management of family funds to the husband, punished female but not male adultery, and did not allow a married woman to bring suit without her husband's permission. The Revolutionary Assembly legalized divorce in 1792, but reaction resulted in a reversal in 1814, when divorce was again forbidden. Legalizing legislation was not finally passed till 1884.

The awful conditions and wages of working women inspired the first socialist women's liberationist; in 1843, Flora Tristan wrote a pamphlet called the *Workers' Union.* In it she advocated both socialism and equal rights for women in politics, education, and work. She admitted that the bourgeoisie resisted her socialism, while the workers resisted her ideas on women's liberation.

In 1849, two women socialists formed a workers' union dedicated to women's liberation and socialism. They and the men

---

[13] Contemporary statistician, quoted in ibid., p. 309.

who joined it were arrested for forming a political association, which was a crime, and sent to prison. The two women, Jeanne Deroin and Pauline Roland, had also launched the first feminist socialist newspaper, *L'Opinion des Femmes.* The newspaper and union were formed in the aftermath of the Revolution of 1848. But the return of reaction in 1851, when they had just gotten out of prison, forced them into exile. No more political activity was undertaken by women until the Paris Commune of 1871, when many women participated and were killed along with the men.

Only very slowly did middle-class women in France win any rights. During the 1870s, they were finally admitted to French universities. Women were allowed to practice medicine by 1875 but not to practice law until 1900. Married women could not dispose of their own earnings until 1907, and they had no independent legal capacity until 1938. Women were not allowed to vote in France until after the liberation from German fascism in 1944!

French women had struggled for the vote ever since 1870, when universal suffrage was granted to men. In 1885, Madame Barbarousse claimed that the law said "all French" *(tout français)* were enfranchised, so women could also vote; but the court held that *tout français* did not include French women.

In spite of the barriers, some French women did distinguish themselves. The most outstanding was Marie Curie, one of only two people ever to receive *two* Nobel prizes. She received the prize for physics jointly with her husband in 1903 and won the chemistry prize by herself in 1911.

Yet France has been more backward than England or the United States in women's rights, the general status of women, and even the number of women working. In 1970, women constituted only 33 percent of the French labor force. The lesser industrialization of France in part accounts for this backwardness, but some of the blame must rest on the reactionary pressure of the Catholic Church and its ideology.

A French woman was not allowed to hold her own bank account or receive mail without her husband's permission until 1965. Only in 1969 did the law allow her an equal say in how to bring up her children—in case of disagreement, the man's decision is still final. As of 1973, there were still only 7 women among the 490 members of the National Assembly.

Even the 1969 laws were obtained only because of the anger

and organized efforts of the French women's liberation movement. Almost all of the French movement has been socialist, and mostly Marxist. Small groups formed in late 1968, influenced both by American women and by their own revolutionary experiences in the May rebellion against the government. Yet when they held their first major demonstration at Vincennes University in 1970, they met violent opposition from men, including radicals: "We had been prepared for significant opposition from men, even afraid of it; but even so we were not prepared for such depth and breadth of outrage. Here were 'movement' men shouting insults at us: 'lesbians,' 'strip,' 'What you need is a good fuck. . . .' "[14]

There are now many women's liberation groups in Paris and in provincial cities. They advocate equality for women in a socialist society and demand publicly run child care centers and the right of women to abortion (a very sensitive subject in a Catholic country). They have attacked the sexist image of women in the media. There is some mention of equality in professional and political jobs, but the main emphasis is on the needs of working women.

WOMEN UNDER BRITISH CAPITALISM

The Industrial Revolution was most rapid in England. It reduced physical work requirements and brought women and children into the factories and the mines—where they could crawl into smaller tunnels than men. Employers generally tried to hire the whole family for the same wage they had previously paid the man alone. The Victorian ethic proclaimed that the family should instill discipline and hard work and that women should produce many children. A number of Protestant sects preached against any freedom for women of the working classes.

Working conditions were so bad and wages so low that thousands of women were forced into prostitution. Men have always had a double standard toward this institution. On the one hand, they condemn the poor women forced into prostitution, and applaud every time the police round them up. On the other hand, society seldom arrests the man who patronizes prostitutes or the pimps and organized criminals who make most of the

[14] A French woman quoted in Juliet Mitchell, *Woman's Estate* (New York: Pantheon, 1971), p. 86.

profits from prostitution. Men often defend it on the sewer theory, first enunciated by St. Augustine: "Rid society of prostitutes, and licentiousness will run riot throughout. . . . Prostitutes in a city are like a sewer in a palace. If you get rid of the sewer, the whole palace becomes filthy and foul."[15] Throughout the Industrial Revolution, women remained at the bottom of society, both as prostitutes and as workers in the dirtiest jobs.

In the England of the early nineteenth century, women still had few legal rights. In 1840 a judge ruled:

> The question raised in this case is, simply, whether by common law the husband, in order to prevent his wife from eloping, has a right to confine her in his own dwelling-house, and restrain her from liberty, for an indefinite time, using no cruelty. . . . There can be no doubt . . . "the husband hath by law power and dominion over his wife, and may keep her by force . . . and may beat her, but not in a violent or cruel manner."[16]

Moreover, a husband could get a divorce on the ground that his wife committed adultery, but a woman could get a divorce only on the grounds that her husband committed adultry *and* extreme cruelty. Only Parliament could grant divorces and almost all divorces were granted to men. Only four women got divorces in 200 years; all four were cases of incest and/or bigamy plus adultery plus cruelty. In the first case, the woman's husband had committed adultery with her sister. Yet divorce was *rejected* for a Ms. Dawson, where it was admitted that her husband committed adultery and beat her with a horsewhip and hairbrush.

Only very slowly and under pressure from organized women's protests were any changes made. In 1856, 26,000 women petitioned Parliament to allow married women to keep their own earnings and inherited property.[17] In 1857, divorced women were finally granted the same rights as single women; married women obtained these rights only by slow degrees in Acts of 1870, 1882, and 1893. These acts concentrated mainly on property ownership and benefited primarily the middle-class women who constituted most of the women's movement up to that point.

---

[15] Quoted in O'Faolain and Martines, op. cit., p. 290.
[16] Quoted in ibid., p. 318.
[17] Ibid., p. 331.

The distinguishing feature of the British scene that affected the women's movement was the very strong hold of elitism and upper-class control of the political process. Thus in much of the nineteenth century, radicals were concerned primarily with extending the vote to working-class men (who were barred by property qualifications) and only secondarily concerned with suffrage for women. On the other hand, many conservatives wanted to extend suffrage to aristocratic or propertied women to increase the vote of the Conservative party. Since the Liberals feared this increase, they opposed all measures that would have enfranchised single women who were property owners. The Liberal politician Lord Acton wrote: "Girls and widows are Tories, and channels of clerical influence."[18]

The first British women's political groups formed in the 1830s to combat slavery around the world. In the 1840s, middle-class women organized the first women's-rights groups in the industrial towns of Sheffield and Manchester—where many middle-class men were radicals because they felt left out of British political life. These groups were local and temporary. The first permanent group was the Manchester Women's Suffrage Committee, founded in 1867 by Lydia Becker. By 1868, more than 5000 Manchester women were organized for suffrage. And in 1869, unmarried women householders were given the right to vote in local elections. Ms. Becker fought for women's rights for the rest of her life and edited the *Woman Suffrage Journal* for 20 years.

At this time, middle-class women were beginning to enter the economy. Florence Nightingale helped found nursing as a proper profession for middle-class women. Thousands of women became schoolteachers and hundreds of thousands became office workers, bookkeepers, and typists.

On the basis of this economic activity, middle-class women exerted more and more pressure for suffrage. Harriet Taylor, whose husband was the philosopher John Stuart Mill, was one of the first writers in England to press for women's rights. In 1867, she persuaded her husband to move an amendment to an election reform bill in Parliament to give women the right to vote. It was defeated by 194 votes to 73, but the strength shown for it was a surprise to everyone. For the rest of the century, similar bills were introduced every year, but all were

---

[18] Quoted in Andrew Sinclair, *The Emancipation of the American Woman* (New York: Harper & Row, 1965), pp. 277–278.

unsuccessful. In 1868 Mill, with help from his wife, wrote *On the Subjection of Women,* in which he advocated equal political rights for women. Many conservative members of Parliament moved bills to enfranchise only propertied women, and these won majorities three times, but they never reached the necessary second reading because the government always took a neutral position on them.

In the 1880s and 1890s, the women's movement grew as Lydia Becker gathered all the local groups into a National Union of Women's Suffrage Societies. This group worked mainly for a limited suffrage restricted to educated middle-class women. There was still, however, unremitting opposition from much of Victorian society. Victoria herself, when she heard that a Lady Amberley had publicly demanded the vote, said: "The Queen is most anxious to enlist everyone who can speak or write to join in checking this mad, wicked folly of 'Woman's Rights' with all its attendant horrors, on which her poor feeble sex is bent, forgetting every sense of womanly feeling and propriety. Lady Amberley ought to get a good whipping."[19]

The women's movement picked up real steam when the militant Emmeline Pankhurst, widow of a radical Manchester Labourite, joined the fight for suffrage. She and her two daughters, Christabel and Sylvia, were at first socialists who worked through the Labour party. They were important enough to be widely slandered. Even a modern British historian, writing in 1971, describes them in an utterly sexist fashion; he is worried primarily over whether they were ladies. He writes:

> Mrs. Pankhurst was a lady, and a lady of immense determination, considerable skill in speaking and . . . [had] no regard for her health . . . or her life itself if they had to be sacrificed for the cause. Christabel was . . . very obviously good-looking, she had immense vitality, she had her mother's skill as a speaker; it was not quite so clear that she was a lady. Sylvia was fairly certainly not a lady.[20]

(Such cutesy writing characterizes most of the male historians of the women's movement, except when they very seriously worry about how many of the leaders were lesbians.)

---

[19] Ibid., p. 283.

[20] Trevor Lloyd, *Suffragettes International* (New York: American Heritage Press, 1971), p. 60.

The British Labour party refused to support the Pankhurst demand of suffrage for a limited number of middle-class women, most of whom would probably vote Conservative. Ms. Pankhurst and her daughters then formed the militant Women's Social and Political Union in 1903. It immediately derived considerable support from the women in the factories due to the efforts of Annie Kenney, herself a mill worker.

The Pankhursts decided that the previously respectable tactics of the suffrage movement would never get anywhere, that publicity was needed, and that spectacular actions would get publicity. In 1905 Christabel and Annie Kenney were arrested for causing a disturbance at a political meeting. In the following decade, hundreds of British women were arrested for stone throwing, hitting policemen (who hit them brutally in return), and chaining themselves to the railings in front of Number 10 Downing Street, the prime minister's residence. The police are usually very, very careful about upper-class women, but they brutally clubbed *any* women demonstrating for their rights. The press reacted with sympathy, as did the general public.

The women protesters particularly heckled Herbert Asquith, prime minister from 1908 to 1916, who bitterly opposed votes for women as a Conservative device. Many were imprisoned for ringing his bell as a nuisance. In 1907 there was a large, peaceful parade by moderate supporters of suffrage. Three days later a parade by the militants was attacked by mounted police who rode down many women. A Ms. Drummond was arrested for breaking into a cabinet meeting and yelling "votes for women." A Ms. Matters dropped leaflets from a balloon high over London. In 1908 Pankhurst's WSPU held a meeting in Hyde Park, which, according to the *London Times,* was attended by 500,000 people.

Also in 1908, Ms. Pankhurst and two others were arrested and convicted of trying to provoke a breach of peace at a meeting. In 1909, they and every other suffragist in prison went on a hunger strike. At first the government released each woman when she grew weak. But that was too easy and made the government look silly. So they started force-feeding the women, which aroused immense public opposition.

In 1910, the Conservatives introduced a bill to allow voting by women who owned property. It got a majority on first reading but was finally killed by the Liberals. The next year, Asquith's government announced that it would introduce a bill to give the vote to all men and would allow amendments to give the vote to women. But the government stalled until 1913, when it killed its own bill by parliamentary maneuvering. Women in this period showed their anger by breaking all the windows in Piccadilly Circus one day, for which 200 were arrested. They also wrote "votes for women" in acid on some golf courses. In 1912 the Labour party conference voted that they would support no further extension of suffrage without suffrage for women—a remarkable stance, since it went contrary to their own immediate objective of expanding the working-class male vote.

Against this rising tide of support for women's rights there was a reactionary backlash. A "distinguished" doctor, Sir Almroth Wright, wrote to the *London Times* that half the women in England go somewhat mad during menopause and that all the militant women were mentally ill.[21] A "distinguished" criminologist named Lambroso said that "even the normal woman is a half-criminaloid being."[22] The government passed a so-called Cat and Mouse Act, by which it could release from prison a militant woman who became weak from a hunger strike, and then rearrest her as soon as she regained her health.

In 1914, the outbreak of the war suddenly ended almost all suffrage activity. Both the moderate women and the militants suddenly became superpatriots. Only a small socialist women's organization led by Sylvia Pankhurst (who had split with her mother and sister as they became more friendly to the Conservatives) remained true to women's suffrage. She went to jail for opposing the war on the grounds that it was both inhuman and a mask for British and German imperialism.

The war, however, did have a major effect on the position of women. Hundreds of thousands went into munitions factories, where they ran the risk of being blown up. Many others kept the rest of the economy and government agencies running during the war. Still others became nurses at the front, drove army trucks, and ran the army communications system. Much of this was amply reported in the British press.

In 1918, partly as a reward for helping win the war and partly under the continued pressure of socialist militants, the government at last gave universal suffrage to men and women. Men were eligible to vote at 21, while women could not vote

---

[21] Quoted in ibid., p. 86.
[22] Quoted in ibid., p. 87.

until they were 30. This age difference was justified on the basis that women constituted a majority of the population. For most women leaders the granting of suffrage largely ended the fight. They continued to argue only for legal rights to property and political equality, all of which were granted in the 1920s. In 1928, women were given the right to vote at 21, and that completely ended the suffrage movement.

Thereafter, the British women's liberation movement lay dormant until 1967. By that time, women constituted 35 percent of the labor force but earned only about 65 percent as much as men for doing the same jobs. The revived British movement has fought for equal pay for equal work. Yet Parliament did not pass an equal pay act until 1970—and it did not take effect until 1975![23] Moreover, there are only 24 women in the 630-member House of Commons.

How do the United States and England compare on economic opportunities for women? Table 9.1 compares the percentages of women in different areas of professional achievement in the two countries, using the latest available data (all are from the 1960s). Although the U.S. economy is better on some aspects and the English is better on others, the general conclusion is that there is little difference.

[23] See Lucy Komisar, *The New Feminism* (New York: Warner, 1972), p. 146.

TABLE 9.1

Women in the economies of the United States and England

	Percentage of women	
Occupation	**United States**	**England**
Lawyer	4%	4%
Doctor	7	16
Dentist	2	7
Engineer	1	0.002
Scientist	7	6
Total labor force	40	35

Sources: U.S. Department of Commerce, *1960 Census of Population, Detailed Characteristics,* PC (1) IDUS (Washington, D.C.: GPO, 1961), Summary, and U.K. General Register Office, *1961 Census of Population* (London: U.K. Government Press, 1962), Summary Tables. Comparable data for other countries in Cynthia Epstein, *Woman's Place* (Berkeley: University of California Press, 1971), pp. 12–13.

By 1968, there was an organized and independent women's liberation movement in England. It received some impetus from radical women, including some Americans, who were working against the Vietnam war. Many women in various socialist parties and in the Revolutionary Socialist Students Federation formed separate caucuses because they did not think these organizations were either treating women equally or putting enough effort into the fight against sexist discrimination. By 1969, many of the caucuses had become independent organizations. Most were socialist-feminist in orientation, though in London women's organizations of every political stripe exist.

In March 1970, the first national conference was held, with about 600 delegates. The conference succeeded in uniting the women's liberation movement to the extent of forming a National Co-ordinating Committee (NCC). The NCC has no powers of its own, but brings together women from liberal, radical, socialist, and anarchist organizations. When the groups agree, it can set up nationwide demonstrations, as it usually does on International Women's Day, March 6. It also holds national conferences three or four times a year. The NCC attempts to direct the various organizations' efforts toward the common goal of women's liberation and away from factional fighting among the organizations themselves.

WOMEN IN SCANDINAVIA

When compared with the rest of Western Europe, the Scandinavian countries have had a much stronger socialist movement, a generally much more permissive society, and a higher status for women in the twentieth century. As early as 1901, women were given the vote in Norway in municipal elections. When Norway became independent of Sweden in 1905, women's rights increased, and women were granted full voting equality in 1913. Finland was under Russian rule, but had a strong socialist movement and a women's movement. In 1907, soon after Finland forced Russia to give it autonomy, women attained complete equality with men in elections.

To bolster national unity during the war, Denmark granted the vote to women in 1915. In 1918, in Sweden, the socialist and left-wing parties demonstrated in the streets and threatened revolution; to appease them, the government granted several reforms, including women's suffrage. Since that time, the Scandinavian countries have had long periods of reformist Social Democratic governments, all of which have tried to improve the position of women. Sweden today has a comprehensive and positively glowing government plan to ensure the overall social, political, and economic equality of women and men.

The Scandinavian countries, however, are still a long way from socialism and a very long way from full women's liberation. In the mid-1960s, women were somewhat better off economically in Scandinavia than in the United States. Whereas women accounted for only 7 percent of all U.S. doctors, in Sweden, Denmark, and Finland the comparable figures were 15 percent, 16 percent, and 24 percent. Similarly, whereas women represent only 2 percent of U.S. dentists, the figure for Sweden was 24 percent, and for Denmark, 70 percent.

The attitudes expressed publicly in Sweden are firmly women's liberationist. Prime Minister Olaf Palme said in 1970 that "nobody should be forced into a predetermined role on account of sex." He said that, in Sweden, "If a politician today should declare that the woman ought to have a different role than the man and that it is natural that she devotes more time to the children, he would be regarded to be of the Stone Age."[24] After very considerable public debate in the late 1950s and early 1960s, the government officially took the position that women should be liberated from the household to do whatever they wish in public and economic life, while men should be liberated from full-time jobs to help in the home. The same proposals for female and male liberation from sex-stereotyped roles were made by the Swedish government in a 1968 report to the United Nations.[25]

In spite of its Social Democratic government, Sweden is still basically a capitalist economy; and in spite of its liberationist policies, women are still basically subordinate and unequal. In the purely economic sphere, women's wages are only 75 percent of men's; and only 42 percent of the women but 84 percent of the men hold paid jobs. Among full-time working women in 1966, only 30 percent made over $3600 a year, while 80 percent of all full-time male workers did so.

---

[24] Quoted in Komisar, op. cit., p. 153.

[25] *Report to the United Nations; 1968: The Status of Women in Sweden*, reprinted in Mary Thompson, ed., *Voices of the New Feminism* (Boston: Beacon, 1971), pp. 155–177.

In 1969, because of these facts and continued chauvinism among many Swedish males, a women's liberation movement was established, mainly in Lund and Stockholm. The women's movement is explicitly Marxist in orientation and works for socialism as well as women's liberation. Similar women's movements exist in the other Scandinavian countries, and strong women's movements also exist in Holland and Belgium.

WOMEN IN CAPITALIST GERMANY

Women in Germany in the nineteenth century suffered all the usual legal and economic disabilities of the rest of Western Europe. In fact, the social situation was so conservative (because Germany was still heavily rural) that women were absolutely prohibited from joining any political organization until 1907. This rule, however, was seldom enforced, and it was attacked in principle by the very important and growing Social Democratic party, the largest socialist party anywhere. Several women became very important in the Social Democratic party, particularly at the party conventions, which were its highest governing body. One such women was Clara Zetkin, who organized women socialists in Germany and internationally.

Most important was Rosa Luxemburg. In conventional terms she had everything against her: She was a woman, Jewish, of Polish origin, and suffering from a physical deformity of her back. Yet she was a wonderful human being, a great orator, and a gifted analytical writer. Her books are considered Marxist classics. She was welcomed by the German Social Democrats as an organizer and a journalist and editor of their newspapers. She was not directly interested in rights for women; she took equality for granted as something any socialist government would have to support totally and any socialist society would be likely to produce.

Luxemburg was one of the leaders of the Social Democrats before World War I. When the right wing of the party supported the war (Germany was "defending itself against British imperialism"), she broke with the other leaders and led the fight in Germany against the war. Her left-wing faction eventually became a new party, calling itself the Spartacists (after the leader of the Roman slave revolt, Spartacus), and Luxemburg became its leader. In addition to fighting against the right-wing leaders over the war issue, she also attacked Lenin for not paying enough attention to the need for democracy within socialist parties and socialist governments. In 1919, she was arrested by the German government, which consisted of right-wing socialists; they murdered her and then claimed she was shot trying to escape.

In the Weimar Republic, from 1918 to 1931, women were immediately given the right to vote and full legal equality; it was, after all, a socialist government long committed to such principles. During this period, many women were prominent in the Socialist and Communist parties; and a flourishing women's movement existed. This movement was strong and far-sighted enough so that it probably would have achieved major advances for women.

In the early 1930s, however, Adolph Hitler and the Nazis came to power in Germany. They killed or imprisoned the leadership of the Socialist, Communist, and even liberal parties, as well as the leadership of the women's movement. Hitler explicitly declared that the concept of women's liberation is a Jewish plot! *Mein Kampf,* Hitler's textbook, stated that women's sphere is restricted to children, kitchen, and church *(kinder, kuche, kirche).* Hitler wrote: "Her world is her husband, her family, her children and her home. We do not find it right when the woman presses into the world of the man. Rather we find it natural when these two worlds remain separate. . . . Woman and man represent two quite different types of being. Reason is dominant in man."[26] Women, he said, are limited to feeling, not reasoning. And the Nazi propaganda minister, Joseph Goebbels, said: "The National Socialist [Nazi] movement is in its nature a masculine movement. When we eliminate women from public life, it is not because we want to dispense with them, but because we want to give them back their essential honor. . . . The outstanding and highest calling of woman is always that of wife and mother."[27]

True to their word, the Nazis set a limited quota on women in universities and excluded them from all public offices. All 30 women representatives were purged from the German congress. All contraception and abortion was made illegal.

Since the war, women in West Germany have had their electoral rights restored to them, but they still lack equality in

---

[26] Quoted in Komisar, op. cit., p. 76.
[27] Quoted in ibid.

many areas. There are no public child care centers, so women have organized their own cooperatives. The abortion laws are still very restrictive. Women get paid much less than men. Women make up 33 percent of the labor force but hold only 3 percent of the country's top jobs. Only 6 percent of the lawyers and 3 percent of the engineers are women.

Edith Neumann, a member of the executive committee of the Social Democratic party of the city of Kiel, resigned her post and attacked that party for its condescending attitudes toward women. They had told her that if women do not get ahead it is their own fault, and despite her protest, continued to use their election slogan, "We have the right men." There is now a significant women's liberation movement in West Germany, which is Marxist in orientation and critical of the existing socialist parties.

WOMEN AND THE MARXIST SOCIALIST MOVEMENT

We have noted that in various countries there were many prominent women in the Socialist and Communist parties, and that these parties have usually supported women's rights. It is also true, though, that socialist men have often given only lip service to women's rights and have not treated women within their own parties equally. For these reasons, many women who have been active in left-wing and socialist parties formed their own caucuses or even split from these parties in the late 1960s. Most of the women's movements in Western Europe continue to fight for both socialism and women's liberation. They believe that women can never be fully liberated until everyone is liberated from capitalism, though even socialism will not automatically liberate women.

Despite the sexism of some leftist males, a concern for women's liberation has always been evident in Marxist ideology. Karl Marx and Frederick Engels founded the modern socialist movement in the 1840s, when women and children worked under the most terrible conditions in factories. In the *Communist Manifesto* (1848) they wrote of the impact of early capitalism on the family:

> On what foundation is the present family, the bourgeois family, based? On capital, or private gain. . . . But this state of things finds its complement in the practical absence of the family among the prole-

tarians, and in public prostitution. . . . The bourgeois clap-trap about the family and education, about the hallowed relation of parent and child, become all the more disgusting, the more, by the action of Modern Industry, all family ties among the proletarians are torn asunder and their children transformed into simple articles of commerce and instruments of labor.[28]

All of their later writings emphasized that there are many forms of the family, each corresponding to different socioeconomic conditions. Marx, in *Capital* (1869), made the new point that although factory work exploited women, their entry into the economy outside the home would eventually lead to a whole new social atmosphere:

However terrible and disgusting the dissolution, under the capitalist system, of the old family ties may appear, nevertheless modern industry, by assigning as it does an important part in the process of production, outside the domestic sphere, to women, . . . creates a new economic foundation for a higher form of the family and of the relations between the sexes. It is, of course, just as absurd to hold the Teutonic-Christian form of the family to be absolute and final as it would be to apply that character to the ancient Roman, the ancient Greek, or the Eastern forms . . .[29]

The first full-scale Marxist work on women's liberation was written by Engels: *The Origin of the Family, Private Property, and the State* (1884). Engels traced various forms of the family and various changes in the status of women to the underlying economic division of labor and the power relations in each society. Although his anthropological data were wrong in detail, he correctly stressed that women have higher status in many primitive societies, where they are responsible for a large part of the economic production. He shows that the dominance of men is established when they come to dominate agriculture through the use of cattle to pull plows, and then start to utilize their war prisoners for slaves to further enhance heavy agriculture and construction.

---

[28] Quoted and discussed in Peggy Morton, "A Woman's Work Is Never Done," in Edith Altbach, *From Feminism to Liberation* (Cambridge, Mass.: Schenkman, 1971), pp. 216–217.

[29] Quoted and discussed extensively in the very useful essay by Hal Draper, "Marx and Engels on Woman's Liberation," in Roberta Salper, ed., *Female Liberation* (New York: Knopf, 1972), p. 92.

Only then, he shows, are women also treated as slaves. Only then is there "monogamous" marriage, in which women must remain faithful though men may indulge in extramarital sex as they will. Only with slavery and private property do "monogamy" and the double standard become institutionalized: "It is based on the supremacy of the man; its express aim is the begetting of children of undisputed paternity, this paternity being required in order that these children may in due time inherit their father's wealth as his natural heirs."[30] Engels showed how male supremacy and this form of the family persisted in all class-divided societies up to and including capitalism. He indicted capitalism for the social inferiority of women and for legal and economic discrimination against them.

Engels believed that all this could change only under socialism. Then relations between women and men would not be dominated by economic considerations but would be for love and companionship alone. Moreover, the form of the family would probably change; at least, marriage and divorce would become much simpler.

Marx and Engels strongly encouraged the practice of women's liberation within the European socialist movement at a very early period. In 1868, Marx wrote that "of course" women could join the International Workers Association on the same basis as men. He proposed a resolution to the General Council of the International to encourage the formation of women's branches of the International, without interfering "with the existence or formation of branches composed of both sexes."[31] Moreover, under Marx's leadership a woman—Harriet Law—was elected a member of the General Council.

Another important book in the socialist movement advocating women's liberation was August Bebel's *Women and Socialism,* written in 1879. Under the influence of Engels and Bebel, the German Marxists strongly endorsed women's liberation. Clara Zetkin published a socialist woman's newspaper, *Equality (Gleichheit),* that had a circulation of 100,000. Not all socialists agreed. In 1875, when the Marxist Bebel moved a resolution for equal rights for women at the Social Democrats' congress, it was defeated. Finally, at the 1891 congress, when the Marxists

---

[30] Quoted in ibid., p. 94.
[31] Quoted in ibid., p. 102.

had a majority, a resolution was passed favoring the full legal and economic equality of women. However, right-wing socialists continued to oppose that program.

Engels and all the Marxist leaders, including the women's leadership—Luxemburg, Zetkin, and Marx's daughter Eleanor—strongly supported all the working women's organizations that fought for socialism and women's liberation. At the same time, they criticized the bourgeois feminist movements, which advocated equal legal and property rights but ignored the need for revolutionary socioeconomic change. Engels commented that for these groups "the separate women's rights business" was a "purely bourgeois pastime."[32] Marxists believe in fighting for equality for women under capitalism, but argue that only socialism can lay the foundation for complete women's liberation.

The Marxist emphasis on equality for women was later to have an important effect on countries which became socialist. Both Russia and China, as we shall see, were very backward at the time of their socialist revolutions. In neither country were the social conditions conducive to women's liberation. Yet, in both countries, under the influence of Marxism and of economic necessity, tremendous progress has been made.

WOMEN IN THE SOVIET UNION

Women in tsarist Russia were badly oppressed. They had few if any rights, either political or economic. According to law, they were required to obey their husbands in all matters. They could be jailed for running away and could not get a divorce. The male supremacist ideology was very strong; women were considered inferior to men in most ways. Although literature depicted some strong-minded heroines among educated women, most upper-class women were idle and suffered from boredom. Peasant and industrial working women often worked all day in factory or field, then took sole responsibility for the housework in the evening.

Women reacted to these bleak conditions with a women's liberation movement of considerable scope. The Women's Political Club, a left-wing bourgeois feminist group, attacked the political and psychological aspects of women's oppression and

---

[32] Quoted in ibid., p. 106.

called for equal rights. A socialist women's movement—the Society for Mutual Help Among Working Women—also existed. The socialist women were critical of the feminists, urging the need for a deeper class analysis of society; they argued that socialism was a prerequisite to complete women's liberation because women could never be free under capitalism. The socialist women had a remarkable leader in Alexandra Kollantai. She was a revolutionary, later a novelist, and still later a diplomat for Bolshevik Russia.[33]

Women fought in the Revolution, and the women's liberation movement expanded afterward. In November 1918, a Soviet women's conference was held in Moscow with 1147 delegates, including many peasant women. In the same year, the Central Committee of the Party established a women's section, called Zhenotdel, to push women's liberation. Yet even the creation of Zhenotdel—which replaced the earlier Society for Mutual Help as the main socialist women's organization—was opposed by some Communist men. They argued that it was too "feminist" to have a separate organization of women, and was totally unnecessary in a socialist state. These arguments reflected both the extreme backwardness of Russian attitudes toward women and the incompleteness of Marxist theory on women's liberation up to that time.

Long before the Revolution, Lenin had endorsed Engels' analysis of the oppression of women and the need for women's liberation. Indeed, he himself did considerable writing in favor of women's liberation. He wrote: "Women grow worn out in the petty, monstrous household work, their strength and time dissipated and wasted, their minds growing narrow and stale, their hearts beating slowly, their will weakened."[34] And he attacked male attitudes: "Very few men . . . think how much labour and weariness they could lighten for women . . . if they would lend a hand in 'women's work.' . . . Our communist labours among the masses . . . involves a considerable effort to educate the men. We must root out the ancient outlook of

[33] The historical background is discussed in Erica Dunn and Judy Klein, "Women in the Russian Revolution," *Women: A Journal of Liberation* 1, 4 (summer 1970), pp. 22–26. Also see Marilyn Goldberg, "Women in the Soviet Economy," *Review of Radical Political Economics,* 4 (July 1972), pp. 60–65.

[34] Quoted in Dunn and Klein, op. cit., p. 24. Lenin has a full pamphlet called "The Emancipation of Women" (New York: International Publishers, n.d.).

the lord and master to the last fiber."[35] Moreover, Lenin lived in a free and open relationship with the revolutionary woman Krupskaya, who was herself an independent leader in the women's movement. Yet Lenin seems to have underestimated the need for consciousness raising among women, since he thought it "feminist" to waste time discussing love and marital problems. He also underestimated, like all socialists of his day, the effort necessary to root out sexism in a socialist society.

Nevertheless, in the 1920s, with Lenin as its leader, the Soviet government propagandized for equal rights, allowed freedom of divorce, legalized abortion, and pushed for women's liberation in many ways (even helping women remove the veil in Central Asia). Marriages and divorces could be registered by a simple postcard, but many intellectuals did not register at all, feeling that registration of marriage was "too bourgeois." Even where marriages were registered, women often used their previous name—while some couples combined the two names. The formal equality of men and women has remained unchanged ever since the Revolution. Article 122 of the Soviet constitution (1936) says that "women in the USSR are accorded equal rights with men in all spheres of economic, cultural, political, and other public activities."

Among the equal rights granted were completely equal property rights within the marriage and the right of either spouse to a divorce by submitting a postcard to the government. At the same time, the women's organization (Zhenotdel) was greatly encouraged and spread to all areas, although it was always stronger in the cities than in the countryside. It published magazines, helped Eastern women remove the veil, and propagandized against arranged marriages and wife beating. It helped organize cooperatives for women through which they could both produce and sell products and buy more cheaply as consumers. Since women had little or no education before the Revolution and were over 90 percent illiterate, an educational drive was launched. Ms. Kollantai wrote a widely read novel, *Red Love,* which described the life and problems of a liberated woman.

But male attitudes were slow to change, especially in the rural areas. In the 1920s, most of the Soviet Union remained

[35] Quoted in ibid.

agricultural, and in most peasant communities, the traditional subservient role of women did not change. As late as 1933, an American woman in the Soviet Union wrote: "On a motor trip I visited many cottages in outlying villages; the women stood while the men sat down and ate; kept their heads bent and their hands folded, not speaking until they were spoken to."[36]

Moreover, the highly democratic processes of government just after the Revolution were replaced by a harsh dictatorship under Stalin by about 1928. The dictatorship resulted from the civil war and foreign intervention of 1918–1921, the lack of literacy and of any democratic tradition in Russia, and—most important—from a need to industrialize backward Russia almost overnight if the Soviet Union was to survive. The terrible economic conditions plus the dictatorship were catastrophic for the women's movement.

In 1929, Stalin abolished the Zhenotdel and all other women's organizations, many of whose leaders had opposed him. In order to encourage industrialization, Stalin and other leaders believed a more regimented society was necessary. This included a more stable family and more difficult divorce. Divorce was made more complicated in 1926, and in 1944 was made quite difficult to obtain and expensive by Soviet standards. The People's Court had to hear the reasons for the divorce—always ultimately granted if the woman persisted, but hard for a man to get if children were involved—and a fee of 100 rubles had to be paid. The court attitude became quite rigid: ". . . the USSR Supreme Court has pointed out that courts trying divorce cases must begin with the task of strengthening the family, and that temporary discord in the family and conflicts between spouses due to random and transient factors must not be regarded as sufficient grounds for divorce."[37]

At the same time, to stabilize the family as Stalin had ordered, the government put out a great deal of puritanical propaganda: "So-called free love is a bourgeois invention and has nothing in common with the principles of conduct of a Soviet citizen. Moreover, marriage receives its full value for the State only

---

[36] Ella Winter, *Red Virtue* (New York: Harcourt Brace Jovanovich, 1933), p. 101.

[37] A. Gorkin, "Concern for the Soviet Family," *Soviet Review* 10 (Fall 1969): 49.

if there is progeny."[38] This was a reversal of the early casual attitude toward marriage.

Stalin's 1944 law ended the father's obligations to children born outside marriage. Before that time, the father's obligations to all children, born in or out of marriage, were the same. In 1968, a new law gave the single mother the right to receive a state allowance and the right to place the child in an institution to be brought up at the state's expense if the identity of the father is not established (and the mother is once again entitled to child support if the father's identity is established).

Immediately after the Revolution, birth control information and devices were made free and available. In 1936, Stalin radically changed the policy. Birth control by contraception was still legal, but discouraged (especially by very, very low production of contraceptives for at least two decades). All abortions not medically necessary were banned. Under Stalin a doctor performing an abortion was imprisoned for two years, and the woman was subject to public censure for the first offense and fined 300 rubles for a second offense.

To increase population in order to provide more labor for industrial expansion, a policy of family subsidies was begun. Payment increased with the number of children. Women who had a great number of children were also given special awards. Women with five children received a Motherhood Medal, Second Class; with six children, the Motherhood Medal, First Class; with seven children, the Order of Glory of Motherhood; and with ten children, the Presidium of the Supreme Soviet presented the woman with a scroll and the title Mother Heroine.[39]

After Stalin's death, the frantic rush to industrialize slackened as the initial goals had been achieved, and some loosening of political control has taken place. Dissenters are still often arrested and sent to jail or to an insane asylum, though no longer executed. In this somewhat better atmosphere, the older Marxist attitude toward the family has begun to reassert itself. In 1955, abortion was again legalized. Abortions were made free for all urban working women but cost 5 rubles for housewives and students and 2 rubles for farm women. The abortion rate has been quite high, especially because of a persistent shortage of contraceptives. Only in the late 1960s was some priority

---

[38] Commissariat of Justice, *Sotsialisticheskaya Zakonnost,* no. 2 (1939).
[39] Dunn and Klein, op. cit., p. 26.

given to the increased production of contraceptives, mostly owing to alarm over the high abortion rate.[40] Therefore, in spite of continuing official propaganda favoring big families, by 1969 the number of children per woman in the USSR had dropped to 1.9 in rural areas and 1.5 in urban areas; the average 1.7 foreshadows a declining population.

In 1955 and again in 1965, the divorce laws were much further liberalized. It still takes three months to get a divorce, but if there are no children, no fee is involved; with children, there are fees and hearings to determine what should be done. The husband or the wife—whoever has a job and does not have the children—must pay child support, but no alimony. The number of divorces has risen sharply but is still far below the U.S. rate. Finally, a 1968 law gives unmarried women the same state subsidies for children as married women, and equal rights to all state facilities.

In spite of all these ups and downs on family policy, the status of women has greatly changed and improved from the oppression of tsarist Russia. The all-out drive for industrialization required the largest possible labor force, and women went to work in unprecedented numbers. They also flooded into the schools and colleges. In 1967, the number of employed women with higher education was 54 times as high as in 1928. Women have made up over 50 percent of the whole labor force ever since 1945. In fact, 70 percent of all Soviet women work. Moreover, the Soviet Union has a vast system of low-cost or free child care facilities; legal dissemination of birth control information and devices; legal and universally available abortion; equal pay for equal work; acceptance of women in all professions; equality before the law; divorce at will; and an insignificant rate of prostitution.

One U.S. specialist says: "Career women get no opposition from men. They are not regarded jealously or as competitors. Neither Russian men nor women feel that the woman intellectual is in danger of losing her sex appeal."[41] Thus women account for 63 percent of all specialists with a secondary education, and 53 percent of all professionals with higher education.

---

[40] See David Heer, "Abortion, Contraception, and Population Policy in the Soviet Union," *Soviet Studies,* 17 (July 1965), pp. 76–83.

[41] Maurice Hindus, *House Without a Roof* (Garden City, N.Y.: Doubleday, 1961), p. 288.

Women constitute 40 percent of all farm experts, 40 percent of all judges, 75 percent of all physicians, and 85 percent of all administrators in health services. In the most traditionally male areas of mechanics and machine adjusters, women rose from 1 percent in 1926 to 9 percent in 1964. In another "male" area, women are now 33 percent of all engineers!

Moreover, women are helped to keep their jobs by an adequate system of maternity leaves throughout industry. They are allowed eight weeks prenatal and eight weeks postnatal leave at full pay. They may also choose to take their annual paid vacation after that (two to three weeks), and an additional three months unpaid leave if desired.[42]

Just before the Revolution, women represented only 25 percent of all university enrollment. Since the Revolution, the number of girls and boys in grades 1 through 10 has been equal, except in the more backward republics, where girls leave school at an earlier age than boys. Through the tenth grade, the curriculum is uniform for both sexes. Beyond that grade, the percentage of women tends to decline. Still, 53 percent of all medical students and even 25 percent of all agricultural students are women.

In 1933, the percentage of women with the degree of *kandidat* (similar to our Ph.D.) was very close to zero. In 1968, women received 31 percent of all *kandidat* degrees. In 1959, 24 percent of all management posts, including department heads, were held by women. In 1967, women accounted for 20 percent of all associate professors and 9 percent of the highest academic ranks, full professor or member of the Academy of Sciences.

If the USSR is compared with the United States in terms of women at work, there can be no doubt that the USSR shows up better, particularly in the prestige professions (see Table 9.2). The same high percentages of women are observable in the professions in Eastern Europe. For example, 30 percent of East German lawyers are women (as opposed to 6 percent in West Germany). In Poland, women constitute 19 percent of the lawyers, 36 percent of the doctors, 77 percent of the dentists, and 8 percent of the engineers.

In general, Soviet women have achieved many of the mate-

[42] William Mandel, *Russia Re-Examined* (New York: Hill and Wang, 1967), pp. 174–175.

rial goals for which American women are still striving. They are highly represented and welcomed in the professions; there are very considerable—though not sufficient—free child care facilities, equal salaries for equal jobs, good maternity leaves, and so forth. There are also equal formal political and legal rights, legal and mostly free abortions, and reasonable divorce laws. These positive features are closely linked with government ownership of the economy (and the continuous full employment that results from it), and they are found to a large degree in all the other countries practicing "socialism" or government ownership—Eastern Europe, China, Cuba, North Vietnam, and North Korea.

TABLE 9.2

Women at work, U.S. and Soviet economies

	Percentage of women	
Profession	**United States**	**Soviet Union**
Lawyer	4%	36%
Doctor	7	75
Dentist	2	83
Engineer	1	33
Scientist	7	38
Total labor force	40	52

Sources: U.S. Department of Commerce, *1960 Census of Population, Detailed Characteristics,* PC (1) IDUS (Washington, D.C.: GPO, 1961), Summary, and Norton Dodge, "Women in the Soviet Economy," in Athena Theodore, ed., *The Professional Woman* (Cambridge, Mass.: Schenkman, 1971), pp. 207–226. Further data and discussion in Cynthia Epstein, *Woman's Place* (Berkeley: University of California Press, 1971), pp. 12–13.

There are, however, also many negative aspects for women in the Soviet Union and the other "socialist" countries. These seem to derive largely from the continuing undemocratic political processes, from the fact that most of these countries are still less developed or rapidly developing, and from inherited sexist attitudes. First, there are no militant women's liberationist movements in any of these countries, though there are women's organizations that try to help women achieve economic success within the given socioeconomic situation. (The degree to which China is an exception is examined later.) Second, although women are well represented in the professions, they are concentrated in the less well-paying ones, and in the lower ranks; there are few women at the top in the political sphere. Finally, traditional attitudes toward women in the home are still very widespread and result in an unequal burden for women.

Men are still expected to enter the higher-paid professions because they are supposed to provide the main support for the family. Women are predominant in teaching and medicine, but these are low-paid and low-prestige professions in the USSR. In the high-paid, high-prestige profession of engineering, women account for only 33 percent of the total (though that is a lot better than the 1 percent in the United States).

Moreover, men have an overwhelming percentage of the top-level positions in every profession. Thus, even in the low-paid teaching field, Soviet women are 72 percent of primary school teachers and 72 percent of primary school directors, but only 24 percent of 8-year school directors and only 20 percent of secondary school directors. In Soviet higher education in 1960, there was a pyramid of pay and prestige with women at the bottom, just as in U.S. higher education (see Table 9.3).

TABLE 9.3
Women in Soviet higher education

Position	Percentage of women
Director	5%
Deputy director	5
Dean	9
Department head	12
Professor	11
Associate professor	24
Assistant professor	41

Source: Norton Dodge, "Women in the Soviet Economy," in Athena Theodore, ed., *The Professional Woman* (Cambridge, Mass.: Schenkman, 1971), p. 218.

In medicine, where 75 percent of the doctors are women, only 57 percent of the directors, deputy directors, and chief physicians are women. Finally, in research institutes, 50 percent of the scientific workers but only 33 percent of branch heads, 21 percent of division heads, and 16 percent of top directors are female.

Men are particularly in evidence at the top of the political heap. In the Central Committee elected in 1971, only 3 percent of the members are women; and only 2 percent of the candidate members are women.[43] In 1970, there was only one woman in the Soviet Council of Ministers (out of 60), although women make up 27 percent of the deputies in the not-too-important Soviet congress (or Supreme Soviet).

Traditional male attitudes still present problems for married women. Most men believe the woman should do all the housework after she returns from the day's work (although educated men under 35 do much more housework than the average). The basic problem of the Soviet woman, in spite of her equal opportunities for education and occupation, is that male supremacy still keeps her doing about three times as much housework as the man, even though her outside job is often equally tiring and time consuming.

The resistance of women to this situation is showing up partly in a skyrocketing divorce rate. In 1950, there were 3 divorces for every 100 marriages. In 1967, there were 30 divorces per 100 marriages. Divorce is most frequent among the intelligentsia.

In 1969, Soviet child care facilities had provisions for nine million children. Nevertheless, Soviet women complain of the shortage of facilities, since there are still places for only 70 percent of urban children and less than that for rural areas. They also complain about the poor quality of the facilities.

Soviet women still have many fewer household appliances and poorer services for the household than American women. Some Soviet women have complained of sexist oppression from lack of sufficient services, such as child care centers (better than in the United States, but still inadequate) and laundries (worse than in the United States). Some progress has been made in helping the housewife in recent years. The USSR made 300 washing machines in 1950, but 5 million in 1969. Seating capacity of restaurants rose 80 percent between 1960 and 1969. The retail sales force per capita has risen one-third since 1960.

On the other hand, the double standard in sex is still evident. A Soviet study on sex attitudes (the first in 40 years) notes that 47 percent of unmarried undergraduate women had had intercourse, although only 38 percent approved of premarital sex. Thirty percent of the men thought it was all right for a woman they love to have sexual relations with others, while

---

[43] Goldberg, op. cit., p. 67.

48 percent of the women okayed it for a loved man. The survey showed that, while the double standard is dying out, men are still "more liberal toward their own sexual behavior than toward that of women, and women are more liberal toward male sexual behavior than toward their own."[44]

Official Soviet sexual morality in the 1970s still demands continence until marriage and associates sex only with children and a family. Extramarital affairs are frowned upon. The cult of virginity is once again glorified. And some women still choose to marry the man with the most material wealth. Finally, a letter to the editor of a Soviet paper in 1967 showed the unenlightened attitude of many Soviet men: "Girls, for all your equality with us men, stay feminine, gentle, and weak (in the best, Marxist sense of this concept). . . ."[45] The writer uses "Marxist" the way Americans use "democratic" to mean anything or nothing. Similarly, an East German slogan in 1974 said: "Having babies is fun and truly Marxist."[46]

The Soviet Union, because of its "socialist" or government-owned economy, has thus succeeded in making women 52 percent of the labor force. Women constitute very large percentages of every profession, receive equal pay for equal work, and are entitled to generous maternity leaves. On the other hand, the USSR's low level of development combined with a one-party dictatorship means that men at the top have their own political and material reasons for perpetuating an authoritarian family, with women doing most of the housework as well as holding a job. Since 1929, the top leadership has always—rightly—feared and prevented the emergence of a militant women's liberation movement because it might jeopardize their own power.

WOMEN IN COMMUNIST CHINA

For thousands of years, most Chinese were peasants, living at the edge of starvation. From 108 B.C. to A.D. 1911, 1828 famines are recorded. The landlord gentry, the ruling class

[44] S. I. Golod, "Sociological Problems of Soviet Morality," translated in *Soviet Sociology,* 10 (summer 1969), p. 13. Fully discussed in the important article by William Mandel, "Soviet Women and Their Self-Image," *Science and Society,* 35 (fall 1971).

[45] Quoted in Goldberg, op. cit., p. 69.

[46] Quoted in *Parade,* June 23, 1974, p. 5.

that ruthlessly exploited the peasants, amounted to less than 20 percent of the population. In both classes, the family was rigidly authoritarian, with female dominated by male and young by old. The Confucian text, *Li Chi*, set the tone: "The woman always follows the man."

In the old China women were a clearly subordinate group. They were not recognized as independent entities under the law; they could not own property or inherit land. Women were taught only one virtue—obedience. Young girls were sold to a strange husband in a strange family. From then on, she was a member of that family and was under the control of her husband or, if he died, her mother-in-law and father-in-law. No matter at what age she might become a widow, she was forbidden to remarry. "She was terrified and often terrorized, frequently beaten by both her husband and her mother-in-law."[47]

Women of the upper classes were kept physically secluded, preparing the meals for men but eating separately. In addition to the first wife, the gentry also had "secondary wives," concubines, prostitutes, or simply female slaves. To show that the man was wealthy and the woman a useless ornament, women of the gentry had their feet bound to prevent them from growing to be more than 2 or 3 inches long! The binding of feet was still common as late as the 1940s.

The peasant women were often used as slaves and prostitutes. Daughters were considered such a curse that they were often killed at birth. When a peasant woman was married, however, her position with regard to her husband might be a little better and the family a little less rigid than among the gentry. Peasant women had to work in the fields in the south and in heavy domestic labor in the north. Therefore their feet could not be bound. Neither could the peasant man afford more than one woman; therefore she usually had more decision-making power than gentry women, and her position was a little closer to equality.

When revolt against the old regime became endemic in the nineteenth century, women immediately joined. Many urban

---

[47] The quotes and the material in the preceding paragraph are from Charlotte Cohen, "Experiment in Freedom: Women of China," in Robin Morgan, ed., *Sisterhood Is Powerful* (New York: Vintage, 1970), p. 388, an outstanding article.

women became bourgeois feminists as early as the 1850s. In the peasant revolt called the Taiping Rebellion, which lasted from 1850 to 1864, women fought in the peasant army. Their program included communal ownership of property, complete equality of men and women, no foot binding or prostitution, and a monogamous family built on love. The emperor, with foreign support, defeated them in a bloody civil war.

In the early 1900s some gentry began to send their daughters to schools, and the bourgeois feminist movement grew. An early leader, Chi'iu Chin, established the first women's newspaper, *Chinese Women's Journal,* and wrote poems like this one:

May Heaven bestow equal power on men, women.
Is it sweet to live lower than cattle?
We would rise in fight yes! drag ourselves up.[48]

Women fought in Sun Yat-sen's liberation wars, but were given only a few new rights in the republican constitution of 1912. Women also joined in the massive student demonstrations of the May Fourth Movement from 1917 to 1921, in which they fought against the restraints of Confucianism, against foreign imperialism, and against the native warlords, but also raised the banner of women's liberation. Many young students, including Mao Tse-tung, refused to marry because all marriages were still arranged and were thus a prison for men as well as for women. When the Communist party was organized in 1921, many women broke with the bourgeois feminist movement, saying it was necessary to go further. The militant Hsiang Chin-yu said: "The emancipation of women can only come with a change in the social structure which frees men and women alike."[49]

From 1921 to 1927, the Communists and the bourgeois republican Kuomintang formed a coalition. During this period both bourgeois and socialist women's movements flourished in the cities. The Women's Department of the coalition organized 1,500,000 women. But in 1927, the Kuomintang broke the coalition and killed every Communist available, as well as every "Communist sympathizer," including every women's leader. Many women organizers were tortured and imprisoned; some had noses and breasts cut off. Any women's emancipation

[48] Quoted in ibid., p. 390.
[49] Quoted in ibid., p. 392.

was suspect, so a girl whose only crime was that she had freely chosen her fiancé was tortured and shot. The Kuomintang soldiers shouted: "You have had your free love now."[50] Although in 1931 the Kuomintang, under Chiang Kai-shek, promulgated a code of equal rights for women, it was never enforced, and the authoritarian family was strongly encouraged.

In contrast, the Communists actively organized a women's movement through groups called Women's Associations. They favored equality both for ideological reasons and because they felt that the strength of women was required in order to make the revolution successful. They had often witnessed "divide and rule" tactics by the conservatives. For example, in a 1924 strike the male union failed to support the women's strike for equal pay, and both unions were weakened. The Communist party admitted that its organizers viewed work among women workers as less important and set out to correct this tendency. A very strong women's movement was launched in the liberated areas of the countryside. The party announced that all marriages must be free and equal and by mutual consent, gave equal property rights, and prohibited concubines, female infanticide, and foot binding. Attracted by this program, women played a vital role in the Revolution.

In 1949, after the Revolution, militant women organized the All China Democratic Women's Federation, which spearheaded the movement for women's rights. In 1950, a new marriage law was promulgated in the People's Republic.

Article 1 of the Marriage Law:

> The arbitrary and compulsory feudal marriage system, which is based on the superiority of man over woman . . . is hereby abolished. The new Democratic marriage system, which is based on free choice of partners, on monogamy, on equal rights for both sexes, and on the protection of the lawful interests of women and children, shall be put into effect.

Article 7:

> Husband and wife are companions living together and shall enjoy equal status in the home.

The law prohibited polygamy, concubinage, child betrothal, infanticide, marriage by purchase, and interference with the

[50] Quoted in ibid., p. 393.

remarriage of widows. It gave equal rights to women and men to pursue any career, to manage the family property, to use their own family names, and to inherit property. Children born out of marriage were given the same rights as legitimate children. Free divorce by mutual consent was allowed: "Divorce shall be granted when husband and wife both desire it." If there was disagreement, a wife could still always get a divorce. A man could get a divorce also, except when the wife was pregnant or had a child under one year old.

China was very poor, and propaganda emphasized the need to work hard if women would be equal participants in society. Women reacted as to a renaissance; one confessed:

> . . . the gongs and drums of "liberation" woke me up like thunder in the spring and I began to crawl out of the dirt. . . . I want to shout with millions of sisters. . . . We want to be masters of the new society. We have to break the chains on our hands and create the garden of happiness for humanity.[51]

The women had to enforce the new ideas and the new marriage law against intense resistance. One important technique was the "speak bitterness" meeting. If a man were found to be oppressing his wife, all the active women in the village would go to him and reason with him. If that failed, as it often did because the women weren't taken seriously, they would put him in jail for two or three days to think it over. Then, the Women's Association would haul him out of jail to a public meeting attended by all the women of the town. The man was allowed to tell his story. Then, whether he spoke or not, the woman was encouraged to speak, usually the first time in her life that she had ever spoken publicly. After that, the accused man was given a chance to confess and promise to act reasonably toward his wife in the future. If he refused, he was beaten, and he was not released until he gave a public promise to behave with equality toward his wife.[52]

The male resistance, however, also resorted to such tactics, especially where the local Communist party cadres were themselves sexist. "In Kwangsi province . . . ten women were ordered to be tortured and made the object of 'struggle' meetings

[51] Quoted in ibid., p. 401.

[52] Diane Feeley, "Speak Bitterness," *Women: A Journal of Liberation,* 1, 4 (summer 1970), p. 5.

for their audacity in desiring to marry for love."[53] The central government, however, always backed the women, so the struggle was largely successful. Moreover, many women were brought into the lower government levels; by Party decree, women must constitute at least 10 percent of every village council.

Another major fight was to eradicate venereal disease and prostitution. George Hatem, an American doctor who spent many years in China, says that in prerevolutionary Shanghai 10 percent of the people had syphilis, and many parents were forced to sell their daughters to brothels in order to stay alive.[54] He adds that in the old China enormous numbers of people had venereal diseases, and prostitution was almost as widespread as poverty. "Shanghai was really a hell-on-earth except for the very rich."[55]

Hatem explains that in Communist China VD was conquered by voluminous propaganda and through educational campaigns involving thousands of volunteers. Prostitution was wiped out in a similar manner. Prostitutes who had been in the business only a short time were given other jobs. Those who were long-time prostitutes were given a rehabilitation course in which they were told that the old society had forced them into such jobs for survival but that the new society would teach them trades and guarantee jobs. The women were encouraged to speak their own bitterness about their past lives at long, friendly sessions, a catharsis that helped many. "Once they were cured and rehabilitated, they were sent out as nurses, teachers, clerks, with the assurance that never again would the government permit poverty to drive them or their children into prostitution."[56]

From 1954 to 1958, much greater emphasis was put on women participating in the economy. But the movement of women into the economy, plus the high divorce rates as women broke up unwanted marriages, led to a very unstable and disoriented family situation. In response, Party policy swung back to an emphasis on family virtues, though a family of equality. People were encouraged to marry late, have fewer children—

[53] Cohen, op. cit., p. 403.
[54] George Hatem, in *Parade,* August 12, 1973, p. 4.
[55] Ibid.
[56] Ibid., p. 5.

a major birth control campaign was launched—and avoid divorce as a bourgeois trait.

There were, however, contradictions within this policy, since women were encouraged to take outside jobs but also told to build stable families, which meant investing a lot of time in child care. This situation was partly resolved in the Great Leap Forward of 1958, when communes were set up in both rural and urban areas. The communes were supposed to take over all housework and childrearing for the working mother. The communes tried to go too far too fast; and the services provided were often inadequate. The resources for communal kitchens and child care often were not available. Nevertheless, there has been no retreat from the basic principle of communal facilities to lighten the women's burden—though many of the initial extremes were quickly abandoned.

One result has been perhaps the world's most extensive free and collective child care system. Two U.S. women journalists[57] reported in 1973 that 90 percent of all Chinese women now work outside the home. Their children, even very small ones, are cared for in nurseries, often right next door to the office or factory where they work. Still, about 50 percent of children under three are cared for by grandparents. From three to seven, only 20 percent are cared for by grandparents, the rest by nurseries.

Since women as well as men now worked outside the home, equality within the home was emphasized even more. In addition, women were further encouraged to raise their consciousness, to get out of purely private life into public life; and many did take on executive responsibilities. The percentage of women on the Party's Central Committee rose from 4.5 percent in 1956 to 8 percent in 1969. The number of women in higher education also began to rise. In 1960, women accounted for 18 percent of the engineering students, 42 percent of the medical students, 28 percent of the agronomy students, and 24 percent of the education students.

Unfortunately, in the period from 1957 to 1960 and since, the women's movement has been set back by the attitude of the government. Perhaps because the government's objective of getting women into the labor force has been accomplished,

[57] Janice Perlman and Lois Goldfrank, "How China Schools Its Children," *Parade,* November 25, 1973, p.11.

the government assets that women's oppression has been completely overcome and that women need no longer strive separately from male revolutionaries. In 1957, the Women's Federation itself claimed that equality before the law had been achieved, "the equality of men and women had been by and large realized, women's oppression had been uprooted, and the fullness of her emancipation would be seen only through the building up of a socialist China."[58] With this outlook, the federation in 1960 declared that its old task was completed and that it would now simply join in the revolutionary work of socialist production and opposition to native reactionaries and foreign imperialists. Its propaganda stopped emphasizing specifically women's issues and has largely switched to general political issues, making it indistinguishable from other organizations. An American observer claims that as a result the Women's Federation declined in influence in the 1960s.[59]

Women are now—since the Cultural Revolution of 1966–1968—exhorted to be revolutionaries first and put private life second. Wei-Feng-ying, a heroine of the Cultural Revolution and a worker-engineer, says: "I put revolution first. . . . After I met my husband concrete problems came up. . . . I could not let love affect my work and studies. In this he fully agreed."[60] When she had a baby but continued working, her grandmother objected. She finally convinced grandmother to take over care of the child, so grandmother could also contribute to socialism indirectly. The press has also attacked Tung Ping, who used to be editor of *Women of China,* for her bourgeois theories that happiness included material goods and a pleasant marriage; she tried to make "us stay all day long in the midst of 'love and marriage,' breaking our revolutionary will. . . ."[61]

What has China achieved? On the one hand, turning millions of women from foot-bound slaves into revolutionary activists in industry and government is a major miracle. In terms of sheer numbers, this is the greatest single emancipation of women in history. The provision of education and communal

---

[58] Charlotte Bunch-Weeks, "Asian Women in Revolution," *Women: A Journal of Liberation,* 1, 4 (summer, 1970), p. 6.
[59] Ibid.
[60] Quoted in Cohen, op. cit., p. 414.
[61] Quoted in ibid., p. 415.

facilities for meals and child care has put real teeth into the Chinese drive for women's equality.

On the other hand, the position that organized women need no longer strive for further progress for women *qua* women is very unfortunate. Real problems still exist. Women in China seem to have some of the same problems as Soviet women. They have made great strides in the economy, in education, and in politics—but they still constitute only a very small portion of those at the top of the economic and political pyramids. They are equal in family rights before the law, but many, many marriages still pursue the traditional path—with the male dominant and the woman doing all the household chores. In 1965, a Chinese woman complained that "women work much more than men. We have two jobs; we work in the fields and in our homes."[62] Thus women bear a double burden. Chinese women have come a remarkably long way, but they still have a long way to go.

WOMEN IN THE THIRD WORLD

While the countries of the Third World vary tremendously in culture and social structure and thus in the position that women hold, they resemble one another in that they all are less economically developed than the countries discussed earlier. They remain very poor, rural, agricultural, with high rates of disease and illiteracy—in other words, they resemble countries in Western Europe in 1750. Many of them, such as India, had very high cultural levels before they were conquered by European or U.S. imperialism. In most cases, imperialism reversed cultural development, plundered and ruined economic development, and lowered the position of women.

In Africa, for example, the women used the hoe to conduct almost all of the agricultural production, while the men limited themselves mostly to hunting and warfare. The advent of European colonialism ended the intertribal war activities of the men. Since the African men then appeared idle to the Europeans, they used every means to force them into farming. The Europeans believed that agriculture is by nature a male job. Therefore, they never perceived that almost all African agriculture was done by women. They assumed that "men could become far better farmers than women, if only they would aban-

[62] Quoted in ibid., p. 413.

don their customary 'laziness.' "[63] Hence, they taught modern farming techniques to the men only.

Modern methods meant introduction of the heavy plow instead of the hoe, which usually means substitution of men for women in farming. This change resulted in the same drastic lowering of the status of African women as had occurred in ancient Neolithic communities when the same substitution was made. The former smooth functioning of African society was totally destroyed as men were forced into farming, for which they were unprepared, while women lost their main economic role and were relegated to comparative uselessness.

In addition to giving men control of the land, the Europeans attracted or coerced many men to the cities to do the lowest work there. Yet the administrators and missionaries often completely blocked the women, who had previously been the main traders, from even entering the towns. Only married women were allowed into the towns; it was assumed that any single woman in the towns would become a prostitute. Because no normal social life was allowed the Africans in the towns, this was a self-fulfilling prophecy.

Since formal independence has been granted, the African countries have gotten rid of most of the legal restrictions on women and have granted them the right to vote (of little use in one-party states) and the right to hold public office. Nevertheless, "few women are in high public office or in the upper echelons of industry and the professions."[64]

In most of the Third World countries, European imperialism relied on the support of the most reactionary groups, so it tended to encourage and support all the most conservative customs regarding women. For example, in India under the British, the custom of arranging marriages, and virtually selling a young woman for her dowry, continued unabated. Even today, "a majority of unmarried young women in India say the men look at their fathers' bankbook even before they look at them as prospective brides."[65] The dowry system persisted under British rule along with laws that gave only men the right

---

[63] Ester Boserup, *Women's Role in Economic Development* (New York: St. Martin's, 1970), p. 54.

[64] Ruby Leavitt, "Women in Other Cultures," in Vivian Gornick and Barbara Moran, eds., *Women in Sexist Society* (New York: Basic Books, 1971), p. 418.

[65] M. G. Srinath, "Indian Marriages Are Made in Counting House, Not Heaven," Riverside, California, *Press Enterprise,* November 22, 1973.

to hold or inherit property. Only men could be educated, and only men could work outside the home in all except the lowest caste. To provide the dowry, many poor families went into debt. Others looked ahead and simply murdered all girl children at birth.

Many Indian women in the cities have rejected the arranged marriage-dowry system and have fought a long battle against it. Aroused women forced the government to ban dowries by law in 1961. Yet these measures have not penetrated at all into the rural areas where most people live. Even in Delhi, in 1973, "a groom's father threatened to call off the wedding at the last moment unless the girl's father produced a transistor radio worth $200 as part of the dowry."[66] The father of the bride didn't have $200 because he has already spent a great deal of money on the wedding—and his salary was only $150 a month. To save his daughter's marriage, he was forced to borrow at exorbitant interest rates from a money lender.

Such vicious practices have begun to change only in Third World areas where women and men have joined to fight liberation wars against imperialism and reactionary rulers. In North Vietnam, women's equality was proclaimed a goal of the Vietnamese Communist party. Women belong to the party as well as to the separate Women's Union, created specifically to fight for women's liberation. They are campaigning for equality in the Party, in the army, in labor, and in the family. In the economy, the number of women has risen from 500 unskilled workers in 1954 to 50 percent of the industrial workers and 70 percent of the agricultural workers in 1973.[67] Moreover, in 1960 new marriage laws outlawed polygamy and gave women equal rights to obtain divorces, equality in the family, and equality in property ownership. Before that, men had sole control of the family and property and the sole right to divorce; a woman could not even remarry if her husband died! Women now get equal pay for equal work, paid maternity leaves, and some child care.

Although this progress is spectacular, men's attitudes are still sexist, and few women have obtained top management or political positions. An American woman visitor was told that there are still three problem areas for women in North Vietnam.

---

[66] Ibid.

[67] Bunch-Weeks, op. cit., p. 6.

First, their self-image is still one of inferiority, so they shy away from responsible jobs. Second, even though the number of women in politics has greatly increased, there are still too few; and there is resistance to putting women into positions of leadership. Third, the woman is still expected to fulfill the traditional role in the family. The Women's Union is fighting on all three fronts, but expects to win only after housework is socialized and adequate child care becomes available.[68]

A full discussion of the position of women in any of the countries mentioned in this chapter would require a book in itself. And, of course, many countries were not discussed at all. Nevertheless, even this quick survey shows that the position of women has varied tremendously over time and from place to place. Women's inferior status is not immutable. In some societies, women have made tremendous progress; but there is much yet to be done.

[68] See ibid., p. 8.

A CENTURY OF STRUGGLE: AMERICAN WOMEN, 1820–1920

10

A few recent historians have noted the neglect of the women's movement in all conventional histories.[1] For example, the suffrage movement gets only two sentences, but prohibition gets three pages in Morison's *Oxford History of the American People.*[2] In his *New Viewpoints in American History* Arthur Schlesinger said: "If the silence of the historians is to mean anything, it would appear that one-half of our population have been negligible factors in our country's history."[3] This neglect is still the case in all general U.S. histories.

The typical history text mentions that women were *given* the vote in 1920. Susan B. Anthony may be mentioned in a condescending sentence or two. That women struggled for almost a century, that many endured ridicule as well as physical hardships, that the early women's leaders were fighting not just for the vote but for full social, political, and economic equality—these facts are never mentioned.

WOMEN'S STATUS IN PREREVOLUTIONARY AMERICA

Many women came to the United States as indentured servants, sold from London prisons or kidnapped from London streets.

---

[1] See Eleanor Flexner, *Century of Struggle* (New York: Atheneum, 1971), Preface. This is the best single work on the women's movement from 1820 to 1920. The most complete documentation is in Elizabeth Stanton et al., *History of Woman Suffrage* (New York: Fowler & Wells, 1881–1922), 6 vols.

[2] Samuel Morison, *Oxford History of the American People* (New York: Oxford University Press, 1965).

[3] Quoted in Flexner, op. cit., Preface.

They were treated as slaves for seven years, then freed, but without money. Most black women were kidnapped in Africa, then shipped as cargo to America, where they were enslaved for their entire lives. (The situation under slavery in the American South is discussed in a later section of this chapter.)

Even "free" women had very few rights in early America, where the laws were based on British common law. A married woman's property, even property from dowry or inheritance, belonged completely to her husband. Married women did not exist as legal entities apart from their husbands. They couldn't testify in court; they couldn't sue or sign contracts; their earnings belonged to their husbands; and they did not have the right to their own children if legally separated. Few women were allowed to remain single, but the harsh frontier conditions created many widows. The widow usually carried on with her husband's farm or other craft. A widow's life was, in fact, freer than a wife's. The laws concerning married women's property were not changed anywhere until the mid-nineteenth century, and many states retained them until much later.

The subordinate status of women was supported by the dominant ideology of the period, the strongest medium of which was religion. In this very religious atmosphere, all of the sects preached "that woman's place was determined by limitations of mind and body, a punishment for the original sin of Eve. However, . . . to fit her for . . . motherhood, the Almighty had . . . endowed her with such virtues as modesty, meekness, . . . piety."[4]

All women on the frontiers—except a few very upper-class women—led a hard life, working from dawn until dusk. Among the pioneers, the men had to hunt and fight wars, build houses, and clear the fields. The women had to plant, tend, and harvest the crops, turn the skins into clothing, and the meat into edible food.[5] This life-style continued on the frontiers in much the same manner from the sixteenth to the end of the nineteenth century.

It is important to understand that women's status in such a society was fairly low and her work was very hard, yet her status was far higher than in contemporary European societies. In a frontier society, ideology must give way to the necessities

---

[4] Ibid., p. 8.
[5] Ibid., p. 5.

of survival, and woman's work was indispensable. Furthermore, women were always scarce on the frontier, as will be shown in some detail in later sections. Since she was both absolutely necessary and very scarce, her status rose. As husband and wife worked side by side, a companionate, though still unequal, relationship often developed. The laws and the ideology had a much firmer grasp in the older communities than in the newer frontier communities.[6] In later sections, we shall see that the frontier perspective was important in making the western states the first in the U.S. to grant women suffrage.

Many women gained political experience when they organized the Daughters of Liberty to support the American Revolutionary War. The Daughters of Liberty educated women to boycott British goods, keep the farms going during the war, and supply clothing to the army.

Tom Paine spoke for women's rights and described women in the 1770s as "robbed of freedom and will by the laws, the slaves of opinion, which rules them with absolute sway and construes the slightest appearances into guilt; surrounded on all sides by judges, who are at once tyrants and their seducers. . . ."[7] In 1777, during the Revolutionary War, Abigail Adams wrote to her husband (the future president): "In the new code of laws . . . I desire you would remember the ladies. . . . Do not put such unlimited power into the hands of the husbands. Remember, all men would be tyrants if they could. If particular care and attention is not paid to the ladies, we are determined to foment a rebellion, and will not hold ourselves bound by any laws in which we have no voice or representation."[8] These isolated arguments made by a few individuals here and there were the sole reflections of women's protest up to the war—and beyond it until the 1830s.

CONDITIONS FROM THE REVOLUTION TO THE CIVIL WAR

Before the Revolutionary War and up to 1820, there was no education for most women. A few rich women were tutored

---

[6] Ibid., p. 9. The fullest discussion of the frontier conditions and effects on the women's movement is in Alan Grimes, *The Puritan Ethic and Woman Suffrage* (New York: Oxford University Press, 1967).
[7] Quoted in Flexner, op. cit., p. 14.
[8] Quoted in ibid., p. 15.

in French, embroidery, painting, singing, and harpsichord playing in institutions called female seminaries.[9]

In 1819, Emma Willard, who had studied and taught mathematics, presented a petition to the New York legislature for a women's seminary. She would not speak publicly because it was considered unladylike, but she lobbied in private. The legislature gave her a charter but no money. She founded her school in Middlebury, Vermont, in 1814. When she finally got money from the city of Troy, New York, she moved the school there and called it the Troy Female Seminary (now called Emma Willard School). She taught not only history and geography and a little math but also the indelicate subject of physiology: "Mothers visiting a class at the Seminary in the early thirties were so shocked at the sight of a pupil drawing a heart, arteries and veins on a blackboard . . . that they left the room in shame and dismay."[10] All of the women's seminaries at this time were on the high school level—there was no higher education for women.

Public education was slow in coming for both males and females in the nineteenth century. By 1840, a free public education was given to 50 percent of the children in New England, 25 percent in the Middle Atlantic states, 16 percent in the West and only 8 percent in the South. New England took the lead because the area needed skilled workers in industry. Women were admitted immediately to the earliest elementary schools but were resisted at the high school level. There were no free high schools for women until after the Civil War.

The first college to admit women (and blacks) as well as men was Oberlin (in 1833). At first women were given a special course, intended to prepare them for homemaking or teaching. Moreover, women students had special duties: "Washing the men's clothes, caring for their rooms, serving them at table, listening to their orations, but themselves remaining respectfully silent in public assemblages, the Oberlin 'co-eds' were being prepared for intelligent motherhood and a properly subservient wifehood."[11] Most women were still trained to be helpmates, not independent scholars. Not until 1841 did the first

[9] The definitive work on women's education is Mabel Newcomer, *A Century of Higher Education* (New York: Harper & Row, 1959).
[10] Alma Lutz, *Emma Willard* (Boston: Houghton Mifflin, 1929), p. 181.
[11] Quoted in Flexner, op. cit., p. 30.

women graduate from the regular (men's) program at Oberlin.

In 1834, the first college for women, Wheaton College, was founded by Mary Lyon at Norton, Massachusetts. In 1837, she helped found Mt. Holyoke. It was little more than a seminary for a number of years and was called one until 1893. Mary Lyon had proposed the idea of such a college, but she stayed in the background until men had failed to raise enough money; then she went out and did it herself.

In the South it was illegal to teach any slave to read. In the North, black men were barred from almost all public schools, even though they paid taxes for them. Black women were treated still worse. In 1833, a private school for black girls was opened by Prudence Crandall in Canterbury, Connecticut. The "respectable" community attacked it with threats, then jailed Crandall for vagrancy, then tried to legislate against the school in the state legislature, then broke windows, then stoned the teachers and students when they went walking, dropped manure in their well, got shopkeepers to refuse to sell them food, forced doctors to refuse to treat them, and finally physically destroyed the schoolhouse.

While the majority of Americans still lived on farms, women were moving into industry during the first half of the nineteenth century. Women did over 100 different industrial jobs before the Civil War, mostly in the textile industry. By 1850, there were 225,000 women in industrial jobs. At first they worked for the textile industry by sewing at home, where it was "respectable"; then they moved into the factories. They worked 13 to 14 hours a day at very low pay. Women were excluded from many other jobs; and, with few skills besides sewing, thousands were forced to compete against each other in the garment industry, so their wages were forced down. Women were paid from one-seventh to one-fourth of what men were paid in the same industries. Many short-lived unions were formed to protest these conditions. In the "good" cotton mills, women worked from 13 to 16 hours a day. In 1835 there was a strike in Paterson, New Jersey, for a 12-hour day!

In 1845, at the Lowell, Massachusetts, textile mills, a union called the Lowell Female Labor Reform Association was formed. It proved that women workers could develop a stable organization, give it dynamic leadership, and carry on a systematic and partly successful campaign. The union spread to all the mill towns, and delegates went to statewide labor conventions. The association took part in a drive for a 10-hour day and presented petitions to the Massachusetts legislature. Sarah Bagley, leader of the union, spoke bluntly to a legislative committee on working conditions, telling how "she worked in a room with more than 150 people, where 293 small lamps and 61 large lamps burned mornings and evenings all winter, making the air foul; sometimes as many as 30 women were sick in one day from the fumes."[12] The 1830s and 1840s thus saw the first women's efforts for equal pay and better conditions. Women in working-class struggles were an important part of the women's movement in several periods; in fact, the three movements—workers', blacks', and women's—have often intertwined in U.S. history.

Married women in the 1840s still couldn't manage their own property, sign legal papers, or control their own wages. Husbands controlled everything, could drink or gamble away all of it, even if nothing was left for wife or children. A woman had no legal existence at all in marriage: she could not make a will, sue or be sued, or help choose where to live. Her husband still had control of her earnings and property, control of her person, and exclusive control and guardianship of their children, even after a divorce.

Between 1839 and 1860, most states passed legislation that enabled married women to hold property. This was an upper-class reform led by wealthy fathers and even by wealthy husbands who sought protection against creditors. When the law permits a married woman to hold property in her own name, her husband's creditors cannot take her property if her husband goes bankrupt. The law left all other inequalities untouched.

One such inequality was the lack of the right to vote. In the democratic atmosphere that existed immediately after the Revolutionary War, many states allowed free blacks to vote, but the vote was not extended to women. Only one state, New Jersey, allowed all men and women to vote if they were over twenty-one and if they owned property worth 50 pounds. But, by 1800, conservatives in almost all states had limited the vote to free, white males who held property. As a result, only 10 to 13 percent of the population could vote. In 1806, New Jersey also fell into line, limiting the vote to "free, white, male citizens with property."

---

[12] Quoted in ibid., p. 59.

American slavery

American slavery before the Civil War was quite similar to slavery in ancient Athens in regard to the position of both slaves and women. Millions of Africans were kidnapped and sent to the United States as slaves. Their first ordeal after being kidnapped was the Atlantic voyage, on which the slaves were treated as "cargo." During a five- or six-week voyage in small, often storm-tossed ships, the slaves were "chained in pairs to platforms . . . sometimes with as little as eighteen inches between the 'floor' and the 'ceiling' . . . occasionally they would have to double up their legs, with no room to move them."[13] Over one-third of the slaves were women, and there are many recorded cases in which they gave birth to children under these inhuman conditions.

When the slaves who survived the voyage reached the United States, the women were sold at auctions, where they were undressed and carefully inspected. A majority of the women were sold for the same job as men, field hand in the cotton states. A few "lucky" ones were made "house servants," in which job they took care of the house and served the sexual needs of the white master. He often got them pregnant, then sold his own children for a profit. Another large number of slave women were sold to the breeding states, Virginia, North Carolina, Maryland, Delaware, Kentucky, Tennessee, and Missouri. In these states the most important cash crop was the breeding of slaves for sale to the cotton states of the Deep South. A typical advertisement of a slave woman read: "Negroes for sale: A girl about twenty years of age . . . and her two female children. . . . She is very prolific in her generating qualities and affords a rare opportunity to any person who wishes to raise a family of strong and healthy servants for their own use."[14]

What kind of life did the wives of slave owners lead? They lived in material luxury, but slavery was a disaster for them in every other way. According to the southern literary image, the white slave-owning woman was a perfect lady, delicate in looks and manner and submissive to her husband; she brought up the children, managed the house, and was very religious. A southern male wrote: "Her life was one long act

---

[13] Ibid., p. 18.
[14] Quoted in ibid., p. 21.

of devotion—devotion to God, devotion to her husband, devotion to her children, devotion to her servants, to the poor, to humanity."[15] She was certainly devoted to God and husband, but we may be more skeptical about devotion to the slaves, whom she too exploited.

The slave-owning woman's religion told her she was inferior to men (though superior to slaves, just as Aristotle had argued in ancient Greece). Religion told her to be meek, obey her husband, and suffer. The same message of "ladylike" obedience and lack of independence or creativity was impressed on her by schools, parents, books, and magazines. It was said to be her only road to respect and love.

As in every other slave society, the power of the man over the slaves made him the authoritarian patriarch of the family. The South remained strongly patriarchal long after the rest of the country had begun to change.

Contrary to the image of romantic love, most marriages among the slaveholders were arranged for economic reasons, just as they were under slavery in Greece. A southern newspaper wrote in 1808 that ". . . when a young man is about to get him a wife, the first inquiry he makes is, Has such a young lady much property . . . ?"[16] Essentially, the young white woman was also sold, but more politely than her black sister. She was often shocked to find that she didn't live romantically but must supervise a hectic operation. One southern white woman wrote: "Her large family, the immense retinue of slaves who all had to be fed, clothed, nursed, not to mention the incessant demands of hospitality, made her the real burden-bearer of the community."[17] No doubt white women found this life a burden, but think what the burden was on the black woman who slaved for her. We might add that much harder work than the slave owner's wife did was done by the small, free farmer's wife in the South, who not only minded house and children but also hoed the cornfields, often cut firewood, and did her own spinning and weaving.

The myth glorified motherhood, but reality even for the white woman included endless pregnancies, many deaths in

---

[15] Quoted in Anne Scott, *The Southern Lady* (Chicago: University of Chicago Press, 1970), p. 5.
[16] Quoted in ibid., p. 22.
[17] Quoted in ibid., p. 29.

childbirth, and numerous children to care for. Because of the lack of contraceptives, white women were often unenthusiastic about sex. The slave-owning men increasingly exploited their female slaves sexually as relations with their wives deteriorated. The wives were then jealous of the slaves and felt demeaned by their husbands' sexual relations with slave women. As one southern white woman wrote: "Under slavery we live surrounded by prostitutes; like patriarchs of old, our men live in one house with their wives and concubines."[18]

The slave-owning woman usually hated black slave women for the sex that was forced on them. Yet a few white women formed alliances and friendships across the slave-master boundary with black women for mutual support against the white male patriarch. For these and other reasons, most white southern women who wrote about it opposed slavery. A few even went north and joined the abolitionist movement.

As in ancient Greece, education for women was very limited, since it was believed that women had inferior minds. Sarah Grimke, a southern white woman who became an abolitionist, wrote: ". . . The powers of my mind have never been allowed expansion; in childhood they were repressed by the false idea that a girl need not have the education I coveted."[19] Just before the Civil War there was some increase in finishing schools for southern slave-owning women. This occurred because it was felt that educated women might be more pleasant companions; the education consisted mostly of learning to read and practicing the fine arts. And what of education for slave women? To teach a slave to read and write was a crime punishable by prison or even death.

THE MOVEMENT FROM THE REVOLUTION TO THE CIVIL WAR

The rise of industry and the creation of a bourgeois class from the eighteenth-century owners of industry and commerce led to several revolutions against feudalism. The most important of these was the French Revolution, which spread the idea of equality across the world. The American Revolution was fought for independence, but it also initiated the slogan of equality that was assumed and amplified by the French Revolu-

[18] Quoted in ibid., p. 52.
[19] Quoted in ibid., p. 64.

tion. These two revolutions shook American society and changed the ideological outlook of many people. At first, the idea of equality was applied only to white males, but it was inevitable that every oppressed group would make this slogan its own.

The Jacksonian movement in the late 1820s and 1830s continued the democratic ferment for equality. At the same time, conflict between the southern slave owners and the capitalist owners of northern industry became evident over who was to be the dominant political-economic power. Using the rhetoric of equality, some northern businessmen supported a movement to abolish slavery. Many women joined the abolitionist movement and gained their first political experience in it. This movement was the most important direct cause of the upsurge of the women's liberation movement that occurred in the 1830s and 1840s.

One other immediate source of the women's movement was the militant unionism in which working women participated during the 1840s. This early unionism was semipolitical in character and was closely tied to the first working people's political parties of the 1840s. Unionism was, of course, another natural result of the spread of industry throughout the northern United States.

Finally, we must recognize that people need time and money in order to participate politically. The rise of U.S. industry and commerce created a class of upper- and middle-class women who had some leisure and a little money. About this time, these women began to have access to some education, which brought them into contact with the theories of equality then prevalent. Working women, on the contrary, had no leisure time or money and no education. The underrepresentation of working women in the nineteenth-century movement can also be attributed to discrimination against them by some of the leaders of the movement. When working women did find any extra energy for organization, most spent it in the fight for higher wages and better working conditions. Some, however, did become involved in the suffrage movement.

The 1830s witnessed an upsurge of the antislavery movement. The American Anti-Slavery Society was formed in 1833. Twenty women attended, but they were not allowed to sign the Declaration of Purposes. So the women formed their own Female Anti-Slavery Society, though they asked a man to preside at their meeting. The society spread, and the women became more confident. By 1837, when a man volunteered to be presiding officer, they wrote to him "that when the women got together, they found they had *minds* of their own, and could transact their business *without* his directions."[20]

All abolitionists—but especially the militant women because they were held to be "unnatural"—suffered persecution and mob violence over and over again. Many women did particularly dangerous work helping slaves escape through the Underground Railroad.

The most successful railroad "conductor" was Harriet Tubman, herself an escaped slave. This black woman actually made many trips into the South and brought out slaves, whom she then delivered to the next person on the railroad to freedom. Her code name in the underground was Moses. "The white slaveholders put a price on her head. They wanted her captured, dead or alive. But the slaveholders couldn't believe that 'Moses' was a woman. One slaveholder even offered a reward of $40,000 for the capture of 'the escaped male slave known as Moses.' "[21] Ms. Tubman fought in the Union Army during the Civil War, and led a successful raid by 300 black soldiers against the Confederates. She was denied a soldier's pension for many years because she was a woman.

The earliest women to speak publicly for the abolition of slavery were Sarah and Angelina Grimke. They were born into a South Carolina slave-owning family, so their hatred of slavery was based on personal knowledge. In the 1830s, they spoke to small groups of women, then to larger groups, and finally to large public meetings of women and men. For this the Council of Congregationalist Ministers of Massachusetts violently denounced them. Speaking publicly was going beyond women's "God-given place." In answering the attack, they began to speak not only for the slaves but for women. Sarah said: "I ask no favors for my sex. . . . All I ask of our brethren is that they will take their feet off our necks and permit us to stand upright. . . ."[22]

---

[20] Quoted in Flexner, op. cit., p. 42.

[21] Susan Brownmiller, *Shirley Chisholm* (New York: Pocket Books, 1972), p. 25. For Tubman's biography, see Earl Conrad, *Harriet Tubman* (New York: International Publishers, 1942).

[22] Quoted in Flexner, op. cit., p. 47.

The male abolitionists, even the radicals, cautioned the Grimkes to be quiet because pushing for women's rights might hurt the cause of abolitionism. This tactical argument divided the black and women's movement time and time again. Angelina replied: "Why, my dear brothers, can you not see the deep laid scheme of the clergy against us lecturers? . . . If we surrender the right to *speak* in public this year, we must surrender the right to petition next year, and the right to write the year after, and so on. What *then* can *woman* do for the slave . . . ?"[23] Here we have a clear instance of sexist ideology used to split and weaken a progressive moment.

In 1840, women delegates to the World Anti-Slavery Convention in London were denied seats and forced to sit in the gallery. This treatment made the women even more aware of their inferior status. Discussion by these women finally led to the first Women's Rights Convention at Seneca Falls, New York, in 1848—though "convention" meant a meeting of interested people, not delegates. They declared: "We hold these truths to be self-evident: that all men and women are created equal."[24] The forms of social, economic, and legal discrimination against women were listed and the women pledged to use every means to end discrimination. The only disagreement was on whether to demand the vote—some said it was too radical and ridiculous—but a suffrage resolution was finally passed by a small majority. Until 1860, there were frequent meetings, primarily just talk aimed at trying to agree on a program; there was no national organization. In fact, the women's movement was run mostly by married women in their few moments of spare time, after doing all the housework and child care.

Many newspapers attacked the women's suffrage movement. For example, the *New York Herald* attacked the suffragist Lucy Stone, who spoke well and might have been a lawyer, saying "How funny it would sound in the newspapers that Lucy Stone, pleading a case, took suddenly ill . . . and perhaps gave birth to a bouncing boy in court."[25] The same nonsense was repeated for decades.

To answer and state their own views, women started their

[23] Quoted in ibid., p. 48.
[24] Quoted in ibid., p. 75.
[25] Quoted in ibid., pp. 81–82.

own newspapers: *The Lily, The Una, Pittsburgh Visiter, Women's Advocate.* No national organization was formed because the women thought it would be cumbersome, might stifle individual initiative, and was not necessary. They concentrated on issues of equality—social, economic, and legal—but very few of the women emphasized the vote. Some didn't see the vote as being really important; others just thought that it was impossible to achieve.

Three women were the most important personalities in the movement: Lucy Stone[26] was considered its most gifted orator; Elizabeth Stanton,[27] its best philosopher and program writer; Susan B. Anthony,[28] its best organizer.

Lucy Stone's upbringing on a poor Massachusetts farm seems to have turned her into a feminist. She saw that her mother worked as hard as her father, yet the father was indisputably the master in the house. She taught school for seven years to earn enough money to attend Oberlin, where she was one of the first women to graduate from the full course. She became a lecturer for the Anti-Slavery Society, but often included women's rights in her talks. Abolitionists, afraid she was hurting the cause, asked her to drop the incendiary topic. Finally a compromise was made; she would speak on abolition on Saturdays and Sundays; on women's rights, the rest of the week. The breadth of issues with which the early women's movement was concerned is shown by Stone's three stock lectures on women. One was on women's social and industrial disabilities, another on legal and political handicaps, and the third on moral and religious discrimination.

The marriage of Lucy Stone and Henry Blackwell in 1855 received wide public attention because of the statement they incorporated into the ceremony. In this statement Blackwell repudiated the superior status the law granted him as husband, and the couple declared themselves equal partners in the marriage. Lucy Stone retained her maiden name throughout her life. Marriage did not hamper Lucy Stone. She continued her

---

[26] See Alice Blackwell, *Lucy Stone* (Boston: Little, Brown, 1930).

[27] See Alma Lutz, *Created Equal, a Biography of Elizabeth Stanton* (New York: Day, 1940). Also see Mary Oakley, *Elizabeth Cady Stanton* (New York: Feminist Press, 1972).

[28] See Ida Harper, *The Life and Work of Susan B. Anthony* (Indianapolis: Hollenbeck Press, 1898, 1908), 3 vols.

lecturing and was active in the suffrage movement throughout the second half of the nineteenth century.

Elizabeth Cady Stanton attended the 1840 World Anti-Slavery Convention in London and was denied a seat because of her sex. Eight years later, she was to be the moving force in calling the first women's rights convention in Seneca Falls, where she introduced a resolution calling for women's suffrage. Despite being married and having seven children, she was to be active in the women's movement for the rest of her life. A good speaker, her greatest contribution was as the movement's philosopher. Her attention was never restricted to suffrage. She called for equality in all spheres; she advocated marriage and divorce law reform at a time when this was considered a topic that should not even be mentioned. She strongly criticized the Bible for its statements on women.

Susan B. Anthony, Stanton's lifelong friend and co-worker, came to the women's movement via the temperance movement. She soon became the movement's greatest organizer. In 1854, Anthony led a petition campaign in New York for women to control their own wages, to have guardianship of their children after a divorce, and to be allowed to vote. She had 60 women "captains," one in each county; they collected 6000 signatures in 10 weeks in spite of harassment. When she presented the signatures and spoke to a Joint Judiciary Committee of the State Legislature, the committee turned down the petition with "humorous" arguments, saying that the ladies ". . . always have the best seat. . . . They have their choice on which side of the bed they will lie . . . if there is any inequity or oppression . . . , the gentlemen are the sufferers."[29] But continuous struggle brought some success. In 1860, Stanton addressed a joint session, and the state legislature passed a law giving women control over their own wages, allowing them to sue in court, and giving them inheritance rights similar to their husbands'.

Unmarried, Anthony bore the brunt of the traveling and lecturing when her married friends could not get away from home. She spent much of her life on the lecture circuit, enduring hostility, ridicule, extreme cold and heat, bedbugs, and miserable food. Although agreeing with Stanton that real equality would require many social and legal reforms, she concen-

[29] Quoted in Flexner, op. cit., p. 85.

trated on suffrage. The vote, she believed, was the prerequisite to other reforms. She also felt strongly that women would not be free until they could support themselves, until marriage became a luxury and not a necessity for women as for men. Education she saw as one key, and because she believed sex-segregated education would always be unequal, she advocated coeducation.

A woman who fought equally well for both abolition and women's rights was Sojourner Truth, a freed slave. At a women's meeting in Akron, Ohio, in 1851, a clergyman argued that women are weak and helpless and ridiculed their ability to vote. The women all hesitated to answer until Sojourner Truth rose and said:

> The man over there says women need to be helped into carriages and lifted over ditches, and to have the best place everywhere. Nobody ever helps me into carriages or over puddles, or gives me the best place—and ain't I a woman? [She raised her bare black arm and said:] Look at my arm! I have ploughed and planted and gathered into barns, and no man could head me—and ain't I a woman? I could work as much and eat as much as a man—when I could get it—and bear the lash as well! And ain't I a woman? I have borne 13 children, and seen most of 'em sold into slavery, and when I cried out with my mother's grief, none but Jesus heard me—and ain't I a woman?"[30]

The women's movement was confined to the North and the West. No women spoke for women's rights in the South before the Civil War. The white women slave owners were supposed to be on a pedestal, but they were (metaphorically) chained to it and supposed to keep silent. Black women were more literally chained.

CONDITIONS FROM THE CIVIL WAR TO 1900

On the farm where most people still lived, full-time work by both sexes was absolutely necessary. Furthermore, in the frontier states women were very scarce. The ratio of men to women was 3 to 1 in California, 4 to 1 in Washington, 8 to 1 in Nevada, and 20 to 1 in Colorado.[31] On the frontier, women worked just as hard as men. A frontier woman wrote about a typical day in her diary: "churned and made a cheese . . . painted

---

[30] Quoted in ibid., p. 90.
[31] Ibid., p. 157.

. . . front door. Washed and cleaned furniture for painting. . . . Dipped 24 dozen candles. . . . Our house [windows] is wholly glassed though to complete it I had to set 47 squares of glass."[32] The obvious indispensability of women's work, combined with the scarcity of women, led to greater egalitarianism in the West and thus to greater receptivity to women's suffrage.

Free high schools for women were first opened in Boston and Philadelphia just after the Civil War. Still, there was great opposition to any higher education for women. It was argued that too much study would fatigue women (because they have smaller brains) and ruin their reproductive organs. In the 1850s and early 1860s, women were permitted to enter some Midwest universities, such as Iowa and Wisconsin. They were turned down until 1870 at Michigan, Ohio, and Illinois. For the most part, these universities admitted women only when they lacked students, particularly when the men went off to fight in the war.

In the East, women were mostly restricted to single-sex colleges, which had to give much remedial work because women lacked good preparation for college. Vassar paid women faculty lower salaries and didn't allow them on faculty committees. A number of women's colleges were established during the second half of the nineteenth century—Vassar in 1865, Smith and Wellesley in 1875, the "Harvard Annex" (later Radcliffe) in 1879, and Bryn Mawr in 1885.

Lack of male teachers resulted in many women going into teaching during the Civil War. After the war, teaching became mostly female, though it had been considered a male job previously. The change occurred, at least in part, because women could be paid lower salaries; in New York in 1853, women teachers were paid 10 percent of the male salary! In most states, women teachers were fired if they married. The reason for this rule was that unmarried women were more submissive because they had no alternative source of support, and so they could be paid less.

In the western pioneer states, women gained the right to control their own property and earnings between 1860 and 1900. In the East, there was some, but less, progress. In 1900, a married woman in Pennsylvania still couldn't sign a contract without her husband's approval. In the South, almost no prog-

---

[32] Quoted in ibid., p. 158.

ress was made in the laws, and almost no women were educated beyond elementary school. Even in the West, as late as 1900 in Minnesota, if a woman was divorced for adultery, she had to forfeit all property, including her own; but there was no similar penalty for men. The same was true in many other states. This was the double standard with a vengeance.

Pioneer and working women dressed roughly, but the mid-nineteenth-century middle- and upper-class "lady" was forced to follow Queen Victoria. Corsets made of steel ribs or whalebone and tight laces were the style, and some young girls had to sleep in them to "narrow the waist." Petticoats and skirts added another 15 pounds. Women could hardly move or breathe, their muscles atrophied, and they fainted with the slightest exertion (no wonder!). A number of early women's leaders attempted to institute a change in style or at least give women an option by adopting the bloomer costume—a short skirt worn over long, full pants. They were subjected to so much ridicule that they came to believe they were hurting the chances of more important reforms and gave up the costume. Women continued to wear long skirts until the feminist upsurge of the 1920s.

During the Civil War women worked in factories, in addition to their traditional work at home. Women kept the farms going. Women became nurses in the Union Army, even though the Army Medical Corps was mostly hostile. Women became teachers in order to keep the schools open.

Although in the mid-nineteenth century women were allowed into industry, they were resisted in the professions. A perceptive woman wrote in 1853 that "millions of women . . . are condemned to the most menial drudgery . . . for one fourth the wages [of men]. . . . They plough, reap, dig . . . chop wood . . . do anything that is hard work, physical labor, and who says anything against it. But let one presume to use her mental powers . . . take up any profession . . . which is deemed honorable and requires talent, and O! . . . unloose his corsets! . . . What a fainting fit Mr. Propriety has taken! Just to think that 'one of the deah creathures' . . . should foresake the sphere—woman's sphere—to mix with the wicked strife of this wicked world.[33]

Elizabeth Blackwell wanted to be a doctor but was turned

[33] Quoted in ibid., p. 113.

down by 29 medical schools. She was then admitted to one as a joke, but persisted and, in 1849, became the first woman M.D. In New York, however, she couldn't find a house or office to rent, had no private patients, and was given no access to hospitals. Finally, in 1857, she started her own hospital, which was run completely by women. After the war there was still no reputable medical school that would admit women, so in 1868 she opened the "Woman's Infirmary Medical School."

In 1872 a woman was prohibited from getting a license to practice law in Illinois. But women were entering law practice in some other states; and Belva Lockwood was admitted to the bar of the United States Supreme Court in 1879.

After the Civil War, vast industrial expansion commenced. Permanent, national unions came into being in the 1870s. Women factory workers increased: 226,000 in 1850; 271,000 in 1860; 323,000 in 1870. Most were still in the sewing trades, which were overcrowded and paid very low wages. Women were admitted to the printers' union and to the cigar markers' union in 1869. Women were important in the militant federation called the National Labor Union in the 1860s and 1870s—but this union lasted only a short while.

Women not only got low wages but often were not paid at all. Many suits for unpaid wages were brought by the Legal Aid Society. Several women at a meeting to discuss legal aid in 1864 said: "Oh, if we could always get paid for our work, we could get along."[34]

In 1868, Susan B. Anthony helped form a "Working Women's Association." Some of the members wanted to teach work skills; Ms. Anthony herself wanted to campaign for suffrage; but most members wanted to fight economic discrimination. In 1869, they organized Women's Typographical Union, Local #1, which was strongly encouraged by some of the men's locals. Because of the male expression of solidarity, the women steadfastly supported the union. The national president of the typographers said: "Though most liberal inducements were offered to women compositors to take the places of men on strike, not a single member of the women's union could be induced to do so."[35] Yet most other union locals did not support the women. A woman organizer reported to the printers' union

[34] Quoted in ibid., p. 132.
[35] Quoted in ibid., p. 135.

convention in 1871 that: "We refuse to take the men's situations when they are on strike, and when there is no strike if we ask for work in union offices we are told by union foremen that 'there are no [jobs]' for us."[36] So the tactic of divide and rule by sexism won again; the women's locals died out. Other short-lived unions run by women in the 1870s were those of the laundry workers, who worked in rooms where the temperature reached 100°; and the shoemakers, who called themselves Daughters of St. Crispin. In all cases, the women's anger at awful conditions and unequal pay led to organization and some success, but sexism by male unions led to eventual defeat.

In 1880, there were 2,600,000 women workers, or 15 percent of the labor force. In 1890, there were 4,000,000 women workers, or 17 percent of the labor force. In 1890, 1,000,000 women were domestic servants, 523,000 were clothing and textile workers, and 109,000 were laundry workers.

In 1881, the Knights of Labor became a national labor federation. It set up craft locals but also established regional "assemblies," covering all the workers in a geographical area. In 1886 there were 113 women's assemblies including all kinds of women workers, from teachers to laundry workers. The Knights had women national delegates—16 women out of 660 delegates in 1886. They also had a woman organizer. Some of their women investigators found that the average woman worker worked 10 hours a day for $5 a *week*. The women organizers complained ". . . many women are deterred from joining labor organizations by foolish pride, prudish modesty . . . religious scruples . . . and expectancy that in the near future marriage will lift them out of the industrial life. . . ."[37] Thus, women's sexist social conditioning as well as male sexism presented obstacles to women's unionization.

In the 1890s, the Knights of Labor died and the American Federation of Labor became the most important labor organization. The AFL mostly organized skilled craft workers. It included few women, gave women no encouragement, and had only one woman organizer (Mary Kenney, for five months in 1892), then none for a long time.

The 1890s saw much social tension. The frontier no longer existed as a safety valve. Millions of workers were in sweatshops

[36] Quoted in ibid., p. 136.
[37] Quoted in ibid., p. 200.

and slums; but there were 4047 millionaires! "Muckraking" journalist attacks on big business were frequent, as were radical proposals for better societies (e.g., Edward Bellamy's utopian novel, *Looking Backward*). In the 1870s and 1880s, many utopian colonies formed. The rise of the Populist party occurred in the 1880s and 1890s. The period was characterized by strikes, much hysteria about communism, anarchism, and bomb throwing, and considerable class polarization.

Nevertheless, many middle-class women joined reform organizations. In 1899 the New York Consumers League exposed the terrible working conditions of women; it had branches in 20 states by 1896 and at its height was led by Florence Kelley. Middle-class women also formed "settlement houses," which gave charity and advice but also helped organize the poor and working women. The main settlement house in Chicago was founded by Jane Addams, who worked closely with organized labor. For the most part, however, middle-class reform movements had little to do with working-class radicals and labor organizations.

THE MOVEMENT FROM THE CIVIL WAR TO 1890

No women's rights activity took place during the Civil War; in the North, women concentrated on propagandizing and petitioning for the abolition of slavery. These women expected equality for blacks *and* women after the war. Thus they felt betrayed when the Fourteenth and Fifteenth Amendments were introduced in Congress in 1866 and restricted the protection of the right to vote to male citizens. This was the first time the word *male* was used in the Constitution. The women knew it would take many more decades to get another amendment for women.

Tragically, the abolitionist movement and the women's movement split. Why? The white male abolitionists consisted of northern businessmen and intellectuals. The businessmen wanted an end to slavery so that northern business could expand. As soon as slavery was abolished, they quit, feeling that their purpose had been accomplished. Social and economic equality for the freed slaves was not a part of their program. The businessmen were against equality and better wages for all workers; many were still for limiting the male vote by property qualifications. They opposed women's suffrage because it might disturb the status quo. Northern politicians wanted the black vote because they believed it would insure Republican victories in the South and enable them to dominate national politics. They could see no gain from women's votes. The intellectuals were middle class; they felt that formal equality for the ex-slaves was sufficient, and they still had biases against women. Black males wanted the vote for blacks urgently because they were still being lynched and physically and legally attacked. Black leaders didn't want to jeopardize the vote for blacks by adding women's votes to the amendment.

The militant women's leaders, who were white and middle class, reacted violently with racist slurs against putting "Sambo" Africans, Chinese, and "ignorant" foreigners ahead of women. Ms. Stanton said that male suffrage "creates an antagonism between black men and all women that will culminate in fearful outrages on womanhood, especially in the southern states."[38]

The joint movement had formed an American Equal Rights Association for pushing both blacks' and women's rights, but it split in May 1869. Stanton and Anthony were for an immediate women's suffrage amendment. When many others opposed it, they formed the National Woman Suffrage Association (called the National hereafter), which did not admit men and worked militantly for suffrage. The National published a paper called *Revolution,* and campaigned not only for suffrage but against the exploitation and terrible conditions of women (and men) workers and the unequal social situation of women. It ran campaigns against the double standard—and published some writers who advocated "free love," which shocked the Victorian world. The *Revolution* even criticized the churches for their sexist ideas and support of discrimination.

In November 1869, the moderates organized the American Woman Suffrage Association (called the American hereafter), which included men in its ranks and whose first president was a man. The organization's main spokesperson was Lucy Stone, and she brought in many middle- and upper-class club women and professionals. The American's newspaper, the *Woman's Journal,* was well financed, unlike the more outspoken *Revolution,* which went bankrupt in just two and a half years. The *Journal* was quite conservative in style and soft-pedaled

---

[38] Quoted in ibid., p. 144.

suffrage. It said nothing about exploitation at work or domination in marriage, and did not attack the churches.

The more radical National also utilized much more militant tactics. For example, in 1876, at a centennial celebration of U.S. independence in Philadelphia—where the emperor of Brazil was the guest of honor—Ms. Anthony suddenly got up on the stage and read a Declaration of Rights for Women, which her supporters then distributed as a leaflet. The National also protested by having 150 women try to vote in 1872. Ms. Anthony was prosecuted for voting illegally. The judge would not even allow her to testify, since women were "incompetent" to do so. She was found guilty and fined $100, but refused to pay; the government never tried to collect because it didn't want the case to be appealed.

In 1872, the National supported a case by Ms. Virginia Minor, who tried to vote on the ground that voting was a privilege granted all citizens by the first section of the Fourteenth Amendment. But in 1874, the United States Supreme Court ruled against Ms. Minor on the grounds that states have the right to set property qualifications or deny the vote to criminals, to the insane, or to women.

The National campaigned for a federal suffrage amendment; known as the Anthony Amendment, it was introduced every year from 1868 on. Actually, the first test in Congress was a bill in 1866 to give women the vote in the District of Columbia. During the debate Senator Williams claimed that if women could hold political views apart from their husbands it would "make every home a hell on earth." Senator Frelinghuysen said that "the God of our race" has stamped on American women a "higher and holier mission" than politics. "Their mission is at home, by their blandishments . . . to assuage the passions of men as they come in from the battle of life. . . ."[39] These two arguments—that women belong in the home, and that the home would be ruined—were used against suffrage by congressmen *ad nauseam.* The bill lost by 37 to 9.

The American worked for suffrage state by state, with success first in the West, where most women in fact worked equally with men. When Wyoming first became a territory, a Ms. Esther Morris lobbied most of the territorial legislators. Her lobbying took the form of serving them both a dinner and a

---

[39] Quoted in ibid., p. 148.

speech patterned on one of Ms. Anthony's. In 1869, Wyoming gave women suffrage, mainly on the argument that women were very scarce and this gesture would attract them. Wyoming also gave women control of their own wages and property and admitted them to jury duty. Ms. Morris was appointed the first woman justice of the peace, and served her full term despite verbal attacks by the newspapers and physical attacks by hooligans.

When Wyoming tried to become a state in 1889, some congressmen argued that it should not be admitted with women's suffrage because the Fourteenth Amendment makes it unconstitutional for women to vote! Southern congressmen argued that *states* have no right to grant suffrage, quite contrary to their usual talk about states' rights. The Wyoming territorial delegate thought that Wyoming would not be admitted with women's suffrage, so he telegraphed his legislature to ask if they would drop women's suffrage to get statehood. The state legislature, elected partly by women's votes, telegraphed back: "We will remain out of the Union a hundred years rather than come in without the women."[40] Finally, in 1890, Wyoming was admitted by a slim margin in Congress, and became the first state with women's suffrage.

The territory of Utah, run by the Mormons, was locked in a battle with the federal Congress over the issue of plural marriages. The issue of women's suffrage became involved as a political tactic on both sides.[41] In 1870, in order to gain political support for plural marriage among women in Utah and elsewhere (and to prove that Mormon women would also vote for plural marriage), the Mormon men's government suddenly gave women the right to vote in Utah. Then, in 1887, when Congress outlawed plural marriages, it added another clause in the same bill revoking women's suffrage in Utah. Finally, in 1896, when Utah became a state, having renounced plural marriage, the state constitution again gave women the vote.

Before women's suffrage was won in 1920, the women's organizations conducted 56 referendum campaigns; 480 campaigns to get state legislatures to allow suffrage referenda; 47 campaigns at state constitutional conventions for suffrage; 277 campaigns to include women's suffrage in state party programs;

[40] Quoted in ibid., p. 178.
[41] Discussed in ibid., pp. 162–163.

30 campaigns to get women's suffrage in national party programs; and 19 campaigns to get the Nineteenth Amendment through Congress.

In Congress, the Nineteenth Amendment did not get out of committee for many years. After much lobbying, it finally got to the floor of Congress in 1886. The southerners spoke against it because, according to them, black women shouldn't get the vote. Senator West said it would ruin the home and make women into dangerous agitators, as they became during the French Revolution—"Who led those bloodthirsty mobs? Who shrieked loudest in that hurricane of passions? Women!"[42] The amendment was defeated 34 to 16, with 22 of the negative votes from the South. It was proposed and defeated every year after that until 1896—after which it didn't appear again until 1913, as we shall see.

Both the National and the American suffrage organizations remained rather small, elite, and ineffectual in this early period. But other women's organizations were formed. The housework of middle-class women in the cities was getting easier with better technology and use of immigrant women as maids. So these middle-class women had more time, and they formed women's clubs. Also, there were more women working as semi-professionals—in 1870 there were 90,000 women teachers; by 1890, the number had increased to 250,000—and they also formed organizations. There were huge numbers of women's clubs, for literary study and "self-improvement," and discussion of reforms. In 1890, the most stable ones formed the General Federation of Women's Clubs. At least 20 black women's clubs also existed but they were rejected for membership by the General Federation, so they formed their own National Association of Colored Women. Once again, racism divided women in a way that allowed them all to be controlled more easily.

Alcoholism was widespread as the last refuge of downtrodden male workers. Its burden fell on wives, whose entire family shopping money might go for their husbands' drink. For this reason, among others, most women reformers favored prohibition. The Women's Christian Temperance Union (WCTU) was formed in 1874, and in 1879 Frances Willard became its president. She was very able and experienced, having been a dean at Northwestern University until she found it impossible

[42] Quoted in ibid., p. 175.

to work with the all-male board of trustees. She organized WCTU chapters in every state and increased its membership to over 200,000. This remarkable woman not only worked for prohibition but openly and strongly pushed for women's suffrage. Before her death in 1898, the WCTU put more money and organizers into the suffrage campaigns than the official associations. The organization's activity also sparked intensified opposition to suffrage by the liquor interests.

THE MOVEMENT IN THE 1890s

In 1890, the National and the American merged into the National American Woman Suffrage Association (NAWSA). The National had grown less radical in its tactics and much less interested in working-class causes, limiting itself to suffrage. The American had become even more strongly in favor of suffrage, and more willing to use political tactics. The merged organization slowly became more conservative and respectable, attracting many former WCTU leaders. It devoted itself to the single issue of suffrage and even gave up on the federal amendment, spending most of its small numbers and limited efforts on state referenda.

Why this change in tone and direction? The women in NAWSA by 1890 were the Boston and New York elite of leisured club women, plus a few professional women. They were fighting for a cause that had become almost respectable among the middle class and in Congress. A highly educated woman speaker was no longer a rarity. The women were totally isolated from working women, whom they often looked down on with contempt. As we have seen, this was an era of growing labor-versus-capital disputes and increasing class polarization.

As the movement became more respectable, the typical member was no longer a nonconformist and iconoclast. Women who agreed with their middle-class contemporaries on every issue but suffrage entered NAWSA. Anti-immigrant and anti-black feeling and rhetoric were very strong at the time, and both were reflected in the new, prosuffrage rhetoric. Partly from belief—and partly as a tactic to win equally prejudiced male legislators, voters, and the business interests of the East and South—the NAWSA leaders often advocated *limited* suffrage for women during this period. They argued that the vote could be limited to all men and women who were educated and propertied, thus excluding most of the workers, immigrants, and blacks.

In 1902, the suffrage leader Ms. Stanton said in answer to the objection that women's suffrage would double the "ignorant vote" of immigrants: "The patent answer to this is to abolish the ignorant vote. . . . There have been various restrictions in the past for men. We are willing to abide by the same for women."[43] In 1903, NAWSA President Anna Shaw said: "Never before in the history of the world have men made former slaves the political masters of their former mistresses. . . . There is not a nation from pole to pole that does not send its contingent to govern American women."[44] Southern suffragists especially pandered to racism, one exclaiming: "How can I, with the blood of heroes in my heart . . . quietly submit to representation by the alien and the negro?"[45]

The women's movement grew out of the abolitionist movement and had its closest ties with the black liberation movement until the Civil War. Conflict began when the Fourteenth and Fifteenth Amendments gave the vote to blacks but not to women. The two movements remained friendly until the 1890s, when the women's movement completely dissociated itself from blacks in order to become "respectable." In the early 1900s, the women's movement became antiblack in order to win the South. Women's suffrage associations affiliated with NAWSA appeared in every southern state by 1900, and two southerners, Laura Clay and Kate Gordon, held seats on the national board until 1910. These southern women argued on every occasion that white supremacy would benefit from women's suffrage because white women would outnumber blacks.

Ironically, southern white males did not buy the argument. White men opposed all change in the status quo; they were afraid women might seek social equality and were most afraid, in the words of an Alabama pamphlet, "that *Woman Suffrage* means a reopening of the entire *Negro Suffrage* question. . . ."[46]

Part of the change in tactics was an end to the old argument,

[43] Quoted in Andrew Sinclair, *The Emancipation of the American Woman* (New York: Harper & Row, 1965), p. 299.
[44] Quoted in ibid., p. 296.
[45] Quoted in ibid.
[46] Quoted in ibid., p. 298.

originating in the American and French revolutions, that justice requires that women as well as men be allowed to rule themselves, that they not be taxed without representation. The suffragists switched to an argument from expediency; they told reformers that women were purer than men and would vote for reforms. Therefore progressive or reform-oriented men need not *share* votes and power with women but could *double* their votes and power.[47]

Similarly, they argued that because women are better and purer that men, politics would improve when good, motherly women were allowed to participate. Thus they accepted Victorian sexist stereotypes as a basis for their arguments. They extended this argument to claim that women should work for various reforms. For example, women should support the pure food and drug acts because they are good for the family, and women should fight for minimum wage and hour acts for women because delicate women need protection—but the vote was the necessary prerequisite for all such struggles.

Why did they concentrate on the sole issue of the vote? Middle-class women had already won the right to a higher education, provided that the family could pay for it. They had also won new property laws that protected a woman's right to control her own property, if she had any. So their immediate needs had been won, and they now mainly wanted formal equality with men in the Constitution. Many believed in sexist stereotypes themselves, and so they felt that it was not "natural" for women to work or to be equal in the family. Hence they largely ignored the two areas of labor and family relations—and some believed that the vote would give them such equality.

From 1870 to 1910, the suffragists were remarkably unsuccessful. This was partly due to their own conservative tactics and racist, elitist positions, which alienated their potential allies. Partly, too, it was due to continued opposition from those who feared women's votes for even more conservative and elitist reasons; this opposition included southern politicians, the liquor industry, city bosses, and big business, as we shall see later. Since NAWSA devoted little attention to it, the federal amendment never even reached the floor of Congress from 1893 to

---

[47] See the excellent and comprehensive discussion in Aileen Kraditor, *The Ideas of the Woman Suffrage Movement, 1890–1920* (New York: Columbia University Press, 1965), pp. 200 ff.

1913. In the states, a huge number of campaigns resulted in only 17 actual referendum votes, almost all in the West. Only two of these were won, those in Colorado and Idaho, where the radical Populist movement was powerful. Since Wyoming and Utah were admitted as states with women's suffrage, the result of all the suffragists' work up to 1910 was four and only four states, all in the West, won for suffrage.

CONDITIONS, 1900–1920

Since the AFL didn't organize women, in 1903 a National Women's Trade Union League was formed by some middle-class, some professional, and some union women. It lobbied Congress to provide money for an investigation of the terrible working conditions of women and children. The report resulting from this investigation, which was issued in 19 volumes from 1908 to 1911, helped pass protective labor laws for women. By 1907, some 20 states had laws limiting women's hours of work. The United States Supreme Court had declared such laws for all workers unconstitutional on the basis that they were an unreasonable, unnecessary, and arbitrary interference with the right and liberty of the individual to contract in relation to his labor. But in *Muller* v. *Oregon* (1908) the Supreme Court held that women are especially delicate creatures who need special protection, and on that basis it upheld protective labor laws for women only.

The number of women workers continued to climb: 4,000,000 in 1890; 5,300,000 in 1900; 7,400,000 in 1910. In 1900, 1,800,000 women were in domestic or other service; 700,000 were farm laborers; 325,000 teachers; 878,000 clothing and textile workers; 174,000 clerical workers; and 217,000 sales clerks.

In 1900, women started organizing the International Ladies Garment Workers Union. The garment industry employed many immigrant women and paid very low wages. Because the immigrant women had no power to collect their wages, they were sometimes not paid at all. For the most part the industry used small wooden buildings, with little or no sanitation and little protection from fire; as a result, several tragic fires occurred. The women worked very long hours in ill-lit rooms amid very noisy machinery. ILGWU officers were mostly white males; and they still are, though the members are now mostly Puerto Rican and black women. In 1909, a strike was considered and a mass meeting was held in New York, at which Samuel Gompers of the AFL, Socialist party leaders, and other union leaders all gave very long speeches. The meeting almost died from too much rhetoric until one young worker got up and said: "I am a working girl, and one of those who are on strike against intolerable conditions. . . . I offer a resolution that a general strike be declared—now!"[48] The strike grew to between 20,000 and 30,000 women. It was helped by the AFL and by the Women's Trade Union League, which called a massive support rally in the New York Hippodrome addressed by the president of NAWSA. Still, the strikers almost starved during a very cold winter. The women picketed every day; the police often assaulted them and arrested many. The courts supported the bosses and approved the police attacks, with one judge telling a striker: "You are on strike against God and Nature, whose prime law it is that man shall earn his bread in the sweat of his brow." To this profound observation, George Bernard Shaw retorted: "Delightful. Medieval America always in intimate personal confidence of the Almighty."[49]

In spite of all the obstacles, women workers continued to organize in this period. During a militant strike in 1912 in the textile industry at Lawrence, Massachusetts, the women said they fought for beautiful lives as well as for money, they fought for both "bread and roses."

As we come marching, marching,
Un-numbered women dead
Go crying through our singing
Their ancient song of bread;
Small art and love and beauty
Their drudging spirits knew—
Yes, it is bread we fight for,
But we fight for roses, too.

As we come marching, marching,
We bring the greater days;
The rising of the women
Means the rising of us all.
No more the drudge and idler,
Ten that toil where one reposes,

[48] Quoted in Flexner, op. cit., p. 241.
[49] Quoted in ibid., p. 243.

But a sharing of life's glories,
Bread and Roses, Bread and Roses.

Another part of the song, which was inspired by the strike, said: "Hearts can starve as well as bodies, Give us Bread and give us Roses."[50]

Led by middle-class presidents until 1921, the Women's Trade Union League organized women, worked for protective laws, and propagandized in support of working women. The AFL was cordial, gave much praise, but offered little concrete help. Only 5 percent of women workers in manufacturing were unionized by 1910, and almost none were organized in the service occupations.

Women workers wanted equal pay, a shorter workday, safer conditions, and less harassment from foremen, including less sexual attention. They were too busy getting a job with decent pay and conditions to worry about the vote. Some early women unionists were suspicious of the suffragists and reformers. Mother Jones, an organizer for the mine workers, said the plutocrats want women to concentrate on "suffrage, prohibition, and charity" rather than the real issues of class struggle, and added: "you don't need a vote to raise hell!"[51] Only in the period from 1908 to 1920 did some socialist women and militant union women join the fight for the vote, but then they were very important in swinging large numbers of working-class men toward women's suffrage. The suffrage movement itself remained white, Anglo-Saxon, and middle class, and never had many working-class members.[52]

The Socialist party and women

The Socialist party helped greatly to make workers conscious of and sympathetic to women's suffrage. At its first convention, in 1901, its program demanded "equal civil and political rights for men and women."[53] It was the only political party to allow

---

[50] The full text of the song, "Bread and Roses," may be found in Irwin Silber, ed., *Lift Every Voice* (New York: People's Artists, 1953), pp. 32–33.

[51] Quoted in William O'Neill, *Everyone Was Brave* (New York: Quadrangle, 1969), p. 54.

[52] See Kraditor, op. cit., pp. 105–128.

[53] Quoted in the excellent article by Mari Jo Buhle, "Women and the Socialist Party, 1901–1914," in Edith Altback, ed., *From Feminism to Liberation* (Cambridge, Mass.: Schenkman, 1971), p. 67.

participation by women. On the other hand, in its early years the party ignored most of the special demands of women, even suffrage, and made no special effort to recruit women.

Until 1908, women made up only a small portion of party members although there were a number of auxiliary or women's locals composed mostly of the wives of members. In 1904, a Woman's National Socialist Union was organized. It was the first radical U.S. women's organization—but it got nowhere except in California, where both socialism and suffrage were already strong among women. At the same time, the party began to eye the growing suffragist numbers as a source of recruits. They proudly pointed to their stand for equal rights, but their own sexism prevented them from doing anything about it. One socialist man admitted that "when we come to practice, we are not always in accord with this highly respectable principle of ours."[54] One woman complained that her husband had been going to socialist meetings for six years, but "he has never yet asked me to attend any of them with him."[55] Most socialists' wives were still expected to conform to the Victorian image by doing nothing but stand at their husbands' sides and "cheer their efforts."

In 1907, however, Josephine Kaneko founded a newpaper called the *Socialist Woman,* which thundered for both socialism and women's rights for the next seven years—during which its circulation rose to 500,000. The *Socialist Woman* immediately complained that the party ignored women's rights and that most locals discussed only men's issues and even met in places where women were not likely to go.

At its 1908 convention the party debated its neglect of women and the need for special organizational forms. A woman delegate said: "It makes very little difference whether we approve of a separate organization for Socialist women or not. We have one—a real, live revolutionary movement, writing its own literature, managing its own newspapers, planning its own campaign."[56] Some delegates at the convention argued that women, like blacks, needed no special demands or special organization but should just join the party. The victory of socialism would solve all problems. Nevertheless, the 1908 conven-

[54] Quoted in ibid., p. 69.
[55] Quoted in ibid., p. 70.
[56] Quoted in ibid., p. 73.

tion approved women's suffrage and other women's rights, elected a National Woman's Committee, headed by May Simons, and provided it with money for one organizer.

The committee helped form a Federation of Socialist Women's Clubs, but this organization only aided coordination of the women's auxiliaries. The local Socialist Women's Clubs often met hostility from the party locals and seldom got any support or funds. Some women belonged both to the Socialist party and the Socialist Women's Clubs, but most belonged only to the Women's Clubs. One woman activist said bitterly that in once instance, the women were using a little local party money for their Women's Club and getting very good results when "the local woke up to the fact that the women were really handling some money, a part of their own dues, and spending it as they thought best! This would never do of course, since in this respect even a Socialist man still has a capitalist mind, and still thinks the purse strings belong to the male sex."[57]

Yet in some areas a little cooperation was given, with ads for meetings saying "Women Especially Invited." In these areas, such as Kansas and Illinois, it was estimated that the number of women in the party rose tenfold in 1908 and 1909.

Just as they did 60 years later, the socialist women debated whether to recruit primarily working-class or middle-class women. As it turned out, their best efforts could attract few women who worked in the factories because they were too tired and lacked the leisure to attend meetings. Socialist propaganda for suffrage, however, attracted and held thousands of professional women and middle-class housewives from 1908 to 1912. In that period many women worked in both movements, women accounted for 15 percent of the party, and several held leadership positions. By 1913–1914, however, the suffrage movement had become so large and respectable that it could ally itself with the far larger and more influential Progressive party, and even some elements of the Republican and Democratic parties.[58] The socialists then stopped getting many

[57] Quoted in ibid., p. 77.

[58] A full-scale discussion of suffrage in relation to the party politics of 1913–1920 is in David Morgan, *Suffragists and Democrats* (Ann Arbor: Michigan State University Press, 1972).

recruits from this source, though many socialist women continued to play a role in the suffrage movement.

THE SUFFRAGE MOVEMENT

NAWSA had two new leaders in this period. One was Carrie Chapman Catt[59] and the other Anna Howard Shaw.[60] Ms. Catt was born in 1859 on a farm in Wisconsin. She graduated from Iowa State College and practiced teaching and school administration, then journalism. She married a successful engineer, who supported her while she worked for suffrage. She was an outstanding organizer of new locals and instituted better procedures at headquarters for keeping track of membership and fund raising. After Susan Anthony retired in 1900, she became president of NAWSA.

Ms. Shaw was born in a western pioneer family. She studied divinity and became a minister. She then studied medicine, received the M.D. in 1886, and practiced medicine in the Boston slums. She was a great orator, first for the WCTU and then for NAWSA. She became president of NAWSA in 1904.

From about 1896 to 1910, NAWSA did little and accomplished almost nothing. It had no national headquarters, and the leaders communicated by mail. Its first significant accomplishment was a petition with 400,000 names collected in 1908–1910. Ms. Stanton's daughter, Harriot Blatch, wrote: "The suffrage movement was completely in a rut . . . at the opening of the twentieth century. It bored its adherents and repelled its opponents. . . . Supporters in private drawing rooms and in public halls . . . listlessly heard the same old arguments."[61]

Ms. Blatch was exhilarated by the far more militant tactics she had witnessed in England; so in 1907 in New York she organized a new group, the Women's Political Union. The Union set out to be more dramatic and to make contact with business and professional women, whereas NAWSA still consisted mostly of "women of leisure." The Union also contacted

---

[59] Ms. Catt gives her view of the movement, including each campaign in detail, in Carrie Catt and Nettie Shuler, *Woman Suffrage and Politics: The Inner Story of the Suffrage Movement* (New York: Scribner, 1926).

[60] See her autobiography, Anna Howard Shaw, *The Story of a Pioneer* (New York: Harper & Row, 1915).

[61] Quoted in Flexner, op. cit., p. 250.

and interested labor unions; it introduced working women to state legislators. The women told the truth about their awful working conditions, thereby shocking the legislators. It initated the first open-air meetings for suffrage in 30 years. Finally, it launched a set of mass parades, which met with opposition by "respectable ladies" but soon became the most successful tactic of the suffrage movement.

There were also a number of other new organizations launched independently among college women, scientists, and union women. Even NAWSA started to revitalize itself, and by 1908 it had 2000 precinct captains in New York City to put pressure on Tammany Hall.

Then, in 1910, a referendum for women's suffrage was won in the state of Washington, mostly by sending speakers to local granges, labor unions, and churches.[62] In California a very important suffrage referendum was won by a narrow margin through imaginative use of speakers and meetings, big billboard ads, plays, pageants, essay contests, and a touring limousine with speakers and a small theater group performing "How the Vote Was Won." The new, splashy, militant tactics were successful in California. There was powerful opposition from business and liquor interests, and thousands of votes were stolen, but enough were protected by militant women poll watchers to win.

In 1910, NAWSA received a gift of $1 million from a millionaire's wife to set up a national headquarters. Moreover, working women became more outspoken as a result of their own militant union struggles. One unionist, Rose Schneiderman, answered a New York State senator who claimed that women would lose their feminine qualities if they voted: "We have women in the foundries, stripped to the waist . . . because of the heat. Yet the Senator says nothing about these women losing their charm. . . . Women in the laundries . . . stand for 13 or 14 hours in the terrible steam and heat with their hands in hot starch. Surely these women won't lose any more of their beauty and charm by putting a ballot in a ballot box once a year. . . ."[63]

---

[62] For a first-hand discussion of the struggles in Washington and Oregon, see Abigail Duniway, *Path Breaking, an Autobiographical History of the Equal Suffrage Movement in Pacific Coast States* (New York: Source Book Press, 1914, 1970 reprint).

[63] Quoted in Flexner, op. cit., p. 259.

In 1912, suffragists, with the aid of radical farmers, won referenda in Arizona, Kansas, and Oregon. They also won in Michigan, but the election was stolen by means of false returns from some precincts. Even the governor accused the liquor interest of election fraud. In the same year, Teddy Roosevelt's Progressive party made women's suffrage part of its program. In 1913 the Progressive party, composed of radical farmers and city reformers, held the balance of power in Illinois, and forced the state legislature to approve women's suffrage.

The Progressive movement

The Progressive movement was not merely a political movement but a pervasive ideology for reform in the 1900–1920 period. With roots in the earlier Populist movement, it advocated reforms intended to restore America to a previous better age. In the cities, it represented small businessmen and artisans who wanted antitrust laws to end industrial concentration, break up the big corporations, and return to a mythical state of pure competition. In the country, it was supported by the small farmers who wanted laws to prevent takeovers by big corporate farmers, laws to break the power of railroads, and laws to break the power of monopolies supplying machinery and fertilizer to the farmer and monopolies buying wholesale from the farmer. To achieve these laws, they also wanted more democratization, such as the popular election of senators and the initiative and referendum, all of which they thought would break the power of the bosses and of the big businessmen who controlled them and return power to the "people" (by which they meant the native-born middle class).

The suffragists promised the Progressives that the vote for women would double the number of reform-minded middle-class voters who could be counted on to vote against corruption and against monopoly. Teddy Roosevelt said in 1910 that "the prime duty of the average woman is to be a good wife and mother," but he agreed that good women might add the duty to vote for middle-class reform "to help the unfortunate."[64] The various women's and Progressive groups were closely linked. As early as 1908, the General Federation of Women's Clubs was a prime mover and lobbyist in the successful Pro-

---

[64] Quoted in Sinclair, op. cit., p. 325. Sinclair gives quite a bit of information on this period.

gressive drive for a Pure Food and Drug Act. By 1914, the General Federation officially supported suffrage.

By 1914, 9 of the 11 states with women's suffrage also had strong Progressive movements and had adopted the initiative and referendum. In fact, many of the same people were in the leadership of the Progressives, NAWSA, the General Federation of Women's Clubs, the Women's Trade Union League, and the settlement house movement. Jane Addams, for example, was a founder of the first settlement house and a leader in all the other organizations.

Militant tactics, 1914–1920

In spite of Progressive and Socialist help and widespread middle-class support, the constitutional amendment was still getting nowhere in 1914. Then Alice Paul came back from England, where she had been impressed by the militant tactics used there. Ms. Paul was made head of NAWSA's Congressional Committee, which had a yearly budget of $10 because NAWSA thought federal action was very unlikely and so gave it a low priority. She gathered new funds, plus a small group of militant women, including the historian Mary Beard. Ms. Paul was a charismatic speaker and leader, and she and her small group managed to organize a parade of 5000 women in Washington, D.C., the day before Woodrow Wilson's inauguration.

> The women . . . had to fight their way from the start and took more than one hour in making the first ten blocks. . . . It was where Sixth Street crosses the avenue that police protection gave way entirely and the two solid masses of spectators on either side came so close together that three women could not march abreast. It was here that the Maryland boys [supporters of the women, from Maryland Agricultural College] formed in single file on each side of the "Pilgrims" and became a protective wall. . . . The parade itself . . . was a great success . . . the marchers, for the most part, kept their tempers . . . few faltered.[65]

Public opinion was outraged by the attack on women and the lack of police protection; the chief of police lost his job.

The committee also organized car caravans to Washington and presented 200,000 signatures for a federal amendment. But its tactics were too militant for NAWSA, so it was expelled.

---

[65] A newspaper account, quoted by Flexner, op. cit., p. 264.

It changed its name to the Congressional Union, then merged with the Women's Political Union to form the Women's party, which still exists. In 1914 and 1916, the Women's party campaigned against *all* Democrats because, when in power, they had not endorsed women's suffrage.

In 1914, only Montana and Nevada, with strong Progressive and Socialist movements, voted for women's suffrage; suffrage lost in five other states. While NAWSA kept changing officers, but doing little more, the militant Women's party held meetings and parades, presented petitions, and lobbied—and finally got the Nineteenth Amendment to the floor of Congress. It was defeated in 1914 by 35 to 34 in the Senate and 207 to 174 in the House.

In 1915, NAWSA pushed referenda in New York, New Jersey, Pennsylvania, and Massachusetts, but after hard campaigns—opposed in Philadelphia by the saloons and in Massachusetts by the Catholic Church—it lost all four. Finally, in 1915, NAWSA tossed out Ms. Shaw and put in its best organizer, Ms. Catt. Ms. Catt, helped by a $2 million bequest from a rich sympathizer, organized in detail both a series of state campaigns and a federal campaign. Also in 1915, the first important antisuffrage organization was formed in the South; its slogan was "Home Rule, States Rights, and White Supremacy."[66]

In 1916, both major parties came out for women's suffrage, but didn't say how or when. Because of southern influence, the Democrats said the issue should be left to the states. Ms. Catt and NAWSA worked closely and politely with President Wilson, even though he still equivocated, at least in public. Ms. Catt designed a secret "winning plan" outlining what each state organization was to do year by year, a plan that proved to be successful.

In 1917, the Women's party turned to all-out militant tactics, picketing Wilson and the White House for doing nothing for women's suffrage. In that year the first woman representative, Jeannette Rankin of Montana, took her seat in the House. Then came war. NAWSA supported the war and worked with the Wilson administration, advocating both patriotism and women's suffrage.

The Women's party, which included many Quaker pacifists, did not support the war or engage in war effort. Jeannette

[66] Quoted in ibid., p. 275.

Rankin, the only woman in the House, voted against the declaration of war. The Women's party picketed the White House with signs saying "Democracy Should Begin at Home."[67] They were attacked by hysterical mobs of hoodlums and soldiers. Then they, and not the mobs, were illegally arrested for exercising their right of free speech; 218 women were arrested and 97 jailed. "When the women protested against the illegality of their arrests, the bad conditions, and the brutality of their treatment by going on hunger strikes, the authorities . . . resorted to forced feeding, and made martyrs wholesale."[68] NAWSA strongly attacked the pickets in several public statements in order to show its own patriotism and respectability.

In addition to the militants' protest, other events helped women's suffrage during the war. Because men were in the army, thousands of women were given jobs in occupations previously excluding them, and thousands more moved from the home into industry for the first time. Women, led by NAWSA, also sold Liberty bonds, raised food in gardens, and did nursing at home and in the front-line hospitals in France. NAWSA Emphasized women's patriotism and participated in a government committee to mobilize women, a committee that led, in 1920, to the formation of the Women's Bureau in the Department of Labor. Only the Women's party and some women socialists actively opposed the war, arguing that it was an imperialist war.

Because of women's war role, the White House pickets, and some usual suffrage activity by NAWSA, in 1917 women were granted the right to vote by state legislatures in North Dakota, Ohio, Rhode Island, Nebraska, Michigan, and Arkansas—still mostly western states. A referendum was defeated in Maine, but in New York a suffrage referendum fared better. After a hard campaign, Tammany Hall was persuaded to remain neutral because it feared revenge by women voters if they did get the vote. Women's suffrage won by 100,000 votes in New York City, and this crucial state was finally won.[69]

In January 1918, Wilson spoke publicly for women's suffrage, and the amendment came to a vote in the House. Last-minute

---

[67] Quoted in ibid., p. 284.

[68] Ibid., p. 285.

[69] The story of the New York campaign is told in detail in Mildred Adams, *The Right to Be People* (Philadelphia: Lippincott, 1967).

efforts were frantic, and the women brought several representatives from hospital beds. The amendment passed by exactly the two-thirds necessary for a constitutional amendment. The deep South still voted almost solidly against it, as did the representatives from a few industrial states—Massachusetts, Pennsylvania, New Jersey, and Ohio.

In this period the militancy of women and the spread of suffrage sentiment was reflected in the explosive growth of NAWSA (see Table 10.1). The Women's party remained quite small, perhaps never comprising more than 40,000 to 50,000 members. NAWSA was happy to recruit anyone, including many who never did anything. Since the women's party demanded and got concentrated activity from all its members, it probably accomplished as much as NAWSA.

TABLE 10.1

Membership of National American Woman Suffrage Association

Year	Number of members
1893	13,150
1905	17,000
1907	45,501
1910	75,000
1915	100,000
1917	2,000,000

Source: Aileen Kraditor, *The Ideas of the Woman Suffrage Movement, 1890–1920* (New York: Columbia University Press, 1965), p. 5. These are very rough estimates.

To get the amendment through the Senate took another year and a half, until late 1919, since its opponents went all-out to delay it. Suddenly, in mid-1918, these opponents thought they could defeat the amendment, so they called it to the floor. In an extraordinary gesture designed to get votes in the next election, Wilson spoke in its favor on the Senate floor. He argued patriotism: ". . . the early adoption of this measure is necessary to the successful prosecution of the war. . . ." He said that the country needed enthusiastic war workers and warriors willing to fight for "democracy" and that most ordinary people "think in their logical simplicity, that democracy means that women shall play their part in affairs alongside men and upon an equal footing with them. . . ."[70] The opposi-

[70] Quoted in Flexner, op. cit., p. 308.

tion argued "states' rights" and fear of black women voters. The vote was 62 in favor to 34 opposed, 2 short of the needed two-thirds. The 34 negative votes almost all came from conservative Republicans in New England and conservative southern Democrats. The southerners spoke against votes for black women; but one newspaper noted that they really represented the cotton industry, which employed thousands of women and children at miserable wages and opposed any strengthening of women's position.

Also in 1918, three more states, South Dakota, Michigan, and Oklahoma, gave women the vote by referenda, in spite of attempts to steal the election in Oklahoma by fraud. Six states (Iowa, Minnesota, Missouri, Ohio, Wisconsin, and Maine) gave women the vote by legislative action. Still, in February 1919 the Senate again defeated the amendment by one vote. In May and June 1919, both houses of Congress finally passed it, though the southerners still voted against it.

Opponents then used every dirty trick to defeat ratification by the states. NAWSA launched a campaign in every state for ratification. Finally it won in 35 states (none in the South), but needed one more that proved very hard to get. By August 1920, the only apparent possibility in the near future was the border state of Tennessee. If the amendment lost there, opponents might delay until postwar conservatism buried it for good. All the forces both for and against poured into Tennessee. The liquor interests handed out so much liquor that on the night before the vote "legislators . . . were reeling through the halls in a state of advanced intoxication."[71] The deep South sent hundreds of men and women to spread racism and sexism. Ms. Catt wrote: "Women, including Kate Gordon and Laura Clay [former members of NAWSA's own board!], are here, appealing to Negrophobia and every other cave man's prejudice."[72]

On the other side, the mother of one legislator wrote to him: 'Hurrah! And vote for suffrage. . . . I notice some of the speeches against . . . were very bitter. . . . Don't forget to be a good boy and help Mrs. Catt. . . ."[73] He changed his position and voted for the amendment, which passed by two votes. The opponents desperately tried to enjoin and overthrow

[71] Quoted in ibid., p. 322.
[72] Quoted in ibid.
[73] Quoted in ibid., p. 323.

Tennessee's vote in the courts, but they failed. And the Nineteenth Amendment became a part of the Constitution!

Who opposed women's suffrage?

Interests opposed were: (1) liquor businesses; (2) big-city bosses; (3) the Catholic Church; (4) southern whites; and (5) big business. The opposition organized antisuffrage organizations, led by wealthy women, as fronts for their own activity. Oppositionists spent huge amounts of money on all kinds of advertising and propaganda. They bought votes wholesale and paid bribes to steal elections. Besides sexist prejudice, they had economic and political interests to protect against possible votes by women.

The liquor industry, fearing women's votes for prohibition, spent millions against suffrage. One brewer wrote to another in 1914 that "a new anti-suffrage association . . . in Illinois . . . is a retail liquor dealer's affair."[74] But he said that the connection should be kept secret.

The big-city machines and bosses were afraid women voters would want reforms, such as no child labor, and—horrors—would want to "clean up" politics.

The Catholic Church felt that women might get out of hand if they voted and might oppose its sexist teachings on "woman's place." In 1916, a cardinal sent a message of support to an antisuffrage convention; and in many state referenda religion-oriented antisuffrage leaflets were sent to Catholic voters.

Southern white politicians denied the vote to blacks in practice. They were afraid to extend suffrage again, or to have any discussion of suffrage, because then the Fourteenth Amendment might be enforced, giving blacks the vote. In 1919, Senator Smith of South Carolina still warned his fellow southerners that votes for women would cause a new "clamor for Negro rights" and argued this could be avoided by adherence to states' rights rather than a federal amendment: "By thus adding the word 'sex' to the 15th Amendment you have just amended it to liberate them all [black women as well as white women], when it was perfectly competent for the legislatures of the several states to so frame their laws as to preserve our civilization without . . . involving women of the black race."[75]

---

[74] Quoted in ibid., p. 297.
[75] Quoted in ibid., p. 303.

Although southern opposition was rooted in social conservatism and fear of blacks, the issue of child labor was also heavily involved. In the years after 1890, textile manufacturing had become of major importance in the South, and this industry depended on cheap female and child labor. Because the suffragists had become associated with child labor reform and because it was assumed that women generally would oppose child labor, cotton textile manufacturers in the South were bitterly opposed to women's suffrage. Some of the racist statements made in opposition to the amendment may even have been a cover for opposition on the basis of protecting the textile interests. In the October 1, 1918 Senate vote, one senator from Mississippi and one from Louisiana, both states with heavy black populations, voted for suffrage. The only southern states that had both senators voting against suffrage were North and South Carolina, Georgia, and Alabama—the four leading textile states.[76]

Big business was worried that any change might disturb its power, and so it opposed women's suffrage as it had opposed popular election of U.S. senators (the Seventeenth Amendment) and the "communistic" income tax established by the Sixteenth Amendment. In every referendum battle women reported huge antisuffrage expenditures by the railroads, oil, and manufacturers. There were large numbers of antisuffrage lobbyists financed by the same interests in every legislative battle. A congressional investigation found that Swift and Company made secret antisuffrage contributions. An antisuffrage appeal in Nebraska in 1914 was signed by nine railroad executives, seven bankers, and two Episcopal ministers. Other antiwomen interests included the Texas Business Association, Santa Fe Railroad, American Express, Portland Cement, and the Union Pacific, Illinois Central, and Southern Pacific railroads. The "Man Suffrage Association" included wives of bankers, wives of railroad and corporate executives, and the son-in-law of J. P. Morgan. The head of NAWSA's Congressional Committee wrote that some senators, who had been put in office by big-business money, "were not really in favor of our form of government. They believed in an oligarchy of the well-to-do, and they were fearful that tariff schedules might be reduced or railroad regulation extended if women had a chance to vote."[77]

---

[76] Morgan, op. cit., p. 175.
[77] Quoted in Flexner, op. cit., p. 302.

Why success in 1920?

In spite of the powerful opposition, women's suffrage was won in 1920. Why? One reason was the support of the Progressives. The Progressives, in turn, were strong at that time because of the last-ditch effort of small business and small farmers to avoid total elimination by big business and big farming interests. Suffrage came to be seen as a middle-class reform expected to expand that group's voting power. A second reason was the support of the Socialists and trade unions, which helped mobilize workers. Perhaps most important were the growing numbers of women in industry and the professions, women with knowledge and some political interest, who could no longer be ignored. Finally, World War I served as a catalyst in that it brought still more women into industry, government, and nursing—and made it useful for Wilson and others to argue for women's suffrage as part of the war for democracy.

FORTY YEARS IN THE DESERT: AMERICAN WOMEN, 1920–1960

11

Suffragist leaders entered the 1920s with bright hopes, but legal changes cannot alter attitudes overnight. For many years after the passage of the Nineteenth Amendment, women voted in smaller numbers than men. It has been estimated that in the 1920 election only 43 percent of the eligible women voted. As late as 1940, 49 percent of the women as compared to 68 percent of the men voted.[1] Many women and men still believed that politics is a male preserve.

Throughout the period, the difference between the percentages of men and women voting has been greatest in groups where sex-role differences are most marked. Among the poor and the poorly educated, in rural areas, and in the South, women have tended to vote in considerably smaller numbers than men.

A women's bloc vote, which the suffragists had hoped for and male politicians had feared, never really materialized. Women tended to vote very much like men. Party affiliation and class, not sex, influenced voting choice.

Few issues have clearly split the sexes. Women have tended to be more in favor of the welfare state—of government intervention and government ownership—and have tended to be more pacifist.[2] The latter tendency has worried male politicians and military men. In 1925, Rear Admiral Fiske said:

---

[1] Martin Gruberg, *Women in American Politics* (Oshkosh, Wis.: Academia Press, 1968), p. 9.

[2] Ibid., pp. 12–13.

No man respects and admires women more than I do, but some women have faults, and the fault most commonly found is a seemingly insatiable desire to interfere in matters they do not understand. War they understand least and from it they instinctively recoil. There is danger in this situation. Women now have the vote and they outnumber the men. There must be some action by the men which will bring women to realize that it is for their comfort and protection that all wars are fought. It is to the interest of women that they permit men to obtain the necessary armament. Only in this way can they be assured of the comfort and protection they need. In spite of themselves, we must protect the ladies![3]

THE WOMEN'S MOVEMENT, 1920–1940

Early data showed some evidence of political independence by women, enough to scare male politicians. In Chicago in 1915, men gave a plurality to the machine candidate for mayor, but women gave as big a vote to the reform candidate. In 1918, women organized a nonpartisan coalition that defeated the antisuffrage Senator John Weeks. In 1918 in Columbus, Ohio, 500 women volunteers registered 21,000 new voters, and a reformer won by 19,000 votes over an incumbent corrupt mayor. In 1921, the National Women's party threatened to run as a third party.[4]

The male politicians caved in before this danger. The Democratic and Republican parties included most demands of organized women in their 1920 platforms. Both parties put women on their national committees and gave them some patronage jobs. In 1920–1921, most state legislatures gave women the right to jury duty; some passed minimum wage and hour laws for women; two passed equal pay laws; and Wisconsin passed a general equal rights bill. Even some southern states passed reforms pushed by women lobbyists. Women lobbyists in Washington got Congress to pass (reluctantly, but under the goad of fear of defeat) the following: (1) in 1921, money for teaching mothers how better to care for babies; (2) in 1921, a bill for meat inspection; (3) a 1922 bill to equalize citizenship require-

---

[3] Quoted in ibid., p. 13.

[4] William Chafe, *The American Woman* (New York: Oxford University Press, 1972), p. 26. The fullest description of the successes of the women's movement from 1920 to 1924 is in J. Stanley Lemons, *The Woman Citizen, Social Feminism in the 1920s* (Urbana: University of Illinois Press, 1973).

ments for men and women; (4) a 1923 bill to extend the merit system in the civil service; and (5) the Child Labor Amendment to the Constitution in 1924. Even the American Medical Association, which ought to know, said that women's organizations were "one of the strongest lobbies that has ever been seen in Washington."[5]

The women's movement was divided over priorities after suffrage was attained, but seemed very much alive. The more militant National Women's party said suffrage had achieved little, that women were still "subordinate to men before the law, in the professions, in the church, in industry, and in the home."[6] The Women's party pledged to work for full equality, and succeeded in getting the Equal Rights Amendment introduced in Congress in 1923 (and every succeeding year until 1972, when it was passed). The Equal Rights Amendment states that "equality of rights under the law shall not be denied or abridged by the United States or by any state on account of sex." The Women's party was the only organization that consistently fought for women's rights from 1920 to 1960.

The Women's party, however, was limited to a relatively small group, having only 8000 members by 1923 (down from 50,000 in 1920). It focused on legal equality and—to a much lesser degree—eventual equality in the home. It never really challenged the Victorian image of women and was horrified by advocates of sexual freedom. It also had nothing to do with battles on behalf of blacks, the poor, or workers. Partly because of its narrowness but mainly because of the hostile sociopolitical climate, it slowly declined after the mid-1920s. Its leaders and members grew older and more isolated, and its influence decreased.

On the right wing of the women's movement was the League of Women Voters, which in 1919 evolved directly from the National American Woman Suffrage Association (NAWSA). Its white, middle-class membership declared that the fight for women's rights had been won with suffrage; in 1931 the league's president claimed that "nearly all discriminations have been removed."[7] The league did very little for women's rights

[5] *Journal of the American Medical Association*, quoted in Chafe, op. cit., p. 28.
[6] Quoted in ibid., p. 114.
[7] Quoted in ibid., p. 115.

and focused mainly on child labor laws, minimum wages and hours laws, pacifism, and many general reforms. It advocated gradualism and attacked all sudden "radical changes." Because it never fought for women's liberation, used conservative tactics, and was generally dull, and because of the hostile political climate, it never gained the allegiance of most American women. Whereas NAWSA had about 2 million members in 1920, the League of Women Voters was down to about 100,000 by 1923.

The league violently attacked the Women's party over the Equal Rights Amendment (ERA). League members argued that the ERA would be used to overturn all the protective labor laws for women (minimum safety, wages, and hours) for which the League had worked. The Supreme Court had voided all protective laws for male workers on the basis that freedom of contract was guaranteed to corporations as "persons" entitled to the due process and privileges given in the Fourteenth Amendment. But in 1908 the Supreme Court had allowed protective laws for women on the basis that women are delicate creatures needing protection. The league favored that decision, philosophy and all. In 1922, the league said "investigations have shown a lower resistance on the part of women to the strain and the hazards incident to industry."[8] The Women's party favored the Equal Rights Amendment and equal protective laws for men and women. But its position was difficult until 1938, when the New Deal passed and, in 1941, forced a reluctant Supreme Court to accept several protective labor laws for both men and women.

Reaction, mid–1920s

In the mid-1920s, conservative reaction resulted in an attack on all progressive legislation and helped wipe out the women's liberation movement. Congress cut down funds for the Women's Bureau and the Children's Bureau, and refused to pass more reforms. Besides the conservative swing throughout the nation, politicians noted that women cast only about 35 percent of the vote in 1923 and 1924, and voted about the same as men on most issues.[9] Many women did not vote because they

[8] Quoted in William O'Neill, *Everyone Was Brave* (New York: Quadrangle, 1969), p. 278.
[9] Chafe, op. cit., p. 31.

still felt that voting was for men. Only slowly did this attitude change, and the percentage of women voting crept up very slowly; it now equals the percentage of men voting.

The Child Labor Amendment (to prevent children from being forced to work) was defeated in the states in the mid-1920s by conservatives, big business, and the church. The National Association of Manufacturers, aided by the agribusiness-oriented National Farm Bureau, led the fight against it. Amid the red-baiting hysteria of the period, it was charged that the amendment was a Bolshevik plot paid for by Moscow gold. The Catholic Church's official magazine said: "There never was a more radical or revolutionary measure proposed for the consideration of the American people than this so-called Child Labor Amendment, that . . . would set aside the fundamental principles of states' rights, . . . would destroy parental control over children, and would commit this country forever to the communistic system of the nationalization of her children."[10]

In addition, there was a general red-baiting smear against all women's groups. In 1924, an employee of the Office of Chemical Warfare of the War Department, run by ex-Senator Weeks (who had been defeated by women's votes and wanted revenge), produced a chart showing that all liberal women's groups were part of a "spider web" directed from Moscow![11] In 1927, a conservative veterans' leader, head of the Military Order, said in a speech to the DAR that the WCTU, the YWCA, and the American Association of University Women were all part of the "radical, pink, or intelligentsia group."[12]

The conservative swing reflected the economic upswing in the 1920s, the continuing decline in the number of small farmers (who had supported radical Populists and Progressives), and the fact that a large, native-born industrial labor movement was still nascent and weak. The women's confused response to the all-out attack on them was also conditioned by the narrow, legalistic ideology of the suffragists that propagandized suffrage as the single goal—neglecting basic social and economic equality. As a result, the women's liberation movement disappeared almost completely after 1923 and, for other rea-

[10] Quoted in O'Neill, op. cit., p. 235.
[11] See ibid., p. 229; also Chafe, op. cit., p. 262.
[12] Quoted in O'Neill, op. cit., p. 229.

sons as well, remained dormant for 40 years (from about 1923 to 1963).

Only the tiny and narrowly legalist Women's party continued the struggle for equal rights—and its members grew fewer and older year by year. The League of Women Voters swiftly declined to one-tenth or less the size of its parent, NAWSA. It became very conservative on women's issues, devoting its time almost completely to general reform issues. The Women's Trade Union League stopped organizing, did purely educational work, and died away in the late 1920s. Similarly, the liberal National Consumers' League became more conservative, electing as president a man who was head of the Cleveland Chamber of Commerce, and likewise swiftly died. The Women's Bureau in the Department of Labor was always very conservative, favoring only some protective labor laws while opposing the Equal Rights Amendment. The bureau continued to argue that woman's place is not at work but in the home. In 1923, the head of the bureau said that equality between the sexes is an impossible myth.[13]

Only a few specialized, middle-class women's organizations survived. Many women did work in pacifist organizations of a reformist, nonrevolutionary nature. In 1919, the National Federation of Business and Professional Women's Clubs was formed. A very narrow and "respectable" organization, it did support the Equal Rights Amendment. In 1921, college women formed the American Association of University Women. The General Federation of Women's Clubs continued, but became mainly social and apolitical; in 1919 its president attacked revolutionaries "of many grades, from certain intellectuals to 'down and outers.' "[14] In 1927, the federation's president advocated a superpatriotic line and told her members to look out for communists in schools and churches, "for I have information from the most authoritative sources that it is among our young people . . . that the communists are working."[15]

The Equal Rights Amendment fight

In 1926, at a meeting sponsored by the Women's Bureau (which was against the amendment), there was a violent fight, with

[13] See Chafe, op. cit., p. 124.
[14] Quoted in O'Neill, op. cit., p. 257.
[15] Quoted in ibid., pp. 261–262.

only the Women's party supporting the ERA. The Women's party won time for a debate on the ERA only by disrupting one of the meeting's other sessions. Using militant liberation tactics, its floor leader said: "Get up and yell—you've got good lungs."

Senate hearings on the ERA in 1931 revealed the different ideologies involved. The Women's party argued that the ERA is necessary because of discrimination against women in wages, employment, education, and numerous laws. It listed at least 1000 discriminatory state laws, including laws in 11 states giving control over a wife's wages to her husband, laws in 16 states forbidding a wife to make a contract, laws in 20 states barring women from jury service, and a law in Minnesota allowing a husband—but not a wife—to collect damages from a lover for adultery!

The ERA was opposed by women connected with the AFL, the Women's Bureau, and the League of Women Voters. They all argued that the ERA might destroy the protective labor laws for women (against long hours, heavy weight lifting, etc.). The league argued that it was getting rid of discriminatory laws state by state, slowly and gradually; "that it is undesirable to interfere with the State-right principle . . ."; and that the League is for protective laws, which are needed for "true" equality, in view of the "actual biological . . . differences between men and women."[16]

The Women's party answered that discriminatory laws had oppressed women for centuries. Getting rid of them on a state-by-state basis would take decades, and it was not willing to wait. Furthermore, it argued in favor of certain protective legislation for both men and women workers. They pointed out that many so-called protective laws actually discriminate against women—for example, laws limiting women to 8 hours work a day in banks or insurance companies—and that many of these were being pushed by male union leaders to force women out of such work.

After the Fair Labor Standards Act was passed in 1938 and was approved by the courts in 1941, protective laws for both men and women became feasible. That basis for opposing the ERA became less tenable. The Women's party got a favorable

---

[16] Quoted in Aileen Kraditor, ed., *Up from the Pedestal* (New York: Quadrangle, 1968), pp. 300–301.

committee report on the ERA to the Senate floor in 1939, and got the Republican party to endorse it in 1940.

Woman as party workers

Some of the suffragists had hoped that once women obtained the vote they would shun the major parties that had treated them so shabbily and act as an independent force or even form their own party. No independent mass women's movement emerged, but many women entered mainstream party politics.

A number of women had been active in the Progressive party before passage of the Nineteenth Amendment. In 1912, Jane Addams seconded Theodore Roosevelt's nomination and campaigned across the country for him. Both major political parties set up women's divisions—the Democrats in 1916, the Republicans two years later. Eager to capture the women's vote, both parties instituted the 50–50 rule on their national committees. Under the rule each state is represented by one man and one woman. "Fifty-fifty looks better on paper than it has worked out in practice," Eleanor Roosevelt said. "Too often the vice chairmen and the committeewomen are selected by the men, who naturally pick women who will go along with them and not give any trouble. Thus they are apt to be mere stooges. . . . Too often the selection of a national committee woman is based on her bank account, social prestige or party service rendered by a deceased husband."[17]

Too often, then, women in party leadership positions were mere tokens. A few women did manage to become powerful in their own right, but the barriers to such achievement were very great.

While women were seldom welcomed into the inner councils of the major parties, they were increasingly making up the rank-and-file work force. Civil service reform radically decreased the number of patronage jobs available, with the result that men willing to do the unexciting everyday party work became hard to attract. Middle-class women with some leisure became the mainstays of the parties, doing everything from envelope stuffing to canvassing.

Work within the party was seldom rewarded with nomination to elective office. According to India Edwards, who was

[17] Quoted in Gruberg, op. cit., p. 62.

for many years vice chairman of the Democratic National Committee, "if the Party backs a woman you can be pretty sure they do it because they think it is a lost cause but they know they have to have *some* candidate."[18]

The first woman to serve in the U.S. Congress was elected in 1916, four years before the passage of the Nineteenth Amendment. She was Jeannette Rankin of Montana, a state that had granted women suffrage in 1914. A leader in the suffrage campaign, she kept the statewide organization she had built for that purpose intact and won the primary and general election handily.

During her tenure she worked for the suffrage amendment in the House of Representatives. She served as ranking minority member on the Woman Suffrage Committee, which she had been instrumental in forming. She led the floor debate on the amendment, which passed the House by the two-thirds vote needed. The measure was, however, killed by the Senate.

Ms. Rankin is best remembered for her vote against the declaration of war. Defeated in 1918 in a try for the Senate, she became a lobbyist for the National Consumers' League and for the Women's International League for Peace and Freedom.

Running for Congress again in 1940, she won on a "keep our men out of Europe" platform. She cast the only dissenting vote against the declaration of war. Realizing that she had little chance of reelection, she retired from elective office but remained active. A strong critic of the Vietnam war, in 1968 she led a women's protest parade to the U.S. Capitol. The antiwar women fittingly called themselves the Jeannette Rankin Brigade.[19]

WOMEN IN POLITICS, 1920–1940

No great flood of women entered the U.S. House of Representatives during the 1920s and 1930s. Between 1920 and 1924, three women each served one term in the House; none was reelected. The three elected in 1924 were to be the first professional congresswomen. Florence Kahn of California succeeded

---

[18] Quoted in Kirsten Amundsen, *The Silenced Majority* (Englewood Cliffs, N.J.: Prentice-Hall, 1971), p. 83.

[19] Hope Chamberlin, *A Minority of Members, Women in the U.S. Congress* (New York: Praeger, 1973), pp. 5–18.

her husband but managed to make a reputation on her own. She served 12 years in the House and was the first woman appointed to the powerful Appropriations Committee. After a long political career on the state level, Mary Norton was elected to Congress from New Jersey. She served for 26 years and rose to the chairmanship of the Labor Committee. Edith Nourse Rogers, also a congressman's widow, served in the House for 35 years. She became chairwoman of the Veterans' Affairs Committee in 1947, and much veterans' legislation bears her name.

Most of the women elected during the remainder of the 1920s and during the 1930s had much less distinguished careers. Seven of the 16 were widows of congressmen; 10 served one term or less.

The first woman senator was appointed in 1922 and served for only two days, at which time her term ended.[20] The second managed to last considerably longer. Hattie Caraway of Arkansas was appointed in 1931 to fill her late husband's seat. She was elected to the Senate on her own and won reelection in 1938. In 1944, she was defeated by J. William Fulbright. As the first woman elected to the U.S. Senate, she broke an important barrier, but she accomplished little else.

During this period only two women were elected governor, and neither won the office in her own right. Ms. Nellie Taylor Ross succeeded her husband as governor of Wyoming when he died in 1925. Lacking political experience and being in mourning, she left campaigning and probably governing to her campaign manager. Miriam ("Ma") Ferguson succeeded her husband as governor of Texas. He had been impeached and therefore could not run. Their campaign slogan, "Two governors for the price of one," indicated that the Fergusons were simply trying to circumvent the Texas constitution. She served from 1924 to 1926 and again from 1932 to 1936.

Women were a little more successful in attaining lower state offices. In a few states, some relatively powerless offices have become women's preserves. In Kentucky, New Mexico, and South Dakota, for example, women were elected secretary of state during the 1920s, and that position has been held almost exclusively by women ever since.

In the 1930s, the Great Depression politically awakened and

[20] Gruberg, op. cit., p. 123.

radicalized millions of women. But their central concern was full employment, not women's rights; so they joined existing movements from the New Deal Democrats and the CIO to the Socialist and Communist parties. Eleanor Roosevelt played a major political role in behalf of liberal causes as did Ms. Roosevelt's close friend, Mary Dewson. Ms. Dewson thought women were different from men, purer and concerned mostly with the "security of the home"; on this basis they would naturally support many New Deal reforms, such as social security. She directed all women's work for the Democratic party in the 1930s. By 1936, she had over 60,000 women out explaining and advocating Roosevelt's policies, door to door.

As a result of women's work for the Democrats, the party convention of 1936 had women (as alternates) equal in number to men on the Platform Committee. The committee passed seven of the eight planks advocated by Dewson. Moreover, these successful activists were paid with patronage jobs: Women got 26 percent of all postmasterships by 1938; Frances Perkins became the first woman cabinet member; Ruth Rhode and Florence Harriman were made ambassadors; and Florence Allen became a judge on the U.S. Circuit Court of Appeals.

It should be noted that the Democrats were not greatly enlightened on women's rights. In 1928, Al Smith ridiculed the notion, saying, "I believe in equality, but I cannot nurse a baby."[21] This strange "logic" forced the Women's party to support Hoover. Even under Roosevelt, the National Recovery Administration codes specifically allowed lower wages for women.

WOMEN AT WORK, 1920–1940

In the very early 1920s, it was fashionable for young middle-class women to go to work, and many looked for liberation by way of a career. "Even the girls who knew that they were going to be married pretended to be considering important business positions."[22] The euphoria and the emphasis on women's emancipation in the mass media was, however, very, very brief.

World War I lasted such a short time that only a few new

---

[21] Quoted in O'Neill, op. cit., p. 292.
[22] Sinclair Lewis, *Main Street* (1920), quoted in Chafe, op. cit., p. 49.

women workers actually entered the economy. As early as 1919, with the number of jobs declining, the usual attempt was made to push women out. In that year, the New York Central Federated Union stated: "The same patriotism which induced women to enter industry during the war should induce them to vacate their positions after the war."[23] Women were forced to give up jobs as streetcar conductors by the unions; 20 women were forced to resign as judges by New York City; and the U.S. government still excluded women from 60 percent of all civil service jobs. The warm myth about women's economic emancipation in the 1920s is deflated by the cold facts (see Table 11.1).

TABLE 11.1
Women at work, 1890–1940

Year	Working women as percentage of all workers	Working women as percentage of all women
1890	17%	18%
1900	18	20
1910	21	25
1920	20	23
1930	22	24
1940	25	29

Source: U.S. Department of Labor, Women's Bureau, *1969 Handbook on Women Workers* (1969), p. 10.

A long-run increase in the percentage of women working and in the percentage of women in the labor force is evident. The first major jump in women's labor force participation occurred in 1900–1910 (a 3-percentage-point jump). Why? Because women were becoming emancipated and wanted to work to be liberated or to have fun?—unfortunately not. Women increasingly *had* to work. The urban population rose rapidly (doubling between 1890 and 1920), and 40 percent of the big-city population was foreign-born by 1900. On top of that, another tremendous wave of immigrants (19 million from 1900 to 1930) filled the new factories. Because the men were paid terrible wages, women (and children) had to work if the family was to survive.

From 1910 to 1920, there was actually a decline in women's

[23] Quoted in Chafe, op. cit., p. 53.

role in the labor force (in spite of the war). Moreover, in the next period, from 1920 to 1930, women's participation rose only slightly. The greatest wave of immigration was over by 1910, and the increase in native-born women working was much less than the increase in native-born male workers. So the "normal" pattern of men dominant in the economy and women relegated to the kitchen continued, with only slight improvement, to 1930.

The next jump in the percentage of workers who are women comes in the 1930s (another 3-percentage-point increase). Perhaps this was due to greater liberation? Unfortunately, no. During the Depression, over half of all U.S. families had incomes of less than $1200 a year. Wives went to work so their families wouldn't starve. They did not go into glamorous occupations; 36 percent of working wives were in domestic and personal services, and 20 percent were in apparel and canning factories—with the highest percentages working in the deep South, which was least liberated but most depressed.[24]

All during the 1930s, employers, unions, and government made the sexist plea that women should go back to the great reserve army of unemployed to solve men's employment problem. By the end of the 1930s, women's unemployment rate was twice that of men, and it has remained so ever since. Mrs. Samuel Gompers said that it was "unnatural" for women to work and that they were taking jobs from men who really needed them. "A home, no matter how small, is large enough to occupy [a wife's] mind and time."[25] Even the Women's Bureau declared: "The welfare of the home and family is a woman-sized job in itself," and wives who work are destroying their families—this despite the fact that the same bureau found that 90 percent of all women who worked in the 1930s absolutely had to do so.[26]

The jobs performed by women were changing in type but not in status. In 1900, most women workers were domestic servants, farm laborers, unskilled factory workers, and teachers. By the 1920s, women had entered white-collar work; in 1930, some 30 percent of all women held clerical and sales jobs. In factory work, 40 percent of the women were in the textile

---

[24] See ibid., p. 57.
[25] Quoted in ibid., p. 64.
[26] See ibid., pp. 63–64.

mills. Ever since, most women have remained segregated mainly in the categories of clerical work, retail sales, domestic service, elementary school teaching, nursing and other service (waitress).

WOMEN AND UNIONS

We saw that there was a long and heroic strike by women garment workers in 1909. By 1920, the International Ladies Garment Workers Union had 65,000 members and the Amalgamated Clothing Workers 66,000. Both unions had a female majority in membership but an all-male leadership. Outside of the garment trades, women were mostly unorganized. One out of every 9 male workers was organized compared to only 1 out of every 34 women workers. This was a major reason for the lower wages of women.

Why were so few women organized? First, for the most part the AFL organized skilled craft workers, while women were primarily unskilled factory workers. Second, many women and most unions assumed that women were transient, not permanent, workers. Third and most important, sexist attitudes prevented unions from organizing women workers, even where the women themselves were enthusiastic. The AFL unions and leaders were openly hostile. Women printers, candy workers, hairdressers, and streetcar workers were all turned down for union membership on the grounds that women weren't serious, wouldn't stick together, wouldn't fit. Samuel Gompers said that the AFL wasn't prejudiced; it just wouldn't accept "any non-assimilable race." When in the late 1930s the CIO (Congress of Industrial Organizations) organized unskilled workers and welcomed women, thousands of women joined and were among the CIO's steadiest and most militant supporters.

THE SEXUAL REVOLUTION OF THE 1920s

Where did most historians get the false idea that women were emancipated in the 1920s? Partly because they focused on suffrage, but mostly because they were struck by the revolution in life-styles. Women's skirts got shorter (these were the "flappers"). Women bobbed their hair, and smoked and drank in public. Men and women danced wildly to jazz bands.

Sex did indeed become freer. The results of a study of white middle-class women are shown in Table 11.2. Many other studies have confirmed the same trend. The greatest increase in premarital intercourse occurred in the 1920s, with comparatively little change since then.

TABLE 11.2
Sexual activity of women

Year of birth	Percentage virgins at marriage
Before 1890	87%
1890–1899	74
1900–1909	51
Since 1910	32

Source: William O'Neill, *Everyone Was Brave* (New York: Quadrangle, 1969), p. 298.

But greater freedom for women to have extramarital intercourse did not mean freedom to get an equal higher education, or to choose a career, or to be paid equal wages, or to be equal in the family. Girls stressed their individual "freedom" (of sex), but showed no interest in women's rights or an equal social position with men. The "revolution" in sexual mores was real, but superficial. The same books and magazines that celebrated the "flapper's freedom" attacked working women. In 1922, a popular novel, *This Freedom,* said that career women are traitors and claimed that "the peace of the home . . . rests ultimately on the kitchen."[27]

Although in the early 1920s some articles defended the right of women to work, the conservative reaction of the late 1920s produced many articles such as the one that said "the office woman, no matter how successful, is a transplanted posey."[28] Others played up the joys of homemaking and said the important thing for women was "no longer smartness, but charm." As we have seen, the scarcity of jobs during the Great Depression greatly intensified the "back to the home" clamor.

EDUCATION

Although large numbers of women were going to college, a change occurred in the women's colleges in the mid-1920s

---

[27] Quoted in ibid., p. 99.
[28] From *McCall's,* quoted in Chafe, op. cit., p. 105.

and after. The high-quality comprehensive training of early years was replaced by an emphasis on preparation for "woman's place" in the home. In 1924, Vassar started offering courses called "Husband and Wife," "Motherhood," and "The Family as an Economic Unit." Even coed colleges, such as Cornell and the University of Chicago, started undergraduate and graduate programs in home economics for women.

The long-run trends are shown in Table 11.3. In the portion of B.A. degrees going to women, there is an incredible jump of 11 percentage points from 1910 to 1920. This reflects to some extent the height of the suffrage movement and its liberating effect on women's thinking. In part, it also reflects the greater willingness of universities to take women when men were drafted for the war. Then, in the 1920s, there is a further jump, but of only 6 percentage points, perhaps reflecting some continuing liberation of middle-class women. In the 1930s, there is a gain of only 1 percentage point, reflecting the very negative impact of the Depression on women's position.

TABLE 11.3

Women's education, 1890–1940

	Percentage of all degrees awarded to women		
Year	**B.A.**	**M.A.**	**Ph.D.**
1890	17%	19%	1%
1900	19	19	6
1910	23	26	10
1920	34	30	15
1930	40	40	15
1940	41	38	13

Source: U.S. Department of Labor, Women's Bureau, *1969 Handbook on Women Workers* (1969).

The trend in the women's portion of M.A. degrees is similar, except that the greatest jump is a 10-percentage-point leap in the 1920s. Since one needs a B.A. degree to get an M.A., this is partly a normal lagged response to the earlier jump in B.A.s, and partly the continued increase in freedom in the 1920s. But in the portion of M.A. degrees going to women, the negative impact of the Depression on women shows up with a 2 percent decrease.

Finally, it was clearly much, much more difficult for women to break into the highest educational sphere, the Ph.D., which is the gateway to many of the higher professions. Only in 1900 did women finally win a significant portion (a mere 6 percent). And there are only two further increases in the portion of Ph.D.s going to women—a 4-percentage-point increase in the 1900s and another 5 percentage points in the 1910s. In the supposedly liberating 1920s, there was no increase. And among the losses of the Great Depression was a 2-percentage-point decrease in the still-small portion of Ph.D.s awarded to women.

PROFESSIONAL WOMEN

The portion of women workers who were "professionals" increased from 12 percent in 1920 to 14 percent in 1930. But 75 percent of these were in the "women's professions" of nursing or teaching, with low status and very low pay. Women remained only 3 percent of architects and lawyers, and the absolute number of women doctors actually declined.[29] From 1925 to 1945, there was a 5 percent quota on women in almost all medical schools—and only 40 out of 482 general hospitals accepted women interns.

Finally, a 1929 survey of women in university teaching found most women faculty discontented, but resigned to the fact that "no matter how much a woman studied or taught, she was likely to remain an instructor, burdened with the greatest teaching load and recompensed with the smallest salary."[30] As an example of discrimination at that time, a woman dean was fired from a midwestern college because she got married; the college president told her this was not discrimination because "marriage itself is for a woman an adequate career."[31]

Things got much, much worse for professional women during the 1930s. As we saw, the portions of MAs and Ph.D.s going to women actually dropped. Even in lower-level professions, such as elementary and high school teaching, men in search of jobs entered and displaced women. Moreover, the new men teachers received higher pay; in 1939, male teachers were paid a median salary of $1,953 a year, while women teachers were paid only $1,394.[32] Finally, the percentage of working women

---

[29] See ibid., p. 58.
[30] Quoted in ibid., p. 91.
[31] Quoted in ibid., p. 101.
[32] Ibid., p. 61.

who were "professionals" (including teachers and nurses) fell during the Depression from 14 percent back to 12 percent.

WAR, 1940–1945

It is one of the great historical ironies that only war could lift the U.S. economy and all its oppressed sectors from the lower depths of the Great Depression. Because of the all-out demand for war production, workers achieved full employment and rapid unionization; blacks came out of the South to industrial jobs and began the long march toward equal civil rights; and women moved in vast numbers into the economy, broke the sexist image, and started their own long march toward liberation. The changes are astonishing: (1) a 50 percent rise in women at work, (2) a large rise in wages, (3) twice as many wives at work, (4) four times as many women in unions, and (5) a vast change in the public attitude toward women.

Even the aggregate data are exciting (see Table 11.4). During the war the portion of women at work jumped 9 percentage points, while their portion of the labor force jumped 11 percentage points. There was a tremendous slip backward immediately after the war, during reconversion and the return of veterans. Then the numbers of women in the economy resumed their upward march; both in absolute numbers and percentages there were many more women working in 1950 than in 1940 (though considerably fewer than at the war peak).

The great increase in women workers did not come without resistance. Of 1,750,000 workers trained for war industries by December 1941, only 1 percent were women. War industry employers claimed women had the ability to fill only 29 percent

TABLE 11.4

Women at work, 1940–1950

Year	Women workers as percentage of all workers	Women workers as percentage of all women
1940	25%	29%
1945	36	38
1947	28	32
1950	29	34

Source: U.S. Department of Labor, Women's Bureau, *1969 Handbook on Women Workers* (1969), p. 10, and U.S. Department of Labor, *Manpower Report of the President* (1973), p. 129.

of the jobs available. Six months later, with millions of men going into the army and a drastic labor shortage, the tune changed. Already, 13 percent of the trainees were women, employers declared that women were able to fill 55 percent of open jobs, and the government said they could do 80 percent of the jobs.[33]

And women did. They shattered the sexist image by becoming—with little training—railroad switchmen, precision toolmakers, crane operators, lumberjacks, acetylene torch operators, and so on *ad infinitum*. Even the giant corporations hired women as chemists and engineers; Wall Street hired women stock analysts; and the U.S. government hired women lawyers and doctors.

Moreover, the war industries, which at first declared it impossible, suddenly were able to provide women with decent rest rooms and toilets. Since these corporations were making astonishing profits from the war and needed workers badly, they were also suddenly able to put in better lighting, chairs, cafeterias, and 40 percent higher wages than the consumer industries.

Furthermore, the unions, which had neglected women, suddenly needed their power. The number of women unionists jumped from 800,000 in 1939 to over 3 million in 1945. Women were concentrated in the CIO unions in the electrical, auto, and steel industries.

Particularly crucial to the changing image of women was the fact that, since it was now encouraged, wives went to work. In 1940, most women workers were young and single. By 1945, over half were married, and their average age was over thirty-five.

Most astounding of all was the change in propaganda. In the 1930s, women were told to stay in the home, that going to work was unnatural. Overnight, with the heavy demand for labor, all of the media, advertising, and government posters declared that it is both natural and patriotic for women to work. Some radio stations had a "Working Women Win Wars Week."[34] Rosie the Riveter, the woman with an acetylene torch, became a national heroine—and *Life* magazine showed women pilots on its cover. The War Department issued a pam-

---

[33] Joan Trey, "Women in the War Economy—World War II," *Review of Radical Political Economics*, 4 (July 1972), p. 44.
[34] See Chafe, op. cit., p. 146.

phlet telling industry in its title: "You're Going to Employ Women." Moreover, it was emphasized everywhere that Hitler's Germany tried to keep women in the home for nothing but sexual reproduction, that fascism tried to push these sexist attitudes on the world, and that American women must fight fascism and sexism by working in the war economy.

And lo and behold! Public attitudes changed—both because of the change in the media and because of the obvious change in reality. In 1935, when over one in four workers was unemployed, a poll showed that 80 percent of Americans thought it was wrong for women to work, particularly if they were married. By 1942, 71 percent thought that more married women could and should be employed.[35]

Yet even during the war there was resistance to women working on the part of some reactionaries. Clare Booth Luce could still tell women to go back to the home to care for their children. The Children's Bureau called working mothers "a hazard to the security of the child in his family."[36] The army refused to commission women doctors until 1943, when Congress commanded it to do so. Private industry kept women as segregated as possible. Industry also gave women the dullest jobs because, as one capitalist put it, they can "do the monotonous, repetitive work . . . that drives a man nuts."[37] In government, the Women's Advisory Commission on War Manpower was kept as an ornament, given no power, and hardly ever consulted, even on decisions about working women.

The government did urge equal wages for women—and some progress was made—but firms could pay women less if they were in a job that was "historically" a woman's; or if they were in a different plant; or if their job was called something different (e.g., General Motors called male jobs "heavy" and women's "light," even though they were exactly the same). The loopholes were thus as big as the rule. Consequently, women were paid much lower wages (about 65 percent of men's), and this was sanctioned in some union contracts by reference to the legal loopholes. Unions and management mostly agreed that women should get seniority on a different list or only "for the duration."

---

[35] Ibid., p. 148.
[36] Quoted in ibid., p. 150.
[37] Quoted in ibid., p. 152.

Even worse was the child care situation. With millions of mothers working, it would seem obvious that child care facilities were urgently needed. But many sexists, like Clare Booth Luce and her husband, believed this would destroy children and the sanctity of the home. As if leaving children unattended wouldn't destroy them—when mothers *had* to work and the war effort needed them. Only when industry found itself inconvenienced because women workers were exhausted or absent trying to care for children and do their jobs as well did the government take some action—much too little and too late. Under pressure from industry and many women's organizations, Roosevelt allotted some emergency funds to child care. Congress then allowed a very little of the funds from the Lanham Act for wartime facilities to be used for child care. Congressman Lanham from Georgia, who didn't want any of "his" funds going to communistic child care, did his best to obstruct. Eventually, only about one-tenth of all children of working mothers received some kind of government-financed child care.

THE END OF THE WAR, 1945–1949

What would happen when the war ended? The Women's Advisory Committee demanded retention of women workers, and in 1944 Senator Harry Truman said "they are entitled to the chance to earn a good living at jobs they have shown they can do."[38] Many, however, feared that there would not be enough jobs to go around. Powerful forces pushed for the "natural" solution of sending women back to the reserve army of unemployed, to wait in the kitchen until they were needed again. By 1945, the head of the National Association of Manufacturers stated the grim message very politely: "From a humanitarian point of view, too many women should not stay in the labor force. The home is the basic American institution."[39] A soldier wrote the Women's Bureau: "Wishing you success in your work, and hoping for the day when women relax and stay in her beloved kitchen."[40] More bluntly, a southern senator, Charles Andrews of Florida, told Congress it should

[38] Quoted in ibid., p. 176.
[39] Quoted in Trey, op. cit., p. 51.
[40] Quoted in ibid.

force wives and mothers back to the kitchen "to give jobs to veterans."

Naturally, after the war, industry followed the sexist urgings. Veterans were given priority and, in the layoffs accompanying reconversion, women were fired at a rate 75 percent higher than men. From 1945 to 1947, the number of women at work declined by 4 million! The percentage of women at work declined from 38 percent back to 32 percent, and the percentage of women in the total labor force declined from 36 percent to 28 percent—almost, but not quite, back to prewar levels. All this occurred in spite of the fact that two-thirds of all women workers said they wanted to keep their jobs.[41]

Fortunately for women, the long expansion of the U.S. economy in the postwar period began very soon. By 1950, the number of women working started creeping up again—and this long-run tendency has continued ever since. In 1950, almost half of all women workers were married, and the median age of all women at work had risen to 36.5—quite a difference from the typically young and single woman worker of the prewar period.

Of course the fact that the economy needed and got more women workers did not mean it needed high or equal wages for women. Discrimination continued. Women's median wage continued to be about 35 percent lower than men's. Women continued to be denied admission to many professional schools, and the percentage of women in well-paying business and professional positions continued to decline.

A few women tried to outlaw such discrimination by political action. Representative Helen Gahagan Douglas fought for an equal pay act in Congress in 1945; the act was defeated then, and was introduced and defeated every year thereafter until it was passed in 1963. Opponents included the Chamber of Commerce, which said capitalists would correct unequal pay voluntarily, and the AFL, whose President Meany said it should be left to collective bargaining.

A second issue pushed anew was the Equal Rights Amendment. Recognizing the "magnificent wartime performance" of women, Harry Truman, Henry Wallace, and both major parties supported it. The Women's Bureau, fearing the amendment might nullify protective legislation, still opposed it. In

---

[41] Ibid., p. 47.

1946, the Senate voted approval by 38 to 35, but this was below the two-thirds needed. The Senate again passed it in 1950 and 1953, but with the rider that sex-specific protective legislation was not affected, which made it meaningless. The ERA never came to a vote in the House.

The third issue of concern to women was continuation of federal help for child care centers. Congress finally extended funding for six months, then refused to do any more. In New York, permanent state funds were refused, but the state agreed to temporary funds for children whose mothers could prove poverty; and the state youth commissioner said it would be better for mothers to go on relief so they could stay home! In 1947, the *New York World Telegram* declared that the child care campaign was masterminded by communists in "social work cells."[42] All New York State child care ended in 1948.

William Chafe says the late 1940s presented "a strange paradox" because "unprecedented numbers of females joined the labor force," but "only minimal progress was made in . . . women's rights" to equal pay, equal promotion, and child care.[43] On the basis of their on-the-job education in the war and the wartime propaganda against fascism (and against the vicious fascist brand of sexism), women briefly renewed the fight for equal rights. Similarly, with their work experience and the volume of propaganda against fascist racism, blacks pressured for more rights. For a time they were supported by millions of veterans whom the war had made more cosmopolitan and liberal—they, too, had been filled with antifascist propaganda. Women were also encouraged by many greatly strengthened radical CIO unions. All these forces coalesced briefly in the Progressive party campaign of 1948.

The counterattack by the conservative advocates of "return to normalcy"—supported by the press, big business, the church, and both old parties—was, however, much too strong at the time. The causes of women's rights, black rights, civil liberties, and better labor laws were all buried under the avalanche of the cold war, the red scare, and the anticommunist crusade. These red herrings justified enormous military spending, which provided enough jobs to allay the workers' discontent. For

[42] See Chafe, op. cit., p. 187.
[43] Ibid., p. 188.

women, the conservative reaction took the form of the "feminine mystique"—a glorification of the traditional female role. Nevertheless, a few determined women refused to stay in their place. In the political sphere, some progress was made.

WOMEN IN POLITICS, 1940–1960

In the 1940s and 1950s, 34 women were elected to the House of Representatives. There were still a large number of congressmen's widows elected—13 of the 34—but more qualified women made it on their own, and a number were to make the House their career.

Frances Bolton, elected in 1940 to succeed her late husband, remained in Congress until 1968 and rose to become ranking minority leader on the House Foreign Affairs Committee. Another widow elected the same year was to have an even more distinguished career. Margaret Chase Smith spent eight years in the House. In 1948, she ran for the Senate without party endorsement. A big vote getter in Maine, she won and was reelected until 1972. She was the first senator to speak out against McCarthyism and the first woman to hold a party leadership post in the Senate.

Helen Gahagan Douglas, an opera singer and actress, was elected to the House in 1944. A liberal Democrat, she had been active in California politics for a number of years. Her liberal activist record was used against her when she ran for the Senate in 1950. Her opponent, Richard Nixon, based his campaign on the red smear—calling her the "pink lady." His vicious campaign during a period of national hysteria about domestic communists was successful, and Helen Douglas, one of the most capable of women politicians, was retired from public life.

Despite the sway of the feminine mystique, the 1950s saw a number of capable women enter the House for lengthy careers. Leonor Sullivan, elected in 1952, became a leading exponent of consumer protection legislation. The 1954 election raised the number of women in the House to 16—a record to that date. The election brought in two women who were to have long and distinguished careers in the House. Edith Green, Democrat from Oregon, made education her specialty and rose to become second-ranking member on the Education and Labor Committee. Martha Griffiths, the first woman appointed to the powerful Ways and Means Committee, was one of the most outspoken feminists in Congress. She worked for laws barring sex discrimination throughout her tenure.

Despite the increase in women in the House, progress for women in politics was slow. No woman was elected governor or mayor of a major city during the 1940s and 1950s. Only two women served in cabinet posts. Frances Perkins, first appointed secretary of labor by Franklin Roosevelt in 1933, served in that post until 1945. Oveta Culp Hobby was named to head the new Department of Health, Education and Welfare in 1953 and served until 1955. Two women served as lieutenant governor and one as attorney general during this period.

Stereotyped notions about woman's place have retarded progress for women in the political arena. For many women the thought of going into politics is simply inconceivable. For those who try, the barriers to success are great. Party pros generally believe a woman's place is stuffing envelopes. Women are not encouraged and are seldom supported as candidates. Being a congressman's widow is more useful in getting a congressional nomination than intelligence and willingness to work hard. A widow has name recognition and presumably sympathy from the electorate. Sometimes, also, a widow is nominated in order to prevent a divisive intraparty fight for the nomination.

The lack of women in politics is often attributed to their family duties. "Edith Green disagrees. . . . Women, she feels, are the victims of a form of psychological warfare, systematically waged by men who consider the political world their exclusive domain. 'When I entered politics,' she says, 'a thousand and one times in a condescending tone, I heard: How did it ever happen that you [meaning a woman] are running for office?' "[44]

Helen Gahagan Douglas was asked during her campaigns, "Hey, Helen, why aren't you home with the kids?"[45] Coya Knutson's congressional career was destroyed by her opponents' use of such sentiments. They extracted from her alcoholic husband a letter saying "Coya come home."[46] She was defeated for reelection. According to columnist Doris Fleeson,

---

[44] Quoted in Chamberlin, op. cit., p. 258.
[45] Quoted in ibid., p. 183.
[46] Quoted in ibid., p. 264.

> Many in Washington, not all of them women . . . feel that she was marked down as "fair game" simply because she was a woman and roughly treated in a manner that the men in her business are not. . . . There are many better stories here than *l'affaire* Knutson and they are about much more prominent people, but it is not considered cricket to use them as a political weapon.

The lesson is that, as a practical matter, women are held to a far higher standard of accountability in politics than men are. Women clearly cannot count on the club spirit for protection.[47]

THE COUNTERREVOLUTION OF THE 1950s

With the U.S. army playing world policeman, with a high level of employment and prosperity at home, and with liberal or radical voices stilled by the witch hunting of Senator McCarthy and others, the Great American Celebration was on. *Conformity* was the catchword, and the best description of students and youth in general was "the silent generation." The cause of women's liberation could not flourish in this atmosphere; it always reflects the general climate and the state of protest movements in particular. We have seen that the women's movement arose with the abolition movement, scored a victory on suffrage in alliance with the Socialist and Progressive movements, and raised its head again, though not in an organized way, in the atmosphere of the all-out antifascist war.

We saw, on the other hand, that the movement died out in the extremely anti-red reactionary period of economic expansion in the mid-1920s. Now we find, as no surprise, that in the prosperity and renewed anti-red hysteria of the 1950s, the possibilities for a revival of the women's liberation movement were cut off. As in the 1920s, the ideological drive of the 1950s, reflected in the media, was toward privatism. It was an apolitical period; idealism or concern with social problems was considered rather weird. Men learned that the highest virtue was money-making; women were told that the highest virtue was to be a child-producing machine surrounded by lots of glittering gadgets in a little box in the suburbs; and sex was glorified, since there was nothing else exciting left to glorify.

Particularly for women, this ideological picture diverged further and further from reality. The ideology declared that men

---

[47] Quoted in ibid., p. 265.

made enormous salaries so women could have "leisure" to care for a huge number of children and mind a beautiful, time-consuming house. In reality, more and more women had to go to work if the family was to earn the minimal socially acceptable income.

Despite the rising tide of back-to-the kitchen ideology, more and more women went to work outside the home (see Table 11.5). Thus both the percentage of women working and the proportion of women to all workers increased steadily each decade. In fact, the trend accelerated. From 1890 to 1940, the portion of women working rose by only 1½ percentage points per decade; from 1940 to 1970, it rose by 5 percentage points per decade!

TABLE 11.5
Women at work 1940–1970

Year	Women workers as percentage of all workers	Women workers as percentage of all women
1940	25%	29%
1950	29	34
1960	33	38
1970	40	43

Sources: U.S. Department of Labor, Women's Bureau, *1969 Handbook on Women Workers* (1969), p. 10, and U.S. Department of Labor, *Manpower Report of the President* (1973), p. 129.

Sexist ideology portrayed all married women and mothers of small children as being at home—otherwise, child care centers might be a reasonable idea. In 1940, married women constituted only 30 percent of all women workers, but that number had risen to 48 percent by 1950, to 54 percent by 1960, and to 60 percent by 1970. The increase of women workers did not come from single women; the percentage of single women at work rose only from 48 percent in 1940 to 51 percent in 1970. But the percentage of married women at work rose from 17 percent in 1940 to 40 percent in 1970.

Particularly contrary to sexist ideology's picture was the rise in mothers at work. The percentage of women at work who had children below age six increased from 13 percent in 1948 to 29 percent by 1967. These greater numbers at work reflected both socioeconomic necessities and changing attitudes, and helped change attitudes further.

BRAINWASHING IN THE 1950s

We were all brainwashed in the 1950s to believe that the Red Menace was about to eat us, so we must spend billions of dollars and thousands of lives to prevent revolution in Korea and Vietnam and Guatamala and everywhere else. But women were especially brainwashed to reverse the effects of the liberating World War II experience.

The old antiwomen interest groups continued to push the sexist view of women's subservience and "place." Big business did not mind the increase in jobs for women; it needed millions of women workers. Knowing their "place," however, meant that these women should be submissive and should not organize for higher wages. Moreover, if women workers think of themselves as transient and "returning" to full-time housework "eventually," then they will more easily accept a low wage in times of prosperity and unemployment in times of depression. Middle-class woman's place was said to be in the home and/or in a "woman's job" on the lowest levels of teaching or nursing or as a humble secretary—but not in positions of power in business or politics. Southern white males continued to oppose any degree of equality for blacks or women. Organized religion, particularly the Catholic Church, continued to urge women's subservience to men and to the church.

The 1950s, however, saw several new twists. Freudian psychology, stated in a sophisticated fashion in university classrooms and in crude ways in the popular media, was used as a major weapon to keep women in their traditional place. The big-selling magazines, such as *McCalls, Life,* and *Ladies' Home Journal,* popularized what Betty Friedan called the feminine mystique. In Friedan's survey of these magazines, "the image of woman that emerges . . . is young and frivolous, almost childlike; fluffy and feminine; passive; gaily content in a world of bedroom and kitchen, sex, babies, and home."[48] The women's magazines mentioned no national and world issues—because these are beyond women—but stuck to recipes and clothing styles. They emphasized as a new, "modern" view the concept of family "togetherness," a sticky mixture of man barbecuing, woman playing with baby, and all praying together ("the family that prays together stays together").

Another "modern" twist was to warn of the dangers of being

[48] Betty Friedan, *The Feminine Mystique* (New York: Dell, 1963), p. 30.

a "dried-up career woman" (à la Freudian psychology), while emphasizing that a woman could be "highly creative" in the home by doing fancy cooking, baking her own bread, sewing, interior decorating, and redecorating. The feminine mystique was extolled in magazine articles like "Femininity Begins at Home," "Have Babies While You're Young," "How to Snare a Male," and "Cooking to Me Is Poetry."[49]

In 1949, only one-third of the fictional heroines in magazines had careers, and they were always psychologically sick and unhappy until they gave it up for the home. By 1959, there were *no* heroines with careers (or a real interest in art or politics), only happy housewives. One typical housewife heroine exclaimed: "I'm so grateful for my blessings! Wonderful husband, handsome sons with dispositions to match, big comfortable house. . . . I'm thankful for my good health and faith in God and such material possessions as two cars, two TV's and two fireplaces."[50]

The politicians echoed the same sexist line. Even the liberal Adlai Stevenson said that a woman's political job was to

> inspire in her home a vision of the meaning of life and freedom. . . . This assignment for you, as wives and mothers, you can do in the living room with a baby in your lap or in the kitchen with a can opener in your hand. . . . I think there is much you can do about our crisis in the humble role of housewife. I could wish you no better vocation than that.[51]

The 1950s were the period in which psychoanalysis reached full bloom; many middle-class men—and women—yearned to be analyzed out of all their problems. The most widely quoted Freudian book was *Modern Woman: The Lost Sex*, by Marynia Farnham and Ferdinand Lundberg, published in 1947. The authors began by repeating all the old slanders against the early women's liberation leaders—that they were sex starved and frustrated, that they envied men's penises and wanted only to castrate all males, that "feminism . . . was at its core a deep illness."[52] Since women were created to be biologically

[49] Ibid., p. 38.
[50] Quoted in ibid., p. 57.
[51] Quoted in ibid., p. 54.
[52] Marynia Farnham and Ferdinand Lundberg, *Modern Woman: The Lost Sex* (New York: Harper & Row, 1947), p. 142.

and psychologically dependent on men, they could not be happy in independent careers. Women's independence and education caused all their neuroses. ". . . The more educated the woman is, the greater chance there is of sexual disorder. . . ."[53] This is contrary, of course, to all known studies, which consistently show women's sexual satisfaction rising with education. On the basis of their faulty analysis, they argued that the government should favor childbearing and larger families by propaganda and subsidies; bar married women from many occupations, even teaching; and pay for psychoanalysis for all neurotics infected by women's liberation.

Similar arguments were made by many sociologists, like Talcott Parsons, who found our present sexist ideology and family structure to be "functional" or useful for preservation of the status quo (true, but that assumes we want the status quo). Even the anthropologists, like Margaret Mead, whose work had shown the great variety of men's and women's role in primitive cultures, went back to look again armed with Freudian categories. And lo and behold! They found what they looked for: that primitive women were very happy because they did nothing but have babies, fulfilling their "true" sexual roles.

All of this was transmitted not only in the popular media but also in the universities. Counselors told women not to prepare for architecture or law or medicine but to take home economics so as to prepare for "the happiest career." Those who were interested in science or any creative subject were discouraged because too much of the wrong education would make a girl unhappy sexually and in general. One women's college boasted, "We are not educating women to be scholars; we are educating them to be wives and mothers."[54] A good education for women, according to Lynn White, former president of Mills College, would not include courses in which men are "naturally" better—like the sciences. It would not only begin with a "firm nuclear course in the Family, but from it would radiate curricular series dealing with food and nutrition, textiles and clothing, health and nursing, house planning and interior decoration, garden design and applied botany, and child development."[55] He urged fellow educators to make a course on the "theory and preparation of a Basque paella" as

---

[53] Ibid.
[54] Friedan, op. cit., p. 150.
[55] Quoted in ibid., p. 152.

difficult and exciting (for women) as a course in post-Kantian philosophy.

Others made use of the same sexist nonsense in more directly "functional" ways. The advertising industry, a multibillion-dollar business devoted to encouraging waste, discovered that women do 75 percent of consumer household buying. When she researched the sexual selling game of the 1950s, one advertising executive told Betty Friedan that "properly manipulated, . . . American housewives can be given the sense of identity, purpose, creativity, the self-realization, even the sexual joy they lack—by the buying of things."[56]

DISCRIMINATION IN THE 1950s

Although reality had little relationship to the picture painted by sexist ideology, we should not assume that the brainwashing was unsuccessful. True, more and more women, many of whom were wives and mothers, worked outside the home. Sexist ideology and overt discrimination, however, were successful in preventing any women's liberation movement in the 1950s; keeping women segregated in "women's jobs"; keeping women's wages low; preventing many women from attaining high education, prestigious professional positions, or positions of power in business or politics; and keeping women as a flexible reserve, easily employable and easily fired.

Since 1950, in every recession the rate of unemployment of women workers has been about twice that of men workers. In the period from 1950 to the present, the wages and salaries of women have shown a *declining* trend relative to those of men (see Table 11.6).

Why did women's wages suffer this relative decline? The answer to this is increased discrimination, but with a change in the forms of discrimination. There was no change in the differential wage that was paid for the same job, but there has been an increase in the percentages of women holding the lower-paying jobs in each occupation. More important, most of the large increase of women in the labor force went into the traditional "women's jobs," so the degree of segregation into the lower-paying occupations increased considerably. Let us examine the evidence for these trends.

There is plentiful evidence that within each occupation the

[56] Quoted in ibid., p. 199.

higher-paying jobs are going to men in ever-increasing proportions. For example, women have remained over 80 percent of all elementary school teachers, but men have increasingly monopolized the better-paying and higher-status administrative jobs (see Table 11.7).

The same trend toward male dominance is observable in the higher-paying administrative jobs in several other "women's occupations," such as social workers, librarians, high school teachers, bank clerks, and telephone operators. The increased predominance of men in the top business and professional posi-

TABLE 11.6
Women's median wage as percentage of men's

Year	Percentage
1950	65%
1955	64
1956	63
1957	64
1958	63
1959	61
1960	61
1961	59
1962	60
1963	60
1964	60
1965	60
1966	58
1967	58
1968	58
1969	61
1970	59

Source: U.S. Department of Labor, Women's Bureau, *Fact Sheet on the Earnings Gap* (1970), p. 1.

TABLE 11.7
Elementary school principals, 1928–1968

Year	Percentage of women
1928	55%
1948	41
1958	38
1968	22

Source: Kirsten Amundsen, *The Silenced Majority* (Englewood Cliffs, N.J.: Prentice-Hall, 1971), p. 38.

tions may also be reflected in the fact that 6 percent of those listed in *Who's Who* in 1930 were women, but only 4 percent of the entries were women in 1970.

The most important type of economic discrimination to increase in this period is the segregation of women into "women's jobs." The increasing numbers of women at work have gone largely into sex-typed jobs, thus intensifying the overcrowding of these areas and further lowering, or at least keeping low, the wages paid in those occupations. Specifically, from 1950 to 1960, sexist ideology and overt discrimination forced 48 percent of the total increase in women in the labor force into occupations that are 70 percent or more female. Moreover, in the same period a startling 59 percent of the growth in number of women at work occurred in occupations in which over half the workers are women.

When we examine detailed classifications, such as telephone operators or stenographers, the pattern is very clear. Yet even in the very broadest classifications encompassing all workers, the long-run trend toward increased segregation is very striking (see Table 11.8).

TABLE 11.8

Economic segregation by sex, 1940–1970

	Women as percentage of total in occupation	
Occupation	**1940**	**1970**
Mainly male occupations		
Foreman	2%	3%
Laborer (nonfarm)	3	3
Farmer and farm worker	8	15
Manager and proprietor	12	16
Mixed occupations		
Factory worker	26	31
Professional and technical	45	39
Salesperson	28	42
Mainly female occupations		
Service (nondomestic)	40	61
Clerical	53	75
Domestic service	94	98
Total	25	40

Source: U.S. Department of Labor, Women's Bureau, *1969 Handbook on Women Workers* (1969), plus current Labor Department publications.

These data tell a grim story. During the years 1940 to 1970, the percentage of all workers who were women increased from 25 percent to 40 percent, but most of this increase came in the segregated "women's occupations." Thus the big jumps are in nondomestic service jobs, such as waitresses, and in clerical jobs. By 1970, three out of every four clerical workers were women, and one in every three women workers was a clerical worker. Both areas are low paying and low status. In domestic service, the lowest paying of all, the percentage of women rose still further, from 94 percent to 98 percent.

In the mixed areas, the relatively low-paying categories of factory worker and sales jobs showed large increases in percentages of women. In the mainly male areas, the only large increase in the percentage of women came in the categories of farmers and farm workers—but more detailed data show that the increase was all in low-paid farm work, while the percentage of female farm owners actually declined.

Foremen remained 97 percent male. The only faint ray of hope was the slight increase in female managers and proprietors, from 12 percent to 16 percent, an increase of 4 percentage points in 30 years.

On the other side of the coin—in this period when the proportion of women to all workers increased greatly—the only major decline in the portion of women in an occupation was in the higher-paying and most prestigious professional areas, a decline that has continued since about 1930. We shall see that women in all the professional areas suffered greatly from the sexist offensives of the 1930s and the 1950s.

The Labor Department's "professional" category is very broad, and we are concerned not only with the declining percentage of women in the whole area but also with their increased segregation within it. Over 75 percent of the women classified as professionals are in the low-paying and low-status occupations of teaching and nursing. The picture in these semiprofessional, mainly female areas of the "professional and technical" category is shown in Table 11.9.

Women held their own in the 1950s (and still do) in elementary school teaching and nursing. The percentage declined somewhat among social workers and librarians, and by 1970 the percentage of female librarians had moved down further, to 80 percent. All of these remained mainly female occupations, but men were moving into them, particularly into the top jobs, taking over most head librarian jobs, social work directorships, and even most elementary principal jobs. Most striking was the male invasion of high school teaching; the percentage of women in this area declined from 60 percent in 1940 to only 46 percent in 1970. Moreover, by 1970, over 95 percent of all high school principals were men.

The greatest losses suffered by women, however, were in the highest-paying and most prestigious professions. For example, the percentage of female college faculty (including instructors, professors, and presidents) continued its decline from the 1930 high point (see Table 11.10).

TABLE 11.9

Low-paid professional occupations, 1950–1960

	Percentage of women	
Occupation	**1950**	**1960**
Elementary school teacher	87%	86%
High school teacher	60	49
Nurse	98	97
Librarian	89	85
Medical-dental technician	57	62
Social worker	66	57

Source: U.S. Department of Labor, Women's Bureau, *1969 Handbook on Women Workers* (1969), plus current Labor Department publications.

TABLE 11.10

Female college faculty, 1910–1970

Year	1910	1920	1930	1940	1950	1960	1970
Percent female	19%	30%	32%	27%	23%	19%	18%

Source: U.S. Department of Labor, Women's Bureau, *1969 Handbook on Women Workers* (1969), plus current Labor Department publications.

The percentage of women scientists also declined in the 1950s, though it was low to begin with (see Table 11.11). Women were barely accepted in the physical sciences in 1950, but the percentage dropped still further in the 1950s and 1960s. The percentage of female natural scientists dropped again in the 1960s; women were only 8 percent of the total by 1970. The percentage of women mathematicians also dropped again, to only 10 percent in 1970. In most of the social sciences the percentages remained low, the highest being in psychology, with 23 percent women in 1970. Several of the lower-paying areas in the humanities have much higher percentages of women.

Another indication of the changing status of women is their educational attainment (see Table 11.12). From their high point in 1930, the percentage of women earning academic degrees drops precipitously to a low point in 1950. The decline is due in some large part to the renewed climate of sexism in the 1930s and late 1940s. It is also due partly to the large influx of veterans from World War II. Yet the low figure for 1950 is not an accident, because the decline begins in the 1930s and because the recovery takes so long. In the face of the sexism of the 1950s, the percentage of women B.A.s slowly recovers until it is slightly higher in 1970 than in 1930, but the portion of Ph.D.s going to women had not yet recovered to the 1930 level.

TABLE 11.11
Female scientists, 1950–1960

	Percentage of women	
Specialty	**1950**	**1960**
Biologist	29%	27%
Chemist	10	9
Mathematician	38	26
Physicist	7	4
Geologist	6	2
All natural scientists	11	10

Source: U.S. Department of Labor, Women's Bureau, *1969 Handbook on Women Workers* (1969), plus current Labor Department publications.

TABLE 11.12
Recipients of academic degrees, 1930–1970

	Percentage of women		
Year	**B.A.**	**M.A.**	**Ph.D.**
1930	40%	40%	15%
1940	42	38	13
1950	24	29	10
1960	35	35	11
1970	42	40	13

Sources: U.S. Department of Labor, Women's Bureau, *1969 Handbook on Women Workers* (1969), and Rudolf Blitz, "Women in the Professions," *Monthly Labor Review*, 97 (May 1974), p. 38.

THE WOMEN'S LIBERATION MOVEMENT: 1940–1960

With two slight qualifications, there was *no* organized women's liberation movement from 1940 to 1960. First, most of the older women's organizations survived. The League of Women Voters continued, though declining; it had inherited a mailing list of 2 million names from NAWSA, but had only about 200,000 members in the mid-1920s, and only 106,000 in 1960. Also continuing were the YWCA, the Business and Professional Women's Clubs, the General Federation of Women's Clubs, and the American Association of University Women. But all had primary interests—social, professional, or reform—not related to women's liberation, or else they saw no relationship. Another continuing conservative influence was the Women's Bureau.

Second, women's liberation was advocated by the National Women's Party and by the old left-wing parties, particularly Communist and Socialist Workers—but all these were small, sectarian, and without influence. The left-wing parties suffered severe government persecution in the 1950s; they also saw women's liberation as only a secondary priority.

In conclusion, we have seen that there was no significant women's liberation movement in the 40 years from the mid-1920s to the mid-1960s. One reason was the limited ideology and elite class base of the suffragists. So strongly had they emphasized the vote, and only the vote, that their successors—like the League of Women Voters—could declare in the 1920s that there was no more discrimination against women and that liberal women should merely fight for general reforms for all people. The sole successor to the most militant suffragists—the Women's party—was narrow in other ways. It continued to fight for equal legal rights but paid little or no attention to women's inferior position in the family, to the exploitation of women workers, or to the special problems of black women. This lack of interest in the major social, economic, and racial issues alienated radical women, while the hostile social atmosphere prevented them from winning over the moderate women.

By the mid-1920s, the relative stability of capitalism, the disappearance of the small radical farmer, the red-baiting and the internal splits destroyed the Socialist and Progressive parties and brought a period of conservatism hostile to the women's movement. The radicalism of the 1930s concentrated on unemployment and, in the late 1930s, on the threat of war with fascism to the practical exclusion of all other issues. Again, during the war other issues could not be raised. The postwar 1946–1960 period was a time of U.S. economic expansion and world dominance, of the cold war and superpatriotism ensured by the witch hunting of McCarthyism. All radical and liberal groups suffered repression; and possible women's liberation causes—such as child care—were smothered with the rest.

THE NEW STRUGGLE FOR LIBERATION: AMERICAN WOMEN, 1960 TO THE PRESENT

12

As the 1960s began, the myth of the American woman as the "happy housewife heroine" conflicted increasingly with reality. Twenty-three million women—36 percent of all women 16 and older—worked for pay. These working women were not just single girls spending a few years in the labor force; over half (54 percent) were married, and many had children. Of all women with school-age children, 43 percent worked for pay. By the end of the 1960s, a *majority* of women between 18 and 64 worked at paid jobs.

While the women's magazines' picture of the full-time housewife and mother was valid for fewer and fewer women, an alternate picture—that of the career woman successfully competing in what had been a man's world—was equally false. Women worked in factories, as domestics and secretaries, as teachers and nurses. The prestigious and remunerative positions in the professions and business were overwhelmingly held by men. Educationally, women were not doing as well relative to men as they had in 1930. In 1960, 35 percent of all B.A.s went to women; in 1930, women had received 40 percent. Whatever a woman's education, when she entered the labor force she encountered discrimination. She made less money than a man with the same education, and her chances of promotion were much less.

Women's position in the public sphere was, if anything, even worse. Forty years after winning the vote, women were voting at almost the same levels as men. Millions worked in political campaigns, stuffing envelopes, typing, canvassing. But despite their numbers as voters and their efforts as party workers, women were barely represented in government decision-making positions. The 1960 elections brought the highest number of women ever into Congress; 15 out of 435 in the House of Representatives and 2 out of 100 in the Senate.[1] There had, of course, never been a woman president or a woman Supreme Court justice. In neither case has a woman ever been seriously considered. Only two women had served in the cabinet, and few had been appointed to other high administrative posts. Federal judges, all appointed by the president, were also overwhelmingly male. On the state level the situation was hardly better. Even by 1967, only about 4 percent of state legislative seats were held by women.[2] No women served as governors in 1960. The only woman to be elected to that office during the 1960s—Lurleen Wallace—was governor in name only, like the two women governors elected previously.

Women's representation was better on the local level, but only when relatively unprestigious and badly paid positions such as library board members and treasury clerks are included.[3] In 1966, there were 100 women mayors, but none of these served as mayor of a major city.[4] Even on school boards, an area that, according to the stereotype, should be of special interest to women, they were underrepresented—only 9.7 percent of board members were women.[5]

Thus, despite doing the major part of the unglamorous but essential political grubby work, women were neither rewarded with high appointive office nor given encouragement and help in running for elective office. John Bailey, one-time Democratic national chairman, expressed the common view of male professionals toward women in politics: "The only time to run a woman is when things look so bad that your only chance is to do something dramatic."[6]

In the other centers of power in the United States, women were again conspicuous only by their absence. The corporate elite was a male preserve. As late as 1967, the boards of direc-

---

[1] Judith Hole and Ellen Levine, *Rebirth of Feminism* (New York: Quadrangle, 1971), p. 401.
[2] Kirsten Amundsen, *The Silenced Majority* (Englewood Cliffs, N.J.: Prentice-Hall, 1971), p. 78.
[3] Amundsen, op. cit., p. 70.
[4] Ibid., p. 79.
[5] Ibid., p. 80.
[6] Ibid., p. 83.

tors of the top 20 industrials, the top 15 banks, and the top 15 insurance companies included no women.[7] By 1970, women were represented on the boards of 2 of the 3 major broadcasting networks. At NBC, 1 out of 18 directors was female; at CBS, 1 out of 16. No woman served on ABC's board of directors. In 37 states, no woman held a top position—president, vice president, or general manager—in any local TV station. In the other states there were a few; for example, in California, of 34 such positions, 4 were held by women. Women did a little better on the boards of major newspapers. There was a woman on the governing board of the *Washington Post,* the *Chattanooga Times,* the *Houston Post,* and the *New York Post.* But in several of these cases, the woman's unquestioned talent was backed up by ownership of the newspaper.[8]

The professedly egalitarian unions provided little more opportunity for women to rise to major decision-making positions. In the late 1960s there was no woman on the 28-member executive council of the AFL–CIO. Of the council's 16 standing committees, none had a woman chairperson. The Amalgamated Clothing Workers of America and the International Ladies' Garment Workers' Union—both with a predominantly female membership—had no woman officer at the national level.[9]

As the 1960s began, then, women were a silent and powerless majority—but not, as the myth of the 1950s had it, a contented one. Even the women's magazines, the prime propagandizers of the feminine mystique, came to recognize the "trapped housewife" syndrome. A Gallup poll taken in 1962 found that 90 percent of the housewives surveyed did not want their daughters to lead the same type of life they had led. They hoped their daughters would get more education and marry later.[10]

The widening of the gap between ideology and reality had reached a critical point. Extreme disparities between social ideology and social reality are conducive to the formation of social movements. This was the situation for women in the early 1960s. According to the ideology, the typical American woman was an affluent housewife, happy and completely ful-

[7] Ibid., p. 91.
[8] Ibid., p. 100.
[9] Ibid., p. 97.
[10] Ibid., p. 122.

filled in that role. In reality, more and more women worked because their financial contribution was needed for family support. Yet the ideology was used to deny them good jobs, promotions, and equal pay. The affluent housewife, on the other hand, was finding that living up to the feminine mystique exacted heavy costs. Generally college educated, she was relegated to housework, which offered little intrinsic satisfaction and no prestige. Thus, many women had been educated too much to find total satisfaction in the housewife role; yet when from choice or need, women went to work, they found themselves discriminated against because of their sex. The preconditions for a social movement were present.

During the early 1960s, however, it was the discontent of blacks, not of women, that became articulate and held center stage. Blacks were saying: We're tired of waiting; we want in *now,* and we're backing rhetoric with action. Sit-ins and freedom rides led to nationwide organizations, and many white students of both sexes became deeply involved in the civil rights movement. Here many young women learned both the rhetoric and the organization of protest. Not surprisingly, as they became more sensitive to the blacks' second-class status, they became aware of their own.

The mid-1960s saw an increased politicization of American college students. Many who started in the civil rights movement became involved in the free speech movement and in Students for a Democratic Society. The antiwar movement attracted additional tens of thousands. Organizing and protesting became a way of life for many on campus. The movement's lack of success in ending the war despite its spectacular growth led to radicalization—to the emergence of the New Left. The early antiwar movement had seen the war as a ghastly mistake; later, the war was increasingly perceived as a natural outgrowth of U.S. imperialism. With this change in view came an increasingly radical critique and analysis of American society. The women in the movement were to learn the New Left lesson well; they were to carry the critique to a more fundamental level than the men expected.

EARLY SYMPTOMS

In December 1961, John Kennedy established a Presidential Commission on the Status of Women. The idea originated with

Esther Peterson, a member of Kennedy's campaign staff and his appointee as head of the Woman's Bureau. Kennedy seemed to have accepted the proposal at least in part because it was a cheap way of repaying the hundreds of women who worked in his campaign, none of whom, with the exception of Esther Peterson, had been appointed to a high-level government job. There has also been speculation that Kennedy saw the commission as a way of finessing the Equal Rights Amendment issue. The amendment had been included in the platforms of both major parties in nearly every election from 1940 to 1960. But the major labor unions, which were important Kennedy supporters, were opposed to it. Such a commission would, at minimum, postpone any need to consider the amendment and, if it were to find no need for the ERA, would give Kennedy an excuse for never bringing it up.[11]

The commission's report did not come out until late 1963, but meanwhile there were other stirrings. In early 1963, Betty Friedan's *The Feminine Mystique* was published.[12] A powerful indictment of the ideology that forced women into the role of full-time housewife and a description of the psychological costs of such a limited life, it became an instant best-seller.

In the summer of the same year, the Equal Pay Act was passed by Congress. This act required that, in the jobs covered by it, women be paid equally with men doing the same job. The act had been introduced in 1945 by Representative Helen Gahagan Douglas and reintroduced in every session until it was finally successful in 1963.[13]

The report of the President's Commission on the Status of Women was made public in October 1963. The report of the commission itself was moderate, although the reports of some of its committees, released at the same time, were somewhat stronger. Its recommendations included greater availability of child care services, removal of the remaining property law restrictions, greater opportunities for women in politics, and equal opportunity in employment. The commission's total lack of militancy is shown by its position on the last point. While it recommended that the president issue an executive order

---

[11] Hole and Levine, op. cit., p. 18.

[12] Betty Friedan, *The Feminine Mystique* (New York: Dell, 1963).

[13] Lucy Komisar, *The New Feminism* (New York: Warner Paperback Library, 1972), p. 118.

embodying the principle of equal opportunity in employment, it recommended no enforcement procedures. Voluntary compliance was to be relied upon.[14] The report favored the removal of all barriers to women's full participation in American society; at the same time, it accepted the assumption that it is the woman who is fundamentally responsible for homemaking and childrearing, even if she also works outside the home. To make this dual role easier, it recommended greater opportunities for part-time workers. The report favored the retention of protective laws for women, at least until such laws could be extended to cover all workers.[15] It also concluded that the Fifth and Fourteenth Amendments provided sufficient basis for the equality of women under the law and that the ERA was not needed.

The importance of the commission lies more in its being an example and a publicizer than in its recommendations. It was the first official body to make a thorough study of the status of women in the United States.[16] By 1963, a number of states had followed the federal example by setting up state commissions on the status of women, and by 1967 every state had such a commission.

Two of the commission's recommendations were of immediate importance. In November 1963, Kennedy, as the commission had urged, set up the Interdepartmental Committee on the Status of Women and the Citizens' Advisory Council on the Status of Women. The first was composed of governmental officials; the latter, composed of private citizens, was to play an important role in pressuring the government to live up to its official nondiscriminatory position.

A major weapon in the fight for equality came into being in 1964. Its inadvertent forger was Congressman Howard Smith, a southern gentleman of the old school—he approved of both women and blacks as long as they stayed in their place. A comprehensive civil rights bill was up for debate, and it looked as if there were sufficient votes to pass it. Smith, the powerful chairman of the Rules Committee and wily leader of the die-hard southern contingent in the House, realized that drastic steps were needed. He could not win on the floor, and

[14] Hole and Levine, op. cit., p. 21.
[15] Ibid., p. 435.
[16] Ibid., p. 18.

he dared not bottle up the bill in committee, as he had done in the past. During his appearance on "Meet the Press," May Craig, a member of the White House Press Corps and a feminist, suggested a strategy by asking him to include women under Title VII, the equal employment section of the bill.[17] Perhaps the bill could be laughed to death.

Congresswoman Martha Griffiths had intended to make that motion, but knowing Smith would bring more votes, she waited to see if he would actually do so. Smith did in fact move to include women in Title VII. Many of the liberal supporters of the civil rights bill, convinced, like Smith, that this might kill the bill, opposed his amendment. Even Edith Green, sponsor of the 1963 Equal Pay Bill and long-time advocate of equal rights for women, worked and voted against Smith's amendment. The other congresswomen supported it, and on February 8, this strange coalition of feminists and southerners passed it by 168 to 133.

Smith must have been surprised, as were others, when the whole bill, amendment included, passed in the House. The Senate might well have dropped the provision had not a lobbying campaign gotten under way. Pauli Murray, a black woman lawyer, wrote a "Memorandum in Support of Retaining the Sex Amendment," which was used by women representing the Business and Professional Women's Clubs in their effort to persuade senators. Caroline Bird reports that Lady Bird Johnson very discreetly let it be known that the administration supported the amendment.[18] Under these circumstances, there were enough senators who decided that voting against the rights of half their constituents was not politically smart. The bill passed, amendment and all.

When the law went into effect in July 1965, it became illegal to discriminate against women in hiring and promotions. But laws are of little use unless vigorously enforced. The Equal Employment Opportunity Commission (EEOC), set up to enforce Title VII, considered the sex provision, in the words of its director, "a fluke . . . conceived out of wedlock."[19] Most of the commissioners seemed to consider the provision at best a joke, at worst a distraction from their real work in behalf

[17] Caroline Bird, *Born Female* (New York: Pocket Books, 1971), p. 3.
[18] Ibid., p. 11.
[19] Ibid., p. 13.

of black men. Perhaps the Playboy Clubs would have to hire male "bunnies," someone said at a White House Conference on Equal Opportunity in August 1965. The press, finding equal opportunity for women at least as funny as did the EEOC commissioners, labeled the amendment the Bunny Law and asked, "Can she pitch for the Mets?"[20]

It became clear to interested women that, given this attitude, little could be expected of the EEOC unless pressure was applied. A particular danger lay in the provision that made it legal to discriminate if sex were a bona fide occupational qualification (bfoq) for the job in question. Interpreted loosely, this could nullify the act. In November 1965, under pressure from the Citizens Advisory Council, the EEOC came out with guidelines that interpreted the bfoq provision narrowly. The council argued and the EEOC accepted the position that exceptions should not be allowed ". . . based on stereotypes of characteristics of the sexes; the preferences of the employer, co-workers, clients, or customers; or assumptions of the comparative characteristics of women (or men) in general."[21] The EEOC, however, rejected the council's recommendation that sex-segregated want ads be outlawed.

NOW IS ORGANIZED

The situation, then, seemed ripe for the formation of a women's organization. In 1965–1966, Betty Friedan was often in Washington conferring with interested women on what could be done to combat discrimination. In the spring of 1966, the controversy over sex-segregated want ads was in full swing, and in June, Congresswoman Martha Griffiths strongly attacked the EEOC for its lack of enforcement. The two EEOC commissioners who were interested in enforcing the sex provision of Title VII had decided that an organization to pressure the government into enforcement was needed and were discreetly letting their views become known.

The third annual meeting of the National Conference of State Commissions, which opened in Washington on June 28, pro-

---

[20] Ibid.

[21] "Report on Progress in 1965 on the Status of Women," *Second Annual Report of Interdepartmental Committee and Citizens' Advisory Council on the Status of Women,* December 31, 1965, p. 25.

vided an opportunity. This meeting, held under the sponsorship of the Citizens Advisory Council and the Interdepartmental Committee on the Status of Women, brought together a large number of concerned women. An informal meeting of some of them to discuss the possibility of an independent women's group produced no results. Some of the state commissioners present felt that such an organization was not necessary, that it would be better to work through the official bodies already established. But when Kathryn Clarenbach, head of the Wisconsin Commission, found that the conference was not allowed to pass resolutions or take action and, thus, that she could not introduce a resolution against the EEOC's position on want ads, it became clear to her and to many others that working through the state commissions would not be sufficient. At the final luncheon, the National Organization for Women (NOW) was formed. NOW's first action, decided upon during the luncheon, was to send telegrams to the EEOC commissioners asking them to change their position on want ads.

NOW announced its existence, with a charter membership of 300, at a press conference on October 29, 1966. Betty Friedan became its first president. Its purpose is stated thus: "To take action to bring women into full participation in the mainstream of American society *now*, exercising all the privileges and responsibilities thereof in truly equal partnership with men."[22]

NOW went into full swing right from the beginning. It immediately got involved in several sex-discrimination cases under Title VII. The EEOC was petitioned to hold hearings on the want-ad guidelines. After considerable pressure, they were held in May of the following year. Task forces were set up to study and make recommendations about discrimination against women in education, employment, and religion. Others worked on the media image of women, the problems of poor women, and the family.[23] Government officials from the EEOC commissioners to the president were lobbied in person and by mail.

During its early years, NOW's tactics included the mainstays of "establishment" protest—setting up task forces, bringing

---

[22] NOW Statement of Purpose, adopted at organizational conference, October 29, 1966.

[23] Hole and Levine, op. cit., p. 86.

suit, lobbying government officials. The organization did not, however, restrict itself to such ultrarespectable activities. In 1967, NOW members picketed *The New York Times* to protest its sex-segregated want-ad policy; NOW organized a national day of demonstration against the EEOC and set up picket lines in cities with EEOC offices. Later, NOW members were to disrupt a Senate committee hearing, demanding that hearings on the Equal Rights Amendment be held.

At NOW's second national conference in November 1967, the growing pains that often afflict a young movement became apparent. As the first national women's group, NOW's membership was extremely heterogeneous, and ideological conflicts were inevitable. At the conference, a major order of business was the drawing up of a women's Bill of Rights. Eight demands were eventually included:[24]

I. Equal rights constitutional amendment
II. Enforcement of laws banning sex discrimination in employment
III. Maternity leave rights in employment and in social security benefits
IV. Tax deduction for home and child care expenses for working parents
V. Child care centers
VI. Equal and unsegregated education
VII. Equal job training opportunities and allowances for women in poverty
VIII. The right of women to control their reproductive lives

Two of the planks engendered major controversies and were adopted only after bitter fights. Women from the United Auto Workers objected to the inclusion of the Equal Rights Amendment plank because their union's official position was still one of opposition. They did not carry out their threat to walk out when the plank was adopted, but they withdrew the secretarial services they had been providing, throwing NOW "into administrative chaos for months."[25] The passage of the abortion plank did lead to a walkout. The opponents argued that abortion was not a women's rights issue and that taking such a controversial position would destroy the effectiveness of the organization.

At the next annual meeting a split-off on the left took place.

[24] Reproduced in ibid., p. 88.
[25] Ibid.

Ti-Grace Atkinson, president of the New York chapter, and some of her radical followers walked out after losing their fight to dismantle NOW's hierarchical structure.

These splits did not retard NOW's growth. By 1971, NOW had over 150 chapters and from 5,000 to 10,000 members. By late 1973, it had grown to about 30,000. During the late 1960s women were becoming aware of their second-class position at a rate sufficient to keep both the moderate and the radical wings of the movement growing at an accelerating pace.

A number of other moderate women's groups were founded in quick succession. The Women's Equity Action League (WEAL), incorporated on December 1, 1968, has been particularly active in cases of sex discrimination in higher education and in the ERA campaign. The group has a fairly conservative style—"League of Women Voter types," according to a member—and its D.C. chapter includes congresswomen and high government officials as members.[26] Federally Employed Women (FEW) was founded in 1968 for the purpose of pressuring the Civil Service Commission to enforce the executive order banning sex discrimination in federal employment. Human Rights for Women, Inc., also founded in 1968, is a nonprofit, tax-exempt organization dedicated to providing legal aid in sex discrimination cases.

RADICAL WOMEN ORGANIZE

The radical wing of the women's movement had somewhat different origins than the moderate wing and developed concurrently. During the middle 1960s, women in the civil rights movement and its offshoots were becoming aware that, even in these groups dedicated to human liberation, they were second-class members—useful at the typewriter, in the kitchen, and in bed, but expected to leave policy making to the men. The first stirrings of organization seem to have occurred in 1964, when a small group of women in the Student Non-Violent Coordinating Committee (SNCC) began to meet and talk about their role in that organization. Ruby Doris Smith Robinson presented a paper stemming from these talks at a SNCC staff meeting. The men's reaction is well expressed by Stokely Carmichael's response: "The only position for women in SNCC

---

[26] Ibid., p. 96.

is prone."[27] The women in these groups found again and again that men considered their complaints trivial. Bringing up the women's issue is "bourgeois," the women were told; it diverts attention from the real problems. A paper written by two SNCC women in 1965 produced such a reaction from male radicals. "Catcalls, storms of ridicule and verbal abuse"—"she just needs a good screw"—greeted attempts to bring up the women's issue at a 1965 SDS conference. Women demanding attention to women's liberation at an SDS convention in 1966 "were pelted with tomatoes and thrown out of the convention."[28]

Despite such treatment, women did not leave the New Left *en masse*. Some did begin to meet together to discuss their position in the movement. These women's caucuses were small and informal. The first effort to organize radical women as women did not occur until 1967.

During the spring of that year, two Chicago women—Heather Booth and Naomi Weisstein—held a seminar on women's issues under the auspices of a free university program. At the same time, a national meeting of New Left groups was being planned for Chicago in the fall. The seminar spurred a group of women to consider presenting a list of women's demands to the National Conference for a New Politics. These women finally decided not to participate as a group. The members who attended as individuals joined with other women to form an ad hoc women's caucus at the convention. The strong women's rights resolution that the caucus prepared was shunted aside by the convention leadership on the basis that there was not sufficient time. When it became clear that the convention did have time to take up additional resolutions as long as they were on other subjects, two of the caucus women, Jo Freeman and Shulamith Firestone, protested. "They were told in no uncertain terms that their 'trivial' business was not going to stop the conference from dealing with the important issues of the world."[29]

"Rage at what happened at the convention kept us going for at least three months," reported one of the participants, and spurred regular women's meetings in Chicago.[30] From

[27] Ibid., p. 110.
[28] Marlene Dixon and Robin Morgan, quoted in ibid., p. 112.
[29] Ibid., pp. 113–114.
[30] Quoted in ibid., p. 114.

these beginnings two groups emerged—the Woman's Radical Action Project and the Westside group. Jo Freeman, a founder of the latter, started the first newsletter of the movement in early 1968, thus providing some link with interested women across the country.

In the fall of 1967, Shulamith Firestone and Pam Allen organized Radical Women in New York. The group's first public action took place during an antiwar demonstration by a coalition of women's peace groups in January 1968. The Radical Women, joined by 300 to 500 women from the Jeannette Rankin Brigade, as the coalition was called, staged "The Burial of Traditional Womanhood" in a torchlight parade at Arlington Cemetery. Many New Left women opposed this action as being nonpolitical and basically irrelevant. The Radical Women responded that before women could hope to influence public policy, they must overcome their own subjugation, that the problem of women in America is social, not personal. Thus dealing with the women's issue was seen as both political and basic. ". . . We cannot hope to move toward a better world or even a truly democratic society at home until we begin to solve our own problems."[31]

The responses to the demonstration highlighted a conflict that had been developing in the new movement. The male-dominated New Left organizations had defined the women's problems as trivial. To the extent that a problem was recognized at all, it was assumed that it would automatically be righted by socialism, increasingly the goal of the New Left. Some New Left women agreed with this position, but those who formed the women's caucuses and then the independent women's groups did not. Nevertheless, even the women who saw the woman problem as important disagreed in their analysis of its origins and thus in their tactics and proposed solutions. Is women's inferior place due to "the system"—to private property and capitalism? Or is it due to men—to the male's psychological need to dominate? Is women's liberation part of the larger struggle for a socialist restructuring of society? Or is it *the* issue—the most basic and first form of exploitation of one human by another? Should women's groups, even if not a part of larger organizations, work closely with the New Left? Or

[31] Kathie Amatniek, "Funeral Oration for the Burial of Traditional Womanhood," *Notes from the First Year,* June 1968.

must they be independent and work alone? This conflict between socialists and feminists was to be a recurring issue in many groups as the movement grew. The two approaches eventually came to be called socialist feminism and radical feminism.

THE MOVEMENT GROWS

Many people first became aware of the women's liberation movement in September 1968. The Radical Women's protest of the Miss America Contest was the first feminist activity to get front-page coverage. The purpose was to "protest the image of Miss America, an image that oppresses women in every area in which it purports to represent us." A Freedom Trash Can into which to throw "bras, girdles, curlers, false eyelashes, wigs" and other such "woman's garbage" was provided and a sheep was crowned Miss America.[32]

By 1969, women's liberation was getting considerable, if often condescending and inaccurate, publicity. But even before the media discovered the movement, it had begun to spread. During 1968, groups were forming throughout the country. Sometimes they were the result of a specific event; sometimes a woman active in one area moved to another and organized a group; sometimes they just seemed to happen, the women involved being unaware of activities elsewhere. The catalyst in the formation of a group in Seattle was a sexist SDS speaker at the University of Washington. "Balling a chick together" is an excellent way of enhancing the political consciousness of poor white youth, he said.[33] Many of the women were active in or dropouts from the New Left. A member of an early San Francisco group explained its origins:

> Some of us had been friends before the group began. We had discussed the problems we had as women. . . . At this time we had heard about women's groups being formed in other parts of the country, but our experience in the "movement" had burned us so badly that anything that hinted of organizing, meetings or objectivity was synonymous with manipulation, rhetoric and ego-trips, so for a long

---

[32] Robin Morgan, ed., *Sisterhood Is Powerful* (New York: Vintage, 1970), p. 521.

[33] Hole and Levine, op. cit., p. 120.

time we didn't seriously consider meeting in any kind of formal way. But finally we did decide to meet.[34]

In August 1968, a meeting of radical women's groups took place in Maryland. Although attendance was small (about 30) and representation was not really national (most being from the East Coast and the Midwest), this was the first attempt at forming a national movement.[35] At Thanksgiving of the same year, a much larger conference was held in Chicago. Over 200 women from across the country and from Canada attended. The conflict between the socialists and the feminists took the form of a debate over the value of consciousness raising. A paper was presented that attempted to formalize and politically justify the technique developed by the New York Radical Women.

While the socialist women had a ready-made ideology that provided an analytic and tactical guide, the feminists had rejected Marxism as inadequate. Most were, in fact, socialists in that they accepted the Marxist critique of capitalism, but they felt that Marxism overemphasized economic determinants and did not provide an adequate analysis of women's subjugation. The feminists had not yet developed an alternate ideology. During the next several years, groups arose that attempted to develop distinctly feminist analyses and tactics.

ORGANIZATION AND IDEOLOGY

In early 1969, several members of the New York Radical Women formed a new group, which they called Redstockings. Intended by its founders to be specifically feminist and militantly activist, the group immediately became involved in the abortion fight. In February, the group disrupted state legislative hearings on abortion reform, demanding repeal instead, and the next month it held its own counterhearings.

The thrust of the group changed rather rapidly, however. A growing commitment to consciousness raising replaced its

---

[34] Pamela Allen, *Free Space* (Washington, N.J.: Times Change Press, 1970), p. 9.

[35] Hole and Levine, op. cit., p. 122. See also Jo Freeman, *The Politics of Women's Liberation* (New York: David McKay, 1975), pp. 106–107.

activism. Redstockings fully developed the theory of consciousness raising, providing an analysis of its uses and purposes. Consciousness raising was likened to the Chinese "speak bitterness" technique—a way of getting one's "personal" problems into the open not in order to adjust but to discover that the problems are, in fact, social and require a collective solution. The Redstocking Manifesto speaks of female *class* consciousness in order to emphasize the political nature of the technique.[36] The value of consciousness raising is now generally accepted by feminists but is seen as a first step to be followed by collective action. The Redstockings, however, turned more and more inward, concentrating on the tecnique to the exclusion of all else. This eventually led to the group's demise.

The history of the Feminists, another group formed at about the same time as Redstockings, illustrates some of the other problems the young movement has had to confront. At the second annual NOW convention, Ti-Grace Atkinson, president of the New York chapter, and some other New York members left the organization after an argument over the decision-making structure of NOW. Atkinson, several NOW members, and some former members of the New York Radical Women formed the October 17th Movement, which was later called the Feminists. The Feminists' objective was to develop a theoretically sound feminist analysis, to work out in practice a new, nonoppressive organizational form, and to take public actions. Their analysis led them to see the source of women's oppression as the male-female role division and to define their goal as the annihilation of sex roles.[37]

Like the Redstockings, the Feminists' first public action was on the abortion issue. In January 1969, they demonstrated at the trial of an abortionist and demanded the repeal of all laws on abortion. To dramatize their position that the family is central to the oppression of women, the Feminists picketed the New York Marriage License Bureau. In a leaflet they distributed, they labeled marriage a "slavery-like practice" and summarized a number of the laws on marriage.[38] They concluded: "We can't destroy the inequalities between men and women

---

[36] Hole and Levine, op. cit., p. 138.
[37] Ibid., p. 143.
[38] Morgan, op. cit., p. 536.

until we destroy marriage. *We must free ourselves. And marriage is the place to begin.*"[39]

The group's most original contribution lay in its experiment with internal organization. Atkinson had left NOW over the issue of organizational hierarchy. All hierarchy is oppressive, she contended. "You cannot destroy oppression by filling the position of the oppressor."[40] Participatory democracy and nonhierarchy had been important ideological tenets of the New Left movement, whatever the situation in actual practice. Women's liberation groups, because of the members' often unhappy experiences in the New Left, were even more strongly committed to nonhierarchy. But often an informal leadership would emerge because of the women's differences in experience and skill—or, structureless, the group would flounder, incapable of any action.[41] The Feminists, too, learned that good intentions are not sufficient.

To overcome this problem, the Feminists devised the Lot System and the Disc System. Tasks were divided into creative and word tasks, and two sets of lots were used. Thus no one could draw the same type of job twice in a row. Not only would this sharing of both the fun and the "shit" work foster a better spirit in the group, but everyone would develop skills and expertise.

The Disc System was used to prevent a few members from monopolizing group discussions. Each woman began with a certain number of discs and every time she spoke she used a disc. At the beginning, the results were more humorous than effective. According to the perhaps apocryphal story, every woman used up all her discs within a quarter hour when the system was first used. The second time, the women were overly careful with their discs, and the meeting dragged on in virtual silence. "Gradually, the device worked its way into everyone's consciousness as a symbol for the need to listen to each other, and not interrupt or monopolize the conversation."[42]

The Feminists' commitment to egalitarianism degenerated into "an anti-individualist mania," in the words of a former

---

[39] Ibid., p. 537.
[40] Quoted in Hole and Levine, op. cit., p. 145.
[41] Morgan, op. cit., p. xxvii.
[42] Ibid., p. xxviii.

member.[43] In the summer of 1969, while part of the membership was on vacation, the remainder passed a new set of rules demanding total commitment to the group. Performing one's assignments and attendance at meetings were made compulsory. To further ensure the dedication of the group, it was decided that at any given time no more than one-third of the membership could be living with a man. Both the new rules and the way they were passed led a number of members to quit, leaving the group in the hands of the ultras. In the summer of 1970, Atkinson left the group. She had been criticized for becoming a "star," and rules to prevent such "star making" were passed. Any contact with the media had to be approved by the group and the spokesperson chosen by lot.

In December 1969, the Stanton-Anthony Brigade, the founding unit of the New York Radical Feminists, was formed. Most of its early members were from Redstockings or Feminists and were determined to avoid these groups' ideological and structural mistakes while incorporating what was useful. The group's manifesto—"Politics of the Ego"—sets forth a clearly feminist position:

> Radical Feminism recognizes the oppression of women as a fundamental political oppression wherein women are categorized as an inferior class based upon their sex. It is the aim of radical feminism to organize politically to destroy this sex class system. We believe that the purpose of male chauvinism is primarily to obtain psychological ego satisfaction, and that only secondarily does this manifest itself in economic relationships. For this reason we do not believe that capitalism, or any other economic system, is the cause of female oppression, nor do we believe that female oppression will disappear as a result of a purely economic revolution.[44]

The early years of the radical movement were very fertile in the development of ideology. Elements of the ideology and the new issues to which the ideology directed women's attention—rape, for example—were to spread to the moderate women's movement. The radical wing was less successful in developing new structures that were both nonhierarchical and effective. Most of the early groups eventually dissolved due to structural problems. Their experimentation did, however,

---

[43] Hole and Levine, op. cit., p. 147.
[44] Reprinted in ibid., p. 440.

sensitize moderate as well as radical women to the need for consciously struggling with the question.

SOCIALIST FEMINISTS

The problems faced by socialist feminists were somewhat different from those of the radical feminists. They did not need to develop an ideology from scratch; they found Marxism adequate and only needed to apply it to the special problems of women. In Engels' *Origins of the Family, Private Property and the State,* a persuasive explanation of the subordination of women as a result of class society already existed. Marxist theory on the need for a reserve army of labor under capitalism could easily be used to explain the discrimination against women in the labor market.

Where the radical feminists emphasized personal and family oppression of women, the socialist feminists emphasized the economic oppression of women (though they also discussed the social oppression). Where the feminists, like Shulamith Firestone, explained the origins of women's oppression in terms of sex differences in strength and in reproductive roles; the socialist feminists pointed to the coming of male predominance in agriculture, and the introduction of private property and slavery as the original causes of female subordination. Radical feminists argued the need for revolution to give the female "class" equality with the male, after which socialism might emerge. Socialist feminists claimed that a socialist revolution is the necessary prerequisite to full liberation for women. However, they opposed the dogma of some male socialists that socialism will automatically lead to immediate women's liberation. Therefore they saw the need for a continuing, independent women's movement under both capitalism and socialism. As this brief outline indicates, the socialist feminists believe they have a consistent theory of the origins, present uses, and solution to sexist oppression—though they are the first to admit a need for much more elaboration.

Relationships with the male Left and with radical feminists were a problem for socialist feminists. Because their ideological stance was close to that of the male Left, they found it hard to break away. Even after they had formed independent women-only groups, many members still felt psychologically tied to the male Left. The male Left's opinion that feminist activities were bourgeois hung heavy over many groups. Working on feminist issues had to be justified in terms of the greater goal of socialism. Bread and Roses, an early socialist feminist group, for a long time accepted Weathermen positions even when they did not "stem from their own understanding or experience."[45] Radical feminists, because of their bad experiences in the New Left, tended to be suspicious of and disdainful toward socialist feminists. They were afraid that socialists saw the movement only as a recruiting ground for new socialists. Because socialist feminists maintained close ties with the male Left, radical feminists did not consider them feminists at all.

With the decline in the New Left and the growth of the women's movement, socialist feminists gained self-confidence and independence. They no longer felt guilty about working on women's issues. Alliances with other groups could be made when the women thought them useful for their own purposes. They no longer felt they must help any Left group to prove their socialist credentials. With the change came a new flexibility and creativity. This was expressed by the Hyde Park Chapter of the Chicago Women's Liberation Union in "Socialist Feminism: A Strategy for the Women's Movement," one of the best statements of the nonsectarian, flexible position.

During the early 1970s, autonomous socialist-feminist groups—frequently called women's unions—formed in dozens of cities. These groups were independent not only of mixed Left groups but of one another. No national organization existed, and frequently little communication among the groups took place. A coalition of socialist feminists from the New American Movement, a nonsectarian socialist group with a heavy feminist emphasis, and from some of the autonomous groups in the East and Midwest decided to organize a national socialist feminist conference in 1975.[46] Six to eight hundred women were expected to attend. Even though the lack of a communications network among the autonomous women's groups meant that publicity was spotty, over two thousand women came. There were physical facilities for only sixteen hundred, so many had to be turned away.

[45] Cellestine Ware, *Woman Power: The Movement for Women's Liberation* (New York: Tower Publications, 1970), p. 67.

[46] Barbara Dudley, for the Berkeley-Oakland Women's Union, "Report on the Conference," *Socialist Revolution,* October–December 1975, pp. 107–116.

RELATIONS BETWEEN MODERATES AND RADICALS

Despite their differences in analysis and style, the moderate wing and the two radical wings of the movement have managed to work together occasionally. The Congress to Unite Women held in November 1969 brought together over 500 women, both moderate and radical. The groups represented ranged from NOW to the Stanton-Anthony Brigade, from the Women Lawyers—Boston to the Daughters of Bilitis. This disparate group managed to agree on a 10-point set of demands, including nationwide, free 24-hour child care centers staffed equally by men and women; abortion law repeal; the ERA; and women's-studies courses in colleges. It also called for an end to sex role socialization of children, and equality in education and employment.[47]

Another case of cooperation, as well as an indicator of the movement's strength and appeal, was the massive Women's Strike for Equality. The strike, set for August 26, 1970, the fiftieth anniversary of women's suffrage, was coordinated by NOW, but the participants ranged across the ideological spectrum and included many women who had not been active in the movement before. Three major demands were agreed upon—24-hour child care centers, abortion on demand, and equal opportunity in education and employment. Thousands of women across the country marched and picketed, held rallies and teach-ins. In New York, women set up a child care center in City Hall Park; in Chicago, sit-ins at restaurants barring women were held. On the West Coast, women were given radio time to discuss women's liberation, and some mayors dedicated the day to equality for women.

Respectable housewives and "hippie" students, secretaries and women lawyers marched together carrying signs that read "Don't Cook Dinner—Starve a Rat Today!" "Eve Was Framed," "End Human Sacrifice! Don't Get Married!!" "Washing Diapers Is Not Fulfilling."[48]

Despite the strike's undeniable success, the differences within the movement were too great to make joint action on a regular basis possible. The moderate groups were afraid of being identified with the "wild, man-hating" rhetoric and tactics of the radical groups. Many radical feminists saw groups

---

[47] Bird., op. cit., p. 222.

[48] Komisar, op. cit., pp. 125–126.

like NOW as hopelessly compromised by their establishment membership and ties, as demanding "let us in" rather than "set us free."

On both sides there was considerable ambivalence. Betty Friedan warned NOW that the basic support for a women's movement comes from young women, however alien their style may be. Some radical women felt that both types of organizations were necessary and valuable. "The more we talk about test-tube babies, the more NOW can demand child-care centers and abortion repeal."[49] Others were ambivalent. They knew that organizations like NOW appealed to women who would never join the more radical groups and they believed that much of the work the moderate groups do is valuable. Yet, they feared that, under the influence of these groups, the women's movement might make the same mistake as the suffragists—that of "creating a bourgeois feminist movement that never quite dared enough, never questioned enough, never really reached beyond its own class and race."[50]

Despite the movement's only occasional success at united action and the splits within each wing, it continued to grow and had an effect on the attitudes of many women who are not members of any group.

FURTHER GROWTH AND RESPONSES

The early treatment of the movement by the media led a few radical women's groups to refuse all contact with media personnel and many to attempt to regulate such contact. The media had promulgated the bra-burning myth—it never happened. The movement was treated with condescension, usually just for laughs. A member of NOW, a group usually less hostile to the media, explained her reaction to TV coverage of the April 26 strike in which she had participated. "I was shocked how warped it was. . . . My reaction was the media was showing the women's movement as silly."[51]

Women's liberation was news. By the spring of 1970, nearly every major magazine had run a cover story on the movement and the networks had given it prominent attention. By fall

[49] Quoted in Hole and Levine, op. cit., p. 92.
[50] Morgan, op. cit., p. xxii.
[51] Honolulu *Advertiser*, July 18, 1973.

of that year, after the strike, 80 percent of a sample of adults knew of the movement.[52] The quality of the coverage began gradually to improve—perhaps because of the radical groups' policy of talking only to women reporters, perhaps because, with the growth of the movement, the media grew afraid of offending a significant portion of its audience.

Despite the often biased coverage, the movement was having an effect on women's attitudes. A 1972 poll[53] showed that 48 percent of women favored efforts to strengthen or change women's status in society, while 36 percent opposed such efforts. A poll taken the previous year had found only 40 percent in favor and 42 percent opposed. Support varied, being highest among single women (67 percent) and black women (62 percent); lowest among the widowed (40 percent), the rural (40 percent), and those 50 and older (41 percent). Asked about the effectiveness of organizations trying to change women's status, 43 percent felt that most or some are helping—up from 34 percent the previous year; 44 percent felt that only a few or none are effective, down from 51 percent. Sympathy for women's liberation groups per se was still not high among women generally—39 percent were sympathetic, 49 percent unsympathetic. But among certain groups sympathy was high—62 percent among single women, 67 percent among black women. While a majority of women (60 percent) agreed that picketing and participating in protests is "undignified and unwomanly," an even larger majority (71 percent) felt that "if women don't speak up for themselves and confront men on their real problems, nothing will be done." Thus women generally were awakening, but many were not yet sure about what could and should be done.

Women who had never before been politically active began to discuss women's issues and sometimes to form groups. OWL (Older Women's Liberation) had formed by 1970 and took part in the Second Congress to Unite Women held in that year. Kaffee klatsches in the suburbs turned into consciousness-raising sessions and sometimes into formal groups such as the Croton (New York) Women's Liberation Organization.

Although the movement is predominantly young and middle

---

[52] Hole and Levine, op. cit., p. 269.

[53] All data in the paragraph from Lew Harris and Associates, Inc., *The 1972 Virginia Slims American Women's Opinion Poll.*

class, it is beginning to penetrate into the working class. Susan Jacoby has described a group in a working-class community of the East Flatbush section of Brooklyn.[54] The women are in their forties; most graduated from high school, married soon thereafter, and quickly had children. A woman who did have contacts outside the neighborhood through her volunteer work and who was hearing more and more about the movement suggested setting up a formal consciousness-raising group. She and her three closest friends quickly recruited others from the neighborhood until they had a dozen members.

Following the advice they got from a copy of *Ms.*, the women decided on regular weekly meetings, agreeing that only a true emergency would be allowed to interfere. Despite the objections of many husbands, the women have managed to stick to their meetings.

Many of the women had joined because, with their children grown, they saw 20 or 30 empty years ahead of them with little idea how to fill them. The groups gave some the confidence to try something new. Ruth Levine, who had never held a job, became the first to begin working. Lacking training, she became a file clerk in an advertising agency; but for her this opened the door to a whole new world. When her young co-workers ask why she is working, she tells them "because it's better than sitting home and being a vegetable and that they should get themselves some more training or they'll be file clerks 20 years from now, whether they get married or not."[55] The money she brings home has also been important. "It makes me feel both that I'm independent and that I'm contributing something to the household." Initially opposed, her husband, a taxidriver, has gradually begun to cut down on his 14-hour workday. They spend more time together and their sex life has improved. "That little bit of extra money makes a big difference to us. We go to bed together more than we did for the last 10 years."

Many of the women have reported an improvement in their sex lives. As in so many consciousness-raising groups, sexual problems were a major topic of discussion during the group's early period. Many of the women who had never discussed sex with their husbands found the courage to broach the subject

---

[54] Riverside, California, *Press Enterprise,* June 17, 1973.
[55] Ibid.

and then found that simply discussing sex could lead to improvement. Masters and Johnson's finding that healthy men and women can and do enjoy sex into their sixties and seventies came as a revelation to many husbands. One woman reported that her husband said, "You know, Rose, we were brought up in ignorance even if we did manage to have four kids. This Masters-Johnson thing you're telling me about—I thought a wife would think her husband a dirty old man if he kept trying to take her to bed when they were 50 years old."

These women have followed the ideal path for a consciousness-raising group—analysis and then action. Although they cannot identify with many of the leaders of the movement ("Gloria Steinem with her streaked hair and slinky figure"), they are concerned about the same issues: child care centers, equal pay for equal work, the right to abortion and contraceptive information, the need to educate young girls to view themselves as independent human beings and not just as wives and mothers. They have attempted to introduce these ideas into the community. One of their specific projects is to provide a health information service for girls and women in their area. A year after its founding, the group took in five new members to replace those who have dropped out because they were too busy with jobs and college courses. "All of the women call that progress," Susan Jacoby reports.[56]

The movement has penetrated into the high schools and below. Groups have sprung up for consciousness raising and action. Individual girls have challenged school policies denying them the right to take shop courses or forcing them to take home economics. A New York girl forced the board of education to desegregate Stuyvesant High School, a highly regarded all-male science school. Girls also protested their exclusion from tennis teams and from participation in other sports. New York State changed its policy in 1971, allowing high school girls and boys to compete in noncontact sports. A 16-month experiment revealed that coed participation had no bad effects. Under intense pressure from feminists, even the Little League agreed to admit girls.

Activities on college campuses vary from consciousness-raising groups to abortion referral services, from the establishment of women's centers to ad hoc actions such as the "nude-

[56] Ibid.

in" at Grinnell College to protest *Playboy's* portrayal of women. When a *Playboy* representative began to speak on campus, a group of students stripped.[57] He left in embarrassment. Pressure from women students and faculty has led to the establishment of women's studies courses. By mid-1971, almost 100 colleges offered at least one credit course on women. Some colleges had set up full-fledged programs; the first was started at San Diego State College in the fall of 1970.

The change in spirit was to be seen everywhere. Women tennis players organized, protesting the much larger amounts of prize money received by men players. Kathy Kusner, an Olympic rider, won her place as the first woman jockey after taking her case to court. Women artists picketed the Whitney Museum, alleging sex discrimination in the selection of works for a show of contemporary American sculptors. Women members of the Washington press corps picketed the Gridiron Club because of its exclusion of women. Colonel Jeanne Holm, director of women in the Air Force, and Hester Turner, chairwoman of the Defense Advisory Committee on Women in the Services, spoke out publicly about the treatment of women in the armed services.

WOMEN IN POLITICS

The change in the climate of opinion and the growth of the women's movement resulted in an increasing role for women in politics. A major increase in the number of women running for and winning election to public office did not occur until the early 1970s. But in the 1960s, women politicians sympathetic to feminist demands found that they finally had an active constituency, and this allowed them to push for prowomen policies with a greater chance of success.

Congresswoman Edith Green was instrumental in getting the Equal Pay Act of 1963 passed. "To get it passed took eight years," she says, "eight years to persuade Congress that a woman doing identical work with a man ought to be paid the same salary."[58] In 1972, with backing from the women's movement, Green got Congress to pass a provision prohibiting edu-

---

[57] Hole and Levine, op. cit., p. 232.
[58] Hope Chamberlin, *A Minority of Members: Women in the U.S. Congress* (New York: Praeger, 1973), p. 257.

cational institutions receiving federal funds from discriminating on the basis of sex.

The inclusion of sex in Title VII of the 1964 Civil Rights Act was a major victory for women, for which Martha Griffiths deserves much of the credit. Less well known is her work on the Ways and Means Committee to make the social security system more equitable. She pushed through a provision allowing divorced women who had been married 20 years or more to collect on their former husbands' social security.[59] As the original sponsor of the ERA, she steered it through the House twice and helped lobby it to success in the Senate.

The 1964 election of Patsy Mink to the House of Representatives signaled the advent of the new breed of women politicians. Young, only 36 when first elected, a lawyer, she made it on her own. Ms. Mink was personally aware of discrimination against women. When, after graduation from law school, she attempted to find a job with a law firm, she was told, "Stay home and take care of your child."[60] In the House, she became an early member of the antiwar group. When Nixon nominated George Harrold Carswell to the Supreme Court, she opposed him because of his sexist views. Carswell had ruled against the female plaintiff in the landmark job discrimination case of *Phillips* v. *Martin Marietta.* Carswell's confirmation would be "an affront to the women of America," Ms. Mink said; he has "demonstrated a total lack of understanding of the concept of equality . . . and the right of women to be treated equally and fairly under the law."[61] Whenever possible, Congresswoman Mink used the powers of her office to change discriminatory practices. The abolition of a Post Office regulation barring women from becoming postal inspectors was one such victory.

Shirley Chisholm had two strikes against her—she is female and she is black. Through hard work, brains, and self-confidence, she made it to the House in 1968. An activist on a wide variety of liberal issues, she has been criticized in her constituency for involvement in the women's movement. Assemblyman Thomas Fortune has accused her of spending "so much time with women's lib and gay lib that she has forgotten

---

[59] Ibid., p. 261.
[60] Ibid., p. 309.
[61] Ibid., p. 312.

all about black lib in Bedford-Stuyvesant."[62] James Farmer ran a blatantly sexist campaign against her. He brought in the issue of "matriarchal dominance" and emphasized the need for "a strong male image" and "a man's voice in Washington."[63] Given such criticism, it is not surprising Ms. Chisholm believes that, in politics, she has faced more discrimination on account of her sex than on account of her race. In 1972, Shirley Chisholm ran for the presidency. Attempting to forge a coalition of youth, blacks, women, and the poor, she amassed 151.95 delegate votes at the Democratic convention.

Bella Abzug, a committed feminist, was elected to Congress in 1970. A lawyer and a founder of Women Strike for Peace, she, like Chisholm, is an activist by nature. As a new member of Congress, she became known nationally. She introduced and worked for a large variety of feminist legislation—comprehensive child care, the right to abortion, and prohibitions against the use of "Miss" and "Mrs." by the federal government.

Chisholm and Abzug were among the founders of the National Women's Political Caucus in July 1971. According to Chisholm, "the function of the NWPC is not to be the cutting edge of the women's liberation movement, but the big umbrella organization which provides the weight and muscle for those issues which the majority of women in this country see as concerns."[64] Women in the moderate wing of the movement felt that, although gains had been made, a specifically political organization was needed. Women should not only influence decision makers, but become decision makers themselves.

The caucus is a multipartisan organization; its basic goal is "to awaken, organize, and assert the vast political power represented by women—53 percent of the population—by: organizing state and local caucuses around the country; raising women's issues at every level of the political process; electing to office women committed to women's concerns; educating women through political action."[65] The swift growth of the caucus showed the need for such an organization. By 1973, every state, the District of Columbia, and Puerto Rico had

[62] Ibid., p. 329.
[63] Ibid., p. 328.
[64] Shirley Chisholm, speech delivered to the national convention of the National Women's Political Caucus (NWPC), 1973.
[65] NWPC pamphlet, 1973.

active caucuses. Caucus members tend to be middle class and politically experienced. Almost nine out of ten members have worked in political campaigns, and 37 percent have held party leadership posts.[66] There seems to be a good deal of overlap between caucus and NOW membership. Although the present chairperson is a Republican, the membership seems to consist predominantly of liberal Democrats.

The caucus played an active part in the 1972 Democratic Convention. The new delegate selection rules resulted in women constituting 40 percent of the delegates. The NWPC had pressured for enforcement of the new rules and held delegate training sessions all over the country. It wrote and successfully passed a women's plank in the Democratic platform. Bella Abzug, a member of the platform committee, had fought for the plank. Federal funding for comprehensive child care programs as well as support for the ERA were included. In order to help women delegates become successful participants, the caucus sponsored a meeting to inform women of key votes and of the Rules, Credentials, and Platform committees' procedures. A "nerve center" where women could get questions answered was set up. NOW was also present in force. To the extent possible amid the usual confusion of a convention, the two groups worked together.

The right to abortion was not included in the platform as passed by the platform committee. At a June meeting between caucus members and George McGovern, he had shown signs of vacillation on the issue. By convention time, the McGovern forces had decided that abortion was too dangerous an issue. Tremendous pressure to drop the issue was applied, but the women decided to fight. At a caucus meeting for women delegates, a vote on the minority plank won by 9 to 1. The women introduced the minority plank, although they feared a humiliating defeat. The fight raged late into the night. When a vote was taken, the women were defeated, but by a narrow margin.

Exhilarated by the near win, the women activists decided to run a woman for vice-president. Frances "Sissy" Farenthold, who had run for governor in Texas and won 46 percent of the vote in the runoff, was chosen as the candidate. There was little time to line up support, yet Farenthold came in second to McGovern's chosen nominee. According to Gloria

---

[66] NWPC press release, August 26, 1973.

Steinem, "in one final, glorious push, our jerry-built system of floor contacts actually worked. Most of the women had never heard of Sissy Farenthold before Miami, yet they trusted their floor leaders' information enough to vote for another woman."[67]

The Republican convention was much less exciting, and progress was more meager. Pressure from Congresswoman Margaret Heckler and from the caucus resulted in a child care plank, but it was much weaker than the one adopted by the Democrats. A bright spot was the increase in women delegates, from 17 percent in 1968 to 30 percent in 1972.

The 1972 presidential election was a disappointment to committed feminists. Nixon, although occasionally paying lip service to feminist aspirations, was a major stumbling block to legislative progress. His statements on abortion, his veto of the child care bill, and his generally conservative stance made most feminists regard him as an enemy. On other levels, the election year had less dismal results. Encouraged by support from women's groups, more women than ever before ran for office, and 28 percent more women were elected to state legislatures.[68] Results of the House elections were also encouraging. Five new women were elected: all were lawyers, four were under 40 when elected, and two were black. The four Democrats, all of whom are liberal activists, soon had an impact on the House. While none of these women ran for office as feminists, all are sympathetic. A number received support from women's groups.

Yvonne Braithwaite Burke became nationally known in the summer before the election, when she served as cochairperson of the Democratic National Convention. The first black woman elected to the House from California, she racked up another first during her freshman year. She was the first congresswoman to have a baby. Asked by reporters whether she would raise her daughter to be a congresswoman, she replied, no, her daughter would be president. Feminists saw poetic justice in Elizabeth Holtzman's victory over Emanuel Celler. For a thirty-one-year-old woman to beat the eighty-four-year-old archfoe of the ERA seemed especially sweet. Not one to rest

---

[67] Gloria Steinem, "Coming of Age with McGovern," *Ms.*, 1, 4 (October 1972), p. 105.
[68] NWPC pamphlet, 1973.

on past victories, Holtzman brought suit against the administration, seeking to halt the Cambodian bombing, and won in the lower court. Barbara Jordan of Texas is the first black congresswoman from the South. As the first woman to serve as president pro tempore of the Texas state senate, she already had party leadership experience. Like Holtzman, she was appointed to the Judiciary Committee and thus was at the center of the presidential impeachment fight.

Patricia Schroeder of Colorado was an unexpected winner. Her male opponent did not take her candidacy seriously enough to campaign hard until it was too late.[69] After a hard lobbying campaign within the House, she was assigned to the Armed Services Committee despite the chairman's objections. According to Schroeder, Chairman "Hébert is a sexist. He doesn't believe that anyone with a uterus can make decisions on military affairs."[70] One of Hébert's first comments to her was, "I hope that you aren't going to be a skinny Bella Abzug." Schroeder has given Hébert plenty of trouble. She insisted on asking unpleasant questions most members of the pro-Pentagon committee never ask. In the dissenting views she attached to the committee's report on the 1974 Military Procurement Authorization Bill, she commented: "Some members gave the impression that doing the hard and tedious work of analysis and criticism of our complicated military program is somehow unseemly, unmilitary—indeed, unpatriotic."

The NWPC's clout and credibility have continued to increase. The caucus was active at the 1974 Democratic miniconvention in Kansas City.[71] For women, the most important issue was the revision of delegate selection rules. Old-line elements in the party wanted to gut the reformed selection rules which in 1972 had for the first time given women and minority males an equal chance to become delegates. The coalition of women and minorities was not strong enough to prevent all change, but they did manage to preserve some elements of the reforms. Women had developed enough clout that they had to be included in the private negotiating sessions.

The results of the 1974 elections were generally encouraging.

---

[69] Chamberlin, op. cit., p. 354.

[70] Judith Viorst, "The Woman Who Has a Bear by the Tail," *Redbook*, November 1973.

[71] NWPC Newsletter, 4 (January–February 1975), p. 2.

All incumbent women members of Congress were reelected, most by a very wide margin. Although 4 congresswomen retired, 6 new women were elected, bringing the total number of women in the U.S. House of Representatives to a record high of 18. The 6 new women were notably representative of states across the nation; they included two from New Jersey, one from Kansas, one from Tennessee, one from Maryland, and one from Nebraska.

At the state level, the most important victory was won by Ella Grasso in her bid for the governorship of Connecticut—the first governorship won by a woman in her own right. Mary Krupsak was elected lieutenant governor of New York; March Fong, secretary of state of California; and Susie Sharp, chief justice of the North Carolina Supreme Court. Janet Hayes was elected mayor of San Jose, California, a city of more than half a million people. All of these are new political records for women. Extremely important for the future is the fact that 27 percent more women were elected to state legislatures. Five of the seven new state senators in Arizona were women, and in Massachusetts, an avowed lesbian was elected to the lower house.

Many of the women who ran were supported by the caucus and by other women's organizations. The caucus has provided technical assistance of various sorts to women candidates. The caucus and the Women's Campaign Committee, an independent group dedicated to supporting progressive women candidates, have also provided financial help.

Preparations for the 1976 campaigns began early. The NWPC's Campaign Support Committee geared up to provide assistance to women candidates. Presidential candidates were polled to ascertain their positions on 16 women's issues ranging from health care to the ERA. Candidates' campaign staffs were scrutinized to determine whether women held decision-making positions. The delegate-selection process was monitored, with many women running for delegate slots. The Democratic Task Force, which consists of caucus members who are active Democrats, worked to ensure that women's interests were included in the Democratic platform.

When the Democratic convention opened, women were organized and ready to take part as a major force. The Democratic Women's Agenda, a coalition of the NWPC's Democratic Women's Task Force and of the Women's Caucus of the Democratic National Committee, held daily morning caucuses for hundreds of delegates.[72] The NWPC established a network of contacts in each state delegation for lobbying, polling, and meeting notification. Abortion and delegate selection procedures were the two major issues. Women successfully pressured the Carter forces to include in the platform a statement saying that a constitutional amendment prohibiting abortion would be "undesirable." Although feminists would have liked a stronger plank, the compromise was an advance over 1972, when no mention of abortion was included.

Under the strong, affirmative-action-oriented delegate-selection procedures in force during 1972, women were elected to 40 percent of the delegate slots at the Democratic convention. The rules were subsequently weakened, and as a result, only 34 percent of the 1976 delegates were women. Because of this decrease, feminists were especially concerned that rules for future conventions include strong affirmative action provisions. Women proposed a 50-50 rule whereby all state delegations would have to have equal numbers of men and women. When the proposal lost in committee, the women threatened a floor fight. Eager to avoid such a fight, which would be broadcast on prime-time TV, Carter was willing to negotiate. A negotiating group from the caucus struck a bargain with Carter which dropped the 50-50 requirement. Instead, the rules would read: "Future conventions shall promote equal division between delegate men and delegate women. . . . The national party shall encourage and assist state parties to adopt provisions to achieve this goal. . . ."[73] In return for this concession, Carter promised to strengthen and make more independent the party's Women's Division and to appoint women to high positions in his administration.

When the negotiation group brought this compromise back to the rest of the women, a spirited debate over whether to accept it took place. Bella Abzug and various caucus leaders

---

[72] The following discussion of the Democratic and Republican conventions is based upon Lucy Komisar, "Women Come Into Their Own," *The Nation,* September 18, 1976; Jo Freeman, "Something Did Happen at the Democratic National Convention," *Ms.,* October 1976; Jo Freeman, "Republican Politics—Let's Make a Deal," *Ms.,* November 1976; National Women's Political Caucus, *Women's Political Times,* July 1976, August 1976.

[73] Quoted in Freeman, "Republican Politics," op. cit., pp. 114–115.

spoke in favor. They knew, from a poll that had been taken, that the 50-50 rule would lose on the floor. Karen De Crow, president of NOW, spoke in favor of a floor fight anyway. The compromise was accepted. Women did not get everything they wanted at the convention but they showed they were a force to be reckoned with. Some symbolic "firsts" also occurred; Barbara Jordan was the first woman to give the keynote address; Lindy Boggs chaired the convention.

Even though female representation at the 1976 Republican convention was up slightly over 1972—31.5 percent in contrast to 29.8 percent—women were much less successful. The NWPC's Republican Women's Task Force was active, but its only victory was preventing conservatives from removing support for the ERA from the platform. A plank supporting a constitutional amendment to prohibit abortion was included in the platform.

Despite the dismal Republican convention, there were other signs that women were being taken seriously as a political force. President Ford had appointed a woman—Carla Hills—to the cabinet. Women played a more prominent role in the campaign than ever before. Two of Carter's deputy campaign managers were feminists. Four of his 10 regional coordinators and 10 of the 48 state coordinators during the primary campaign were women.[74] On October 2, 1976, Carter spoke to the National Women's Agenda Conference and thus became the first presidential candidate ever to give a major speech on women's issues.

From a feminist viewpoint, the results of the election were mixed. Carter's victory was generally applauded, as a Democratic administration was thought likely to be more sympathetic to women's concerns than previous Republican ones. All incumbent congresswomen who ran were reelected, even though some faced strong challengers. An issue in Martha Key's reelection campaign in a Kansas district was her marriage to a congressman from Indiana. Would her loyalties now be divided between Kansas and Indiana, some asked. Needless to say, her husband's constitutents did not raise such questions about his loyalties. Two new congresswomen were elected. One, Barbara Mikulski of Maryland, had been a long-time NWPC activist. Despite these victories, the total number of

[74] Komisar, op. cit., p. 232.

women in the House of Representatives actually declined from 19 to 18 because several women retired. The United States Senate remained all male. Congresswomen Patsy Mink and Bella Abzug gave up safe seats to run for the Senate, but both were defeated in primaries. The only woman to win a senatorial primary lost in the general election. Dixie Lee Ray became governor of Washington. A woman for the first time won statewide elective office in Oregon. Women again increased their numbers in state legislatures, but still make up only 9.1 percent of the total membership.[75]

Caucus efforts did not end when the campaign was over; a new phase centering on making sure Carter kept his promises to women began. Under caucus leadership, an Ad Hoc Coalition of Women's Groups, including representatives of over 40 national women's and public interest organizations, was formed to pressure the administration to appoint women to high-level positions.[76] The coalition compiled a list of qualified women which it made available to the administration. After considerable pressure, Carter met with leaders of the coalition, and meetings with other officials also took place. The pressure had some results. Two women were appointed to cabinet posts—Juanita Kreps as secretary of commerce and Patricia Roberts Harris as secretary of housing and urban development. Midge Constanza, a NWPC member, became a presidential assistant, and Eleanor Holmes Norton was nominated to chair the EEOC. Although Carter far surpassed previous administrations in appointing women to top positions, the number—40—is still dismally low.[77] On the plus side, many of the women appointed to such positions are strong feminists.

Speaking about the caucus in 1973, Sissy Farenthold, its chairwoman, commented, "Two years ago we were considered a 'burlesque show.' Today we are invited to make recommendations for White House Councils, asked for advice on issues from Congressional offices, and called upon to testify on legislation that we support."[78] The NWPC's clout is even stronger today.

Another form of political activity in which most of the nationally organized groups engage is legislative lobbying. NOW, the

---

[75] *Los Angeles Times,* November 14, 1976.
[76] National Women's Political Caucus, *Women's Political Times,* winter 1977.
[77] *Los Angeles Times,* June 19, 1977.
[78] *NWPC Newsletter,* July 1973.

caucus, and Women's Equity Action League have all been heavily involved in lobbying on women's issues. A group exclusively devoted to this activity is Women's Lobby, Inc., which women active in lobbying for the ERA formed in late 1972. The lobby has developed amendments to two bills that have passed. One prohibits sex discrimination in all medical, dental, osteopathic, and veterinary schools aided by the 1972 Health Manpower Assistance Act; the other gives wives, widows, and dependents of veterans the right to apply for apprenticeship training under the auspices of the Veterans Administration. The lobby's top priority is child care. It also worked to extend the minimum wage to domestic workers and to block the antiabortion constitutional amendments.

According to Carol Burris, lobby president, the Women's Lobby motto is, "If you don't do something to Congress, Congress will do something to you."[79] This motto, extended to the whole political system, expresses the convictions of the feminists who have been active in politics. A political system in which women do not participate as decision makers will be antiwomen. Only by getting into the seats of power can women bring about the changes needed for a truly nonsexist society. The women who have been elected to Congress and the state legislatures have affected legislation. Even though small in number, the women have frequently worked together closely, thus combining their strength. In early 1977, the congresswomen institutionalized their informal cooperative arrangement by forming a Congressional Women's Caucus.

LESBIANS

The new femininist movement attracted many lesbians. Oppressed both for their sex and for their sexual preference, such women saw the need for organization and action. They, after all, could not rely on men to support them and thus felt the brunt of job discrimination. Many had rejected the feminine role and could see its oppressiveness and its absurdity.

At first, lesbians in the movement hid their sexual orientation. They were afraid of being rejected by their straight sisters, who constituted the vast majority, and they were afraid of hurting the movement. In the early years, the taunt of lesbian

[79] Riverside, California, *Daily Enterprise*, June 28, 1973.

had often been used against women's liberationists. At that time, everyone seems to have believed that if the women's movement became tainted with lesbianism, it would be destroyed. With increasing gay consciousness and the growth of the gay liberation movement, lesbians active in women's groups became less willing to stay in the closet. "Why, in a movement dedicated to the liberation of all women, must we hide our sexual orientation?" they asked. Equal rights for lesbians should be a demand of the women's movement. With this change in attitudes and this new militancy, the issue could no longer be swept under the rug. How the lesbians' demands were to be received was to be a test of the movement. Was it to remain dedicated to the liberation of all women, or would it abandon sisters whenever politically expedient?

In some groups and areas, a gradual change in attitude took place, and lesbian demands were incorporated without bitter battles. In others, the issue proved extremely divisive. New York NOW was almost destroyed by internal struggles over lesbian demands. Betty Friedan had always opposed any recognition of the lesbian issue, calling it the "lavender herring." NOW had, however, never barred lesbians from membership and had allowed at least one lesbian couple to use the reduced "couple rate."

In 1969, Rita Mae Brown joined New York NOW and became very active. She refused to hide her lesbianism and spoke out on homosexual oppression. Considerable pressure was applied, and in January 1970 she resigned, saying "Lesbianism is the one word which gives the New York N.O.W. Executive Committee a collective heart attack."[80] At the national level, the issue was also heating up. The national director who had supported the lesbians' demands was forced out of office. A gay feminist group was formed in response to these events. Rita Mae Brown called a meeting to discuss sexism within the movement. From this group, which was later to call itself the Radicalesbians, came the position paper, "The Woman-Identified Woman."

In 1970, the lesbians decided to force the movement to confront the issue at the second Congress to Unite Women. On

---

[80] Quoted in Sidney Abbott and Barbara Love, *Sappho Was a Right-On Woman* (New York: Stein and Day, 1973), p. 112. The following account is based on the excellent discussion in Abbott and Love.

Friday night, when congress participants were all assembled in a large hall, the lights suddenly went out. When they were turned on again, 20 lesbians wearing "Lavender Menace" T-shirts were at the front of the hall. They spoke of their oppression both within and outside the movement and invited sympathetic members of the audience to join them. One of the women who spoke was a member of the scheduled panel. It was the first time Kate Millett talked about her bisexuality. Reactions among straight women were varied. Some felt that an important issue had finally been brought out into the open; others were dismayed and felt that the congress had been destroyed.

A few feminists did begin speaking to lesbian groups. Ti-Grace Atkinson made a rather ambivalent speech to the Daughters of Bilitis (DOB), an older lesbian organization. Caroline Bird, after at first refusing, spoke very positively. Many NOW members still hoped they would be able to contain the issue. A candidate for NOW president spoke to DOB members, telling them they were welcome so long as they were not openly homosexual. When the mass media got into the act, however, containment proved impossible.

At a Columbia University Forum on Sexual Liberation, a lesbian challenged Kate Millett to openly declare her bisexuality. Ms. Millett did so. A *Time* reporter with a tape recorder was in the audience. On December 8, 1970, *Time* printed a vicious attack on Ms. Millett and on the movement. Under the title, "Women's Lib: A Second Look," the article said that Millett's admission of bisexuality had ". . . contributed to the growing skepticism about the movement. . . . The disclosure is bound to discredit her as a spokeswoman for her cause, cast further doubt on her theories, and reinforce the views of those skeptics who routinely dismiss all liberationists as Lesbians."[81]

Such an attack could not go unanswered. A lesbian woman persuaded the Women's Strike Coalition to make support for Millett part of a march already planned in New York. On December 12, 1970, both gay and straight women marched wearing lavender arm bands handed out by the president of New York NOW. The leaflet handed out to members and to the press explained the crux of the issue as well as it has ever been explained:

---

[81] "Women's Lib: A Second Look," *Time*, December 8, 1970, p. 121.

> It is not one woman's sexual preference that is under attack—it is the freedom of *all women* to openly state values that fundamentally challenge the basic structure of patriarchy. If they succeed in scaring us with words like "dyke" or "Lesbian" or "bisexual," they'll have won AGAIN. They'll have divided us, AGAIN. . . . *Time* Magazine wants us to run scared, disown Kate and all our gay sisters. . . . That's why we're all wearing lavender Lesbian armbands today—to show we all stand together as women. . . . They can call us all Lesbians until such time as there is no stigma attached to women loving women.[82]

Gay and straight women found they could work together openly. Yet the media completely ignored the event. Something further had to be done. On December 17, 1971, a press conference was held. Its purpose was to show movement support for Millett. Movement luminaries like Ti-Grace Atkinson, Gloria Steinem, and Florynce Kennedy participated. Bella Abzug and NOW National President Aileen Hernandez sent supporting statements. This cast was too much for the media to ignore. Press coverage was extensive and fair, and media lesbian-baiting decreased.

Within NOW the controversy still raged. At the national level, the executive committee attempted to come to a decision. An angry closed session disclosed that the committee was split almost evenly, and no decision was reached. The New York NOW elections of 1971 turned into a dirty political brawl with accusations of lesbianism used as weapons. A woman who had shown sympathy toward lesbians was, in effect, purged.[83]

In other parts of the country, change came much more smoothly. In April 1971, the West Coast regional membership passed a resolution demanding acceptance of lesbians and lesbianism. They voted to present their resolution to the full NOW membership in the fall. Other chapters also had come to terms with the problem and were prepared to bring it up at the convention.

The fifth annual conference of NOW, held in Los Angeles in September, passed a strongly worded prolesbian resolution. There was no bitter floor fight, and the vote was nearly unanimous. The resolution recognized and admitted NOW's culpability:

---

[82] Quoted in Abbott and Love, op. cit., p. 122.

[83] Ibid., p. 127.

> Afraid of alienating public support, we have often treated lesbians as the step-sisters of the movement, allowed to work with us, but then expected to hide in the upstairs closet when company comes. Lesbians are now telling us that this attitude is no longer acceptable. Asking women to disguise their identities so they will not "embarrass" the group is an intolerable form of oppression, like asking black women to join us in white face.

It then resolved:

> That NOW recognizes the double oppression of women who are lesbians,
>
> That a woman's right to her own person includes the right to define and express her own sexuality and to choose her own lifestyle,
>
> That NOW acknowledges the oppression of lesbians as a legitimate concern of feminism.[84]

THIRD WORLD WOMEN

Although a few Third World women have participated in the women's liberation movement from the beginning, the movement has been predominantly white and middle class. How to get more Third World women involved has been a constant topic of conversation in women's groups. Socialist feminists concerned about building a class movement have been especially worried about their white, middle-class membership.

Many black and Chicana women have been repelled by the racial and class composition of the women's movement. Especially during the early years, they felt that they had little in common with movement women and that the movement did not attack problems of central concern to them. In class and color, movement women looked too much like "Miss Ann," the employer and oppressor of the black woman domestic. Even when militant Third World women became aware that they were playing the traditional subservient feminine role in black or Chicano liberation groups, racial or ethnic loyalty often kept them from public revolt.

The first feminist protest by radical minority women occurred in the Student Non-Violent Coordinating Committee. In 1964, Ruby Doris Robinson, a black woman, presented a

---

[84] Fifth Annual Conference of the National Organization for Women, Los Angeles, September 3–6, 1971, *Revolution: From the Doll's House to the White House* (a report from NOW to its membership), pp. 15–16.

paper protesting women's role in the organization. The men's violent reaction, however, made it clear that women would have to choose between feminism, which was labeled bourgeois, and black liberation. At that time the men were not willing to incorporate feminist demands into their basic program. Many Third World women still feel that they must choose—they can either become feminists or support their brothers. They must decide whether their basic identity is racial or sexual. Most have chosen to work within the black or Chicano movements.

But ideological tendencies within parts of the black movement eventually led many black women to decide that a black feminist movement was necessary. Black women found that too many black men were blaming them for their situation. Black matriarchy and the castration of the black male by the black female became accepted tenets of "revolutionary" rhetoric. Black men were telling their women to take a subordinate position so as to build up the damaged black male ego. In effect, women were being told that the black liberation movement could succeed only at their expense.

Some black men had swallowed basic tenets of white establishment ideology, which they believed they had rejected *in toto.* The black woman who is economically and socially oppressed for both her sex and her race, who makes less money and is more frequently unemployed than the black man, yet who frequently must rear her children alone, was seen as a problem, not a sister. She was called an ugly black bitch for not looking and acting white, a castrating bitch for having the strength that made her and her children's survival possible. According to Cellestine Ware, a black woman and a founder of New York Radical Feminists, "it is the fear and anxiety of the black male that led to the construction of the 'evil' black female. By now, the superstructure of the 'black bitch' bears as little relation to the real black woman as any myth to the reality."[85]

The black movement's position on birth control and abortion disturbed many women. Male radicals charged that white America planned genocide. Forced sterilization and the availability of birth control and abortions were all part of the plan.

---

[85] Cellestine Ware, "Black Feminism," *Notes From the Third Year,* 1973, p. 25.

Black women should refuse to use the pill; they should breed and rear warriors for the revolution. Many black women agreed with the analysis, but not with the recommendation. The "no pill/have-kids/mess-up-the-man's-plan notion" is oversimplified, they charged.[86] "Seems to me the Brother does us all a great disservice by telling her to fight the man with the womb. Better to fight with the gun and the mind."[87]

Many black women felt that neither the white women's movement nor the male-dominated black movement addressed some of their basic concerns. A black woman's organization was the obvious solution, but because women feared that such a group would be considered divisive, it was not until 1973 that a national group was formed. In August 1973, 30 black women, all of whom had been active in the women's movement, formed the National Black Feminist Organization. Margaret Sloan, NBFO chairwoman, explained, "We decided we needed a group of black women to come out and say 'We're here, we understand feminism—it's okay.' "[88]

The group's membership grew to over 1000 by the end of 1973. Four hundred women attended its first convention in December of that year. The organization admits only black women, but intends to work with both the women's and the black movements. Keynote speaker Shirley Chisholm brought up one issue—that of stereotypes. "One of the cruelest labels has been that the black woman is a matriarch. First society forces her into that condition, then it criticizes her for it. Black women had to have strength and power to survive, but their strength is no sign of liberation, nor do they have power in terms of society."[89]

Black feminists' priorities differ somewhat from those of the white movement. A minimum wage for domestics and safeguarding the rights and improving the position of welfare mothers are high on the list. According to Eleanor Homes Norton, New York City Commissioner on Human Rights, "what the women's movement as a whole badly needs is a black nuance and nuances from Spanish-speaking women. The move-

---

[86] Toni Cade, "The Pill: Genocide or Liberation?" in Cade, ed., *The Black Woman* (New York: Signet, 1970), p. 168.
[87] Ibid., p. 167.
[88] *Newsweek,* December 17, 1973.
[89] Shirley Chisolm, quoted in ibid.

ment will only be truly sensitive to them when they join up." Black and white feminists do agree on most basic issues. Child care is, for example, considered a priority by both. The chances for fruitful joint work look good. A militant black feminist organization may also act as a prod on the moderate women's groups to live up to their stated principles of equality for *all* women.

Chicana women have been active within the La Raza Unida party. In 1972, the Chicana Caucus at the National Chicano Political Conference held in San Jose, California, adopted a lengthy statement on the concerns of the Chicana. The statement covered everything from the position of Chicanas in the party to jobs, child care, education, and abortion. At the first national convention of La Raza Unida in September 1972, the party pledged "support to Latina women in their struggle for equal rights in all spheres of life."[90]

The Chicana may, then, be able to work for her own liberation as a woman within the Chicano movement. Not all Chicanas believe this will be possible. Guadalupe Valdés Fallis writes:

> With the 'back to the roots' movement and 'let us find out who we are' emphasis, the idealization of all things Mexican has taken hold. And with that, an idealization of a system with all its antiquated and oppressive treatment of women.[91]

In California, with its large Mexican-American population, Chicana feminist groups have formed. Conferences to discuss the special problems of the Chicana are frequently held. Like black women, Chicana feminists are committed to fighting both sexism and racism.

UNION WOMEN

The class composition of the women's movement is slowly beginning to change. Working-class women's lack of interest in the movement seems to have been due to several distinct factors—their greater acceptance of sexist ideology, lack of time, and the perception that the movement did not address their

---

[90] Reprinted in *Ms.*, 1 (December 1972), p. 128.

[91] Guadalupe Valdés Fallis, "The Liberated Chicana—A Struggle Against Tradition," *Women: A Journal of Liberation*, 3, 4 (1974), p. 20.

special problems. In working-class families, sex role socialization tends to be even more intense than in middle-class ones. The effect on attitudes can be seen in a 1973 survey.[92] Noncollege women were less likely than college women to believe that women are discriminated against (42 and 63 percent, respectively, said yes); noncollege women were less likely to agree that the statement "women's place is in the home" is nonsense (47 percent to 64 percent). Because most working-class women are employed and are also solely responsible for the housework, time is always a problem. Furthermore, the women's movement has been perceived as alien and radical. "Women's libbers" have been seen as "women who want to be men" or as persons advocating sexual promiscuity.

Nevertheless, the women's movement does seem to have had an effect on working-class women. Union women especially are becoming aware of job discrimination and are determined to do something about it. In March 1974, over 3000 women members of 58 labor unions met in Chicago and formed the Coalition of Labor Union Women.[93] Olga Madar, vice president of the United Automobile Workers and an active feminist, was elected president. The organization's objectives include fighting sexism within unions as well as in society at large. Unions will be encouraged to place a greater emphasis on organizing unorganized women, to give women a greater policy-making role within the union, and to be more aggressive in fighting job discrimination. The women also agreed to work for child care legislation, an increased minimum wage law, ratification of the ERA, and the extension of protective laws to men.

The majority of working women are not union members. Getting these women, who are usually the lowest paid and the most discriminated against, involved in the movement will require the movement to develop a greater sensitivity to their needs. Working-class women are concerned with survival issues; changing the content of sexist commercials and electing women to Congress are of little concern to them. The media's portrayal of the movement will have to be countered by an educational campaign. Television, particularly, has concentrated on the most colorful activities of the movement. The

[92] Study by Daniel Yankelovich, reported in Riverside, California, *Daily Enterprise,* June 3, 1974.

[93] Riverside, California, *Daily Enterprise,* April 3, 1974.

very considerable effort to end job discrimination against working-class women has been ignored.

WOMEN AND THE CHURCH

The world's major religions have played a role in preserving women's subordinate status. Founded at a time when women's social position was that of an inferior, they have maintained forms reflecting an earlier social reality. Women were excluded from the priesthood by the Catholic and Episcopalian churches and by some Protestant sects. Among Orthodox Jews, women are physically segregated in the synagogue and are not counted in the *minyan*, the quorum of ten needed for a service.

The development of feminist consciousness led women to question church practices and to attempt to change them. "Church authorities, usually entirely male, have misused the Bible to reinforce their prejudices against women," charges Virginia Mills, a member of the United Presbyterian Task Force on Women.[94] Nuns have formed a liberation group and are demanding freedom from domination by priests. The publication of a new Roman Catholic Missal supposedly extending women's rights within the Church received a sharp reaction from NOW's Ecumenical Task Force on Women and Religion. The missal stated that women could read the Bible and act as lectors during mass, but only when there were no men available—and women could not stand within the altar rail, as men did. The Task Force burned the missal and sent its ashes, tied with a pink ribbon, to the president of the American bishops.

On August 27, 1973, a group of Hawaiian women calling themselves the Ad Hoc Committee for Equal Rites for Women protested in front of Our Lady of Peace Cathedral in Honolulu. On the day proclaimed Women's Rights Day by the governor, the biblical passage used for the prescribed second reading was Ephesians 5:21–32, which reads in part: "Wives be subject to your husbands, as to the Lord. For the husband is the head of the wife as Christ is head of the Church. . . . As the Church is subject to Christ, so let wives also be subject in everything to their husbands. . . ." Reactions to the protest were mixed. "It's a good example of liberation in action," one female parish-

[94] Komisar, op. cit., p. 139.

ioner said. "I wouldn't want one of my grandchildren out there," another responded. The Church hierarchy attempted to defend itself, claiming that the women were misinterpreting the passage. Bishop Scanlan's defense that the Catholic Church has exalted women "more than any organization that ever existed," showed, however, that there was no real understanding of the women's point. Ms. Leopold, the organizer of the protest, had the last world. According to newspaper reports, a priest attempting to end a discussion with her said, "God bless you." "Thank you," Ms. Leopold replied, "She will."[95]

Women have demanded the right to become priests, rabbis, and ministers. In most Protestant denominations, there are no formal barriers, but finding a church willing to accept a woman minister is still difficult. As late as 1975, only 2 percent of all ministers were women.[96] The first woman reform rabbi was ordained in 1972, and several others have been ordained since. Jewish feminists have also gotten some changes in ritual.[97] More congregations now allow women to receive *aliyahs* (the honor of blessing the Torah) and count women in the *minyan*. The *bar mitzvah*, the celebration of a boy's coming of age, is increasingly being extended to girls.

The most intense and well-publicized conflict over women's right to serve as priests took place in the Episcopal Church. Under pressure from feminists, the church's general convention voted to allow women to be ordained as deacons in 1970. In 1973, a proposal to ordain women priests was voted down. Feminists and sympathetic priests decided some dramatic move was needed. In July 1974, four bishops ordained eleven women as priests. Because the ordination was unauthorized, the House of Bishops voted to censure the bishops who had taken part. The publicity attendant upon these proceedings resulted in a great deal of support both for the unofficially ordained women and for the prowomen bishops. In 1976, the church reversed its 1973 position and voted for the ordination of women. Since then, over 40 women have become Episcopal priests.[98]

Roman Catholic feminists have had considerably less success

---

[95] Honolulu *Advertiser*, August 26 and September 1, 1973.
[96] *Newsweek*, October 13, 1975.
[97] *Newsweek*, May 31, 1976.
[98] Riverside, California, *Daily Enterprise*, September 16 and 17, 1976.

in changing their church's centuries-old practices. Feminist agitation for women priests seems to have precipitated Pope Paul's declaration reaffirming the traditionalist view. The declaration said:

> The same natural resemblance is required for persons as for things; when Christ's role in the Eucharist is to be expressed sacramentally, there would not be this natural resemblance which must exist between Christ and his minister if the role of Christ were not taken by a man; in such a case it would be difficult to see in the minister the image of Christ. For Christ himself was and remains a man.[99]

The Vatican statement was intended to cut off the debate, but it has not done so. The arguments used were not persuasive to groups such as the National Coalition of American Nuns and the National Assembly of Women Religious, which will continue to push for the ordination of women.

WOMEN'S STUDIES

The rising feminist consciousness quite naturally created a demand for women's studies programs in universities. Movement women realized that they knew very little about woman—about female sexuality and psychology, about women's history and literature. The college curriculum, designed by men and largely taught by men, sets up male culture as the standard and frequently completely ignores the female.

Using the black experience as an example, feminists pushed for women's studies courses and programs. Perhaps because administrators did not want to repeat the often bitter battles that had preceded the acceptance of black studies, feminist success came relatively quickly. By the beginning of 1974, women's studies programs were functioning at 78 institutions, and about 2000 courses were being offered at another 500 campuses.[100] State colleges, less tradition-bound than more prestigious universities, have been most receptive. San Diego State College set up the first women's studies program in 1970. Now almost every college and university offers women's studies courses, and some of the material is being taught at the precollege level.

---

[99] Quoted in *Los Angeles Times*, January 28, 1977.
[100] *Newsweek*, December 10, 1973.

Most feminists agree that the purpose of women's studies is not just to teach about women but to prepare women to change society. This activist thrust dictates a close relationship between women's studies programs and the movement. Ideally, the program should serve all university women—secretaries, cafeteria workers, and faculty wives, as well as students and community women. The program should serve as a mobilizing device. Given the breadth of the constituency to which the programs try to address themselves and the movement's emphasis on nonhierarchy, the question of administrative structure has frequently caused problems. University administrators are less than friendly to a nonstructured program in which no one is in charge. Most programs have set up a coordinating board or committee with representation from faculty, students, and sometimes staff. Involvement of community women has been spotty.

Feminists criticized traditional education not just because of its course content, but also for its structure. The usual relationship between student and instructor is characterized by sharp differentiation of roles and by power. In such a situation all students are, in effect, passive objects to be acted upon by the instructor. Emphasis on objectivity, on learning the material that is given you, guarantees that the student will keep academic knowledge and her own life experiences separated. To break out of this sterile, power-dominated form of education, feminists have deemphasized lectures and have used small-group discussions as much as possible. Team teaching, in which both students and faculty are involved as instructors, is used, especially in beginning classes. Students are encouraged to work together on projects to break down the feelings of competitiveness the educational system fosters. Students in advanced classes often do original research in the library and in the field, and thus are adding to knowledge of the female experience. There are still many experiments to be tried. But in providing participatory, noncoercive education, women's studies have been more successful than traditional programs.

The relationship of women's studies to the university has raised problems to which no ideal solution has yet been found. In some colleges, the women's studies "program" consists of courses on women given within the traditional departments. Under this arrangement, feminists have no control over staffing or course content. Women's studies programs set up as separate units do have greater autonomy. Control over hiring is usually far from complete, but the program board at least has considerable say and finds it easier to hire women who are not "qualified" according to traditional criteria. Community women without the necessary degrees but with valuable experience are sometimes used as part-time instructors. The independent program makes experimentation much more feasible. Unfortunately, autonomy may result in isolation and vulnerability. The existence of an independent women's studies program may take pressure off the traditional departments to hire feminists. Such a program can be easily dismissed as academically unsound, composed of a bunch of kooky females, and, when financial adversity hits the college, easily cut. The innovative and highly successful program at SUNY/Buffalo found itself in this position in 1972. Because it had established close working relationships with other units on campus, however, it came out of the struggle in good shape.[101] At present, women's studies programs need allies if they are to survive and grow.

Some women have decided that the compromises necessary to stay on campus are not worth the result and have started independent feminist liberation schools. Breakaway in Berkeley, for example, has declined to affiliate even with a free or people's school: "The only way we can learn without intimidation, inhibition, and frustration is from and with each other. Women must have their own school where they can meet together in a warm, supportive atmosphere to share experiences and knowledge."[102] Breakaway has offered courses on everything from "Women Over Thirty" and "Women Who Are Coming Out" to karate, carpentry, and auto mechanics. The student body is fairly heterogeneous—street women, students, and housewives.

FEMINISTS IN PRINT

In March 1968, Jo Freeman and other Chicago feminists began putting out *Voices of the Women's Liberation Movement.* The little newsletter—only six mimeographed pages—was the first

---

[101] Christine Grahl et al., "Women's Studies: A Case in Point," *Feminist Studies,* 1, 2 (fall 1972).

[102] Quoted in Kirsten Grimstad and Susan Rennie, eds., *The New Woman's Survival Catalog* (New York: Coward-McCann, 1973), p. 123.

modern feminist publication.[103] As the movement grew and as more and more small groups formed across the country, so did the need for a means of communication. Many of the women active in the movement had had experience with New Left underground publications. Newsletters and journals began publication across the country. By 1971, over 100 were being published. By 1977, both the number and their circulation had increased many times over.

Publications range from local newsletters in mimeo form to slick magazines with a national distribution. Some are special interest journals such as *Women and Film;* most range widely, including coverage of the movement locally and nationally, legal developments, personal testimonials, theoretical articles, and frequently feminist fiction and poetry. Some of these publications are one-woman enterprises; a few are run along traditional lines. Most are put out by a group of women who share all the tasks, grubby as well as creative, as equally as possible.

The financial success story among feminist publications is that of *Ms.* A group of women with publishing experience decided a feminist magazine that would reach nonmovement women was needed. Substantial financial backing was required if the magazine was to have a national circulation and look respectable. Such backing was not easy to find; people who controlled sufficient funds were convinced there was no market for such a publication. Finally *New York Magazine* was persuaded to put out a sample issue. The 300,000 copies of the sample were sold out in eight days. The women editors were left without enough copies to honor their promises for free ones.[104] Regular publication was begun in July 1972. By October 1973, *Ms.* had a monthly circulation of 350,000 and a 70 percent renewal rate.[105] With the magazine doing so well, the women have branched out into television, books, and records. Marlo Thomas's record for children, "Free To Be . . . You and Me" was produced by *Ms.* and was an instant hit, selling 95,000 copies.[106]

Within the more radical segment of the movement, senti-

---

[103] Hole and Levine, op. cit., p. 270.
[104] See "A Personal Report," *Ms.*, 1 (July 1972).
[105] *Newsweek*, October 15, 1973.
[106] Ibid.

ments toward *Ms.* are mixed. The sexist advertising run in the sample issue appalled most feminists. The women who put out the sample, however, had no control over advertising in that issue. Since beginning an independent publication, they have refused the worst sort of advertising. Virginia Slims ("You've Come a Long Way Baby") has repeatedly attempted and failed to get its ads accepted, even though Billie Jean King has spoken for them. Nevertheless, sexism is so ingrained in our society that a totally pure policy is not possible. Ads offensive to feminists still appear. To their credit, the editors print letters criticizing their choices and attempt to take such criticism into account. There has been criticism, both within *Ms.*'s staff and from the feminist community, on content as well. Not enough space is devoted to the problems of blue-collar women, Third World women, and lesbians, it has been charged. The magazine is not radical enough; it reflects a middle-class bias.

Despite such criticism, most feminists would agree that, on balance, *Ms.* has had a good influence. *Ms.* is reaching women who wouldn't be caught dead reading *Ain't I A Woman?* or *No More Fun and Games.* According to Onka Dekker, writing in *Off Our Backs,*

> *Ms.* is making feminist converts of middle class heathens from academia to condominium-ville. A slick, reputable-looking magazine breaks down defenses and lets the word worm its way into the brain. *Ms.* is almost in violation of Truth in Packaging laws. There is a female mind-set on those glossy pages slipping into American homes concealed in bags of groceries like tarantulas on banana boats. . . . Curious girl children will accidentally discover feminism in *Ms.* the way we stumbled onto sex in our mother's *Ladies' Home Journal.*[107]

From newsletters and magazines, feminists expanded into books, not just writing them but publishing them as well. A number of feminist presses are in operation, turning out beautifully printed and inexpensive feminist works. Diana Press, Inc., of Baltimore is owned and operated by three women. It grew out of an ideologically heterogeneous women's collective. One of the owners explains: "The name, Diana Press, for example, was agreed upon as a compromise between those who wanted to commemorate weatherwoman Diana Oughton and others

---

[107] Quoted in Grimstad and Rennie, op. cit., p. 35.

who saw Diana as a symbol of ancient woman's culture."[108] Diana Press operates both as a publisher and as a commercial printshop, in which capacity it has done much work for women's groups.

The Feminist Press of Old Westbury, New York, pioneered in the publication of nonsexist children's books. In addition to its substantial list of adult and children's books, it publishes a women's studies newsletter. Since until recently no nationally organized women's studies association existed, the newsletter provided a much-needed communication channel among feminists around the country involved with women's studies.

Among women's presses KNOW, Inc., is unique and has become an institution of the movement. Members of Pittsburgh NOW founded the press in the fall of 1969 to reprint movement articles for use at local NOW meetings. When word got around, KNOW discovered there was a great need for such reprints and decided that the press could be supported by selling them at slightly over cost.[109] The demand proved so great that KNOW found that it could actually pay a staff member. By late 1973, the press was run by six full-time and four part-time staffers, who work as a collective. KNOW's vice president is an ex-typical housewife whose male-chauvinist husband never wanted her to work. "He still looks at me in amazement some days," she says. "I just say to him—'You're not Vice-President of your company.' "[110] KNOW's list includes some 200 articles and pamphlets, some full-length books, and a Female Studies series that consists of course syllabi and essays on women's studies.

This outpouring of feminist literature made women's bookstores possible, and they have sprung up across the country. The typical feminist bookstore is a place to meet other women, discuss literature, and find out what's going on around town. Browsing is encouraged; comfortable chairs and cheap coffee are often provided. The women who work there are not "hired help" but committed feminists ready to help the beginner find what to start with or discuss feminist theory with the experienced.

Most women's bookstores carry a wide selection of feminist

---

[108] Quoted in ibid., p. 9.
[109] Ibid., p. 10.
[110] Quoted in ibid.

literature—nonfiction from both standard and feminist presses, novels by women past and present, a full range of feminist periodicals, and a section of nonsexist children's books. Most also have a bulletin board where news of movement events can be posted.

The *New Women's Survival Catalog,* published in 1973, and its 1975 successor, *The New Woman's Survival Sourcebook,* provide an overview of the state of the movement. Produced by an all-woman collective, the books list and provide information about everything from feminist speakers' bureaus and establishment women's organizations to self-help clinics and lesbian poetry collectives. From these books one can get some notion of the scope of the movement. Exciting things are happening in Santa Fe and Iowa City as well as in New York and Berkeley. Because the radical wing of the movement has shunned national organization, it is difficult to get any kind of overview of the state of the movement. These books show that it is healthy and growing at an incredible pace.

INTERNATIONAL WOMEN'S YEAR AND THE WOMEN'S AGENDA

The United Nations declared 1975 International Women's Year. Each member country was expected to draw up a plan to equalize the status of women. When it became clear that the U.S. government did not intend to take the UN mandate seriously, women's groups decided to act. With the Women's Action Alliance acting as coordinator, over 100 women's groups were contacted and asked to submit a list of goals. Sufficient areas of mutual concern were found to draw up the U.S. National Women's Agenda. The 90 groups representing 30 million women supporting the agenda ranged from the YWCA and the Future Homemakers of America through the National Women's Political Caucus and the National Black Feminist Organization to the National Gay Task Force.[111] Despite the diversity of the support, the document is strongly feminist. Specific goals are listed under eleven headings: fair representation and participation in the political process, equal education and training, meaningful work and adequate compensation, equal

---

[111] Nancy Seifer, "Best-Kept Secret of Women's Year," Riverside, California, *Press Enterprise,* October 5, 1975.

access to economic power, quality child care for all children, quality health care and services, adequate housing, just and humane treatment in the criminal justice system, fair treatment by and equal access to media and the arts, physical safety, and respect for the individual (including extension of civil rights legislation to prohibit discrimination based on sexual preference).[112]

In the media, the June announcement of the agenda was overshadowed by the International Women's Year Conference. Held in Mexico City, it really consisted of two conferences—the official UN conference, the delegates to which were appointed by and represented UN member governments, and the unofficial Tribune sponsored by nongovernmental organizations. The official conference was a disappointment to feminists. According to Elizabeth Reid of Australia, one of the few feminists among the official delegates, "government 'politicos' were permitted to carry on their old-hat squabbles without even feeling embarrassed by the fact that these squabbles, as they presented them, in no way related to women."[113] The official delegates' behavior showed that, by and large, the governments they represented did not care about women. Governments used the conference to continue the on-going rhetorical conflict over Zionism, imperialism, racism, and the redistribution of the world's wealth. Some of these issues are of major concern to women, yet the way in which they were presented indicated that few delegates understood this. The level of feminist consciousness of the conference is indicated by the fact that a man was chosen as chair.

Despite the diversion of the conference from its stated aim, the World Plan of Action adopted did contain elements important to women. Political participation, education, employment, health and nutrition, and population were areas in which governments were urged to better the position of women.[114] That these women-related matters remained in the draft plan is largely due to the conference running out of time before the draft could be extensively amended.

The unofficial Tribune attended by approximately 7000 women was, in the words of most participants, "where the

---

[112] The full agenda is reprinted in *Ms.*, December 1975, pp. 110–111.

[113] Elizabeth Reid, "Between the Official Lines," *Ms.*, November 1975, pp. 88–89.

[114] Ibid., p. 90.

action was." Here too bitter conflicts erupted; attempts to disrupt meetings occurred. Yet real communication also occurred. In the words of a participant, "There, the primary concern was the lives of women—how women work, eat, learn, participate, reproduce, survive. Without doubt, political issues also disturbed the peace at the Tribune but it was, in most cases, a fruitful disturbance, exploring the relationship of female oppression to other forms of oppression."[115]

NOW women organized several large sessions called "Global Speak-Outs" which were chaired by a panel of representatives from all over the world. Innumerable smaller workshops and informal get-togethers were held. Out of the Tribune came a plan for strengthening and implementing the World Plan of Action. Unfortunately, the official conference refused to consider it because it did not come from an official body.

In December of 1975, the UN General Assembly endorsed the World Plan of Action and proclaimed 1976–1985 UN Decade for Women. A world conference to evaluate progress on the plan is scheduled for 1980.

In the United States, meanwhile, feminists continued to push the Women's Agenda. December 2, 1975, was declared Agenda Day and women around the country sought endorsements of the agenda from political figures at all levels of government. In 1976 women attempted to get as much of the agenda as possible included in the party platforms.

BACKLASH

Social change is painful for many, and thus inevitably a backlash developed. When social roles and expectations are changing rapidly, many people will feel insecure and anxious. The values and behavior patterns they were taught as children are challenged. The world becomes a confusing and threatening place. The reaction to the changing role of women has taken a number of forms. Some academics have revived pseudoscientific theories which purport to show that traditional sex roles are biologically based. Attempts to "fool mother nature" will result in disaster, they claim.

---

[115] Ellen Boneparth, "International Women's Year: The Ecstasy and the Agony." Paper presented at the 1976 Annual Meeting of the Western Political Science Association, April 1–3. See also Mary Jo McConahay, "Trials at the Tribune," *Ms.*, November 1975; *Do It Now*, July–August 1975.

The success of books like *Total Woman* and *Fascinating Womanhood* is another reaction. Both tell women that if they return to traditional patterns, total happiness will be theirs. "It is only when a woman surrenders her life to her husband, reveres and worships him, and is willing to serve him, that she becomes really beautiful to him,"[116] writes Marabel Morgan of *Total Woman*. Outward submissiveness, manipulation of the feminine wiles sort, and plenty of slightly exotic sex (greet him at the door wearing only net stockings and a frilly apron) is the recipe for holding onto one's husband and meal ticket.

Courses propounding these views have been set up by the authors and have attracted sizable numbers of women. Those who attend—mostly not very affluent wives with children—seem to feel that something is missing from their lives and their marriages, that somehow the American dream has eluded them. That these women turn to solutions like *Fascinating Womanhood* indicates that feminists have not been successful in conveying their message to all segments of society. In part, this is the fault of women's groups themselves; the media treatment of the movement also must bear much of the blame. The media generally and television in particular report primarily the picturesque, the exotic, and the outrageous. Thus mass marches, sit-ins and demands for test-tube babies get covered; the hard and less glamorous work such as attempting to secure laws providing financial security for housewives does not. In the process, the real effects of the changes advocated by the women's movement are distorted.

Such misinformation accounts for the defeats in 1975 of state equal rights amendments in New York and New Jersey. Because both are liberal states that easily ratified the national ERA, proponents were overconfident. Many neither gave money nor worked for ratification. In contrast, opponents went all out. In New York, Conservative party members, fundamentalist churches, Right-to-Lifers, the John Birch Society and some conservative Catholics were the backbone of the organized opposition.[117] This coalition is similar to that which has worked against the national ERA in the unratified states, and the same

[116] Quoted in Joyce Maynard, "Different Kind of Liberation," Riverside, California, *Daily Enterprise*, October 5, 1975.
[117] Lisa Cronin Wohl, "The ERA: What the Hell Happened in New York," *Ms.*, March 1976, p. 66.

falsehoods were used. The ERA would result in unisex toilets, homosexual marriages, and husbands no longer supporting their wives, they claimed. That such a campaign succeeded shows again that the women's movement must do a better job of communication. Some of the opposition to the changes the movement advocates is based on deep-seated ideological differences. Much, however, is due to a diffuse fear of social change and can at least be alleviated by an understanding of the true roots and effects of such change.

THE MOVEMENT IN THE MID-1970s

The strong reactions the women's movement has provoked are a sign that it has had an impact on society. Although the backlash has not stopped the movement's growth, internal conflicts have created problems. As NOW's membership expanded, the organization became more heterogeneous. Feeling the need for some national organization, many radical women joined NOW while still maintaining their roles in local autonomous groups. The logic of feminist analysis radicalized some NOW members. They began to see that major structural changes were required to make true equality possible. At the 1975 NOW convention, the brewing conflict between such women and more conservative members came to a head.[118] One group, which called itself the majority caucus, advocated a greater emphasis on improving the quality of life for the masses of women through worksite organizing of women in stereotypic women's jobs, recognizing the bond between oppression based on sex, race, sexual preference, poverty, and ethnic background, and struggling against them simultaneously. It called for greater recruitment of minority women and more militant tactics. The opposition consisted of women who considered this program ideologically uncongenial and of others who believed that because of the backlash, NOW should adopt a more moderate program even though they themselves agreed with the majority caucus position. The caucus, led by Karen DeCrow, won a close but decisive victory. Considerable

[118] For descriptions of the convention, see Judy MacLean, "N.O.W.," *Socialist Revolution,* July–September 1976, pp. 39–50; and Pam Proctor, "Has the Feminist Movement Reached a Turning Point," *Parade,* February 15, 1976, pp. 13–16.

bitterness resulted from the conflict and at first a lasting split within NOW seemed possible. That this has not occurred indicates that much of the opposition was based upon tactical rather than ideological considerations. At its 1977 national convention NOW was clearly united again. Ratification of the ERA was adopted as the top priority. Other resolutions passed called for working to pass displaced homemaker legislation, legislation to establish a homemakers' "bill of rights," full employment, a comprehensive child care act, and a guaranteed minimum income.[119]

With a membership of almost 60,000 and internal conflicts under control, NOW is entering its second decade in good shape. Problems do remain. Given its ambitious program, the allocation of scarce money and of womanpower will, as in the past, remain a problem. Ideological conflict will undoubtedly appear again. On balance, however, NOW seems stronger than ever and ready to carry on its tasks.

An overall assessment of the autonomous women's groups is less easy to make. The radical feminist groups that have survived seem to be those which have devoted themselves to a specific task or project. Some of these will be described in the next chapter. A multitude of specialized women's groups have formed during the 1970s. The National Congress of Neighborhood Women, a Brooklyn-based, multi-ethnic organization, is devoted to issues affecting working-class women. California Women in Higher Education includes faculty, administrators, and staff women from colleges and universities working to end discrimination in higher education. The Appalachian Women's Rights Organization attempts to deal with the special problems of poor mountain women. Women's caucuses within professional organizations are still going strong. A number of groups dedicated to organizing women working in clerical occupations have formed. Even in smaller cities, a number of women's groups with no official ties to one another often exist. The number usually runs into the dozens in metropolitan areas. Women's centers, which have been established on many campuses and in many cities, frequently provide some coordination. Some centers serve as umbrella organizations and are run by

---

[119] Judy MacLean, "United NOW Enters Its Second Decade," *In These Times,* May 3–9, 1977, pp. 12–13.

representatives of a number of groups. Almost all function as information clearinghouses. Joint activities are often planned through the centers.

The demise of some of the autonomous radical feminist groups and the conflict within NOW have led some commentators to declare the death of the movement. The women's movement has changed, but this is a sign of life, not death. The easy victories have been won; the struggle for more difficult to achieve but more significant changes continues.

HOUSTON: THE IWY CONFERENCE

The Houston Women's Conference in November 1977 demonstrated that the movement had truly come of age. The meeting showed that women of all ages, races, and economic conditions are concerned with feminist issues and that, despite their diversity, they can work together.[120]

The Conference was the result of federal legislation authorizing the International Women's Year Commission to "convene a national women's conference, preceded by state conferences, to evaluate the status of women and issues of concern to them." Five million dollars was appropriated for this purpose.

Many of the state meetings at which delegates to the Houston Conference were to be chosen saw feminists challenged by right-wingers opposed to the most basic feminist positions. Some meetings were disrupted and there were numerous charges that, in the western states, the Mormon Church had instructed its members to attend. In Utah, a resolution to deny women the right to vote was proposed; it failed. In several states, men with walkie-talkies seemed to be directing strategy. Altogether 130,000 women attended the state and territorial meetings, and although a few meetings were dominated by conservatives, feminists prevailed in most. Most of the resolutions approved by the state meetings were strongly feminist. The 1442 delegates chosen to go to Houston were a diverse group—17.4 percent were black, 8.3 percent Hispanic and almost 10 percent members of other minority groups. The con-

---

[120] The following account is based upon Karen Wellisch, "Winning Big in Houston," *In These Times* (Dec. 6–12, 1977), Lucy Komisar, "Feminism as National Politics," *The Nation* (Dec. 10, 1977) and Lindsy Van Gelder, "Four Days that Changed the World," *Ms.* (March 1978).

servatives had won less than 20 percent of the delegate slots.

Nevertheless many women worried that Houston would become a confrontation between feminists and the right wing. The media had played up the dissension in the state meetings and seemed to be anticipating, rather gleefully many women thought, a battle of major proportions.

The meeting started on a high note. A torch that had been carried by relays of women runners from Seneca Falls, site of the first women's rights convention in 1848, was handed to Susan B. Anthony, great-niece of the nineteenth-century women's leader. Bella Abzug, presiding officer of the International Women's Year Commission and sponsor of the legislation mandating the conference, and Billie Jean King, the feminist tennis star, joined the runners for the final yards. The opening session was addressed by Rosalynn Carter, Betty Ford, Lady Bird Johnson, Coretta Scott King and Congresswoman Barbara Jordan.

The large number of delegates and the existence of the right-wing minority made organization mandatory. The Pro-Plan Caucus formed by leaders of various feminist state delegations and supported by NOW, the NWPC, the labor caucus, and many other groups provided the coordination. The agenda for the Houston meeting was the 26-point national agenda put together by the IWY Commission from resolutions passed by the state meetings. The Pro-Plan Caucus was formed to support this agenda. The Pro-Plan conveners held meetings with state delegations, special interest caucuses, and national organizations to urge acceptance of the plan without change. The conveners believed this the safest strategy because they feared that once the convention began to amend the plan, the process might get out of control. Eventually the strategy was agreed to with exceptions being made for the minority, disabled, and welfare caucuses. The substitute minority women's resolution, which the Pro-Plan Caucus agreed to support, was developed by the American Indian-Alaskan Natives caucus, the Asian-Pacific caucus, the Hispanic caucus, and the black caucus working together.

The long consultations and careful planning paid off when the time to consider resolutions came. The debate was often passionate, and many demonstrations briefly interrupted the proceedings; but all sides including the right wing (dubbed the "antis") were given an opportunity to speak, and the agenda was considered in a timely and orderly fashion. The plan was passed almost in its entirety. Although the resolution on abortion, the ERA, and lesbian rights received the most press attention, the plan covered the full spectrum of women's concerns from better treatment for homemakers to welfare reform, from equal opportunity in employment and in politics to help for older women, disabled women, and rural women. Only a resolution calling for the establishment of a cabinet-level women's department failed, and on this measure, feminists were split.

The "antis," finding they were massively outnumbered, did not make a serious attempt to disrupt the meeting as some had feared. A counter rally of some 10,000 held in the Astro-Arena was addressed by Phyllis Schlafly, a leader in the anti-ERA movement, and did receive considerable press coverage. Ironically the influence of the "antis" was the opposite of what they had intended. The prospect of a catfight among women resulted in much more media coverage of the Houston meeting than probably would have occurred otherwise. For the overwhelming majority of feminist delegates, the threat from the "antis" made it clear that unity was essential. After the tone of press coverage of the Mexico City IWY meeting, feminists knew that dissension at Houston was a luxury the women's movement could not afford. Even so, the press did give disproportionate coverage to the minority of "antis"; but what was accomplished by women at Houston was so impressive that the media did present a largely favorable image.

The National Plan of Action approved by the Houston meeting was submitted to the President and the Congress. For action to follow will require considerable pressure from women. The euphoria of Houston will have to be translated into a lot of hard work.

CURRENT ISSUES OF THE WOMEN'S MOVEMENT

13

The women's movement in the decades before 1920 focused almost all its attention on a single issue—the vote for women. The women's movement of the 1970s concerns itself with the full range of women's oppression. Struggles concerning a wide variety of issues are in full swing.

This chapter records the arguments used and the campaigns launched on the main issues currently being fought by the women's movement. These are (1) changing the way women are portrayed in the media, (2) equal opportunity in employment and education, (3) child care, (4) upgrading the position of the homemaker, (5) woman's right to control her own body, (6) violence against women, and (7) the Equal Rights Amendment. These issues all grow out of the fundamental principle of the movement: that all internal and external barriers to women attaining full personhood must be destroyed. Increasingly, women are realizing that, to attain this goal, society itself must be fundamentally changed.

CHANGING THE IMAGE

Movement women agree that the image of women in the print and broadcast media is both a symptom of and a contributor to sexism in our society. Without a change in this degrading and not really human picture of women, changes in other spheres will be much more difficult.

The treatment of women in the adult media is bad enough; that in children's books and TV programs is really dangerous. What children read and see during their preschool and early school years will strongly influence their view of what the world is like and what sorts of behavior are expected of them. Women who became involved in the movement began to look at their children's schoolbooks in a new light. What they saw led several groups to make detailed studies. A group studying elementary school texts in New Jersey found that girls are portrayed as passive, fearful creatures who cry a lot and provide an adoring audience for their assertive, curious, and brave brothers. Women are housewife/mothers, often as fearful and incompetent as their daughters. The group, an offshoot of NOW, published its findings under the title *Dick and Jane as Victims.*[1] Other studies have found that the same situation prevails across the country. Pressure has been brought on both publishers and school boards. Task forces have been organized in many cities, including Berkeley, Dallas, and Minneapolis, that attempt to introduce nonsexist materials into the public school curriculum and run workshops for teachers on the subject. But progress has been slow. The authors of *Dick and Jane as Victims* report that their examination of 1973 copyrighted texts shows no real progress. Both publishers and educators have frequently refused to see a problem. "It might confuse young children a little bit to be shown women out working," said Daniel E. O'Connel, director of curriculum development from the Boston schools.[2] "Concern about sexism is a bunch of baloney—it is just something else to clutter up thought processes," one teacher said.

Nevertheless, the pressure has had some effect. In Detroit, Evanston, and Seattle, official policy calls for the rejecting of blatantly sexist material. In Wellesley, Masschusetts, a committee has been set up to screen textbooks for sexism. The New York City Board of Education has warned more than 150 textbook publishers to pay "special attention to the relative neglect . . . of the rôle of women," and said that "books and materials should concern themselves, among other things, with the new roles of women in the economy and the changing patterns of family life." Some publishers have also reacted favorably. Both the American Book Company and Scott, Foresman, among the largest textbook publishers, have said there would be changes in their new editions.

Other children's books have also been scrutinized. A wom-

---

[1] *Dick and Jane as Victims, Women on Words and Images,* 1972 (P.O. Box 2163, Princeton, N.J., 68540).

[2] Quoted in Riverside, California, *Daily Enterprise,* June 14, 1973.

en's group studying 1000 such books found that only 200 could be labeled nonsexist. The list of "good" books has been widely distributed, and many women's bookstores stock nonsexist children's books. Some women have even decided to write children's books to fill the void.

Kathi Gibeault, a California woman, found that by age six her daughter was already affected by the negative image of women in children's books. She decided to do something about it. *Susan in the Driver's Seat* is a "blow-by-blow account of several weeks of running around with her daughter to actually meet women with exciting careers." Her second book, *Mommies Are People Too,* is the "story of the adjustment a young girl goes through when she realizes her mother is determined to go back to work and no longer spend all her time in the home."[3]

Children's TV programs have not escaped criticism. Jo-Ann Gardner, a movement activist and psychologist, has raked "Sesame Street" over the coals. "Virtually all [the programs] emphasized that there is men's work and then there is women's work—that men's work is outside the home and women's work is in the home."[4] She accused the show of "promoting 'femininity,' motherhood and homemaking as the most desirable and only appropriate roles for females."[5] Joan Cooney, the executive producer, agreed to make some changes, but the staff felt, according to one member, that "our target audience—ghetto and culturally deprived children—needs strong male figures with which to identify."[6]

Criticism of the adult media for their portrayal of women predates the movement. In *The Feminine Mystique,* Betty Friedan bitterly attacks the women's magazines and advertisers as accessories in the creation and prime transmitters of the mystique. The women's magazines portrayed women only as full-time housewife-mothers interested in a beautiful house, a happy husband, and lots of children. Being feminine, which meant being not only pretty and submissive but also childlike and basically incompetent at anything other than housework,

---

[3] Ibid., May 31, 1973.
[4] Quoted in Judith Hole and Ellen Levine, *Rebirth of Feminism* (New York: Quadrangle, 1971), p. 251.
[5] Quoted in ibid.
[6] Quoted in ibid.

was the most important thing in life. True fulfillment for a woman meant giving birth—the more often the better. All news of the world outside was resolutely kept out of the magazines. An editor explained to Friedan, "Our readers are housewives, full time. They're not interested in the broad public issues of the day. They're not interested in national or international affairs. They are only interested in the family and the home. They aren't interested in politics, unless it's related to an immediate need in the home, like the price of coffee."[7] Women's lack of interest in the "broad public issues" is the result, not the cause, of these magazines' policies, Friedan claims. "Ideas," she points out, "are not like instincts of the blood that spring into the mind intact. They are communicated by education, by the printed word."[8]

Friedan's discussion of advertising is concerned mostly with its manipulative aspects—with advertisers' exploitation of the void in most housewives' lives to get them to buy more and more, with their claims that a woman can express herself by using 10 different types of cleaners rather than an all-purpose one, that fulfillment lies in having the cleanest laundry on the block.

The movement has launched an all-out attack on the portrayal of women by advertisers. In the world of TV commercials, two types of women exist. One is the housewife-mother—usually blandly pretty, always interested exclusively in trivia, the whitest laundry and the shiniest floors, and often stupid. Some man has to tell her what products to use even in her supposed area of expertise, and she will listen to any man no matter how strange his form—tornado, knight, or disembodied voice from the ceiling. The other variety is the sex kitten. She is also not very bright, but then she clearly is good for only one thing, and that presumably doesn't require brains. Very infrequently a deviant like Josephine the Plumber is thrown in, obviously for comic relief. She, of course, is neither young nor pretty.

The campaign against sexist advertising has taken several forms. Women have been encouraged to write to the offending company to criticize and threaten a boycott of its products.

---

[7] Quoted in Betty Friedan, *The Feminine Mystique* (New York: Dell, 1963), p. 31.

[8] Ibid., p. 45.

NOW presents its "Barefoot and Pregnant in the Kitchen" awards to advertising agencies that produce particularly blatant ads. Stickers have appeared on billboards and subway and bus ads, particularly those depicting women as sex objects, reading "this ad exploits women."

The campaign seems to have had at least some marginal effect. The Geritol commercial in which a man, speaking of his wife, says, "I think I'll keep her" is no longer being run. Rollei, a German camera manufacturer, which intended to advertise its new tiny camera in France as especially for women because it is foolproof, was persuaded to advertise on a nonsexist basis in the United States.[9] A few ads that depict women as independent human beings have even appeared. The Zest soap ad that showed two women on a cross-country camping trip received a "Positive Image of Women" award from NOW.[10]

NOW has decided that advertising can be a tool as well as being a target. One of its members, a woman active for many years in advertising, set up and coordinates its ad campaign. After prolonged negotiations, the Advertising Council, which handles public service campaigns, endorsed the project in February 1973. Both magazine ads and TV and radio commercials were prepared and run across the country. One shows a toddler. The copy reads, "This healthy, normal baby has a handicap. She was born female. As she grows up, her job opportunities will be limited, her pay low. She may earn half of what a man does. Isn't it time to change all that? Job discrimination based on sex is against the law. And it's a waste. Think about your own daughter—she's handicapped too." Another, showing a fancy college diploma, says, "Congratulations, you just spent twelve thousand dollars so she could join the typing pool."[11]

Although advertising has been a special target, other aspects of the media have not escaped attention. TV has been attacked for the horror of its daytime programing—TV executives seem to agree with their counterparts at the women's magazines that housewives' IQs are at about the level of the average six-year-old and that their interests are a good deal narrower. Prime-time programs show women in a restricted set of tradi-

---

[9] *Parade,* September 2, 1973.
[10] Honolulu *Advertiser,* August 24, 1974.
[11] Ibid., July 18, 1973.

tional roles. Even "career girls" (never "women") like Mary Tyler Moore really don't do much at work; the plots revolve around their love lives.

In 1971, NOW began a campaign to monitor network and local TV broadcasting across the country. Members and other interested women were asked to keep tabs on their local stations and fill in detailed forms on the image of women portrayed and the quantity and quality of new programs about and for women. The purpose was to collect sufficient data so that stations with a particularly bad record could be identified and their licenses challenged before the FCC. In May 1972, NOW filed its first suit, against WABC-TV in New York.[12]

Newspapers have been criticized for their condescending attitude toward women and toward the movement. The women's page, with its assumption that women's interests are restricted to recipes, fashion, and bridal announcements, is considered an affront. The constant references in news stories to women as divorcees or grandmothers, blondes or brunettes, when these facts have absolutely nothing to do with the story and when no man would ever be thus labeled, are considered even worse. Edith Green reports that when she was first elected to Congress all the newspapers wanted pictures of her in the kitchen. A classic in the "putting down women" category was achieved by a highly respectable newspaper when it headlined a story about a physicist receiving the Nobel Prize "Grandmother Wins Nobel Prize."

Pressure has resulted in at least one newspaper officially changing its policy and in some others being a little more careful. Reportedly, rumors that women reporters at the *Washington Post* were planning a women's liberation group led the editor of the paper to issue a memorandum directing reporters to stop using degrading descriptive words such as brunette, cute, and the like and to stop being condescending in their stories about successful women.[13]

The most dramatic action against the women's magazines was the sit-in at the *Ladies' Home Journal.* The Media Women, a feminist group, occupied the offices of the magazine's editor-in-chief and publisher for 11 hours on March 18, 1970. In a

---

[12] Hole and Levine, op. cit., pp. 264, 428.
[13] Ibid., p. 263.

press release the women charged that the *Journal* "deals superficially, unrealistically or not at all with the real problems of today's women; . . . the *Journal* depicts no life style alternative for the American woman, aside from marriage and family."[14] Of the demands made—a woman as editor-in-chief, a child care center, a $125-per-week minimum wage, a less hierarchical structure, a "liberation" issue put out by the protesters—only the last was, in part, agreed to. The women were paid for producing a short supplement to the August 1970 issue, and used it to explain feminism and various women's issues to the *Journal*'s readership.

Although some of the women who participated in the action felt that it was a failure because no permanent changes resulted, the women's magazines have begun to change. Probably due more to the growth of the movement than to any specific pressures, they have started to run articles on abortion, child care, and even jobs. After the defeat of the state ERAs in New York and New Jersey, editors of several magazines decided the defeats resulted from a lack of reliable information and that the traditional women's magazines could provide such information to women unlikely to get it elsewhere. The joint effort eventually grew to 36 magazines, including *Ladies' Home Journal, Family Circle, Good Housekeeping, Playgirl,* and a number of the confession magazines,[15] all of which published stories about the Equal Rights Amendment in July 1976.

There are other signs of change as well. Several major publishers now send their authors instructions on how to avoid sexist language. Dr. Spock, in the latest revision of his best-selling *Baby and Child Care,* has significantly changed his earlier sexist outlook. The new version emphasizes the role of the father and includes a chapter on working mothers.[16] Instead of their usual man of the year, *Time* Magazine honored twelve outstanding women as the 1975 women of the year. Very gradually, advertising seems to be improving. A study by the National Advertising Review Board may result in further change. The study found that not just feminists but also very conservative women were offended by the portrayal of women in advertising.[17]

---

[14] Media Women, press release, March 18, 1970.
[15] Riverside, California, *Daily Enterprise,* July 4, 1976.
[16] *Newsweek,* May 3, 1976, p. 86.
[17] *Los Angeles Times,* January 24, 1977.

This is one indication that attitudes generally are beginning to change. Another is the continuing increase in the proportion of women who favor efforts to strengthen and change women's status in society. In 1972, 48 percent expressed support; in 1975, 65 percent.[18] Change is particularly great among young women. A 1976 survey found that only 25 percent of 18- to 25-year-olds wanted to be full-time housewives.[19] Even the 1976 most admired woman poll reflects the change in attitude. Among the 20 top scorers were Barbara Jordan, Barbara Walters, Shirley Chisholm, Margaret Mead and Bella Abzug—all career women who made it on their own.[20]

But a great deal still needs to be done. Parents attempting to raise their children in nonsexist ways often feel the whole world is conspiring against them. Schools, peers, and TV still convey sexist attitudes. The sexist messages may be somewhat less blatant than they were a few years ago, but they certainly haven't disappeared. Thus, feminists must keep the pressure on those who determine the content of all media. Everything from textbooks to TV commercials must continue to be monitored and protests made when necessary. NOW's National Media Reform Committee is one of the groups working in this area. Positive strategies must also be pursued. Feminists produced several television programs which have been shown on the networks. A number of women's groups now produce radio shows, and numerous feminist films are being made.

EMPLOYMENT AND EDUCATION

When stated abstractly, equal pay for equal work and equal opportunity in the labor market are the least controversial tenets of the women's movement. These demands are so directly derived from the mainstream American ideology that few are willing to take issue with them publicly. Furthermore, the Equal Pay Act of 1963 and Title VII of the 1964 Civil Rights Act have made these views the law of the land. The women's groups found, however, that given the pervasive sexist assumptions in our society and the vested interest of many groups in keeping women in their place, these laws were not solutions, only weapons that could be used in the fight for equality. With

[18] *Ms.*, March 1976, p. 67.
[19] *Los Angeles Times,* November 21, 1976.
[20] Ibid., January 19, 1977.

the passage of these bills the battle had but begun; much hard and sustained work was required if the laws were to have any impact.

Keeping a watchful and threatening eye on the Equal Employment Opportunity Commission became one of NOW's first activities. How effective Title VII would be depended on how strict the EEOC guidelines on sex discrimination were and on how vigorously they were enforced. Most of the EEOC commissioners were clearly not interested in enforcing the sex provision in Title VII. After considerable pressure from the Citizens Advisory Council, the EEOC had issued guidelines giving a narrow interpretation to the provision for "bona fide occupational qualifications" (bfoq), restricting its applicability to situations such as male actors for male roles. Nevertheless, the EEOC had allowed sex-segregated want ads to continue, claiming that the headings simply "indicate that some occupations are considered more attractive to persons of one sex than the other."[21] Congresswoman Martha Griffiths attacked the EEOC on the floor of Congress, labeling its attitude toward the sex provision "specious, negative and arrogant. I would remind them that they took an oath to uphold the law, not just the part of it that they are interested in."[22]

NOW pressure resulted in EEOC hearings in May 1967 on the sex discrimination guidelines. Both the want-ad policy and the problem of so-called protective laws were discussed. In December, keeping the pressure on, NOW picketed EEOC offices across the country, and in February 1968 it filed a suit against the EEOC to "force it to comply with its own governmental rules."[23] In August, the EEOC reversed its position, declaring sex-segregated want ads illegal. The American Newspaper Publishers Association sued the EEOC but lost, and the order finally went into effect in January 1969.

Suits have also been brought against individual newspapers under Title VII and under various state and local laws. In December 1968, when charges were filed against New York City newspapers with the New York Fair Employment Practices Commission, they gave up sex-segregated want ads. Although a number of papers complied either voluntarily or under court

---

[21] *Congressional Record,* June 20, 1966, p. 13055.
[22] Ibid.; p. 13054.
[23] Quoted in Hole and Levine, op. cit., p. 406.

order, there were many holdouts. In June 1973, a suit brought by NOW was decided by the Supreme Court. Rejecting the argument that freedom of the press is endangered, the Court ruled that a city ordinance outlawing sex-segregated advertising is constitutional.[24]

The relationship between Title VII and state protective labor laws for women has presented an especially difficult problem, and the EEOC's policy has vacillated. Most women's groups argue that such "protective" laws really protect jobs for men, that their effect most often is to prevent women from getting higher-paying jobs. An incident that took place during a drive to revise the New York State protective laws seems to bear out their contention. Assemblywoman Mary Ann Krupsak reported that a memo distributed by organized labor to legislators "simply said in essence, 'We must protect jobs for men.' "[25] Furthermore, by 1970 about 75 percent of all women workers were covered by the federal, non-sex-specific Fair Labor Standards Act; and most of the rest are in occupations such as private household work that are not covered by the state laws. Women's groups were especially concerned that state protective laws not be interpreted as making sex a bfoq for jobs covered, since this would, to a large extent, have nullified the sex provision of Title VII.

In December 1965, the EEOC's first guidelines did allow state protective laws to be interpreted as a bfoq exception to Title VII so long as the laws actually protected rather than discriminated against women. It did not, however, specify how this distinction was to be made. In its next set of guidelines, issued in August 1966, the EEOC claimed it did not have the authority to determine the relationship between the protective laws and Title VII. This was up to the courts to decide. Reversing itself in February 1968, the EEOC said it would decide on a case-by-case basis whether state laws were discriminatory and thus superseded by Title VII. Finally, in August 1969, the commission decided that state protective laws were superseded by Title VII.

While bringing pressure on the EEOC, women's groups were also bringing suit under Title VII in the federal courts. A num-

[24] Riverside, California, *Daily Enterprise,* June 22, 1973.

[25] New York City Commission on Human Rights, *Women's Role in Contemporary Society* (New York: Avon, 1972), p. 334.

ber were specifically on the protective law issue, resulting from women having been denied promotion on the basis of state or company regulations on weight lifting or hours. The court decisions tended to invalidate state laws. (For a discussion of these cases, see Chapter 7.)

Complaints to the EEOC have snowballed—some resulting in accommodation, some in court suits. Airline stewardesses have challenged company rules firing them on marriage or on attaining the age of 32 or 35. In 1970, a group of stewardesses filed suit in court against TWA, charging the airline with sex discrimination because it paid pursers, who are male, $2500 to $3500 more per year than hostesses who do the same work.

Also in 1970, editorial staff women at *Newsweek* and *Time* charged their companies with sex discrimination. In both cases a settlement giving women greater opportunities for promotion was reached without court action.

The Department of Justice filed its first sex discrimination suit under Title VII in 1970. Brought against Libbey-Owens and the United Glass and Ceramic Workers of North America, the suit charged that women were hired in only one of the five plants in Toledo, Ohio, and were assigned to the less desirable and lower-paying jobs. The consent agreement that settled the case included an agreement by Libbey-Owens to change its policy and to publicize the change to its women employees, but did not include back pay.

The years 1972 and 1973 saw some significant progress in the area of equal employment opportunities. Vigorous lobbying by feminist groups resulted in an extension of the EEOC's powers. The commission may now directly sue an employer in federal court for violation of the civil rights laws. Title VII was extended to apply to educational institutions and to government employment. Also in 1972, the Equal Pay Act was extended to cover executive, professional, and administrative jobs. In 1973, AT&T was forced to give $50 million in back pay to women and minority workers. The EEOC, NOW, and the NAACP had challenged AT&T's rate increase request on the basis that 1800 individual discrimination complaints had been filed against the company. The agreement worked out with the EEOC was much below what women and minorities were really owed—that was figured at $3.5 billion for the period 1965 to 1973. Still, it was the largest back-pay settlement reached to date.

In contrast, the settlement with the steel industry that was announced in April 1974 was severely criticized by both NOW and the NAACP. The settlement included $30.9 million in back pay to about 40,000 minority males and about 4,000 women and it committed the steel companies to opening up more jobs to minorities and women. In return, however, the companies will not be subject to any equal employment opportunity suits for five years.[26] The latter provision as well as the inadequate back pay for women led NOW to challenge the settlement.

With its new powers and an expanded legal staff—up from 30 to 220 during 1973—the EEOC seemed to become more vigorous. In September 1973, discrimination charges were filed against a number of large corporations and unions, including General Motors, Ford, General Electric, Sears, the United Automobile Workers, and the United Electrical Workers. Continued understaffing, poor management, and lack of support from Republican administrations, however, hindered the effectiveness of the EEOC. By early 1977, the backlog of cases had grown to 126,000.[27]

Because of these problems, women have frequently been forced to hire private attorneys. Helen O'Bannon, for example, filed a class-action sex discrimination suit against Merrill Lynch.[28] She had applied for a job as account executive and had passed the early screenings. On the final test, which included such questions as "When you meet a woman for the first time, what impresses you most?" ("correct" answers—beauty and affectionateness), she did not do well. She filed a complaint with EEOC, but when nothing had happened after fifteen months, she filed a suit on her own. Later, the EEOC did join her suit. Merrill Lynch agreed to a $3.5 million settlement that committed the firm to pay compensation to women and minorities against which it had discriminated and to recruit and hire women and minorities.

Numerous other women are pursuing the same strategy. Thus, women employees at *The New York Times* are suing the paper for discrimination and have won the early rounds in the legal battle.[29] Bringing suit is, however, expensive and time-consuming and thus is not a tactic available to most

---

[26] Riverside, California, *Daily Enterprise,* April 16, 1974.
[27] *Los Angeles Times,* April 21, 1977.
[28] *Ms.,* January 1977, p. 19.
[29] *In These Times,* May 18–24, 1977.

women. An overhaul of the EEOC to make it more effective is essential. The Carter administration seems more likely than its predecessors to attempt the task, but pressure must be applied to ensure that Carter lives up to his commitments. Certainly the appointment of Eleanor Holms Norton, a black and a committed feminist, to head EEOC is promising.

From 1972 through 1976, enforcement of existing antidiscrimination laws seemed to be the major problem in the employment area. The EEOC's administrative rulings interpreting Title VII were strongly prowomen and most precedent-setting court cases favorable. The Supreme Court decision on pregnancy handed down in late 1976, however, indicated that women would have to go to Congress for more legislation. The EEOC's rulings state that pregnancy must be treated like any other temporary disability, but the Court ruled that General Electric could exclude pregnancy from its temporary disability plan even though almost any other imaginable disability is covered. Immediately after the Court rulings, representatives of women's groups got together to form the Coalition to End Discrimination Against Pregnant Workers.[30] The coalition is determined to get Congress to pass a law overturning the Court's ruling, and chances of passage look good, with the Senate having passed such a bill in late 1977.

Another weapon that has been used in the fight for equal employment opportunities is Executive Order 11375. In October 1967, after intense lobbying by women's groups and by the head of the Women's Bureau, President Johnson signed this executive order. Banning discrimination on the basis of sex in federal employment and by federal contractors and subcontractors, it was a revised version of an order signed two years previously that banned discrimination on the basis of race, color, religion, or national origin.

With the signing, the campaign to get the order enforced began. The Department of Labor, which is charged with enforcement in most cases, was pressured to hold hearings and issue tough guidelines. But when new guidelines were finally published in February 1970, they did not refer to women at all. Contractors were required to come up with affirmative action programs with specific goals and timetables for minori-

---

[30] *The New York Times,* December 15, 1976.

ties, but presumably, given the omission, not for women. After more pressure, guidelines on sex discrimination were issued, but they were much weaker than those applicable to minorities, lacking any requirement for specific goals or timetables. Secretary of Labor James D. Hodgson expressed the department's attitude when he said he had "no intention of applying literally exactly the same approach for women" as for minorities.[31] He backed down to a certain extent when the outraged reactions began coming in, saying that new guidelines incorporating "some kinds of goals and timetables applying to some kinds of federal contractors" would be issued. New guidelines were finally issued on December 4, 1971.

Even without strict guidelines, women's groups began to make use of the executive order. Because a federal contract may be denied a contractor found in violation—a very costly result—the order is potentially a powerful weapon. The Women's Equity Action League was the first to make use of the order against an educational institution. In January 1970, the group filed charges of sex discrimination against the University of Maryland. By the end of 1971, suits had been brought against over 300 colleges and universities by various women's groups. NOW brought a suit against Harvard, and federal contracts were held up for two weeks. WEAL filed suits against the entire public university system in Florida, New York, and California. Until these suits were filed, the government had made no attempt to enforce the sex provision of the executive order.[32]

Suits have also been filed against all U.S. medical and law schools charging them with discrimination in admissions policies. NOW has charged 1300 major U.S. corporations with sex discrimination under the order.

Attempts to combat sex discrimination also took place within the professions. In September 1969, women's caucuses were formed at the annual meetings of the American Political Science Association, the American Sociological Association, and the American Psychological Association. By the end of 1971, a women's caucus existed in nearly every professional association.

---

[31] Quoted in Hole and Levine, op. cit., p. 46.

[32] Irene L. Murphy, *Public Policy on the Status of Women* (Lexington, Mass.: Heath, 1973), p. 37.

In some cases the caucus was established by moderate women. Thus Alice Rossi, an established scholar and a founder of NOW, was instrumental in the formation of the caucus in sociology. More frequently, younger women who had come to feminism via the New Left took the lead and, in some cases, continued cooperation with the radical mixed caucus in the association.

These groups demanded that commissions be established to study the place of women in their professions. Often the caucuses hold panels to present and discuss research on women. Child care facilities at the convention is another demand often made and frequently obtained. Some caucuses have run their members for association offices and have won a few positions.

Discriminatory practices in graduate student admissions and in the hiring and promotion of faculty have been much harder to influence. Caucuses have attempted to get their associations to require open listing of all faculty positions. Because so much hiring, especially at the prestige schools, is done by the "old boy" system—the chairman at one school asking his buddies at other schools to recommend a good young man—women often do not hear what positions are open, much less get a chance to interview for them. Open listing, then, is a small step toward equalizing opportunity.

Although many women lawyers have been active in the movement, no feminist groups were formed within any of the established lawyers' associations until 1972. Women's caucuses seem to exist at every law school where there are female students. In 1971, the *Women's Rights Law Reporter,* intended to keep lawyers informed about the "changing legal condition of women," began publication.

The Professional Women's Caucus was formed on April 11, 1970, with the intention of bringing together women working within the various professional caucuses as well as women unaffiliated with any feminist group but interested in bettering the position of professional women. It has set up task forces to do research and political and legal work. In 1971, the caucus instituted a class action lawsuit against every U.S. law school receiving federal funds, charging sex discrimination in admissions policy.

Little true progress has been made in opening up job opportunities on college and university faculties. Many universities have set up affirmative action programs, but most of these are mere window dressing. Because qualifications for academic positions are much more a matter of subjective judgment than are those for factory jobs, enforcement is more difficult. The academic establishment has mounted a massive campaign against affirmative action.[33] Its members claim that hiring minorities and women will lower standards. The Nixon and Ford administrations seemed to be in sympathy with this position and put no real pressure on the universities to comply with the law.

Enforcing legislation that runs counter to the vested interests of powerful groups in the society is always difficult. When the administration is hostile, it becomes almost impossible. According to Irene Murphy, who has made a careful study of public policy on the status of women, Nixon made no effort "to give strong and continuous support to antidiscrimination programs"[34] and opposed most bills designed to strengthen such programs.

During the last year of the Ford administration, a battle to prevent weakening of the Executive Order took place.[35] During the summer of 1976 rumors that the Office of Federal Contract Compliance Programs intended to weaken affirmative action regulations began to spread. A leaked copy of the proposed regulations allowed women's groups to prepare for the battle ahead. Published in mid-September, the proposed regulations would have exempted approximately 20 percent of the companies doing business with the government from preparing an affirmative action plan. In addition, the review of a potential contractor's affirmative action plan before a contract was awarded would have been practically eliminated.

Leading the fight against these changes were several working women's groups, including "9 to 5" and Women Employed. Their strategy was to delay issuance of the regulations as long as possible. If Carter won the election, the regulations probably would be scrapped. A public hearing on the changes was demanded; sympathetic congresspeople were asked to contact the secretary of labor; and a letter-writing campaign was

---

[33] See Gertrude Ezorsky, "Fight over University Women," *The New York Review of Books,* 21, 8 (May 16, 1974).
[34] Murphy, op. cit., p. 42.
[35] For an excellent account, see Judy MacLean, "Coalition Winds Ford Benign Neglect in Its Own Red Tape," *In These Times,* April 6–12, 1977, p. 6.

started. When OFCCP capitulated and held public hearings, so many people asked to testify that the hearings lasted twice as long as originally planned. By this time the election was over, but preventing the regulations from being issued before the inauguration was still necessary. A telegram blitz and threats of a lawsuit won the day. "The strategy of winding up the bureaucracy in its own red tape worked," said Day Creamer of Women Employed. "We learned that a coalition of women's and civil rights groups can be incredibly powerful. If we work together, we can win, even against incredible odds."[36]

This was, however, a defensive battle. Although Carter is more sympathetic to women than his Republican predecessors, making the Executive Order effective will require a great deal of sustained pressure. There have been some successes. Some women have gotten into better-paying, nontraditional jobs in industry. Several sex discrimination complaints against universities—notably one against Cal Tech and another against the University of Pennsylvania—have resulted in the reinstatement and promotion of the woman plaintiff.[37] Given the magnitude of the discrimination against women and the potential of the Executive Order for rectifying such practices, the record of the OFCCP is indeed a sorry one. Only if subjected to intense pressure is it likely to do better in the future.

Equal education opportunity is a prerequisite to equal job opportunities. As we saw in Chapter 6, some progress has been made in admissions to professional schools such as those of law and medicine. Title IX of the Education Amendments of 1972 provides women with another lever for increasing educational opportunities. The act prohibits sex discrimination by any school or college that receives federal funds. The history of Title IX shows again the obstacles to women's equality. To get the act passed, numerous compromises had to be made. Single-sex high schools and undergraduate colleges, for example, may continue their discriminatory admissions policies.[38]

After the act was passed, the Department of Health, Education and Welfare undertook the writing of specific guidelines interpreting the legislation. Lobbying by interested groups was

---

[36] Quoted in ibid.
[37] *Los Angeles Times*, May 21, 1975, and April 3, 1977.
[38] Riverside, California, *Daily Enterprise*, June 19, 1974.

hot and heavy. Women's groups wanted strong, explicit rules. The most vocal opposition came from spokespeople for men's sports.[39] Groups representing high school and college coaches attempted to have sports exempted from the guidelines. Almost all schools have blatantly discriminated against women in sports. There are fewer choices available to women, funding levels are much below those for men's sports, and women have access to facilities such as basketball courts only when the men have finished. Coaches in big-time men's sports such as football and basketball, which have benefited most from these unequal arrangements, lobbied hard against any rules that would lessen their privileged position.

The guideline-writing process dragged on and on; final regulations did not go into effect until July 1975. In athletics, the guidelines require equal opportunity to participate, but not equal expenditures.[40] Another important area not covered is sexism in textbooks.

Although guidelines are far from perfect, they are strong enough to make a difference if effectively enforced. Women's groups, having learned that enforcement occurs only when sufficient pressure is applied, set out to monitor progress. The most ambitious effort is run by the Project on Equal Education Rights (PEER) of the NOW Legal Defense and Education Fund. PEER women are reviewing every complaint of sex bias from women employed in or students enrolled in primary and secondary schools filed in four regional offices, which cover 17 states.[41] From this monitoring, PEER will be able to make an assessment of how effectively the law is being enforced, and the knowledge that they are being watched will undoubtedly affect the behavior of officials charged with enforcement.

Although women are increasingly entering better-paying nontraditional fields, the vast majority still work at jobs that are overwhelmingly sex-segregated. Economic equality for women requires not just women having an opportunity to enter previously male jobs, but also the upgrading of traditionally female jobs. At least ten independent working women's organizations dedicated to this task have formed in cities around the country. Groups such as "9 to 5" in Boston, Women Em-

---

[39] Ibid.

[40] Riverside, California, *Daily Enterprise*, June 4, 1975.

[41] *The New York Times*, August 31, 1976.

ployed in Chicago, and Women Organized for Enforcement consist of women employed in clerical jobs.[42] One focus is assisting individual employees with job problems—sex discrimination, harassment, unfair firings. Thus when Iris Rivera, a secretary at the Public Defender's Office in Chicago, was fired for refusing to make coffee, members of Women Employed demonstrated on her behalf.[43] The publicity that ensued resulted in Ms. Rivera's reinstatement. These organizations also engage in political action such as lobbying for legislation and pressuring for the enforcement of affirmative action laws. The groups took a leadership role in the fight against the Ford administration's attempt to weaken affirmative action rules.

Boston's "9 to 5" has gone one step further and formed a union.[44] Since one-third of all women are clerical workers and most clerical workers are not unionized, this may be the most promising strategy for upgrading women's jobs. Unions run by women could give clerical workers the clout to obtain both better wages and respect and dignity on the job.

NOW has also decided that the upgrading of traditional women's jobs must be a top-priority goal. As Ellie Smeal, NOW president, said: "The jobs that women do are often complicated and highly skilled. A secretary needs training on business machines, a command of the English language, discretion, the ability to make decisions. We have to ask why she is paid on a lower end of the scale than men in less skilled jobs."[45] The thrust among feminists is to demand "equal pay for work of equivalent value—work that is not identical to that of men, but is equal in terms of training, skill and importance."[46] Developing effective strategies for implementing this goal is one of the most pressing challenges to the women's movement today.

CHILD CARE

By 1969, child care had become a major issue not only in the movement but among women generally. The inclusion of child

---

[42] *Moving On,* March 1977, pp. 6–10; *New American Movement,* January 1976; *Do It Now,* March 1977.
[43] *In These Times,* February 23–March 1, 1977.
[44] *Do It Now,* op. cit.
[45] *Los Angeles Times,* May 26, 1977.
[46] Ibid.

care in NOW's bill of rights had occasioned no controversy. "We demand," the statement read, "that child care facilities be established by law on the same basis as parks, libraries, and public schools, adequate to the needs of children from the preschool years through adolesence, as a community resource to be used by all citizens from all income levels."[47] The disparate groups that participated in the Women's Strike for Equality made 24-hour child care centers one of their three central demands.

Nonfeminists—education experts, liberals, people interested in getting welfare mothers to work—are also active on the issue. The feminists' analysis and justification for child care is, however, very different from the traditional arguments:

> A basic cause of the second-class status of women in America and the world for thousands of years has been the notion that . . . because women bear children, it is primarily their responsibility to care for them and even that this ought to be the chief function of a mother's existence. Women will never have full opportunities to participate in our economic, political, cultural life as long as they bear this responsibility almost entirely alone and isolated from the larger world. . . . [We believe] that care and welfare of children is incumbent on society and parents. We reject the idea that mothers have a special child care role that is not to be shared equally by fathers.[48]

Feminists do not see child care simply as a way of making women's dual role—both mother and worker—easier, but as a first step toward breaking down society's view that the sole responsibility for child care necessarily rests with the woman. All agree that men should participate in the running of such centers on the same basis and in the same numbers as women.

Cooperative child care centers have sprung up all over the country. Because of state licensing requirements and high cost many have folded, but some have survived and new ones continually start up. Perhaps the most unusual is the Artemis Child Experience Center, which was set up and is staffed by antisexist men.[49] The increasingly vocal demand for child care has also led some companies to set up centers. It has even attracted

---

[47] Reproduced in Hole and Levine, op. cit., p. 439.
[48] NOW, quoted in ibid.
[49] Kirsten Grimstad and Susan Rennie, *The New Women's Survival Sourcebook* (New York: Knopf, 1975), p. 73.

private entrepreneurs. Several franchised chains of child care centers have been started.

Radical women are especially concerned with these trends. Realizing the desperate need for child care, they still feel that commercial and some types of governmental centers would be worse than none at all. Commercial centers run for the sake of profit, not for children, would only train children even earlier and thus more thoroughly to be compliant workers, unthinking order-followers. The centers must be community and parent controlled, they contend, if they are to serve the function of helping to break down sex role socialization.

Some of the moderate women's groups have also participated in setting up child care centers. NOW and Princeton University joined in sponsoring a nursery school in Princeton, New Jersey. Being less mistrustful of governmental activity, however, they have spent the greater part of their effort in lobbying for federal assistance. At the White House Conference on Children in December 1970, NOW organized a strong feminist lobby, with the result that the conference recommended to the president a federally financed national child care network.

In December 1971, Congress passed the Office of Economic Opportunity bill, which included a comprehensive child development program. The bill authorized $2 billion for the program in 1973 and stipulated that care was to be available to all children regardless of parents' economic status. Debate was vigorous, with opponents using the same arguments employed during World War II. James Buckley said that no need for such a program had been established, that costs would be prohibitive, and that "the proposal threatens the very foundations of limited government and personal liberty."[50] Walter Mondale then a senator and author of the proposal, responded, "The whole purpose behind the child development provisions in the bill is to improve and strengthen the family relationship. The program is entirely voluntary. It builds upon parentally controlled committees. The whole purpose is to strengthen the family and to run it at the local level."[51]

The bill, while far from perfect, was a good one. It met two of the major feminist criteria for child care. Considerable control was to be vested in parent- and community-staffed commit-

---

[50] Quoted in *Congressional Quarterly Report,* 20 (January 29, 1972), p. 216.
[51] Quoted in ibid.

tees. The centers were to be open to all children. Poor families would not have to pay; a sliding scale of payments based on income was to be established for other families. On December 9, 1971, President Nixon vetoed the OEO bill because he objected to the comprehensive child development program. Echoing the most conservative congressmen, he claimed that the bill had "family-weakening implications." A veto override attempt failed in the Senate.

Various comprehensive child care bills have been introduced in each house of Congress since then. Even though such bills had no real chance of passage so long as Nixon or Ford was president, a right-wing scare campaign against federally funded child care began.[52] Flyers claiming such a bill would take control over children away from parents, that it was a Communist scheme, spread across the country and led to masses of hysterical mail being sent to Congress. With a Democrat in the White House and the Senate sponsor of the child care bill as vice president, the prospect for passage looks somewhat brighter. Women must, however, expect the virulent right-wing campaign to resurface and be prepared to counter it. With more and more women employed outside the home, the need for high-quality child care continues to grow. This is a battle that must be won.

UPGRADING THE POSITION OF THE HOMEMAKER

The work the full-time homemaker does has been estimated as being worth from $10,000 to $20,000 per year. Yet the homemaker lacks the most elementary protection afforded most employed people.[53] If she is hurt, she is not eligible for disability pay. If she is divorced or widowed, she does not get unemployment compensation. She is not eligible to receive social security payments on her husband's account until she reaches age 60. And if at the time of divorce she had been married less than 20 years, she has no claim on her husband's social security. She cannot build up social security or pension rights on her own. If her children are over 18, she is not even eligible for welfare.

The women's movement has begun an attack on the laws

[52] *Newsweek*, April 5, 1976.
[53] *Ms.*, January 1977.

and customs that place the full-time homemaker in such a vulnerable position. Attempts are being made to change social security laws so as to provide homemakers with accounts in their own names. A recent law makes it possible for housewives to establish individual retirement accounts. There is considerable discussion of changing state family laws to give the housewife some present interest in her husband's income, and the possibility of a salary for housework has even been brought up.

At present, the greatest effort is going into the passage of displaced homemaker legislation. A woman divorced or widowed after many years as a full-time housewife confronts immense emotional and financial problems. Lacking employment experience, confronted with discrimination on the basis of both her sex and her age, she frequently can get only the most menial of jobs. Displaced homemaker legislation is intended to help women in this situation. The Displaced Homemakers Center set up under a recently passed California law provides job training and placement, peer counseling, assertiveness training, and a variety of information programs. Two other states have passed similar legislation, and it is under consideration in 17 others.[54]

Congresswoman Yvonne Braithwaite Burke has introduced a Displaced Homemakers Bill at the national level which President Carter endorsed during his campaign. The bill provides funding for pilot centers that would operate much like the one in California. It also calls for studying the feasibility of including homemakers under federal programs such as unemployment compensation and disability insurance.

The coalitions fighting for passage of these bills at the state and national levels include feminist groups and traditional homemakers who have never previously been involved with and sometimes have opposed feminist concerns. The coordinators of the NOW Task Force on Older Women, which is very active in the Alliance for Displaced Homemakers at the national level, are hopeful that a bill will be passed soon and that the experience of traditional women and feminists working together will broaden and deepen the movement.[55]

---

[54] *Do It Now,* December 1976.
[55] Ibid.

A WOMAN'S RIGHT TO CONTROL HER OWN BODY

In the years before 1970, about one million abortions were performed every year in the United States; of these only 10,000 were legal.[56] One expert estimated that as of 1970, over 350,000 patients were admitted to hospitals every year with complications resulting from abortions.[57] Although the number of deaths yearly was disputed—estimates range from over 10,000 to a low of 500—it is well known that it was the poor, the black, and the brown who died. Unable to pay for a safe illegal abortion, they turned in desperation to back-alley butchers.

While most Americans resolutely ignored these grisly statistics, there were individuals and groups working without much success to change the laws before the women's movement emerged. Occasionally a particular incident would bring the abortion problem into public view. In 1962, Sherri Finkbine's attempt to obtain a legal abortion received front-page coverage. She had been taking thalidomide, which results in severely deformed babies, yet she was denied an abortion in the United States. The birth of over 20,000 deformed babies after a German measles epidemic also stirred up discussion for a while.

The early groups, for ideological or tactical reasons, worked for abortion law reform. They often pushed for laws modeled on that suggested by the prestigious American Law Institute. This group recommended that abortion be legal not only if the woman's life was at stake but also if pregnancy would gravely impair her physical or mental health, if the baby was likely to be deformed, or if pregnancy was the result of rape or incest.

The women's movement, which became involved in the abortion fight soon after its inception, demanded repeal, not reform. Instead of basing its argument on the need for population control or on the fact that an abortion properly performed is safer than having a baby, it argued that a woman's right to control her reproduction is a matter of simple justice:

---

[56] Lucinda Cisler, "Unfinished Business: Birth Control," in Robin Morgan, ed., *Sisterhood Is Powerful* (New York: Vintage, 1970), p. 258.

[57] Robert Hall, "The Abortion Revolution," in Arlene and Jerome Skolnick, eds., *Family in Transition* (Boston: Little, Brown, 1971), p. 260.

> Repeal is based on the quaint idea of *justice;* that abortion is a woman's right and that no one can veto her decision and compel her to bear a child against her will. . . . [Other justifications] are only embroidery on the basic fabric: *women's right to limit her own reproduction.*[58]

The Association to Repeal Abortion Laws in California, founded in July 1966 by Patricia Maginnis, seems to have been the first total-repeal group. The group compiled and distributed lists of abortionists, intending to provoke arrest in order to test the laws in court.[59] In January 1969, the New York chapter of NOW founded New Yorkers for Abortion Law Repeal. This was the first repeal group to justify abortion in strictly feminist terms. Its activities included publicizing the issue, lobbying, and some referral work.

The radical women's liberation groups often preferred more dramatic action. Redstockings disrupted New York State legislative hearings to protest the list of witnesses—14 men and a nun! When they were not allowed to testify as they demanded, Redstockings held counterhearings. Before a large audience, women told about their own abortions.

In Detroit, women staged a funeral march mourning women murdered by back-alley abortionists. In Minneapolis, they presented a guerrilla theater skit on the issue. In Washington, D.C., women's liberation groups, joined by welfare women and the Medical Committee for Human Rights, picketed a hospital that had approved a legal abortion for a woman and then at the last moment withdrew the approval.

Abortion referral groups, some set up by radical feminists, some chapters of NOW, some independent, sprang up across the country in neighborhoods and especially on college campuses.

During the period 1968–1970, court actions against abortion laws were under way in more than 20 states. Some favorable rulings had resulted at the lower court levels. But the first real breakthrough occurred in 1970 at the state legislative level. Between 1967 and 1970, 12 states had reformed their abortion laws along American Law Institute lines, but this was not considered much of a step forward. In 1970, Hawaii, Alaska, and

---

[58] Cisler, op. cit., p. 276.
[59] Hole and Levine, op. cit., p. 295.

New York passed much more liberal laws that came close to allowing abortion on request.[60]

Public opinion supported the change. A Lou Harris nationwide poll in the spring of 1969 found that 64 percent of the people believed that the decision on abortion should be a private one; 60 percent of the Catholics questioned agreed.[61] Nevertheless, in New York, where the Catholic Church is strong, the battle was a vicious one. Women's groups lobbied for total repeal, the Catholic hierarchy for no change. During the fight, New York's eight Catholic bishops several times issued joint pastoral letters that were read from 1700 pulpits, reaching an audience of six and a half million.[62] The deciding pro vote was cast by a Catholic assemblyman, despite the knowledge that he was jeopardizing his career. He was denied reendorsement by the local Democratic party and defeated by his heavily Catholic constituency. The liberalized laws, though a step forward, still did not meet the criterion of total repeal. Most required the permission of the woman's husband or, if she was a minor, of her parents. Frequently the operation had to be performed in a licensed hospital and by a licensed physician and could not be done after a certain date.

Feminists argue against all such restrictions. The decision, they say, should be the woman's alone; no one should be able to force her to have a baby she does not want. An abortion done early is a simple and safe procedure that can be done in a doctor's office and by well-trained paramedics under a doctor's supervision. If both hospital and doctor are required, the cost of abortions will be prohibitive for the poor and difficult for everyone to get because of the shortage of hospital beds and of physicians. Finally, a woman's right to an abortion should not be limited to a certain number of months after conception. If a woman decides to terminate a late pregnancy, she undoubtedly has a very good reason and should have the right to make that decision.

By 1972, a large number of cases challenging various state laws had been brought, and lower courts had declared some state abortion laws unconstitutional. Then, in early 1973, the Supreme Court handed down decisions on *Roe* v. *Wade* and

[60] Hall, op. cit., pp. 268–269.
[61] Cisler, op. cit., p. 277.
[62] Hall, op. cit., p. 277.

Doe v. *Bolton.* Although not establishing abortion on demand, the decisions were a major victory. The state may still prohibit abortion during the last three months of pregnancy and may regulate abortion to ensure the woman's health during the second three months; during the first three months, the decision must be left to the woman and her doctor.

The opponents of abortion greeted the decision with dismay, and an organized movement to overturn it was soon formed. Right-to-life groups, backed by the Catholic Church, launched an extensive and well-financed campaign. The National Right-to-Life Committee has opened an office in Washington, D.C. Right-to-Lifers have organized mail campaigns directed at officeholders; as a result, mail to Congress ran 100 to 1 in opposition to freedom of choice. Pressure at the local level resulted in the Supreme Court's decision being ignored in many areas. These groups seem willing to use almost any tactics. The children of abortion advocates have been harassed; a Minneapolis hospital that was performing abortions had its phone lines jammed.[63]

The Catholic Church has poured a great deal of money into the antiabortion fight.[64] Pressure is being brought on both legislators and parishioners. The executive secretary of the Maryland Catholic Conference in effect threatened Catholic legislators with excommunication if they voted for legalized abortion.[65] The bishop of the San Diego diocese ordered priests in his diocese to refuse communion to Catholics who publicly admitted membership in NOW or any group that supports the right to abortion.[66] The move led NOW to call a Day of Outrage against the Catholic Church on Mothers' Day, 1975. In Washington, NOW members picketed the Vatican embassy; in cities across the country, protests were staged.[67]

Although the bishop's action seems to have backfired, the concerted antiabortion fight has influenced public officials. Congress passed a bill allowing an institution to refuse to perform abortions on the basis of moral or religious convictions. Both Congress and a number of state legislatures have passed bills

---

[63] *Ms.,* October 1973, p. 92.
[64] Ibid., p. 92.
[65] Ibid., p. 94.
[66] Riverside, California, *Daily Enterprise,* April 9, 1975.
[67] Riverside, California, *Daily Enterprise,* May 12, 1975.

cutting off Medicaid funding for elective abortions, and on June 20, 1977, the Supreme Court declared such a law constitutional. A constitutional amendment banning abortion, the right-to-lifers' ultimate aim, is still a possibility. In late 1975, the Catholic bishops unveiled a plan to create "tightly knit and well-organized"[68] anti-abortion groups in all congressional districts to pressure members of Congress. A year later, the National Conference of Bishops launched a political pledge drive for support of an amendment.[69] An anti-abortion candidate ran in the 1976 Democratic primaries and even managed to qualify for federal funds. Both major party candidates met with the bishops during the campaign, and although neither supported an amendment outlawing abortion, neither took a clear right-to-choose position.

Feminist groups have attempted to counter this barrage through lobbying and letter-writing campaigns. Since all public opinion polls show a considerable majority of Americans favor the right to choose, one might think the fight will be easily won. Unfortunately, the anti-abortion forces are lavishly financed, well organized, and single-minded; feminist groups have much less money and are fighting on many issues. Too many women are unaware of the real danger that the gains so painfully won may be wiped out unless they take an active part in the struggle.

The right to choose must, of course, include the right to choose to have children. When cases of forced sterilization of women on welfare came to light, pressure was brought on HEW to write guidelines protecting women from this indignity. The new rules are now much stricter in ensuring that the woman's informed consent is obtained, but enforcement will have to be monitored.

As their self-awareness grew, women increasingly began to realize that control over one's own body required knowledge about one's body. Many found they actually knew very little about their bodies. Little girls are taught not to touch or look at their genital area—"it's not nice," "it's dirty." "Sex" education in the schools, when it existed at all, tended to be restricted to the film on menstruation put out by Kotex. Gynecologists

[68] Quoted in *The New York Times,* November 21, 1975.
[69] *Do It Now,* April 1977.

often treat women as if they are children; they seldom explain what they are doing, much less provide the background information women need.

The self-examination movement grew out of the felt need for knowledge as a prerequisite of control. With the help of some trained person—a paramedic, a nurse, or a doctor—women have learned how to do pelvic examinations on themselves and how to teach others to do so. Self-examination makes women more comfortable with their own bodies; it demystifies the gynecological examination given by doctors. The attitude of male doctors during such examinations had only increased women's feelings of helplessness and incompetence. By becoming familiar with their own bodies, women were serving notice that they would no longer let doctors play God; they would know enough so that they could ask intelligent questions and would demand answers.

The Feminist Women's Health Center in Los Angeles grew out of a consciousness-raising group that became a self-help group.[70] The center, which offers courses on self-examination, free pregnancy screening, and counseling, opened a gynecological clinic in August 1973. There a patient may choose a private examination by a woman gynecologist. Women paramedics demonstrate self-examination as well as provide traditional treatment. Alternately, the patient may be treated along with a group of women with similar problems, in which case she can observe the treatment given other women. The center has opened a licensed abortion clinic where cheap and nontraumatic abortions are available. Each woman is accompanied during the procedure by a woman counselor, and women paramedics handle everything but the abortion itself. The Los Angeles group has helped organize self-help groups, as well as two other Feminist Women's Health Centers in Santa Ana and Oakland.

A number of other women's clinics have sprung up around the country. Women's unwillingness any longer to put up with gynecologists who degrade them is one spur. The high cost of abortions and the often unsympathetic treatment given by the medical establishment to women requesting abortions is another. The women's health movement is growing so quickly

[70] Quoted in Kirsten Grimstad and Susan Rennie, eds., *The New Woman's Survival Catalog,* (New York: Coward-McCann, 1973), p. 71.

that it is difficult to estimate the number of clinics and centers in operation. By 1975, there were at least 42 in the United States, and a number were known to be operating in Canada, Australia, and England.[71] Groups often start by offering counseling and training in self-examination, then include lab work and treatment for VD and vaginitis, and then, where funds and facilities are available, offer abortion services. A newsletter, *The Monthly Extract,* keeps workers in the area informed of what others are doing.[72] The Feminist Women's Health Centers run seven-week summer sessions to train women to staff these health facilities.

As such services become increasingly available, gynecologists will have to change their behavior or lose their patients. The self-help movement thus may have an impact far beyond the women it actually treats. "Health Care is for People not for Profits," reads the caption on a poster from the Chicago Women's Graphics Collection. It is a fitting motto for the self-help movement.

VIOLENCE AGAINST WOMEN

In the early 1970s, rape became a major feminist issue. The increase in rape and the growing feminist consciousness led to a questioning of society's views on rape and a new, specifically feminist analysis.

The common view holds that rape is committed by a few sick men driven by insatiable sexual urges. Not infrequently, it is assumed that the crime is usually committed by black men on white women. But society's view toward the victim is at best ambivalent. It is frequently assumed that she asked for it; nice women don't get raped. Even if the victim can show that the attack was completely unprovoked, she is stigmatized. Somehow she is to blame for having been raped. These attitudes are lodged deep in the consciousness of most men and women. All consciousness-raising groups include sex and female sexuality as a major topic of discussion. Such discussions frequently begin with the participants' sexual hangups and progress to an analysis of the socialization process that pro-

[71] Grimstad and Rennie, *Survival Sourcebook,* pp. 35–36.
[72] *Survival Catalog,* op. cit., p. 73.

duced them. Early consciousness-raising groups often did not carry the analysis much further, but as the movement's awareness increased, women came to see the relationship between sex and dominance in our society. Men often see sex as something men do *to* women, an act that certifies the male's superordinate position. The connection between sex and violence is not restricted to hard-core pornography; words like *fuck* and *screw* signify both sexual intercourse and doing someone in. Women came to see that frequently their sexual relationships had included masochistic-sadistic overtones, at least on the psychological level. Whatever their rhetoric, many men still regard sexual relationships as conquests.

When the topic of rape came up, most women would say, Yes it's a problem, but it's never happened to me. As the discussion progressed, however, women would frequently realize that their denial was not completely accurate. Almost all had been sexually harassed by men. Being shouted at and followed on the street, being pressured into bed through the use of psychological warfare ("cock teaser, frigid bitch") were common experiences. Even the use of threats and physical force by "dates" was not unusual. Such experiences left women feeling not just sexually used but psychically put down. The essence of such situations was not sex but domination. Sexual harassment was men's way of asserting their supremacy, of warning women to stay in their place.

From an understanding of the sex-dominance relationship, a new analysis of rape emerged. Rape is a political, not a sexual act. It is a political act of terror against an oppressed group. According to one of the first feminist analyses of rape, "rape teaches . . . the objective, innate and unchanging subordination of women relative to men."[73]

Kearon and Mehrhof's 1971 analysis has become a feminist classic. They say:

> [In our sexist society the] sexual act [is] a renewal of the feeling of power and prestige for the male, of impotence and submission for the female. Rape adds the quality of terror. . . .[74]

---

[73] Pamela Kearon and Barbara Mehrhof, "Rape: An Act of Terror," *Notes from the Third Year,* 1972, p. 80.
[74] Ibid.

Society's real attitude toward rape is shown by the treatment given the victim. Frequently the accused rapist is treated better than the victim. Police often refuse to believe rape took place unless the victim can show severe injuries. They ask demeaning questions: Did you enjoy it? Did you come? The victim is repeatedly forced to describe the rape in excruciating detail to various male police officers. Her past sex life is scrutinized. A woman who once says yes to a man not her husband is assumed to have lost her right to say no to any male. Eva Norman, a founder of the Los Angeles Commission on Rape, says: "The crime of rape has no parallel. It is the *only* crime in which the victim is treated like a criminal by the police, the hospitals, the courts."[75]

Not infrequently the police will make only a nominal effort to catch the rapist. "If he is white, and middle class, forget it. They figure that the chances of getting a conviction in court wouldn't be that good."[76] If a woman has let a man into her apartment and he has raped her, she might as well forget it too. Both the police and juries take that as consent. If the accused rapist is black or lower class and the woman is white, the police are more likely to pursue the matter.

In 1972, 46,497 forcible rapes were reported. Criminologists estimate that only 1 out of 10 rapes is reported.[77] Given the police harassment of the victim, the low reporting rate is hardly surprising. But even if a woman is willing to endure the experience of going to the police, the chances of conviction are very slim. In 1972, 3,562 rapes were reported in Chicago; 833 arrests were made, 23 defendants pleaded guilty; and 8 were found guilty and sentenced after a trial. Thus fewer than 1 percent of the rapes resulted in jail sentences.

The situation is not new, nor was it a well-guarded secret. But it required a strong feminist movement and a new analysis of rape to make women see that collective action was necessary. The first political action was a Rape Speak Out organized by the New York Radical Feminists in 1970.

The first rape crisis center seems to have been the one in Washington, D.C. Formed in the summer of 1972, it at first

---

[75] Quoted in Grimstad and Rennie, *Survival Catalog*, p. 155.
[76] Quoted in ibid., p. 145.
[77] Ibid., p. 150.

concentrated on counseling and giving emotional support to rape victims. Since then it has gone more heavily into helping women deal with hospitals and the police. Members accompany the woman to the hospital and to the police. They make sure the medical examination form is filled out properly. This is necessary for conviction, but according to one of the members, "the intern, either out of ignorance or not wanting to testify, fudges the report" unless watched.[78]

The presence of rape crisis center members not only provides emotional support to the victim but results in better treatment by the police and the hospital. The police take the case more seriously and moderate their behavior. The Washington center's existence has even had an effect on the treatment of victims they do not know about. A member explained: "When we first started, we wouldn't say that we were members of the Rape Crisis Center—we would simply say that we were friends of the victim. So, now, whenever a woman comes in with a friend, they assume that she is from the Crisis Center, even if she's really not, and they behave very nicely."[79] Members accompany the women to court and can refer her to a free lawyer. They are also involved in the D.C. Task Force on Rape, which is working for changes in the police, hospital, and court procedures.

Such services, while essential, will not directly prevent rape. The center has also set up self-defense classes to aid women in protecting themselves. Karate, judo, and street-fighting techniques are taught. Asked how effective the classes were, a member replied:

> No matter how much karate or self defense you know, it's not worth shit if you don't have the mind set to use it. What we try to do is politicize the women. Middle-class women, especially, are very afraid of being aggressive. We try to break that down and make women realize that if someone is fucking her over, she has the right to hit him back—just enough so that she can get out of the situation and run.[80]

Rape crisis centers have sprung up by the dozens. According to Mary Ann Langen of NOW, "In 1972 there were three rape

[78] Quoted in ibid., p. 145.
[79] Ibid.
[80] Quoted in ibid., p. 146.

crisis centers in this country. Today there are over 150."[81] Frequently centers are started by former rape victims. Many are modeled on the D.C. center; its booklet, "How to Start a Rape Crisis Center," is often used as a guide. Every center has a crisis line that women who need help can call. Most try to staff the line 24 hours a day, but because this is often difficult, compromises are frequently made. Center members check out hospitals to determine which offer the best and most sympathetic care. They compile lists of gynecologists, VD clinics, and Planned Parenthood chapters where further medical help can be obtained. A list of sympathetic, nonsexist psychiatrists and psychologists is also necessary.

Some women will need professional help, but many find that talking to previous victims working at the center is even more useful. Because society tends to blame the victim for the rape, women often need reassurance that they are still worthwhile people, that in fact they are not responsible. The Washington, D.C., center sets up meetings at which rape victims and their families can discuss their reactions and learn from each other to overcome their shame and fear. Rape crisis centers frequently get calls from women who were raped years before. Often it is the first time the woman has told anyone about the experience. Center members will accompany a victim to the police if she decides to report the crime. The decision is left up to the woman; the center will help her, whatever she decides. Most women agree in principle that all rapes should be reported and prosecuted, but the emotional ordeal involved is such that few women feel they should persuade someone who is reluctant to go to the police.

Some centers have managed to establish reasonable relationships with police and prosecutors' offices. In a number of areas, rape crisis personnel are even involved with police training. Janet Taggart of Seattle's Rape Reduction Project says, "We do a part of each new patrol person's training. It is very extensive and it's generally been successful."[82] Even if these officials cannot be made more sympathetic by reasoned discussion, the presence of an active center often has a salutary effect. If they know that any misbehavior will be publicized, they tend to be more careful.

---

[81] Quoted in *In These Times*, March 9–15, 1977.
[82] Quoted in ibid.

A center organized on different lines began operation in May 1973 in Philadelphia. Women Organized Against Rape (WOAR) has its headquarters in Philadelphia General Hospital, the institution where rape victims who report the crime are examined. When a rape victim enters the hospital, the WOAR room is notified and a member on duty is immediately available for help. Because of its location, WOAR sees all rape victims who report the crime. A member explained why they worked so hard to get into the hospital: "It was obvious to us that hotlines and crisis centers which work outside the system would reach mostly middle-class and movement women. We felt we had to be available to poor and Third World women who are particularly vulnerable to rape, and who are the most abused by medical and legal agents of the patriarchy."[83]

Getting into the establishment took a three-year campaign. In August 1970, women began to collect the names of women interested in starting a rape crisis center. In November, WOAR was formed by 150 women. WOAR talked to various prominent Philadelphia women—a district attorney, a judge, members of the city council, and several black leaders. WOAR's documentation of the abusive treatment of rape victims persuaded these women to serve on the WOAR board of directors and to use their influence to get the group into the hospital. Opposition collapsed under this kind of pressure, and during its first three months, WOAR counseled over 300 rape victims. Of these, 90 percent were black and 60 percent were girls under 16.[84] This approach has begun to spread; in several other cities, centers are now located in hospitals.

Action against rape has taken a variety of other forms. Most centers do some community education such as giving talks at schools and to local organizations. Self-defense for women has become more prevalent. Classes and how-to booklets and even schools are proliferating. Some women have taken direct action against rapists. Los Angeles women active in the Crenshaw Women's Center for a time experimented with street patrols. They prevented several rapes, turned in one rapist the police had been looking for, and scared away a man who had been following a woman for several days. They followed him until he became frightened and disappeared.[85] Rumors that known

[83] Quoted in Grimstad and Rennie, *Survival Catalog*, p. 147.
[84] Ibid.
[85] *Ms.*, September 1973, p. 16.

rapists have been beaten up by groups of women surface occasionally. Some women's groups are said to have compiled lists of known rapists.

Active campaigns to change laws and judicial proceedings are being waged and are beginning to show results. Over half the states have made some reforms in their rape laws, with the most frequent change being a restriction on the admission of evidence about the victim's previous sexual history. But although some progress has been made, a recent rape case shows that the old antiwomen assumptions are far from dead. In Madison, Wisconsin, a teenaged boy convicted of raping a 16-year-old girl was "sentenced" to a year of supervision by his parents. In explaining his leniency, the judge called the rape "a normal reaction . . . to sexual permissiveness and provocative clothing."[86] Feminist groups and other outraged citizens organized a recall petition drive, obtained almost twice the required number of signatures, and the judge was removed from the bench in September 1977 in the first judicial recall election in Wisconsin history. He lost to a feminist candidate.

The feminist movement is forcing people to look at other ugly aspects of reality that many would rather pretend did not exist. One of these seldom discussed subjects is wife-beating. Contrary to myth, this is not a rare occurrence, nor is it restricted to the "lower classes." During 1973, approximately 14,000 wife-abuse complaints reached the New York State Family Courts.[87] The cases that get to court are only the tip of the iceberg. Virtually all police personnel agree that wife-beating is the most underreported of all crimes; it has been estimated that a million women a year are subjected to domestic violence.[88]

Guilt and fear frequently prevent battered women from reporting the crime. As with rape, prevalent attitudes in our society are such that women who have been beaten often believe that somehow it's their fault. Many feel a public admission would expose them as failures at the role of wife. Economically dependent upon their husbands, lacking anyplace to go, battered wives fear that calling the police will only increase their husbands' wrath.

---

[86] *Los Angeles Times,* June 3, 1977; *The New York Times,* January 4, 1978.

[87] Judith Gingold, "One of These Days—Pow Right in the Kisser," *Ms.,* August 1976, p. 52.

[88] *In These Times,* May 18–24, 1977.

If a battered wife does call the police, her complaint is often not taken seriously. The husband will be arrested only at last resort and only if the injury inflicted is considerable. Police do not like getting involved in domestic conflicts, and unfortunately, too many seem to believe that there's nothing very wrong about a husband slapping his wife around a little. Yet according to a Kansas City study, 96 percent of that city's family homicides had been preceded by at least one "domestic disturbance" call.[89]

The magnitude of the problem first became apparent in London. A Women's Aid center, opened in 1971 to provide advice and support to women, found battered women coming to them seeking shelter. The refuge that was established provided shelter to almost 5000 women and children in its first three years.[90] There are now about 50 such shelters in England. The first center in the United States had a similar history. Women Advocates of St. Paul, Minnesota, started in 1972 as a phone service for answering women's legal questions.[91] Staffers were soon deluged by women seeking emergency housing, which was not available. A fund-raising campaign resulted in enough money to open a shelter in 1974. Rape hot lines also frequently received calls from battered women desperate for someplace to go.

Although a number of privately funded shelters have been opened by women's groups around the country, the need much exceeds the supply. Lengthy waiting lists are intolerable when delay may mean serious injury or death. Because the costs of operating shelters are high, government funding is increasingly being sought. A group in Orange County, California, obtained federal grant money to open a shelter. The NOW Wife Assault Task Force in Ann Arbor, Michigan, which provides emergency housing as well as other services, pays one full-time staff member with Federal Government Comprehensive Employment and Training Act (CETA) funds.[92] A Brooklyn program operated jointly by the YWCA and the National Congress of Neighborhood Women received a $200,000 grant from New York State as startup money.[93] In California, a bill providing money

---

[89] Gingold, op. cit., p. 54.
[90] Grimstad and Rennie, *Survival Sourcebook*, p. 214.
[91] *Do It Now*, June 1976.
[92] Ibid.
[93] *In These Times*, May 18–24, 1977.

for a pilot program to establish four to six shelters is under consideration by the state legislature.

Providing shelters for all battered women who need them is essential; too many women endure abuse because they simply have nowhere to go. A 1973 NOW study showed that although Los Angeles had approximately 4000 emergency beds for men, there were only 30 for women with children.[94] This situation seems typical across the country. But emergency housing, while clearly important, is by no means a solution to the problem. Social service agencies and the police must be made more sensitive. Perhaps legal changes will be necessary; women's groups are studying possible reforms. In New York, a class action suit on behalf of 12 battered wives charges that police "deny the existence, prevalence, and seriousness of violence against married women or treat it as a private privilege of marital discipline."[95] A similar suit has been filed in California. Both are requesting a court order directing the police and the courts to enforce the law.

The roots of the physical abuse of women lie in our society's beliefs about appropriate sex roles and in the institutional arrangements that result from these beliefs. Men are expected to be aggressive and physically assertive, to be head of the household. Women are expected to be dependent and passive. Within the traditional family structure, women are economically dependent upon their husbands and thus basically powerless. Under these circumstances, it is not altogether surprising that men take out their frustrations by beating their wives—often the only persons over whom they have power. A real solution thus requires basic changes in attitudes and power relationships.

Some of the uglier symptoms of the underlying attitude toward women in our society are the prevalence of violence against women in films and the bizarre record jackets put out by a number of reputable firms. On the record jackets, women have been shown badly beaten and seemingly enjoying it. Women Against Violence Against Women was recently formed to combat such outrages. The group forced the removal of a billboard advertising one such record and is attempting to organize a boycott of the companies involved. In a society in

---

[94] *Los Angeles Times,* March 27, 1977.
[95] *Ms.,* April 1977, p. 19.

which women are so frequently the victims of violence, to encourage further violence and to imply that women actually enjoy it is close to criminal.

THE EQUAL RIGHTS AMENDMENT

The Equal Rights Amendment has been introduced in every session of Congress since 1923, but in 1963 the possibility of favorable action seemed more remote than ever. In that year, the President's Commission on the Status of Women opposed the ERA, declaring that it was unnecessary and in fact undesirable, since it would void state protective laws for women. The AFL–CIO, the United Auto Workers, the Women's Bureau, and the League of Women Voters all opposed the amendment. Only the tiny National Women's party and the National Federation of Business and Professional Women's Clubs supported it—and the latter was not actively working in its behalf. With the resurgence of feminism, interest in the amendment revived. Passage of the ERA was included in NOW's bill of rights, although only after a struggle. In late 1967, President Johnson said he personally favored the amendment, and Nixon came out in support during the 1968 campaign. Nixon's Task Force on the Status of Women supported passage in its report, and the Citizens Advisory Committee strongly urged passage.

The voiding of some state protective laws as being in conflict with Title VII of the 1964 Civil Rights Act made it easier for some groups to change their position. At their national convention in 1970, the United Auto Workers reversed themselves and came out for the ERA. While the national board of the AFL–CIO remained opposed, a statewide AFL–CIO women's conference in Wisconsin endorsed the amendment and stated its opposition to state protective laws. Elizabeth Koontz, head of the Women's Bureau, persuaded the Department of Labor to change its position by June 1970.

In May 1970, hearings on the amendment began in a subcommittee of the Senate judiciary committee. As a result of pressure by NOW—members had disrupted Senate hearings on the 18-year-old vote, demanding hearings on the ERA—the hearings were devoted predominantly to friendly witnesses and reported the amendment to the full committee with a favorable recommendation on June 28, 1970.

The House judiciary committee, under the chairmanship of

Emanuel Celler, a long-time opponent of the ERA, refused to hold hearings or issue a report. To get the amendment out of committee, Martha Griffiths, the primary sponsor, resorted to the use of the discharge petition. This tactic is considered an insult to the chairman and to the committee and thus is seldom successful. Since 1910, only 24 bills had been brought to the floor in this way.[96]

Griffiths filed the petition on June 11; by July 20, she had gathered the necessary 218 signatures. "I didn't let anyone forget this one," she says.

> I chased fellow congressmen ruthlessly. I'd even listen to roll calls for the names of any who hadn't signed. Having spotted the face, I'd promptly corner him for his autograph. Louisiana's Hale Boggs, Democrat whip, was opposed to the amendment. But he promised to sign as Number 200, convinced that I would never make it. You may be sure that when I had Number 199 signed up, I rushed to his office, and Hale Boggs became Number 200.[97]

Pressure from women's groups had made opposition politically dangerous. On August 10, the House passed the ERA by an overwhelming 352–15 vote.

The ERA fared less well on the Senate floor. An amendment by Senator Sam Ervin exempting women from the draft was added. A totally unrelated amendment guaranteeing the right of nondenominational prayer in the public schools also passed. These crippling amendments sealed the ERA's fate for that session. No further action was taken.

Pressure by women's groups continued. On June 22, 1971, the House judiciary committee reported out the ERA by a 32–2 vote. Chairman Celler was still opposed, but other committee members, fearing another successful discharge petition and the wrath of their women constituents, voted overwhelmingly against him. The victory was only a partial one. The committee had added the Wiggins Amendment, which allowed Congress to exempt women from the draft and permitted either Congress or the states to enact laws allowing different labor standards for men and women. As Don Edwards, an ERA

---

[96] *Congressional Quarterly Almanac* (Washington, D.C.: Congressional Quarterly, 1970), p. 707.

[97] Quoted in Hope Chamberlin, *A Minority of Members* (New York: Praeger, 1973), pp. 259–260.

supporter, pointed out on the floor, the Wiggins Amendment was added to kill the ERA. It would, he said, in effect repeal the portion of Title VII that prohibits sex discrimination in employment. Bella Abzug said that the clause intended to retain protective labor laws will "protect women from only one thing—from participating effectively in society, despite the fact that many are compelled by economic conditions to work and participate. Believe it or not, my friend, some of us even choose to work and participate."[98] Martha Griffiths, the original sponsor of the ERA, said that if the Wiggins Amendment were approved, she would vote against the ERA as amended and would ask others to do so. Celler, a diehard opponent to the end, supported the Wiggins Amendment on the floor, but it was defeated 87 to 265. On October 12, the House passed the ERA by a 354–23 vote. Nine of the eleven congresswomen voted for it; one, Edith Green, did not vote; Lenore Sullivan, who is dependent on labor backing for reelection, voted against it.

The Senate judiciary committee reported out the ERA on March 14, 1972, without amendments. In committee, only Sam Ervin voted against it. The committee's report said that "the basic principle on which the amendment rests may be stated shortly: sex should not be a factor in determining the legal rights of men or of women. The amendment thus recognizes the fundamental dignity and individuality of each human being."[99]

On the floor of the Senate, Sam Ervin was the major opponent. "During the debate he quoted the Bible, recited poetry, spun North Carolina tales and discoursed at length on constitutional law."[100] If the amendment were ratified, women would be drafted and "sent into battle to have their fair forms blasted into fragments by the bombs and shells of the enemy."[101] Amending the Constitution to get rid of discriminatory state laws, he said, "would be about as wise as using an atomic bomb to exterminate a few mice."[102]

Ervin offered amendment after amendment: to exempt

---

[98] *Congressional Quarterly Almanac,* op. cit., p. 657.
[99] *Congressional Quarterly Weekly Report,* 20 (March 25, 1972), p. 693.
[100] Ibid., p. 692.
[101] Quoted in ibid., p. 694.
[102] Quoted in ibid.

women from the draft, from combat service, to retain protective laws, to secure sexual privacy, and so forth. Supporters countered all his arguments and voted down all his amendments. If any one had passed, the ERA would have been doomed. If a conference to resolve House-Senate differences had been necessary, Celler, the archfoe, would have represented the House.

Finally, on March 22, the Senate passed the ERA without change by an 84–8 vote. Two southern Democrats and six Republicans voted against it. Martha Griffiths, aided by Congresswoman Margaret Hickler, had lobbied hard in the Senate and won.

The *Congressional Record* noted there were demonstrations in the galleries when the vote was announced. Women's groups had worked hard for passage. They had lobbied, organized letter-writing campaigns, and put out publicity to inform women across the country. One group of middle-aged women lobbied every Wednesday afternoon for months on Capitol Hill. They called themselves Crater's Raiders after Flora Crater, organizer of the Virginia Women's Political Caucus and later the feminist candidate for lieutenant governor. Without such pressure the amendment would have failed. Other groups, such as Common Cause, had participated in the effort.

There was little time to celebrate passage. For ratification, approval by 38 states would be needed. The first states came easily. Hawaii ratified the ERA only minutes after congressional passage. By the end of 1972, 22 states had ratified. NOW, the National Women's Political Caucus, the League of Women Voters, and other women's groups lobbied vigorously in many states. Personal visits with state legislators and letter-writing campaigns were organized. In many places, statewide coalitions of women's groups have been formed. Pro-ERA speakers are present to testify at legislative hearings; close watch is kept on the position of each legislator. In those states where the ERA had not been ratified, women challenged anti-ERA legislators in the 1974 elections and defeated many of them.

Early in the ratification fight, major opposition came from the AFL–CIO, which still based its argument on the protective laws. Most of the major groups on the far right joined in fairly quickly. The John Birch Society, the National States' Rights party, the White Citizens Council, Young Americans for Freedom, the Ku Klux Klan, and the Christian Crusade are prominent among opposition groups.[103] Phyllis Schlafly has surfaced as the most prominent opposition spokesperson. A self-proclaimed ordinary housewife and author (she has written a number of right-wing tracts including *A Choice Not an Echo*), she heads STOP ERA, a nationwide organization of indeterminate size.[104] Her arguments are the usual ones and are stated in the most inflammatory way possible: Rest rooms and prisons will be desegregated; unwilling mothers will be forced to go to work; women will be sent into combat. Misstatements and half-truths seem to be a basic part of her strategy. Expounding the virtues of the present support laws on William Buckley's "Firing Line," she told of a case in which the court had forced a husband to buy his wife a mink coat.[105] She implied that this was his obligation under the support laws; she did not explain that the woman had charged the coat, and under a law protecting creditors, the husband was liable for the woman's debts. Nor did she add that if the man had charged the coat, the woman would have been liable.

Schlafly travels around the country speaking against the ERA. Anti-ERA legislators have been very generous with their time, and she has testified at many legislative hearings. Whenever an ERA proponent appears on TV or radio, Schlafly requests and usually gets equal time. Thus, she has received a great deal of media exposure.

Business involvement in the anti-ERA campaign, if it has occurred, has been very discreet. NOW has charged that in Nebraska the opposition was heavily funded by the insurance industry, and similar rumors have surfaced elsewhere.[106]

Eight more states ratified the ERA during 1973. In late 1974, the AFL–CIO reversed itself and endorsed the amendment. Reportedly, pressure by union women and the organization's increasing discomfort with the company it was keeping caused the reversal. Even with this new support, victories became more and more difficult. In 1974, three additional states ratified,

---

[103] See Lisa Cronin Wohl, "The Sweetheart of the Silent Majority," *Ms.*, March 1974; and *Do It Now: Monthly Newsletter of the National Organization for Women*, April 1974, p. 10.
[104] Wohl, op. cit., p. 55
[105] Ibid., p. 56.
[106] Ibid., p. 88.

in 1975, one; 1976 saw no new states added to the list; 1977, only one.

Although only three additional states are needed, time is running out; the deadline is March 22, 1979. Most of the remaining unratified states are in the South or are states in which the Mormon Church, a strong opponent of the ERA, is powerful.[107] The ratification campaign now has the support and active assistance of the Carter administration, but the opposition is increasingly well organized and very well financed.

Several strategies are being pursued. In the electoral arena, attempts to replace opponents with supporters are going forward. Legislators who were declared supporters and won with movement support but then voted against the ERA will get special attention. NOW and other women's groups have urged organizations not to hold conventions in states which have not ratified. By late 1977, over 45 organizations—ranging from the American Association of Law Librarians to the American Home Economics Association—had joined the boycott and cities such as Chicago and Atlanta were losing millions as a result. An effort to get Congress to extend the ratification deadline is also underway. The ERA may still be won, but victory will require swift and massive effort.

CONCLUSION

In all the areas discussed, some progress has been made; for a young movement, the achievements are impressive. Yet in none of these areas is victory in sight, and the opposition is becoming stronger. In order to bring about real and lasting change, women must continue and intensify their efforts. As the struggle progresses, new issues will continue to arise. Sexist ideology still distorts our perceptions. As we struggle together, our sight begins to clear and new problems requiring action become evident.

The list of needed changes is almost endless. Can they be accomplished within the system? In order to create a humane and nonsexist society, will a revolution be necessary? Movement women are split in their answers to these questions. Their differing views will be explored in the next chapter.

---

[107] Lisa Cronin Wohl, "Mormon Connection?" *Ms.*, July 1977, pp. 69–85.

THEORIES OF WOMEN'S LIBERATION

14

All feminists agree that women at present have lower status than men; that women are discriminated against socially, economically, and politically; and that this state of affairs is unjustified and must be changed. They differ in their analysis of the origins of women's inferior status, of why the lower status has persisted, and of what changes are necessary to end sexism.

Within the women's movement, the three major ideological positions are those of the moderate or women's rights feminists, the radical feminists, and the socialist feminists. Not all women active in the movement can be neatly placed into one of these categories, nor do all adherents of any one position agree among themselves on all matters. The ideologies are still flexible and in the process of development. The discussion that follows will sketch the ideas prevalent within each of the three groups at present.

SOCIALIST FEMINISM

Having the rich tradition of Western socialism to draw upon, socialist feminist ideology is the most elaborate and extensive of the three. Following Engels, socialist feminists see the oppression of women as stemming from the class system. Women did not always occupy an inferior place. "Throughout primitive society, which was the epoch of tribal collectivism, women were the equals of men and recognized by man as such."[1]

---

[1] Evelyn Reed, *Problems of Women's Liberation* (New York: Pathfinder Press, 1969), p. 65. The discussion of the socialist theory of origins closely follows Reed.

Women were, in fact, the social and cultural leaders in an egalitarian society because during the hunting and gathering stage their labor was the more important. Hunting, which was done by the men, is an unreliable source of food; the vegetable foods the women found and prepared were the staples of primitive peoples' diet. Women discovered agriculture, domesticated small animals, and developed the arts of pottery and weaving. Thus, in primitive society there was a sexual division of labor and women worked very hard. But the assumption of some anthropologists that women were therefore oppressed is completely wrong. "The primitive woman is independent because, not in spite of, her labor."[2]

How, then, did women lose their position of equality? "The downfall of women coincided with the breakup of the matriarchal clan commune and its replacement by class-divided society with its institutions of the patriarchal family, private property and state power."[3] Hunting and gathering were gradually replaced with agriculture and stock raising. A more complex division of labor developed. Increasingly, a surplus product above subsistence needs was produced. Society, which had been homogeneous, began to be differentiated into groups that differed in the labor in which they engaged. These divisions eventually led to classes, in which some produced and others received the surplus.

> By virtue of the directing roles played by men in large-scale agriculture, irrigation and construction projects, as well as in stock raising, this surplus wealth was gradually appropriated by a hierarchy of men as their private property. This, in turn, required the institution of marriage and the family to fix the legal ownership and inheritance of a man's property. Through monogamous marriage the wife was brought under the complete control of her husband who was thereby assured of legitimate sons to inherit his wealth.[4]

Thus women's inferior status is due to the institution of private property and class-divided society and to their corollary, the family. The family did not develop to fulfill human needs for companionship, emotional support, and children—needs amply fulfilled by the communal clan. Its function at origin was the preservation of wealth within the paternal line. Wom-

---

[2] Robert Briffault, quoted in ibid., p. 43.
[3] Ibid., p. 65.
[4] Ibid.

an's function within the family was preeminently that of breeder; she became in effect a possession of her husband.

Women have continued to be oppressed as a sex in all succeeding class societies. In modern capitalism, women are oppressed by their subordinate role in the family and are doubly exploited as workers. Women are still defined in terms of the traditional female role as primarily housewives, and this is a role with little status. As Margaret Benston points out, "in a society in which money determines value, women are a group which works outside the money economy. Their work is not worth money, is therefore valueless, is therefore not real work."[5] Even when women do work at paid jobs, their position in the labor force is not taken seriously—it is not really where they belong. Therefore women serve as a reserve army of labor—to be employed when needed and fired, without political repercussions, when not.

Sexism, like racism, is seen as functional for the capitalist system.

> . . . It is not just male supremacist ideas, or individual men, who keep women doing unpaid labor in the home and low paid labor outside. It is capitalism's need for a reserve labor force, to keep wages down and profits up. The system cannot afford to free women. It cannot afford the social services necessary to allow women to be out of the home. . . . Nor can capitalism afford to give women control in areas like child-raising and reproduction, because they would then be free to demand jobs that do not exist.[6]

The nuclear family, in which the husband is the major breadwinner, also serves important functions in a capitalist society. As an economic unit, the nuclear family is a valuable stabilizing force in capitalist society.[7] Because the husband is solely responsible for supporting his wife and children, his ability to strike or to change jobs is limited. Because the wife is economically dependent, she is also likely to become emotionally dependent and passive. Her economic vulnerability is apt to make her

---

[5] Margaret Benston, "The Political Economy of Women's Liberation," in Edith Hoshino Altbach, ed., *From Feminism to Liberation* (Cambridge, Mass.: Schenkman, 1971), p. 202.

[6] "Working Draft—Socialist Feminist Paper," in *Women's Studies Program: Three Years of Struggle* (Publication of Inside the Beast, California State University at San Diego, May 1973), p. 12.

[7] Benston, op. cit., p. 205.

fearful and interested only in security. Therefore, she will exert a conservative influence on her husband and children. The family, as currently organized, keeps both men and women from making trouble.

Capitalists thus gain from sexism. The low wages paid "working" women result in higher corporate profits; the unpaid work women do in the home is essential for the reproduction and maintenance of the work force. If women did not cook, clean, and do laundry for their husbands and children, society would have to provide these services. Sexist socialization makes women docile as workers and easily fired when not needed. The present family structure supports the economic and political status quo. The inculcation of the sexist ideology through education and the media makes sexism, like racism, a basis for dividing the working class. When workers are split along sexual and racial lines, unions are weakened and the workers' economic bargaining power is decreased. Furthermore, such divisions make workers easier to rule politically and thus contribute to the capitalists' hold on power.

The socialist feminist explanation of women's oppression, then, places major emphasis on economic factors. The oppression of women is traced to the institution of private property and the first division of society into classes. Sexist ideology and structures such as the family, which maintain women's inferior status, persist because they are an integral part of and perform important functions for the capitalist system.

Juliet Mitchell, an English socialist feminist, enriches this analysis by emphasizing that, in analyzing the position of women at a given point in time, reproduction, sex, and the socialization of children as well as production must be considered. Women's position at any given point in history is determined by the particular combination of these elements in force at that time.[8] The extent to which reproduction is voluntary, the extent to which the socialization of children is considered primarily the women's task, and the extent of sexual freedom all affect the position of women. These factors are ultimately related to but not directly derivable from the economic factor—the mode of production:

---

[8] Juliet Mitchell, "Women: The Longest Revolution," in Altbach, op. cit., p. 99.

> The contemporary bourgeois family can be seen as a triptych of sexual, reproductive and socializatory functions (the woman's world) embraced by production (the man's world)—precisely a structure which in the final instance is determined by the economy.[9]

Since private property and class divisions are at the root of women's oppression and since that oppression is useful for the capitalist system, a socialist revolution is needed to free women. "As long as a system works better with sexism and racism, it will not be able to 'reform' them out."[10] The women's struggle is a part of the larger struggle based on class.

Unlike earlier socialists, socialist feminists do not believe that socialism will automatically free women. The position of women in the Soviet Union and China, while much improved from that of prerevolutionary days, is still not equal to that of men. Women must make sure, through their struggle, that the revolution is a socialist feminist one:

> Socialism that is really feminist will only come about with sharp and conscious struggle led by women. The ideas and concepts of sexism . . . will persist for a long time. In addition to changing these ideas, men's concrete power and privilege will have to be done away with. Some Socialist groups argue that men are sexist only out of false consciousness, since sexism divides the working class and keeps it from uniting against its real oppressors. But men also benefit from sexism: they gain material advantages (skills, jobs, positions), status, power and service. . . . Men, too, will benefit from ending sexism—by ending their own oppressive roles (tough, hard, competitive, etc.) and by having more human relationships—but they will also have to give up that power and privilege.[11]

To free women, the objective conditions and structures that now keep women in their place must be changed. Margaret Benston emphasizes that fighting for free and equal entry into the productive sector is not sufficient. Housework must be socialized. Otherwise the "working" woman simply ends up with two jobs. Child care, cooking, cleaning, and the other work that is done in the home must not remain the woman's private responsibility. Mitchell makes the same point in a more general

---

[9] Ibid., p. 121.
[10] "Working Draft—Socialist Feminist Paper," op. cit., p. 12.
[11] Ibid., pp. 12–13.

way when she calls for changes in all four factors that determine women's position. While economic demands are most basic, the other elements must not be neglected. Furthermore, strategy will sometimes dictate emphasizing one or another of the noneconomic elements over the economic.[12]

Working for present reforms so long as the ultimate objective is not forgotten is imperative. Marxist women should struggle with their sisters for equal pay for equal work; equal opportunity in education and employment; free abortion on demand; and free community-controlled child care centers. "Mobilizing women behind these issues not only gives us the possibility of securing some improvements but also exposes, curbs and modifies the worst aspects of our subordination in this society."[13]

Women must maintain their independent struggle for liberation but must not fall into the trap of believing that men per se are the enemy. "No segment of society which has been subjected to oppression . . . can delegate the leadership and promotion of their fight for freedom to other forces—even though other forces can act as their allies."[14] During the course of the struggle men can and must be reeducated. Male workers must learn that "their chauvinism and dominance is another weapon in the hands of the master class for maintaining its rule."[15]

What, then, is the socialist feminist vision of the good society after the revolution? No one has drawn up blueprints, but the general outlines are clear. The society would be democratic both politically and economically. The means of production would be publicly owned and the fruits of production equably distributed. Factors like sex and race would no longer predetermine one's status or life-style. Most of the functions the family now performs—child care, for example—would be socially performed, and as a result, the oppressiveness of the present bourgeois family would cease. According to Mitchell, the result would be not the destruction of the family, but "a plural range of institutions—where the family is only one. . . ."[16]

---

[12] Mitchell, op. cit., p. 121.
[13] Reed, op. cit., p. 75.
[14] Ibid.
[15] Ibid., pp. 75–76.
[16] Mitchell, op. cit., p. 123.

RADICAL FEMINISM

Because it is a newer ideology, radical feminism is less fully developed than socialist feminism, and there is less agreement among its adherents. All radical feminists agree, however, that the oppression of women is the first and most basic case of domination by one group over another. "Male supremacy is the oldest, most basic form of domination. All other forms of exploitation and oppression (racism, capitalism, imperialism, etc.) are extensions of male supremacy: Men dominate women, a few men dominate the rest."[17]

The problem, then, is the sex class system through which women have been relegated to being breeders and have been excluded from the creation of and any real participation in culture. "Radical feminism recognizes the oppression of women as a fundamental political oppression wherein women are categorized as an inferior class based upon their sex."[18] The function of sexism is primarily psychological, not economic. According to the New York Radical Feminists,

> the purpose of male chauvinism is primarily to obtain psychological ego satisfaction, and . . . only secondarily does this manifest itself in economic relationships. For this reason we do not believe that capitalism, or any other economic system, is the cause of female oppression, nor do we believe that female oppression will disappear as a result of a purely economic revolution. The political oppression of women has its own class dynamic; and the dynamic must be understood in terms previously called "non-political"—namely the politics of the ego. . . . Man establishes his "manhood" in direct proportion to his ability to have his ego override woman's, and derives his strength and self-esteem through this process.[19]

Among radical feminists, only Shulamith Firestone has developed a comprehensive theory of the origins of women's oppression. The origins of the sex class system, she says, lie in the biologically determined reproductive roles of men and women: Women bear and nurse children. "Unlike economic class, sex class sprang directly from a biological reality: men and women

---

[17] "Redstockings' Manifesto," in Betty and Theodore Roszak, eds., *Masculine/Feminine* (New York: Harper & Row, 1969), p. 273.

[18] "Politics of the Ego: A Manifesto for N.Y. Radical Feminists," in Anne Koedt, Ellen Levine, and Anita Rapone, eds., *Radical Feminism* (New York: Quadrangle, 1973), p. 379.

[19] Ibid., pp. 379–380.

were created different and not equally privileged."[20] Until reliable birth control methods became available, women were "at the continual mercy of their biology."[21] Biology made women dependent on males for their physical survival. Thus "the biological family is an inherently unequal power distribution."[22] The result is power psychology and the economic class system. "Natural reproductive differences between the sexes led directly to the first division of labor at the origins of class."[23]

The exploitation of woman by man and of man by man has its origins in biology, not economics. The male's biological advantage in not being the bearer of children made the female dependent on him. This dependency of female on male is the prototype of all power relationships and the origin of the power psychology—the desire to dominate others. The first division of labor—that between man and woman—contained a power component. From this developed the exploitative economic class system. According to Firestone, "current leftist analysis [is] outdated and superficial because this analysis does not relate the structure of the economic class system to its origins in the sexual class system, the model for all other exploitative systems and thus the tapeworm that must be eliminated first by any true revolution."[24]

Women's oppression has its origins in biology but is not therefore immutable. Technological developments—reliable birth control and, in the future, artificial reproduction (i.e., test-tube babies)—have the potential for freeing women. However, oppression will not cease just because its biological determinants are overcome. The supporting structures for maintaining that oppression are still functioning. A feminist revolution is needed, and its first stirrings are already occurring.[25]

While not all radical feminists would subscribe to Firestone's exclusively biological explanation, all would agree that all past and present societies are patriarchies. Men institutionalized their domination over women via social structures such as the family and religion. "The oppression of women is manifested

---

[20] Shulamith Firestone, *The Dialectic of Sex* (New York: Bantam, 1970), p. 8.
[21] Ibid.
[22] Ibid.
[23] Ibid., p. 9.
[24] Ibid., p. 37.
[25] Ibid., p. 31.

in particular institutions, constructed and maintained to keep women in their place. Among these are the institutions of marriage, motherhood, love, and sexual intercourse (the family unit is incorporated by [these])."[26] To free women, these institutions and the sexist ideology they foster must be destroyed. Revolution, not reform, is needed.

According to Firestone, revolution is possible because of the control over reproduction technology has made possible; it is necessary simply for survival. The population explosion must be controlled, and soon, if disaster is to be averted. But the family structure and the psychology it fosters make such control impossible. People have too many babies and for the wrong reasons—to satisfy ego needs by possessing and living through a child. The reduction of population growth and the rearing of psychologically healthy children will be possible only when the family is destroyed.

The revolution, then, aims at a total restructuring of society. The abolition of capitalism and the institution of a socialist economy, while necessary, are not sufficient. Nor is it reforms in the status of women that are sought. "The end goal of feminist revolution must be . . . , not just the elimination of male *privilege* but of sex *distinction* itself: genital difference between human beings would no longer matter culturally."[27] Thus all sex role typing must be abolished. Integrating women into the male world is not the answer.

> We believe that the male world as it now exists is based on the corrupt notion of "maleness vs. femaleness," that the oppression of women is based on this very notion and its attendant institutions. . . . We must eradicate the sexual division on which our society is based.[28]

Women must make the revolution; they can expect little help from men. The first step is to free themselves from the self-destructive, sexist notions they have internalized:

> We must begin to destroy the notion that we are indeed only servants of the male ego, and must begin to reverse the systematic crushing of women's egos by constructing alternative selves that are healthy,

---

[26] "Politics of the Ego: A Manifesto for N.Y. Radical Feminists," op. cit., p. 381.
[27] Firestone, op. cit., p. 11.
[28] Bonnie Kreps, "Radical Feminism 1," in Koedt, et al., op. cit., p. 239.

independent and self-assertive. We must, in short, help each other to transfer the ultimate power of judgment about the value of our lives from men to ourselves.[29]

The destruction of the sex class system will ultimately benefit men by freeing them from the masculine role, which is also oppressive, and thus make possible genuinely human relations. Men cannot, however, be expected to realize this. They have been warped by the power psychology, and they derive real benefits from the present system. *"All men* receive economic, sexual, and psychological benefits from male supremacy. *All men* have oppressed women."[30] Thus only women working together can bring about a nonsexist, nonoppressive society.

What, then, will the new society be like? Firestone sets out four conditions that it must fulfill.

1. Women must be freed from the "tyranny of their reproductive biology."[31] Childrearing and even childbearing will become the responsibility of society as a whole. Men, as well as women, will be involved. Further advances in the biological sciences should make artificial reproduction possible for those who wish to make use of it. Changes in childrearing require radical social reorganization.
2. "The full self-determination, including economic, of both women and children"[32] will be necessary. Feminist socialism in a land of plenty will provide economic independence for everyone whether they "work" or not. With increasing automation, work as we know it would disappear. Dull, repetitive, uncreative tasks would be done by machines. Human beings would be free to occupy themselves at whatever they found interesting, whether socially useful or not.
3. "The total integration of women and children into all aspects of the larger society"[33] would be required.
4. Full sexual freedom must be guaranteed to both women and children.[34]

The fulfillment of the first two conditions would strip the family of its reproductive and economic functions and thus destroy

[29] "Politics of the Ego: A Manifesto for N.Y. Radical Feminists," op. cit., pp. 382–383.
[30] "Redstockings' Manifesto," op. cit., p. 273.
[31] Firestone, op. cit., p. 206.
[32] Ibid., p. 207.
[33] Ibid., p. 208.
[34] Ibid., p. 209.

it. The latter two would ensure an end to any form of social oppression.

While disclaiming any intention or desire to provide a detailed blueprint of the future society, Firestone does present sketches meant to stimulate further thought. "The most important characteristic to be maintained in any revolution is flexibility."[35] There should, she says, be a multitude of options. People should be able to choose the life-style that suits them best and change it at will. This would be possible in an affluent, highly automated, socialist society in which no one had to work.

She suggests two nonreproductive styles—single professions and "living together." The first she describes as "a single life organized around the demands of a chosen profession, satisfying the individual's social and emotional needs through its own particular occupational structure."[36] More satisfactory for some people would be "living together"—the "loose social form in which two or more partners, of whatever sex, enter a nonlegal sex/companionate arrangement the duration of which varies with the internal dynamics of the relationship."[37]

These two forms provide for various combinations of privacy and companionship, and one or both would probably be the choice of most people for at least part of their lives. They are not, however, suitable for children. For children and adults who like and want to be around children for part or all of their lives, there would be households—a group of adults and children living together. To provide the stability needed for the children, the adults would contract to live together for a specified time—seven to ten years, Firestone suggests. After that period each individual and the group as a whole could decide whether to remain together. Both child care and other chores would be equally shared by all the adults and thus would not be burdensome. Children born into a household would have the right to transfer out if they so wished. This setup makes it possible for children to form close relationships with adults and other children without being anyone's "property," as is the case in the nuclear family.

Radical feminists and socialist feminists thus differ over the

[35] Ibid., p. 227.
[36] Ibid.
[37] Ibid., p. 228.

origins and the present function of women's oppression. Socialist feminists see the origins in the institution of private property and the division of society into classes; radical feminists emphasize female biology—particularly the woman's reproductive role. Sexism, according to the radical feminists, primarily serves a psychological function for men. Socialist feminists, in contrast, see sexism as primarily serving an economic function for the capitalist.

Radical feminists, then, see patriarchy (male supremacy) as the defining characteristic of our society; for socialist feminists, the defining characteristic is capitalism. They agree that to free women a revolution that is both socialist and feminist is necessary; but, differing in their prior analysis, they place differing emphases on the two elements. Socialist feminists see a socialist revolution as a necessary but not sufficient condition for a nonsexist society. Participation by active, committed socialist feminists in the revolutionary struggle and in the new society will ensure the demise of sexism. Radical feminists believe that a feminist revolution against the patriarchy will destroy sexism and also institute socialism. The two groups' ideals of the good society, then, do not differ greatly.

Socialist feminists and most radical feminists believe androgyny to be a major defining characteristic of the good society. With the destruction of sex roles, both male and female would be free to develop and express the full range of valued human traits. Creativity, independence, nurturance, and sensitivity would be considered desirable characteristics in all human beings. Liberation consists not in women "becoming" men but in both male and female being free to become truly human. In a good society both men and women would be different from what they are in our society. Personality differences among people would still exist, but they would not be related to sex. Furthermore, society would be structured so as to encourage the development of traits such as cooperativeness and sensitivity toward others.

A few women have rejected androgyny and substituted the notion of matriarchy. These women have tended to glorify all traits presently labeled feminine—even those that most feminists see as self-destructive. One version of this position is based on the biological differences between the sexes. Women are, by nature, mothers, it is claimed; but rather than justifying women's inferior place, the capacity for motherhood makes women superior. "Female biology is the basis of women's powers."[38]

Although this position is rare in the movement, the publication in the August 1973 *Ms.* of an open letter by Jane Alpert gave it considerable publicity. Alpert, formerly closely associated with the Weathermen, presents a theory of "mother right." The feminist revolution, she says, "must be an affirmation of the power of female consciousness, of the Mother."[39] The good society will be one in which women are revered and powerful because of their capacity to bear children. ". . . [T]he point of Mother Right is to reshape the family according to the perceptions of women, and to reshape society in the image of this new matriarchal family."[40]

This position is unlikely to gain many adherents because of the theoretical and practical problems it presents. To base the argument for women's liberation on the female's capacity to bear children at a time when motherhood will occupy decreasing amounts of women's time seems foolhardy. A reversal in the status of present sex roles will not end oppression. The sex roles themselves must be destroyed.

WOMEN'S RIGHTS FEMINISM

Moderate feminists have been less inclined toward abstract analysis and theorizing than their more radical sisters. Their ideology is the least integrated and least clear-cut of the three major positions. Most start from liberal principles—that all people are created equal and that there should be equal opportunity for all. They see that these principles have not been applied to women and demand that henceforth they should be.

No moderate has written on the origin of women's lower status. Most would probably subscribe to a biological explanation similar in content to Firestone's but very different in tone. Before reliable contraceptives and baby bottles were available, a woman had no choice but to spend the greater part of her life bearing and rearing children. By the time the technology to free women from this biologically determined role became

---

[38] Jane Alpert in *Ms.*, August 1973, p. 91.
[39] Ibid., p. 94.
[40] Ibid., p. 93.

available, the male-female division of labor had been so completely accepted as natural and right that little changed. Thus tradition maintains a form of social organization that is no longer necessary.

In *The Feminine Mystique,* Betty Friedan analyzes the costs of maintaining the traditional male-female division of labor. She concentrates on the sterile life of the middle-class housewife. Under mid-twentieth-century circumstances, housework and childrearing are not sufficiently challenging for any adult. Yet women have been taught that true self-fulfillment lies in being wife and mother exclusively. When women do not realize the promised self-fulfillment and, in fact, become miserably unhappy, they blame themselves, not their situation. Friedan's solution is an education and a profession for women.

Since 1963, when her book was published, Friedan's analysis has broadened considerably. She and other moderates no longer concern themselves only with the plight of middle-class women. Friedan's early analysis implied that only the brainwashing of women by the schools and the media kept them from achieving professionally. Moderates now realize that legal inequalities, employment discrimination, and the lack of facilities such as child care centers are also real barriers. They realize that women's secondary status has been institutionalized and that women cannot free themselves individually through a change in consciousness. A mass movement of women is needed.

Moderates do not carry their critique of motherhood and the family to the same basic level as the radical feminists do, but they agree that as now constituted, the institution of the family is oppressive. Betty Friedan says that as long as women are relegated to being mothers and mothers only, "motherhood is a bane and a curse."[41] When women are free to be full, equal human beings, the family will no longer be oppressive. Moreover, other life-styles will also be available for those who prefer them.[42]

Although moderates have picked up some of the vocabulary of the other wings of the movement—they speak of the oppression of women—and see many of the same problems, their

[41] Betty Friedan, "Our Revolution is Unique," in Mary Lou Thompson, ed., *Voices of the New Feminism* (Boston: Beacon, 1970), p. 36.
[42] Ibid., p. 38.

analysis of the functions sexism serves is quite different. In *The Feminine Mystique,* Friedan points out that keeping women in the home is profitable for business because it fosters overconsumption. Middle-class women with nothing interesting to occupy their time will go out and buy unneeded products. More generally, however, moderates see sexism as dysfunctional for society—it deprives society of the talents of half its members. Furthermore, moderates do not see sexism as performing a vital function for an appreciable segment of society. It doesn't really help anyone. Opposition to feminists' demands is interpreted most frequently as stemming not from self-interest but from false consciousness due to sexist socialization.

Given this analysis, moderates place great emphasis on the benefits to men from ending sexism. "Man . . . is . . . the fellow victim of the present half-equality."[43] Radical feminists point out that men will also have to give up advantages they now enjoy. The moderates, because they do not see men as truly benefiting from sexism, do not consider men the enemy.[44]

Moderate feminists have been relatively optimistic about working with men. Organizations like NOW admit male members. Nevertheless, moderates believe that women must depend primarily on themselves. ". . . It would be as much of a mistake to expect men to hand this to women as to consider all men as the enemy, all men as oppressors."[45] Like "any other oppressed group," women must lead the fight for their own liberation.

While moderates are increasingly using the term "revolution," they do not mean it literally. A nonsexist society can be attained by working through the present system. Many may hope that an accumulation of reforms will transform society, but radical restructuring, such as that envisioned by the socialist or radical feminists, is not considered necessary.

Two beliefs explain the moderates' optimism that the needed changes can be accomplished within the system. As no significant segment really benefits from sexism, opposition to feminist demands should eventually wither away under the impact of education. Furthermore, the moderates, working from a liberal

[43] Ibid., p. 32.
[44] Ibid., p. 36.
[45] Ibid., p. 39.

ideology, see the distribution of power in the United States as pluralist. Competition among many groups determines government policy; no single group dominates. Organized women can get into the game and, like other groups, can expect to have their demands met if they put on enough pressure.

The moderates have not sketched out their ideal society very clearly. They are often accused by their more radical sisters of demanding "let us in," not "set us free"—of simply wanting a slice of the pie. Although this may have been a fair criticism in the early days of the movement, it is considerably less so now. Moderate groups have increasingly concerned themselves with the problems of poor women—welfare mothers, for example—and of social outcasts—lesbians and prison women in particular. The notion of androgyny has also taken hold. Moderates do not advocate that women adopt the more unattractive male traits, such as aggressiveness and supercompetitiveness, in order to be successful. Like socialist feminists and radical feminists, moderates believe that each person should be free to develop his or her full humanity independent of what is now labeled masculine or feminine. In a good society, valued human traits such as independence (now labeled masculine) and tenderness (now labeled feminine) would be characteristic of both men and women.

FROM IDEOLOGY TO ACTION

The three major groupings in the movement are more clearly distinct in ideology than in tactics and strategy. Much cross-fertilization has taken place. Forms of action that originated in one segment of the movement have spread to others.

Consciousness raising

Consciousness raising was developed as a feminist technique primarily by radical feminists. Rejecting the male New Left's emphasis on antiseptic, abstract theorizing, the early feminists insisted that theory must grow out of their feelings and experiences.

They quickly discovered that becoming aware of women's secondary status was only a first step. Through the socialization process women have internalized many of the assumptions of patriarchal society. Recognizing that society's notions of masculinity and femininity are assumptions, not facts, and tracing out the ramifications of these assumptions and truly freeing oneself of them is not an easy process. A sudden revelation brought on by some blatantly sexist incident may provide the impetus for further examination; it does not make one a free woman or a true feminist.

Becoming a feminist requires both an emotional and an intellectual understanding of the patriarchal nature of society. A woman must discover how she herself has been molded by that society and how its structures affect her. To do so, she needs the warm, supportive environment provided by other women going through the same process.

From these realizations grew the theory of consciousness raising (CR). Of course the first CR groups, frequently called rap groups at the time, developed without the aid of theory. Dissatisfied and increasingly angered by their treatment within the New Left, women got together to discuss their problems. They soon realized that their problems were not personal and idiosyncratic but systemic and thus political. Such discussions led to increased awareness of the sexist nature of society and thus to more basic analysis and criticism.

The male Left ridiculed women's problems as trivial and CR groups as bourgeois therapy. Feminists countered that CR is highly political because it is aimed at fundamental change, not at adjustment. Theory and analysis, if it is to be valuable as a guide to action, must stem from personal feelings and experiences. In a CR group, women discuss their own feelings and experiences. In discovering how similar these are from woman to woman, women discover the political nature of their problems. The individual woman learns that she is not a misfit, a kook, or sick but rather that society is sick. From such discussion comes an analysis that is truly meaningful because it was developed by the women themselves and because it is based not on abstractions but on the women's own life experiences. Such an analysis becomes an integral part of the way a woman looks at the world; it shapes the way she thinks and behaves. From this analysis strategies for action are developed. The ideal course for a CR group is from discussion of feelings and experiences, to analysis, and then to action. Each succeeding stage should grow organically from the preceding stages.

Although the consciousness-raising technique was developed by radical feminists, it has spread to all sections of the movement. Most NOW chapters have set up CR groups; all women's centers serve as a way of bringing together women who want to form groups; and many suburban homemakers otherwise unaffiliated with the movement have participated in independent CR groups.

Most groups consist of 5 to 15 women who meet weekly for a period ranging from 6 to 18 months. A general rule is that attendance should take precedence over anything but a true emergency. How structured the discussion is varies from group to group. In some cases a woman who has previously been through CR acts as facilitator—she guides the discussion, attempts to keep participants on the topic, and helps them move from personal experiences to societal analysis. In others, all the women are new to the process and either rotate the position of facilitator or do not use it. Most groups will set a particular topic for each session—early childhood experiences and learning what being a girl means, relations with parents and siblings, first menstruation and adolescence, sex, marriage, motherhood, growing old. To what extent discussion is kept on the topic varies from group to group. Ideally, all members should participate equally and should be absolutely honest. Because of the very intimate nature of the matters discussed, reaching the ideal is not easy. Many women find it difficult at first to open up and then painful to be honest with themselves. Again ideally, the atmosphere should be so warm and supportive as to make complete honesty possible. Because the discussion brings out such basic beliefs and values, conflicts do occur and feelings sometimes run high.

Despite the problems, women who have participated in CR groups almost universally consider the experience not just worthwhile but one of the most important of their lives. Reexamining the notions one has held since childhood and being truly honest with oneself is painful, yet it is necessary if one is to start on the long journey toward becoming a free woman.

A critique of the CR technique frequently voiced a few years ago is that, whatever the theory, in practice it often has not led to action. The problems encountered in translating analysis into action are, however, due not to the CR technique but to feminists' notions on structure.

The problem of structure

Radical feminists again took the lead in making a critique of traditional organizational structures a central tenet of feminism. A dislike of hierarchy was evident in the New Left. Despite this, feminists were offended by the power tripping they had seen in New Left organizations. In their new movement they were determined to prevent the same structures and behavior patterns from arising.

Starting from the premise that all hierarchy and leadership is oppressive, many radical feminists concluded that the only good structure is no structure at all. All tasks should be shared; no one should be in the position of telling anyone else what to do. Decisions should be made by consensus. "Elitist" or "star" became the worst epithet one could hurl at a sister. Women who assumed responsibility and got something done frequently were not praised but accused of ego tripping or self-aggrandizement.

The notion that no structure at all was necessary made action very difficult, if not impossible. With no agreed-upon mechanism for making decisions, decisions frequently were not made; with no one responsible for a task, the task frequently was not performed.

After a time frustrations built up and a reaction set in. Joreen's article, "The Tyranny of Structurelessness,"[46] was well received when it appeared in 1972. She points out that while structurelessness inhibits action, it does not prevent the development of an elite. If a group lacks a formal structure, a friendship clique within it will become an informal elite, and because it was not chosen by the members, it cannot be held responsible by the members. "If the movement continues to deliberately not select who shall exercise power, it does not thereby abolish power. All it does is abdicate the right to demand that those who do exercise power and influence be responsible for it."[47]

Radical feminists have increasingly come to realize that the structureless, leaderless group appropriate to consciousness raising is not appropriate to action. They have not, however, given up their commitment to nonoppressive organization. Most groups do attempt to come to decision by consensus whenever possible. Tasks are shared; no one is left with all the grubby work while others do the more creative tasks. Increasingly, an apprenticeship system is being used. Instead of expecting a woman to undertake a task with which she has had no experi-

---

[46] Joreen, "The Tyranny of Structurelessness," in Koedt, et al., op. cit., pp. 285–299.

[47] Ibid., p. 297.

ence—frequently the result of rotating tasks without attention to participants' skills—a younger woman and a more experienced one will work together. Leaders are more frequently officially designated, but their titles—facilitator or coordinator—indicate a real difference in function. They are expected to facilitate, not direct or dominate. The group as a whole makes policy.

These less extreme ideas about organization are now prevalent throughout the movement. NOW chapters are, in reality, autonomous. They are no longer required to get their bylaws approved by national NOW, and each chapter decides on its own what activities to undertake. Many have abandoned traditional officers' titles such as president for those favored in the rest of the movement. As in the more radical groups, great stress is placed on consensus decision making.

The problem of structure has not been solved. Developing organizational forms that make possible effectiveness without hierarchy or coercion is no simple task. Groups still flounder for lack of structure; others disintegrate because of conflicts over structure. When groups have organized for a task, the pressures of operating in this society often create new and unforeseen quandaries and conflicts. What should be the relationship between full- and part-time workers at a self-help clinic? Should the full-timers, who do know more about the task, have greater say in its operation? Should women working at a feminist bookstore, at a self-help clinic, or on a feminist periodical pay themselves a salary? Are they taking advantage of their sisters, or are they simply making it possible for them to spend full time on feminist causes? If some women are paid, will a professional feminist elite emerge?

Despite the problems and the further need for experimentation with organizational forms, many groups are engaged in actions. The types of activities undertaken can be broadly divided into two categories: the setting up and running of counterinstitutions and attempts to bring about changes in governmental policy through political action.

Counterinstitutions

Feminist analysis bears heavily on the many legitimate needs of women that the institutions in our society do not adequately fulfill. One feminist response has been the setting up of counterinstitutions such as women's clinics, independent feminist schools, rape crisis centers, and child care centers. Women's centers, bookstores, periodicals, and publishing houses also can be placed in this category.

Radical and socialist feminists took the lead in the development of such counterinstitutions, and most are staffed by women from these groups. Moderate feminists have, to a lesser extent, also become involved in this form of action. KNOW, Inc., discussed in the last chapter, was begun by NOW members; and moderate women have been active in rape crisis work in some areas.

Women engaged in such work see it as serving several purposes. A needed service is provided—support for rape victims, nonoppressive and inexpensive gynecological care, feminist psychological counseling, nonsexist child care. These counterinstitutions are also intended to raise women's consciousness. A rape victim helped by feminists will not only have an easier time surviving the trauma but will be more likely to interpret the experience in feminist terms. A woman who has learned self-examination will never again let herself be cowed into silence by the coldly superior manner of a gynecologist. Made aware that there are better alternatives, women will question the way Establishment institutions treat women. Thus consciousness raising through experience takes place. Its effects are not limited to women who use the services or hear about them through friends or the media. For the women who provide the services, their work is a continuation of the consciousness-raising process. Other women's experiences enrich their understanding of sexist society and increase their dedication to change.

For radical and socialist feminists, these counterinstitutions are also intended to serve as models for structures in the future good society. Some women may hope that, through an evolutionary process, their counterinstitutions will replace Establishment institutions. Most believe that this is impossible without major structural change. However great the need for the services provided, our present society will limit the growth of feminist institutions and will not allow them to become a threat to the system. Constrained by lack of money, harassed by Establishment groups who see them as a threat to their monopoly position, feminist counterinstitutions will be able to fill only a fraction of the need for their services.

They are, nevertheless, of real importance as experiments and as models. Nonoppressive forms of organization must be developed, and these institutions serve as laboratories. If post-revolutionary society is to be better than what exists at present, there must be models. That is a function feminist organizations can serve.

Change through the polity

All segments of the movement have been involved in traditional forms of political action aimed at changing government policy. The emphasis placed on such action and the rationale for engaging in it differ.

Moderate groups have devoted the greater portion of their effort to getting legal changes and to seeing that feminist-supported laws are actually enforced. Because most moderates believe significant change can be accomplished within the system, their emphasis on influencing government follows logically. Their form of organization—national in scope and more structured than in the rest of the movement—is well suited to such action.

Moderates use the full gamut of political tactics. They lobby, testify at legislative hearings, and organize letter-writing campaigns. They have also picketed and disrupted legislative hearings. Moderate groups have brought thousands of suits charging sex discrimination.

Lacking the money and frequently the organization for the more Establishment type of political activity, socialist and radical feminists have tended to use demonstrations and the like to bring political pressure. Still, in terms of types of action, no sharp distinction between segments of the movement can be made. Groups like the New York Radical Feminists have testified at legislative hearings on rape laws; petitions opposing anti-abortion amendments to the Constitution are circulating throughout the movement.

The rationale given by radical and socialist feminists for such action does differ from that of the moderates. They do not believe reform is sufficient. Certain kinds of reforms—those that pacify people through tokens—are, in fact, pernicious. Still, some reforms will ameliorate conditions. Bringing up demands around which a mass movement can be built and keeping pressure on the system will bring the revolution nearer. Thus, for socialist and radical feminists, reforms are not an end in themselves but a means toward a more distant goal.

The diversity of viewpoints and the number of independent groups involved in the women's movement is a strength—not a weakness. There is a great need for experimentation, both in organizational forms and in tactics. As long as there are many groups, if one or another gets sidetracked into nonproductive activities or even disintegrates, the movement is not endangered.

Building a movement that is viable for an extended period of time is crucial. We cannot expect a quick and easy victory. But if we can avoid the mistakes of the suffragists, who limited their goals too much and were too easily satisfied, our chances of building a humane, nonsexist society are good. After all, women do constitute more than half of the world's population.

Women, even movement women, are not yet all sisters. Class and race divide us. Old fears, prejudices, and suspicions are hard to overcome. Yet we do have many basic interests in common. Even those women who benefit materially from the status quo do so, by and large, only as adjuncts to men. They pay for their comforts through dependency. As more and more women begin to realize that the present system does not serve their interests—that it serves only the interests of a few upper-class white males—a mass movement aimed at basic socioeconomic change may emerge.

FURTHER READINGS

Those who wish to explore in greater depth any of the topics covered in this book will find the materials cited in the footnotes useful. Many of the books cited include bibliographies and most are heavily footnoted.

Because extensive bibliographies already exist, this listing is not intended to be exhaustive. I have included only those works that I consider to be especially useful.

CHAPTER 1

Figes, Eva, *Patriarchal Attitudes* (Greenwich, Conn.: Fawcett Publications, Inc., 1970). A beautifully written historical study of sexist ideology—guaranteed to both anger and amuse.

Morgan, Robin, ed., *Sisterhood is Powerful* (New York: Vintage Books, 1970). Gornick, Vivian, and Barbara Moran, eds., *Women in Sexist Society* (New York: Signet, 1971). These are two of the earliest and still among the best collections; both contain articles on sexist ideology and its effect on the lives of women. They provide a good introduction to the range of concerns that have activated the women's movement.

CHAPTER 2

Weisstein, Naomi, "Psychology Constructs the Female, or the Fantasy Life of the Male Psychologist," in Michele Hoffnung Garskof, ed., *Roles Women Play* (Belmont, Calif.: Brooks/Cole, 1971). This particular article is also available in many other collections. A devastating critique of psychologists' views on women, its author is a psychologist and movement activist. The article is a movement classic.

Maccoby, Eleanor E., and Carol N. Jacklin, *The Psychology of Sex Differences* (Stanford, Calif.: Stanford University Press, 1974). This is a thorough and scholarly recent survey of the psychological literature on sex differences.

Chester, Phyllis, *Women and Madness* (New York: Avon Books, 1972). A powerful book about the damage that psychiatry has done to women.

Hyde, Janet Shibley, and B. G. Rosenberg, *Half the Human Experience* (Lexington, Mass.: D. C. Heath, 1976) and Deaux, Kay, *The Behavior of Women and Men* (Monterey, Calif.: Brooks/Cole, 1976). These two brief texts are highly readable for the beginner, and both are written from a feminist point of view.

CHAPTER 3

Bem, Sandra L., and Daryl J. Bem, "Training the Woman to Know Her Place: The Power of a Nonconscious Ideology," and Freeman, Jo, "The Social Construction of the Second Sex," both in Garskof, ed., *Roles Women Play.* Both articles survey the socialization process from a feminist theoretical perspective.

Women on Words and Images, *Dick and Jane as Victims* (P.O. Box 2163, Princeton, N.J. 68540, 1972). This is an excellent study of sexism in elementary school textbooks.

The books by Shibley and Rosenberg and by Deaux cited earlier also discuss the socialization process.

CHAPTER 4

Friedan, Betty, *The Feminine Mystique* (New York: Dell, 1964). An important book in the history of the contemporary feminist movement, it is an excellent study of the problems faced by middle-class housewives and a good analysis of the institutions that perpetuate the feminine mystique.

Bernard, Jessie, *The Future of Marriage* (New York: Bantam, 1973). A survey and analysis of the sociological literature on marriage, the book confirms Friedan's contention that marriage, as presently constituted, is not good for women.

Rubin, Lillian Brestow, *Worlds of Pain* (New York: Basic Books, 1976). This is an excellent recent study of the working-class family.

CHAPTERS 5 AND 6

The Women's Bureau, U.S. Department of Labor is the best source of data on women in industry and the professions. Its *Handbook on Women Workers,* 1975, contains a mass of relevant data. The Bureau periodically issues new bulletins, and a list of those available can be obtained by writing the Bureau.

Review of Radical Political Economics, vol. 4 (July 1972). This special issue on women in the economy includes a number of interesting articles and an extensive bibliography.

New York Commission on Human Rights, *Women's Role in Contemporary Society* (New York: Discus Books, 1972). This book consists of testimony given before the New York Commission. It includes much material on women in industry and in the professions.

Edwards, Richard, Michael Reich, and David Gordon, *Labor Market Segmentation* (Lexington, Mass.: D. C. Heath, 1975). This book presents a new theory of the labor market which explains why women are relegated to the worst jobs. Some of the articles are technical, but the Introduction and Chapters 8 through 11 can be read by the noneconomist.

Blaxall, Martha, and Barbara B. Reagan, ed., *Women and the Workplace: The Implications of Occupational Segregation.* Published as Spring 1976 Supplement of *Signs: Journal of Women in Culture and Society* (Vol. 1, No. 3, Part 2). This is a good collection of articles on sex segregation in employment.

CHAPTER 7

Babcock, Barbara Allen, Ann E. Freedman, Eleanor Holmes Norton, and Susan C. Ross, *Sex Discrimination and the Law: Causes and Remedies* (Boston: Little Brown, 1975). The 1000-page volume is the most comprehensive single source on women and the law.

Ross, Susan, *The Rights of Women* (New York: Avon, 1973). One of the American Civil Liberties Union's series, the handbook is written for the layperson.

Women's Rights Law Reporter. Published twice a year, this journal is exclusively devoted to reporting on the legal status of women. Each edition includes analytic articles and a summary of recent cases. It is the single best source on the fast-changing legal scene.

CHAPTER 8

Leacock, Eleanor, Introduction to Frederick Engels', *The Origin of the Family, Private Property, and the State* (New York: New World

Paperbacks, 1972). This is an excellent contemporary discussion by an anthropologist of the issues raised by Engels.

Reiter, Rayna R., ed., *Toward an Anthropology of Women* (New York: Monthly Review Press, 1975). In this excellent collection, women anthropologists present a feminist analysis of women's status in various "primitive" societies.

Mead, Margaret, *Sex and Temperament in Three Primitive Societies* (New York: Dell, 1935, 1971). Mead's very readable study shows how sex roles vary across societies.

O'Faolain, Julia, and Lauro Martines, eds., *Not in God's Image* (New York: Harper & Row, 1973). This collection contains selections on women written by people in each of the periods from ancient times to the nineteenth century.

CHAPTER 9

Bell, Susan, ed., *Women: From the Greeks to the French Revolution* (Belmont, Calif.: Wadsworth, 1973). This is a collection of historical documents and writings.

Flexner, Eleanor, *Mary Wollstonecraft* (Baltimore: Penguin, 1973). This excellent biography of a great woman is a pleasure to read.

Boserup, Ester, *Women's Role in Economic Development* (New York: St. Martin's, 1970). A study of the changes in women's role that occur during the process of economic development, it documents the importance of women in the economy of many "primitive" societies.

Iglitzin, Lynne B., and Ruth Ross, eds., *Women in the World* (Santa Barbara, Calif.: Clio Books, 1976). This is a comprehensive collection of articles on women in both developed and developing societies.

CHAPTER 10

Flexner, Eleanor, *Century of Struggle* (New York: Atheneum, 1971). This is the best single work on the women's movement in the United States from 1820 to 1920. It is a social as well as a political history and is very well written.

Kraditor, Aileen, *The Ideas of the Women Suffrage Movement, 1890–1920* (New York: Columbia University Press, 1965). This is an excellent history of the ideological issues raised and arguments used by the suffrage movement.

Newcomer, Mabel, *A Century of Higher Education for American Women* (New York: Harper & Row, 1959). This is the definitive historical work on the education of women in the United States.

Friedman, Jean E., and William G. Shade, eds., *Our American Sisters: Women in American Life and Thought* (Boston: Allyn and Bacon, 1973). This collection of articles by contemporary historians covers the Colonial period to the present.

Lutz, Alma, *Emma Willard* (Boston: Beacon, 1970); *Created Equal: A Biography of Elizabeth Cady Stanton* (New York: John Day, 1940); *Susan B. Anthony* (Boston: Beacon, 1959). All of Lutz's biographies are informative and truly enjoyable to read.

Wertheimer, Barbara Mayer, *We Were There: The Story of Working Women in America* (New York: Pantheon Books, 1977). This is a readable history of American working women.

Linda Gordon, *Woman's Body, Woman's Right: A Social History of Birth Control in America* (New York: Grossman, 1976). This fascinating book is written by a feminist historian.

CHAPTER 11

Chafe, William, *The American Woman, 1920–1970* (New York: Oxford, 1972). This political and social history contains much useful information.

The Friedman and Shade reader cited earlier includes some useful articles on this period.

Trey, Joan, "Women in the War Economy—World War II," in *Review of Radical Political Economics* 4 (July 1972). This article gives a good detailed description of the enormous increase in participation by women during World War II.

Gruberg, Martin, *Women in American Politics* (Oshkosh: Academia Press, 1968). This book provides a great deal of data on women in politics during this period.

CHAPTERS 12 AND 13

Hole, Judith and Ellen Levine, *Rebirth of Feminism* (New York: Quadrangle Books, 1971). An excellent history and analysis of the contemporary women's movement, it is must reading for anyone interested in the movement.

Ware, Cellestine, *Woman Power: The Movement for Women's Liberation* (New York: Tower Publications, Inc., 1970). The development of the movement is discussed in this interesting book by an early participant.

Freeman, Jo, *The Politics of Women's Liberation* (New York: David McKay, 1975). Freeman, another early participant, presents an excellent description and analysis of the development of the movement.

Brownmiller, Susan, *Against Our Will: Men, Women and Rape* (New York: Bantam, 1976). An extremely provocative book, it has caused a great deal of discussion within the movement.

Tolchin, Susan and Martin, *Clout: Woman Power and Politics* (New York: Capricorn, 1976). This is a good discussion of women in politics with especially good sections on the 1972 Democratic convention.

Off Our Backs, Majority Report, and *Ms.* These publications are good sources of news on the movement.

CHAPTER 14

Reed, Evelyn, *Problems of Women's Liberation* (New York: Pathfinder Press, 1969). Reed presents the orthodox Marxist position. Her discussion of the origins of women's oppression is especially interesting.

Mitchell, Juliet, "Women: The Longest Revolution," reprinted in Edith Altbach, ed., *From Feminism to Liberation* (Cambridge, Mass.: Schenkman, 1971). This seminal article that first appeared in the *New Left Review* has had an important impact on the thinking of socialist feminists.

Firestone, Shulamith, *The Dialectic of Sex* (New York: Bantam Books, 1970). The most complete statement of radical feminist theory, it is extremely thought provoking.

Koedt, Anne, Ellen Levine, and Anita Rapone, eds., *Radical Feminism* (New York: Quadrangle, 1973). A number of articles from the very influential *Notes* are reprinted in this collection. Also of interest is Joreen, "The Tyranny of Structurelessness," which is an excellent analysis of the problems that the movement has had with questions of organization and structure.

Friedan, Betty, "Our Revolution Is Unique," in Mary Lou Thompson, ed., *Voices of the New Feminism* (Boston: Beacon Press, 1970). A founder of the moderate wing of the movement briefly presents her position in this article.

INDEX